The Rise of American High School Sports and the Search for Control

Sports and Entertainment
Steven A. Riess, *Series Editor*

The Rise of
American High School Sports
and the Search for Control

1880–1930

R O B E R T   P R U T E R

Syracuse University Press

∞ The paper used in this publication meets the minimum requirements
of the American National Standard for Information Sciences—Permanence of Paper
for Printed Library Materials, ANSI Z39.48-1992.

For a listing of books published and distributed by Syracuse University Press,
visit our website at SyracuseUniversityPress.syr.edu.

ISBN: 978-0-8156-3314-3

Library of Congress Cataloging-in-Publication Data

Pruter, Robert, 1944–

The rise of American high school sports and the search for control, 1880–1930 /
Robert Pruter. — First edition.

pages cm. — (Sports and entertainment)

Includes bibliographical references and index.

ISBN 978-0-8156-3314-3 (cloth : alk. paper) 1. School sports—United States—History.

2. School sports—Social aspects—United States.

GV346+

796.04'20973—dc23   2013020402

Manufactured in the United States of America

To Margaret and Robin

Robert Pruter, a librarian at Lewis University, in Romeoville, Illinois, has contributed articles and reviews to the *Journal of Sport History, International Journal of the History of Sport, Sport History Review,* and a number of sport history encyclopedias. He has also written extensively on African American popular music and is the author of two award-winning histories, *Chicago Soul* (1991) and *Doowop: The Chicago Scene* (1996). He lives in Elmhurst, Illinois, with his wife, Margaret, and his daughter, Robin.

Contents

ILLUSTRATIONS

PREFACE

High school sports from their beginnings in the late nineteenth century have played an outsize role in the US educational system and have subtly permeated the fabric of our society to such a degree that for most Americans, their presence seems to go unnoticed next to the far more media-grabbing collegiate and professional sports. In 2008 there were slightly more than 27,500 secondary schools in the country enrolling more than 16 million boys and girls, probably more than a third of them participants on their high school sports teams, making interscholastic sports the largest organized sports program in the nation.[1] Besides engaging millions of family members in the day-to-day drama of their sons and daughters playing for their high school teams, interscholastic sports take up a sizable chunk of the sports pages and considerable airtime on radio and television, and they are well represented in our literature, fine arts, and popular culture. Through more than a century of our history, high school sports have engaged variously our educators, our medical and psychological experts, our politicians, our military leaders, and our families who have debated their role, their moral worth, their value, their very existence. The nation's high school sports programs, reflecting society at large, became an arena by which Americans fought some of the most contentious issues in society—involving race, immigration and Americanization, gender roles, the position of the military, and commercial exploitation of our youth.

American educators have debated the worth of high school sports in various ways since their beginnings, but above all they saw high school athletic competition as something that helped make their charges better students, better people, and better Americans. In the nineteenth century, in which private boarding schools largely prevailed, the headmasters saw sports as of value not only in building strong bodies, but also in building strong minds and a solid Christian-imbued morality. The educators of the next century in their secular public high schools saw sports in a similar manner, but without religious underpinnings and more broadly one of character building, useful for redirecting high school youth away from the common social vices of drinking, smoking, gambling, and sexual exploration.

High school sports were thus seen as building whole persons, that is, physically fit and healthy American boys and girls, not only capable of book learning but also imbued with a host of values learned on the hardwood courts and playing fields of their high schools, including sportsmanship, teamwork, the following of rules, courage, leadership, democratic ethos, and a sense of right and wrong. These values were high-minded, to be sure, but the educators were not unmindful that athletics were invaluable in instilling social control over potentially antisocial students.

On the other hand, high school sports from their beginnings were inherently subversive of the educational mission of producing students of good character. Under pressure of producing winning teams, the players, coaches, fans, and community supporters saw elevation of the few talented athletic stars to excessive glorification, the skirting of rules to keep players eligible, the erosion of scholarship standards, and paradoxically the lack of sportsmanship, fair play, and acceptance of the rules, values that sports were presumably supposed to instill. This history answers the question of how American educators developed their system of high school sports, all the while having to contend with essential contradictions between the worthy values they wished to impart through sports and the apparent evils of popular sports that corrupted educational values and eroded all-important character development.

Throughout the history of high school sports, the educational establishment worked to rein in and take control of them, which had their birth outside the classroom domain, and this governance took place on increasingly larger plateaus—on the school level, on the league level, on the state level, and finally one fully national in scope. I see the process as follows, roughly divided into three distinct eras, which this work uses as a framework for the history:

1. Student Initiative and Adult Alliances, 1880–1900, an era of largely student initiation and direction, when the sports and interscholastic competition were introduced into the schools and became a part of the cultural life of the high schools, but also saw student alliances with adult authorities largely outside the schools, such as athletic clubs and colleges, that supported interscholastic sports with facilities, officiating, and sponsorship

2. Establishment of Institutional Control, 1900–1920, an era of co-optation by educational authorities, who, having developed physical education as a part of the curriculum, brought high school sports under institutional control, on the school level, league level, and state level, both to end reputed abuses in interscholastic athletics and to bring them under the umbrella of physical education

3. Triumph of National Governance, 1920–1930, an era when interscholastic sports became a national phenomenon and when they came under national control and governance of the state high school associations organized into a national federation, which forced the universities and clubs out of sponsorship of high school sports

The culmination of this fifty-year development of high school sports was their full integration into the American educational system and their outsize role in the formation of modern American high school youth. The essential structure of interscholastic sports being established in 1930, the epilogue of this book will take the story up to the present day.

There are necessarily a number of smaller narratives in this history as well, namely, the stories of how Catholics, African Americans, and private schools worked to provide the same structure of organization and sponsorship and the same character-building athletic experiences that the public schools were providing to their boys and girls. The female experience with interscholastic sports in America has been far more contentious than with the boys and involves three distinct periods—namely, the Progressive Era, when high school sports for the "new athletic girl" briefly flourished but were suppressed; the Roaring 1920s era, which saw communities providing an inter–high school sports experience for the new liberated female that was likewise suppressed again; and the post–Title

IX era at the end of the century, which saw nationwide adoption of inter-scholastic sports for high school girls. The role of girls in high school sports was tied into gender in terms of their character-building value, and therefore was sometimes highly explosive in terms of the definition of American womanhood.

Despite their undeniable importance in our history, high school sports have never previously been the subject of a general published history. The topic no doubt can be vast and daunting, with a myriad of issues involving thousands and thousands of high schools in a variety of settings and time periods. Not surprisingly, no broad history of the subject has appeared. Even in this history, I have forced myself into a bit of narrowing, confining it largely to the crucial years of high school sports creation, roughly from 1880 to 1930, with a strong focus on Chicago and Illinois.

The Rise of American High School Sports and the Search for Control, 1880–1830 has been preceded, however, by a number of doctoral dissertations over the years that have attempted a general history. The most ambitious and impressive dissertation is Timothy Patrick O'Hanlon's, whose "Interscholastic Athletics, 1900–1940: Shaping Citizens for Unequal Roles in the Modern Industrial State" was submitted as a PhD dissertation at the University of Illinois in 1979. The dissertation was animated by a thesis not wholly subscribed to by this researcher—namely, that educators saw interscholastic sports as a means for producing docile and cooperative workers for the new industrial state—but the examination is impressive in both its research and the conveyance of key aspects of interscholastic history. Because O'Hanlon begins his inquiry with 1900, which is appropriate in his focus on high school sports in modern society, the reader nonetheless gets a sense that he is examining high school sports almost in medias res. Although O'Hanlon has published pieces of his dissertation in some respected journals, he has never seen fit to revamp the dissertation for a book.

Sport history has also benefited from some impressive books published on nineteenth-century secondary sports. In England J. A. Mangan produced *Athleticism in the Victorian and Edwardian Public School*, first in 1981 and then in a revised edition in 2000, and Tony Money produced

Manly and Muscular Diversions: Public Schools and the Nineteenth-Century Sporting Revival in 1997. Mangan explained the "why and how" of English schoolboy sports emergence, and Money explained the "what and when" of their emergence sport by sport. Whereas the English interscholastic sport history was unlike the American history in many respects, US nineteenth-century preparatory schools were similar to the English public schools in that they educated a social elite, were largely boarding schools, and were the origin of secondary-school sports. As Mangan's and Money's works on the English public schools were groundbreaking for their English readers, so was Axel Bundgaard's *Muscle and Manliness: The Rise of Sport in American Boarding Schools* (Syracuse University Press, 2005) on the American side. The book details the creation of interscholastic sports in American boarding schools, under the influence of muscular Christianity and the direction of visionary headmasters, paralleling similar development in the mother country in the famed English boarding schools.

Relatively speaking, with regard to research journals devoted to sport and sport history, the number of articles relating to interscholastic sport history is as limited as it is in the book world. The articles that have been published have constituted a far-larger proportion dealing with female high school sports than is found in other areas of sport history. They have been produced by academic sport historians (who try to explain why boys and girls are playing high school sports), but I have also made use of many articles in popular magazines written by journalists and sport enthusiasts (who try to explain why boys and girls win or lose). Sources directly relating to high school sports that I have found useful for this work are listed in the bibliography, which is by necessity selective.

When Axel Bundgaard's work on nineteenth-century boarding schools appeared in 2005, a reviewer of the book, Timothy J. L. Chandler, opined that "Bundgaard has provided a solid foundation for the further study in elite American high schools. . . . [I]f Bundgaard is disinclined to follow Tom Brown through the twentieth century in these U.S. schools, I hope his fine work will encourage someone else to take up the challenge."[2] I was well on my way in my research and writing, having already taken the baton from Bundgaard when the review came out, and found work on such a book a considerable challenge. *The Rise of American High School Sports*, then, should be seen as a groundbreaking product that could be built on and expanded by future sport and educational historians.

I recognize that sport history becomes a history of value only if it helps to illuminate and explain the history of our society, as I hope this history does, but I also know the importance of getting the story. The reader should come away from this strongly empiricist study knowing the answers to what, where, and how high schools have in the past century and a half adopted most of the sports that have been and are currently played on the secondary-school level. I have given much coverage to the formation of interscholastic competition in the various sports, but not neglected the debates, disputes, and struggles surrounding their adoption, issues that always hark back to the basic values of interscholastic sports for American youth. The scope of this book is national, but I have drawn heavily on how interscholastic sports developed in Chicago and Illinois as case studies that illustrate how the sports and changes in governance were occurring from the school level all the way up to the national stage. The focus on Chicago is both a practical consideration and, fortuitously, one based on sound historical reasons. I am based in Chicago, and although trips to New York City, Milwaukee, Los Angeles, and Washington, DC, were possible for some research elsewhere, by necessity most of the archival evidence had to be gathered in my hometown and environs. With the advent of the Internet, I found while in the process of researching the book that newly available digitized sources kept appearing, which helped tremendously in my research on other cities and states.

Chicago and Illinois have also played an outsize role in the history of high school sports. In the late nineteenth century, Chicago high schools as much as any other part of the country helped create high school sports that superbly exemplified what was going on nationally. Then through the next two decades of the new century, all eyes were on Chicago, as the city served as the host for many of the national high school tournaments that were conducted in the various sports, notably the basketball and track and field extravaganzas sponsored by Amos Alonzo Stagg and the University of Chicago and the Catholic basketball tournament sponsored by Loyola

University of Chicago. At the same time, Illinois and its high school association leaders were central in the movement by which state high school athletic associations were formed and came together in the National Federation of State High School Athletic Associations and brought high school athletics under their control and sponsorship.

ACKNOWLEDGMENTS

Although sitting before a blank computer screen and with a pile of notes may seem like a lonely endeavor at times, in this history project I have been involved with a host of people—family, friends, colleagues in the field, and librarians and archivists—all of whom have helped me in matters small and large.

My colleagues in sport history who have given their assistance have been many, and most are members of my favorite academic society, the North American Society for Sport History (NASSH). My deepest indebtedness goes to Steven Riess, Northeastern Illinois University, who helped me to see this research as a book-length project and encouraged me to work on it to completion. He wisely counseled me on my initial submission and encouraged me to rework the manuscript and make it considerably better. Gerald Gems of North Central College helped me in showing what sport history is, both by the example of his pioneering work in high school sports, which I consider a model, and by his personal guidance and professional advice.

Robert Barnett of Marshall University shared with me his work on black high school athletics in the era of legal segregation in West Virginia and suggested good pathways for this work. Longtime NASSH member J. Thomas Jable shared some of his work with me, and as one of the readers of the manuscript, he made a number of helpful corrections and helped me to see the major themes in my work. There are a number of other NASSH historians to whom it would be remiss not to extend my appreciation and thanks both for their personal advice and for the excellent work they have published that has served my research, namely, Linda Borish of Western Michigan University, Stephen Hardy of the University of New

Hampshire, David K. Wiggins of George Mason University, Mel Adelman of Ohio State University, James Odenkirk of the University of Arizona, and John Watterson, one of NASSH's preeminent football historians.

I am also indebted to longtime colleague and fellow high school sport historian Scott Johnson, whose work has encouraged and who has provided me considerable research assistance in his position as vice president of the Illinois High School Association. My good friend and NASSH member Raymond Schmidt has been invaluable to this project; he gave the manuscript line-by-line scrutiny, and his astute and knowledgeable suggestions helped make the book a better work than it would have been. Finally, heartfelt thanks go to my copy editor, Annette Wenda, who improved the book in many little ways, fixing grammatical mistakes, ensuring consistency of use, and saving me from a few errors.

As a librarian and archivist, I should not forget the valuable assistance of my colleagues in these professions, some of whose names include Lesley A. Martin of the Chicago History Museum; Richard Seidel of the Chicago Board of Education Archives; Morag Walsh and Lorna Donley of Special Collections, Harold Washington Library Center, Chicago Public Library; Julie Lynch of the Sulzer Branch, Chicago Public Library; and Wayne Wilson of the LA84 Foundation Sports Library. My gratitude goes out to all those other unnamed librarians and archivists who assisted me at the University of Chicago Special Collections, Chicago Public Library, Columbia University's Butler Library and Columbia University Archives, New York Public Library, and Library of Congress and to the librarians and other custodians of school publications at the high schools I visited, namely, Lane Tech, Lindblom, Hyde Park, Roosevelt, Schurz, Phillips, Austin, and Senn High Schools, all in Chicago, as well as such Chicago suburban high schools as Proviso East (the author is a 1962 graduate), Oak Park, Evanston, Highland Park, and Morton.

Last, I wish to extend my gratitude to my family, my wife, Margaret, and my daughter, Robin, both of whom provided not only needed encouragement for me to persevere but also helpful suggestions on approach and scope.

PART ONE

Student Initiative and Adult Alliances, 1880–1900

1

BASEBALL AND FOOTBALL
PIONEER HIGH SCHOOL SPORTS

High school sports first emerged in the boarding schools of the East. They began as casual sports and games, usually ball games, played by students as far back as the late 1700s. The earliest boarding schools were largely located in New England, namely, Atkinson Academy and Phillips Exeter, both in New Hampshire, and Lawrence Academy, Deerfield Academy, Wilbraham Academy, Governor Dummer Academy, and Phillips Andover, all in Massachusetts. Schoolmasters of the day tried to discourage ball playing in proximity to the highly precious windows, but generally looked at the boys' games as being good for their health and physical development. We know about these students' early engagements in bat and ball games and football from the various regulations imposed by the schools and local towns to reduce noise and damaged windows. Such play, however, did not fall under the school curriculum, but instead took place during "unsupervised recess activities" and in nonschool hours.[1]

In the first few decades of the nineteenth century, nonschool hours were not that plentiful. A typical school day would last from 8:00 a.m. to 6:00 p.m. The early boarding schools wanted to leave little idle time on the hands of their charges, feeling that freedom could lead to "immoral purposes." Gradually, the boarding schools shortened the hours, leaving time for the boys to generate sports activities during their off-school hours. The very nature of the boarding school, however, fostered the development of sports. First, the absence of parental control in their daily lives encouraged students to join together in organizing their lives outside the school hours. Second, in most boarding schools, instruction came not only from degreed educators but also from teachers who were still attending college, a place where students were forming organizations to engage literary societies, debating clubs, as well as clubs organized around sports. This influence encouraged similar development in the boarding schools.[2]

Round Hill School, founded in 1823, in Massachusetts, was the first prep school to introduce physical education into the curriculum. Under its gymnastics instructor—the first in a secondary school in the United States—Charles Beck, the school introduced such pastimes as horseback riding, gymnastics, bathing, and dancing as prescribed recreations. A passel of other sports soon flourished at the school, including team sports like early forms of baseball and football, plus cross-country running, swimming, wrestling, and boxing. Winter sports included hockey, sledding, and ice skating. Similarly, around the same time, in Lawrenceville, New Jersey, Isaac Brown introduced a program of gymnastics and swimming. Thus, by the 1830s, in the private secondary schools, boys under their own initiative and direction were adopting sports, while at the same time headmasters and other school authorities were instituting formal recreations.[3]

Organized competition began in the 1850s, first early in the decade with informal intramural competition between class teams, and then at the end of the decade with a scattering of interscholastic contests. Such contests were limited to schools in New England and the Middle Atlantic states, most notably Phillips Academy (founded in 1778), in Andover, Massachusetts; Phillips Exeter (1783), in Exeter, New Hampshire; and Lawrenceville School (1810), in Lawrenceville, New Jersey. They would be joined by Worcester Academy (1832), in Worcester, Massachusetts; Episcopal High (1839), in Alexandria, Virginia; Williston Seminary (1841), in Easthampton, Massachusetts; the Gunnery (1850), in Washington, Connecticut; Hill School (1851), in Pottstown, Pennsylvania; and St. Paul's School (1856), in Concord, New Hampshire. These schools emerged at the forefront in the establishment of interscholastic athletics in the preparatory world.

Lawrenceville boys were playing interclass football games by 1852. The following year, the Phillips Andover schoolboys were playing baseball games against the older Andover Theological Seminary students, and the St. Paul's schoolboys were engaged in boat races, cricket, and hares and hounds (an early form of cross-country running). But as the decade wore on, more organization took place, as the schoolboys formed clubs in imitation of athletic associations in colleges and amateur clubs in the towns and cities. The year 1859 was "pivotal" for the emergence of schoolboy athletics into an organized framework under the control of student sport leaders, notably with the organization of the first boating club at Williston Seminary and the first baseball club at Phillips Exeter that year. These sports clubs helped to codify rules, appoint captains and officials, and finance the activities.[4]

The example of the English public schools, where sports were beginning to flower, inspired private-school educators in America to emulate the British example of athleticism in the schools. What particularly energized them was the Thomas Hughes novel *Tom Brown's Schooldays*, published in 1857, which was loosely based on Hughes's memories of his schooldays at Rugby and the devout headmaster, Thomas Arnold. Also influential was Thomas Wentworth Higginson's *Atlantic Monthly* article "Saints and Their Bodies," from March 1858, that argued the importance of a healthy body and manliness for a Christian upbringing, that is, a "muscular Christianity." These publications were widely read in the United States and inspired American schoolmasters to encourage their students to take up sports as part of a good Christian education.[5]

Just as schoolboy sports were about to take off, however, the Civil War erupted, deferring growth to the latter part of the 1860s. The end of the war saw not only the well-known flowering of baseball activity, but also a steady expansion of schoolboy sports in the preparatory schools. At this time, students in most of the prep schools organized athletic associations and clubs to support and sponsor interscholastic competition, and particular rivalries developed, notably between Phillips Exeter and Phillips Andover. The schoolboys engaged primarily in baseball and football, and to a lesser extent crew and cricket. Whereas the boys were largely responsible for organizing and competing, school authorities assisted by developing playing fields. The experience of Phillips Exeter is typical, in which during the 1860s the schoolboys supported rowing, baseball, and cricket. The purchase of an athletic field by the trustees in 1871 brought greater interest in sports, and the boys played their first outside game of baseball in 1875, against the Eagle Club of Exeter. In 1878 Exeter played Andover in their first interacademy game.[6]

The post–Civil War era also saw the establishment of a specialized kind of preparatory school called the military academy, which provided a secondary education within the strictures of military organization and discipline. Early military academies included Michigan Military Academy (Orchard Lake), organized in 1877, and Culver Military Academy (northern Indiana), in 1894. The military academies helped fuel the growth in such military sports as rifle, fencing, and polo.[7]

The earliest sports were all outdoor endeavors, but in the 1890s indoor sports developed with the building of gymnasiums. The first preparatory school to build a gymnasium for its students was Williston Seminary, which completed its facility during the 1864–1865 school year. The building contained an "exercise floor" plus bowling alleys. Other gyms soon followed: Peddle in 1869, St. Paul's in 1878, and Exeter in 1886. By the 1890s, with the help of donors, prep schools across the country significantly increased the number of gymnasiums in secondary education. Wilbraham Academy with its new gymnasium in 1896 featured one of the first basketball courts. During this time, the academies appointed gymnasium directors to provide formal exercise programs.[8]

The private boarding-school academies thus paved the way for the development of interscholastic sports in American public schooling, and as with the private schools, it took many decades before a full-fledged system of interscholastic sports developed in the public high schools. Massachusetts pioneered the state provision of a secondary-school system in 1826. The states initially began public school systems for primary-grade students. This growth of public common school education in the primary schools fueled the rise of public high schools. These schools, initially requiring tuition, were gradually made free, setting them apart from the academies, which for the most part charged tuition. Said Elmer Ellsworth Brown in 1907, "The public schools were now regarded as the schools of the people, in contrast with the academies which were represented as schools for the few who were able to pay."[9]

Some early states that adopted provisions for free public secondary-school education were Ohio in 1848, New Hampshire in 1849, Iowa in

1858, and California in 1851. After the Civil War, the states increasingly made provision in state law for the maintenance of public and free high schools, notably Maryland in 1865, Wisconsin in 1875, and Minnesota in 1881.[10]

Boston Latin, founded in 1635, was the first public secondary school, but it did not set the precedent for such schooling. The precedent was set with the founding of Boston English, in 1821, regarded as the pioneering event in the development of the public high school. Other schools quickly followed, sometimes called "high schools" and sometimes called "free academies." Philadelphia founded Central High in 1838, and the establishment of other central high schools followed in Baltimore (1839), Providence (1843), Hartford (1847), and Pittsburgh (1849). By the 1850s, high schools were being established farther west, in St. Louis (1853), Chicago (1856), Detroit (1858), and San Francisco (1858). Brooklyn developed two high schools, one for boys and one for girls, in 1878. New York City was the last major city to establish public high schools, opening in 1897, in Manhattan, Boys High (later DeWitt Clinton) and Wadleigh High School for girls and, in the Bronx, Mixed High (later Morris) for girls and boys.[11]

The 1890s saw a tremendous sea change in the country's secondary education system, when the number of public high schools increased dramatically, far outstripping private schools. As late as 1887, private schools were still enrolling a greater proportion of secondary-school students, but the following year saw the public schools pass the private schools in the number of secondary-school students. In the 1889–1890 school year, the country could count slightly more than 220,000 students in 2,526 public high schools, as opposed to about 145,000 students in 1,634 private schools. By the end of the 1890s, the number of public schools had increased to 6,005, serving some 530,000 students, compared to 1,978 private schools, serving about 189,000 students. The 1890s likewise saw a tremendous concomitant growth of interscholastic sports in the public schools. The growth of the public high school, from 100 in 1850 and 800 in 1880 to 6,000 in 1900, also forced a parallel decline in the private secondary schools. In 1890 one-third of all high schools were private, enrolling about one-third of the secondary-school students; by 1900 the public schools were enrolling more than 80 percent of the students, which by 1918 had increased to 91 percent.[12]

The growth in the public high school systems was not uniform across the country. In the South, growth lagged considerably behind the rest of the country. The region in the late nineteenth century was still suffering from the effects of the Civil War, and economic and social backwardness in the region retarded public school development. There was also a cultural preference by the better-off southerners for private-academy education, particularly military academies. As late as 1888, there were only 67 high schools in the southern states, and in 1898, there were only 796, which, although representing considerable growth, still reflected a lag compared to growth nationwide. The growth of public school education from 1890 to 1930 was twenty times greater than the population, and in this period the public high schools took the lead in the development of interscholastic sports.[13]

Interscholastic sports first emerged during the 1870s and 1880s through the adoption of three sports—baseball, football, and track and field—and although the private schools took the lead during this era, there were many public schools with students that likewise engaged in creating these new extracurricular activities. The first sports that captured the schools were baseball and football. Track and field largely emerged in the late 1880s and served to generate and encourage the formation of leagues. In these following narratives on the development of baseball and football competition in the high schools, the focus is largely on what was transpiring in Chicago schools, and we can see the students in the act of creating the norms and traditions of interscholastic sports. Progress would come only after struggles over the concept of who could represent a school team, over sustaining a league, over what should constitute winning prizes, and over drawing spectators.

CREATION OF INTERSCHOLASTIC BASEBALL

Baseball was the first sport adopted by the high schools, and it certainly preceded in places the emergence of the extracurriculum in the schools in the 1880s. Yet an examination of organized youth baseball yields unmistakable evidence that the primary organizing impetus of youth baseball came not from students in educational institutions, but from youth in the system of amateur team competition.

The amateur baseball nines of the 1860s and 1870s were organized along the lines of American fraternal organizations with a formal club organization. They had constitutions, bylaws, and officers—primarily president, secretary, and treasurer. Members paid dues and met regularly to conduct business. Baseball clubs with large memberships might include a "first nine" (the club's nine best members), "second nine," and even a "third nine." There were also junior clubs of younger players that were auxiliary to senior clubs. Competition for a club was arranged by its secretary, who would normally issue a written challenge, such items often appearing as a notice in the newspaper. If such a challenge was accepted, the teams would play a "match game," or a series of match games, often a best-two-out-of-three series. If a team played out of town, the secretary would make the travel arrangements. A team was led by a captain, whose job was to train the team as well as to direct and lead the team on the field.[14]

The junior teams of the day patterned their organization after the structure of the senior teams. In the major cities, there were dozens of junior teams. For example, in 1858 there were at least sixty junior teams in the New York City area alone. The ages of the players on junior teams have not been consistently or well defined. In practice, the use of *junior* in the name more often than not implied a roster of players in their late teens, who nowadays might be called "young men." Roughly, early baseball was organized into three levels—boys (sixteen and under), juniors (young men under twenty-one), and seniors.[15]

In Chicago youth participants had developed a more nuanced system of organization based on several age-group levels below the age of twenty-one. As in the East, there were originally three levels of organization, but the Chicago versions were slightly different—namely, pony (fourteen and under), junior (seventeen and under), and senior. These pony and junior clubs formed the basis of youth baseball in Chicago, by which high school players in the city's secondary schools patterned their baseball organization.[16]

A post–Civil War baseball fever that gripped the nation would eventually bring secondary schools in regions throughout the country together in competition. In the 1860s and 1870s, however, secondary-school students had yet to develop the whole array of sport and club activities that is called the extracurriculum. Thus, in the absence of school publications such as yearbooks, magazines, and newspapers, and such attendant customs of the extracurriculum as fight songs, cheers, and school colors, the bonds that linked students in identification with their schools were weak. The movement toward the creation of baseball teams as representative of the schools was a long one that developed in fits and starts over two decades.

Sport historian Harold Seymour gives a flavor of early high school ball by relating the adventures of high school teams as presented in two dime novels written by William Everett, *Changing Base* (1868) and *Double Play* (1870). In the former, in a school modeled after Boston Latin, the students form a team to play against a pugnacious Irish nine, and in the latter, a high school team is challenged by an amateur team in a nearby town, the Wide Awakes. And this portrayal was exactly how high school youth largely competed during that period, against club teams.[17]

Throughout New England, especially in the famed boarding schools, baseball teams were being formed during the early 1860s. Phillips Exeter organized its first team in 1859, Williston Seminary in 1860, and Phillips Andover in 1865. The first recognized outside competition for the academies took place in 1866, when Andover played two games, against Tufts College and an amateur team, the Lowell Club. Worcester High in Massachusetts has traditionally been recognized as the first secondary institution to form a team (1859) that competed against teams outside of the school. The amateur baseball club was so preeminently the model for organizing a baseball team that many early high schools patterned their baseball organization after an amateur club. Thus, the Worcester High School players thought they were forming just another amateur team in the town rather than a team designed to represent the school in competition against other high schools. When Worcester High formed the "Worcester High School Baseball Club," the team included two players who were not enrolled in the school. The idea that all the members of the team should be students of the school had not yet taken hold. Worcester's first opponent was a community club called the Eaglets.[18]

Among the nation's public schools, Philadelphia Central was another pioneer, forming a baseball team in 1863 and playing local amateur teams, namely, the Olympics and the Minervas. But again the model for the team was the amateur club, in which the high schoolers formed the Active Club within the school to play other amateur clubs. In the 1870s, Central found competition against local academies, but competition against other public schools did not emerge until the founding of Central Manual Training in 1883. Meanwhile, in Boston the English and the Latin schools were competing against each other as early as 1870.[19]

There was only one public secondary institution in Chicago during the early 1870s, Chicago High School (founded in 1856), and in the surrounding suburbs there was only Hyde Park (founded in 1869). In 1875 Chicago High School was broken up into separate North Division, West Division, and South Division schools. They were at first two-year institutions, with the old high school building serving to provide the final two years of secondary education. There is no evidence of interscholastic baseball at Chicago High during the 1860s and 1870s, but the city during this era boasted several private academies, which did play baseball. Local academies that fielded baseball teams, and sometimes played each other as well as other teams, were the Chicago Academy, Dyhrenfurth's Educational and High School, and the Beleke Academy. The earliest interscholastic contest in Chicago dates back to mid-October 1868, when the Chicago Academy played the Beleke Academy in a season-ending game.[20]

The earliest reference to Chicago High School playing baseball dates to May 1870, when the *Chicago Times* reported that "a match game of base ball was played on yesterday afternoon at the corner of May and Lake streets between the junior A and junior B classes of the Chicago High School." The following summer, Chicago High School competed against the freshman class team of Chicago University (not the same institution as the later-formed University of Chicago). During 1873–1874 the newspapers provided various reports on Chicago High playing amateur teams in the city, notably the McVickers (a team of employees at the McVickers Theater), Eagles, Leavitt Street Nine, and Highlanders (from the far-northern suburb of Highland Park).[21] Thus, in the Chicago second-ary schools, the game began as an intramural activity, where it proved to be a popular interclass contest. Eventually, there came a point when the schoolboys looked at the amateur clubs, private schools, and university or college in their community as a possible opponent and issued a challenge. This pattern can be extrapolated to apply to the experiences of many other secondary schools across the country.

Baseball as it was played at Evanston illustrates how the model for organization was the amateur club. In 1878, for example, the Evanston High boys formed a team called the Resolutes. There was no conception of "school colors," and there was no strong sense that the team was representing the school primarily. The Resolutes began the season playing a practice game with the high school freshmen, followed by a game against the Northwestern freshmen, and then a schedule that included such amateur teams as the Pastimes, Aetnas, Wilmettes, and Rogers Parkers. The Resolutes wore uniforms. A report in the *Evanston Index* said, "Noting the continued success of the Resolutes, the Northwestern University nine has adopted the same uniform, and appears in brown trimmed suits and brown stockings."[22]

The Resolutes were not the only amateur team formed by Evanston High School students. Three other teams in the school were the Oneidas, Stars, and Mohawks, which likewise played local amateur teams, but no other high schools. That a school, which had only twenty-three graduates in 1878, would form so many teams is indicative that these teams did not consider that they were primarily representing the high school itself. The local newspaper considered them to be "village clubs," understanding them to be amateur teams representing the community. These Evanston High teams could afford to invest in school uniforms, being of upper-middle- and upper-class backgrounds. Two members of the Resolutes went to college and became lawyers, one of whom ran for office as US senator from Illinois. The Oneidas, perhaps lower on the social scale, represented the entrepreneurial merchant class, in which one member became director of wholesale grocery sales and another became an owner of a wholesale dry-goods business. By 1880 all the other teams at Evanston High had disappeared, and only the Stars remained.[23]

For most young baseball players of the 1860s and 1870s, getting actual baseball experience in high school was rare, even if they were attending school. The experience of Hall of Famer Albert Spalding is instructive. He attended Rockford High in Illinois and belonged not to a school team but rather to a pony-level team called the Pioneers that played against amateur teams at all levels throughout the city. After his junior year, young Spalding dropped out of high school to work at a newspaper, but mostly to play with the Forest City club. In the following years, with Spalding pitching, the Forest City team emerged as one of the top amateur teams in the nation.[24]

The common experience of high school boys playing on their high school teams has to wait until the development of the extracurriculum, which in Chicago high schools has been placed in the 1880s. In the first years of the decade, the extracurriculum began with the founding of school newspapers and the development of interscholastic athletic competition in football and baseball, and later expanded to include other sports competition, plus yearbooks, glee clubs, student government, debating societies, and fraternities and sororities.[25]

The extracurriculum in Chicago public schools, and by extension the development of interscholastic baseball competition, began during 1880–1882 when West, South, and North Division schools changed to four-year institutions. One can imagine a considerable change in student atmosphere once the schools expanded to include junior and senior classes. There must have been increased identification by the students with those schools, which in turn engendered the desire to have athletic teams to represent their schools. Suburban schools in the area were growing in population from a couple of dozen students to a couple hundred or more—figures high enough to provide nine good men throughout the baseball season. Because high schools at this time were considered to be largely teacher training centers for girls, the student population was about two-thirds female, and the dropout rates were high, particularly for boys.[26]

The 1880s involved years of struggle for Chicago high schools to get interscholastic baseball off the ground. Up until the mid-1880s, the predominant baseball activity in the schools was still intramural contests, typically played between two classes or two literary clubs at a picnic. In

1884, however, in the immediate Chicago suburbs of Lake View and Hyde Park, the schools of Hyde Park and Lake View, along with North Division, formed a league and played a double round-robin schedule during May and June. The winner of the league received a pennant emblematic of the "championship of the high schools of Cook County." The opening game of the schedule at Lincoln Park between Hyde Park and North Division attracted some three hundred spectators. Despite the propitious start, the league disappeared after its second year. Besides the schools in the league, area schools Evanston High and South Division also fielded teams.[27]

In a letter to the Chicago schools' student newspaper, *High School Journal*, dated December 20, 1885, a student lamented, "For several years past there has been so-called 'baseball leagues' among our high schools, but very few schools participated. Let 1886 be different from this." Most of the teams were not yet wearing uniforms. An Oak Park High graduate from 1884 recalled, "We had no baseball uniforms. We made one effort at it by the girls starting to make us caps, but after four were finished the attempt died."[28]

The year 1888 gives first evidence that high school baseball in Chicago had finally taken hold. Whereas the big city newspapers ignored the activity, local newspapers, such as the *Evanston Index*, give evidence of a remarkable resurgence at Evanston High, with considerable reporting by high school correspondents on games with Lake View High, Northwestern University, Lake Forest University, and West Division. In the spring of 1889, interscholastic baseball rapidly picked up steam, as there was a plethora of games reported in the large Chicago newspapers, involving North Division, West Division, Manual Training, Hyde Park, and Northwest Division teams. Competing against them were such prep schools as Harvard School, University School, and Brown School.[29]

What happened at Evanston High during these years is indicative of how baseball had emerged from being a sandlot activity to something close to a full-fledged interscholastic sport. For example, when the 1888 team obtained uniforms, apparently for the first time in years, it became something of an event, with members of the team showing up in class in their uniforms to preen before their classmates. One girl classmate after seeing a game with the players in their "striped blue and black" outfits

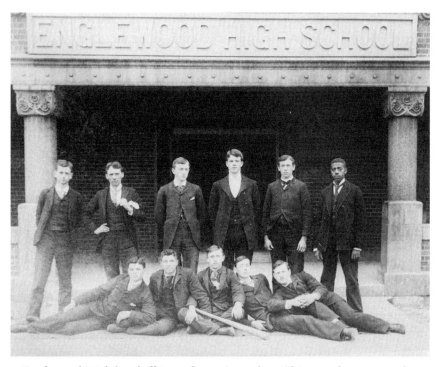

1. Englewood High baseball team from 1892, when Chicago educators saw baseball as a sport that could shape gentlemen. Note that there is no color line. The boy standing at the far left is Harold Ickes, who would in his prime serve in President Franklin D. Roosevelt's cabinet. Courtesy of the Chicago Public Library, Special Collections and Preservation Division, EHS 1.10.

gushed that the uniforms were "just too lovely for anything." Evanston reported the following year that they had "secured a lot and fixed it up for a ball ground. Located two blocks west of the school, [it] has a backstop, and will have a shanty and a grandstand."[30]

In early 1890, the students of the Cook County schools finally established a baseball league on a permanent basis, when on February 7 student delegates met at a downtown Chicago hotel and formed a conference. Behind the scenes were some faculty members. The person credited as being most instrumental in the launching of the baseball league was Henry L. Boltwood, principal and baseball coach at Evanston High, who saw the character-building value of properly supervised high school sports.

He was an early advocate of athletic competition for schoolboys, and as part of his role in attending games he said, "A teacher can make every such contest an occasion for emphatic lessons in conduct, and do much to educate his boys to despise any and all unfair conduct, to avoid profanity, and betting, and to play like gentlemen."[31]

High school baseball flourished in a few Chicago-area secondary private and public schools during the 1870s, but student involvement in baseball was conceived at the time not as representing a high school, but rather as using the high school as the organizing focus for an amateur or community team. These club teams disappeared by the late 1870s, and when baseball had reemerged in the late 1880s, as part as the development of the extracurriculum, it was as though organized baseball competition were reinvented anew, as though such competition had never existed earlier in the secondary schools.

CREATION OF INTERSCHOLASTIC FOOTBALL

Football in some high schools emerged as early as the 1850s, but it was not until the early 1880s that it became established as an interscholastic sport, albeit somewhat tentatively throughout the decade. The earliest games were no more than sandlot scrimmages, but as the years wore on some schools developed programs with uniforms, formally refereed games, and laid-out playing fields. As in baseball, football in the high schools experienced much the same evolution over several decades from casual interclass games on the school yards to interschool matches and finally to the formation of leagues.

Interscholastic football arose first in the Boston public and private schools during the late 1850s, namely, Boston English, Boston Latin, and Dixwell Latin in Cambridge (the latter a private school). Another public school joined the competition in 1863, suburban Dorchester High. The games disappeared near the end of the 1860s and did not resume until 1874. By the 1870s, the New England boarding schools, notably Phillips Andover and the Adams Academy, were regularly competing in football.[32]

The earliest public high school outside of Boston to have competed in football appears to have been Philadelphia Central, which was meeting such private academies as Eton and Episcopal as early as 1876. By 1877, in New Jersey, Stevens Prep of Hoboken was playing Brooklyn Polytechnic Institute (later Polytechnic Prep). That year Brooklyn Polytechnic also began annually competing against Adelphi Academy. In New York City, the private schools of the Interscholastic Association were already playing games among themselves in 1878. In California San Francisco Boys High was meeting Oakland High as early as 1876. By the end of the 1870s, there were some thirty secondary schools, most all in the northeastern section of the country, playing various forms of football, which included association (soccer), rugby, and American intercollegiate.[33]

Elsewhere in the East, in Washington, DC, Episcopal High was fielding a team as early as 1881, and Washington High started a team in 1885, their opponents being local colleges and club teams. A long-time football rivalry between the Baltimore City College High School and Baltimore Polytechnic High began in 1888. Likewise, in Michigan, Detroit High and Ann Arbor High both competed for the first time in football in 1888.[34]

A look at Chicago-area high schools during this time reveals a slightly later development in the game and illustrates how these schoolboys went about creating football as a high school sport. They patterned their approach after the organization of the colleges and universities, forming athletic associations to sponsor the teams and adopting the ever-changing rules of the intercollegiate game. The first school in the Chicago area to adopt the game was Evanston High. The schoolboys from the local high school put together a sandlot team in the fall of 1879 and played a couple of games against Northwestern Academy and one against Northwestern University. By the fall of 1881, Lake View High, in Chicago, was also playing football, playing a couple games with Evanston High and a couple with the Northwestern University academy boys. The middle- and upper-class character of the contests can be gathered by the nature of the entertainment after the games. "In the evening," reported the community's newspaper, the *Lake View Telephone*, "the Evanston team with their ladies received the high school boys in handsome style at the residence of John Barnum. The judge was in a happy mood, Prof. and Mrs. Nightingale were present, and the whole affair was highly enjoyable." The practice of providing after-game receptions and refreshments in the evening, usually hosted by the "ladies," was a common one during the 1880s.[35]

The manner in which high schools, as well as universities, organized football teams was first to establish a club around which an "eleven," to use the vernacular of the day, would be built. The clubs then issued challenges to other schools to participate in games. There were no teachers, no coaches, and no uniforms. Occasionally, there were schedules and leagues, and there was a crudely laid-out field. The Cook County schools made it a practice to play at what they called "the Hollow," which was apparently a field at the south end of Lake Park, around Twelfth Street and Michigan.[36]

In 1884 the *High School Journal*, a collective newspaper for all the county's high schools, began publication. An early issue of interest dates from November 1884, when a South Division student reported that "our boys have organized 'The Football Association of S.D.H.S.' The club is ready to play against any similar organization in or out of our neighboring high schools, and would suggest to the boys of any school in which there is no club, the advisability of forming one. On October 10th and 17th, we defeated Manual Training, 2 to 1 and 1 to 0, respectively, and hope in the near future to play the Chicago University club." Other high schools also reported forming clubs.[37]

Five Chicago-area schools with the approval of teachers formed the "High School Foot Ball League" in 1885, drawing up a constitution, a set of football rules, and a schedule of games. The pages of the *Journal* during the fall and winter were alive with reports of competition. A North Division High correspondent reported: "We are glad to see so many of the young ladies in attendance at the football games. We don't doubt that they look on us 'footballists' with feelings of envy, and would like to help us win more games." Some of the games ended because of darkness, and some never took place because one or both schools failed to show. Only three of Lake View High's seven games were completed. By this time there were some seventy-five schools across the country playing football, but still mostly in the Northeast.[38]

Chicago schoolboys formed a new football league in the fall of 1886 and adopted "intercollegiate rules," meaning the evolving game of

American football. A representative of North Division suggested that there was a need of a tangible prize and suggested a pennant. He also thought there should not be a money prize. A pennant became the typical award for Chicago schools, as opposed to plaques and trophy cups. The football season of 1886 quickly deteriorated. West Division's team had to disband when some parents objected to their boys playing. North Division withdrew from the league in opposition to the adoption of intercollegiate rules, and Lake View's team got so battered and bruised that its correspondent reported, "We had one man knocked senseless and another laid up for a week, while several received lesser pummelings. Some members of the team have taken to tennis and have no time to practice. Have hopes of reorganizing." Dubious practices, such as the importation of ringers (players not members of the school), had already developed. In an anonymous letter to the *Journal*, a North Division fan chided the South Division team members, asking, "How many don't go to school at all?" By December the football league had died.[39]

After a virtually moribund season in 1887, the 1888 football season saw an explosion of activity, with considerable competition among more than a dozen public and private schools in the Chicago area. A true and permanent football league was finally established in the fall of 1889, when the *Chicago Tribune* reported on the formation of the "Cook County High School Football League" by a group of student representatives who established a constitution and bylaws, elected officers, and drew up a schedule.[40]

The creation of a football league in the Chicago area was indicative of what was happening in the rest of the nation in the years 1888–1892, when most areas that supported interscholastic football formed leagues. At this time some two hundred secondary schools were now fielding football teams. The earliest interscholastic football league of permanence was the Interacademic League of Philadelphia, which brought together five private schools in the fall of 1887. Notwithstanding the pioneering aspect of that league, it is New England, and especially Boston and its environs, in the 1880s that had the most flourishing interscholastic football scene in the nation, with dozens of public and private secondary schools regularly competing among themselves. Thus, it was Boston that formed the largest and most successful of the early football leagues, in 1888, when eight city

2. Lake View High football team from 1892, when the football league was student run and managed. Indicative of the early development of high school football at this time are the makeshift, home-sewn uniforms. Courtesy of the Chicago Public Library, Sulzer Regional Library, LVHS 5/4.

and suburban public and private schools came together in a full-fledged league—with uniforms, referees, and fields. Other New England states followed slowly; Connecticut, under the lead of Yale University, formed its first interscholastic football league only in 1893.[41]

The New York–New Jersey area developed a variety of football leagues in this period. In 1888 New York City's Interscholastic Association held a championship game at Polo Grounds, but there was no league schedule at this time and the "championship" was more of a match game. Also in 1888 in Brooklyn, Adelphi Academy and the Bedford Institute played for the Brooklyn Scholastic League championship. The league did not survive after the initial year, being replaced by another short-lived league, the Interscholastic Football Association, made up of Stevens Prep (of

New Jersey), Columbia Grammar (of Manhattan), Polytechnic Prep, and Adelphi Academy (both of Brooklyn). This league lasted only through the fall of 1890. By the fall of 1892, the Interscholastic League saw enough of its schools permanently adopting football (Berkeley, Cutler, Barnard, Trinity, and Dwight) so that it could initiate a regular schedule, leading up to a championship game. The following year, the public and private schools of Long Island, which included Brooklyn Boys, Polytechnic Prep, Adelphi Academy, and Bryant and Stratton, formed an all-around athletic league that included football, called the Long Island Interscholastic Athletic League. These two leagues would carry on interscholastic football in the New York area until the formation of the Public Schools Athletic League (PSAL) a decade later.[42]

Baseball and football were the pioneering sports in the secondary schools. Whereas early interscholastic contests during the 1870s and 1880s were not much more than sandlot affairs, eventually schoolboys adopted uniforms, formal fields, greater levels of organization and leadership of the teams, and some incipient league creation. From their very beginnings, these student-led interscholastic programs, as was true of all athletic competitions of the day, were producing disquieting issues regarding sportsmanship and fair play, but educators were not paying attention at this time. From their observation of the private schools' long earlier history with sports, they apparently assumed as a given that athletic contests fostered Christian manly and moral virtues. Educators were not yet searching for control. Sustained leagues and formal schedules developed only near the end of the 1880s and would then blossom in the next decade. League formation was in part precipitated by the organization of track and field meets, which could bring many schools together in one contest and served as the keystone in the building of high school leagues.

2

The Rise of Schoolboy Track and Tennis

Interscholastic sports in the 1890s experienced an explosive growth, one that was haphazard, messy, and inchoate. Students and educational authorities were pioneering the establishment of a new sports institution, and the directions were not always clear and sure on how it should be done. The students took the lead in forming teams and leagues, and although the understanding in many histories is that interscholastic sports were originally initiated by students and run by students, the story is a bit more complicated. When interscholastic sports were in their initial stages, students came together on their own to compete against each other, as when Chicago high school students played football in the early 1880s. But by the 1890s, to conduct a schedule of sports students had to reach out to adult authorities for the use of facilities, for officiating, and for the awarding of trophies and prizes. Thus, when the early leagues were formed, the students formed alliances with private athletic clubs and other groups that could provide these things, which were particularly needed in such sports as indoor and outdoor track, tennis, and football. At this time, adult authorities were unaware of, or, if aware, indifferent to, emerging problems of sportsmanship and other ethical abuses surrounding incipient high school sports.

The initial focus of league formation and the development of a high school league was usually the track and field meet. Whereas football and baseball lend themselves to one-on-one competition, track and field call for more than a dual meet—for participation by a whole group of schools. Many of the earliest league competitions thus first involved a track and field meet, around which other sports would eventually be added to the schedule. This pattern emerged in the big cities, notably in New York, and also in rural areas where schools first came together in county competitions. In Chicago, likewise, track and field proved to be the anchor sport that spurred the development of league organization in other sports.

TRACK AND FIELD SPURS LEAGUE FORMATION

The Chicago area typified national developments in the formation of high school leagues, both public and private, city and suburban, during the late 1880s and early 1890s. Although there were short-lived leagues representing Cook County (encompassing Chicago and its suburbs) prior to this period, the Cook County High School League first came together permanently with a track and field meet only in the spring of 1889. Then a football conference was formed in the fall of 1889, and a baseball conference came together in the spring of 1890. The high school sport leagues of the decade formed alliances with adult groups to build their programs, particularly for indoor and outdoor track and field.

Sports activities in the high schools at this time were solely generated by the high school students, and Chicago students followed the pattern of organization found elsewhere in high schools and colleges. The students would form an "athletic association," through which the collection of dues would raise money for sports activities. Field days along with baseball teams were two of the first sponsorships undertaken by such associations.[1]

The first track and field meet of the Cook County schools came only after individual development in the schools, which began with the custom of holding intramural meets called "field days." The earliest reference to track and field dates back to December 1886, when a West Division correspondent for the *High School Journal* noted that "there has been a great deal going on in athletic sports down at our school. The question of racing has been agitated, and several races have been spoken of between the North-Siders [North Division High], who are anxious to be beaten. Of course we have accepted all challenges, but will not run until next spring." Evanston held an intramural field day in November 1887, and Hyde Park held a field day for its athletes in June 1888, the latter attended by some five hundred members and their friends, including many ladies. The field day included two events for girls, the 25-yard race and a baseball-throwing contest.[2]

All these activities by the various schools built up to the first interscholastic track and field meet ever held in Illinois, in 1889, by an assemblage of Cook County schools. In April the schools sent student delegates to a meeting for the express purpose of forming an interscholastic field day. The *High School Journal* reported that many of the delegates made an attempt to form an athletic league but were outvoted, and the delegates narrowed the meeting to merely organizing for a county-wide track meet. Delegates were chosen from each school to form a committee to carry forward the plans for the field day and to elect a captain.[3] Hyde Park, a leading school in athletics, and its delegates were not happy with the results of the meeting. They had wanted an organization to include "not only field days but athletics in general."[4] The Hyde Park delegates were farsighted in seeing the need for a permanent all-sports organization.

The delegates decided that financial support would partly come from the contestants, charging a fee of twenty-five cents for each event entered. The type of events for which the delegates chose to conduct competition shows that the sport of track and field was still evolving. Track and field events that would be recognizable to the twenty-first-century fan were the 100-yard dash, 440-yard run, half-mile run, mile run, 120-yard hurdles, 220-yard hurdles, half-mile walk, mile walk, running broad jump, running high jump, shot put (six pounds), and pole vault. But there were other events peculiar to the time, namely, the high kick, throwing the baseball, batting the baseball, and the mile bicycle race, as well as informal picnic-type events—the potato-sack race, 50-yard carry race, tug-of-war, girls baseball throw, and a janitors race.[5]

The field of competition was the Wanderers Cricket Grounds (Thirty-Seventh and Indiana). Only five schools attended—North Division, South Division, Hyde Park, Oakland, and Evanston. The winner of each event received a prize donated by a local business, usually an item of sports equipment or an article of clothing. Prizes included a tennis racket donated by A. G. Spalding, a gold-headed cane from F. M. Shroad jewelers, a pair of athletic shoes from C. W. Lapham, a baseball from Jenny &

Graham, and a scarf pin from Joseph & Fish jewelers. Local newspapers donated medals for winners of certain events. For example, the pole-vault winner received a medal from the *Chicago Tribune*; the high-kick winner, a medal from the *Inter Ocean*; and the half-mile winner, a medal from the *Herald*. The awarding of these prizes should not be considered a first step toward professionalism. Undoubtedly, the organizers in 1889 considered these prizes harmless, and rules were not so stringent regarding exactly what constituted "professionalism."[6]

In late June 1890, the Cook County schools held another field day at Wanderers with some six hundred competitors and spectators and an increase in the number of participant schools, with eleven represented. In most events, gold medals were given to the winners and silver medals to the second-place finishers. Other more practical prizes were dispensed to the contestants, including a set of Indian clubs, a tennis racquet, a suit of clothes, boxing gloves, athletic shoes, and a tennis shirt. This time a team championship was recognized.[7]

By March 1891, enthusiasm for a grander and more formal field-day championship was growing. A letter to the *Journal* from a student at Lake View gives an idea how the field day was viewed as a social event:

> I would like through your columns to raise my voice in regard to a Field Day of the Cook County High Schools. Let us have one! . . . Personally I favor a rousing big picnic at Washington Park. In the morning we can have the last of the league baseball games—the schedule can be so arranged—and possibly some of the sports, especially the long runs, a team race—with teams from each school—tennis and other school contests. In the afternoon—about four o'clock—have the individual events. Save some of our dinner. There may be enough of what the contestants dare not eat before and cannot now, and have a moonlight supper, boat ride, and wind up with a glorious contest of singing on the water.[8]

On March 28, the delegates met and voted to "make the Field Day organization a permanent one," satisfying the desires first voiced by Hyde Park two years earlier. The delegates also voted to award a pennant to the school that won the most events, and again expenses were defrayed by charging a twenty-five-cent entrance fee; spectators were also charge twenty-five cents for admission. On June 13, Cook County schools held their third annual field day.[9]

The Cook County meets, although organized by student delegates, could not have taken place without the support and sponsorship of adult authorities. The material prizes and medals were donated by various city newspapers and retail shops, the grounds were provided by independent athletic clubs, and the judges and other officials were adults. T. S. Quincy, who was president of the Wanderers club, also served as the chief judge. By the 1893 Cook County meet, the material prizes were no longer evident, and winners were given the standard medal prizes. Perhaps the organizers had second thoughts on the kinds of prizes they had been awarding in the previous years' meets, thinking they were not suitable for amateur high school contestants.[10]

In February 1893 the University of Illinois announced its sponsorship of a meet for all the Illinois high schools, the first state tournament in the country. It sent a circular to each school announcing the meet, addressed to each school's captain of the track and field team or head of its athletic association. For example, one recipient was future college football coach Wallie McCornack, captain of Englewood's track and field team as well as the student-run athletic association. As the university's athletic association was likewise student run, the relationship between the institution and high schools was almost like one of big brothers to little brothers. On the other hand, there was a considerable degree of adult institutional control, in that the university's athletic department under E. K. Hall (who later became a prominent head of the college football rules committee) was the main sponsor of the event, and the games committee consisted wholly of University of Illinois staff. The fact that the students needed to defer to their schools' principals for permission to attend is also significant. Still it was each high school's athletic association or team captain who corresponded with the university and arranged the team's participation. There was no adult coach, and a student captain and a student manager handled each track team.[11]

An attempt at the meet to form a permanent statewide organization for all the high schools anticipated by a decade the formation of the Illinois High School Athletic Association (IHSAA). All the invited parties to the meeting the night prior to the state meet were student delegates,

3. Inaugural University of Illinois–sponsored track and field tournament, 1893, the first state high school track and field meet held in the nation. Courtesy of the Chicago History Museum.

who were presented a draft of a constitution for the Inter-Scholastic Athletic Association. A student from Hyde Park objected to clauses giving the University of Illinois a vote on the executive committee, but after being laughed at by the delegates and dismissed by the chairman, he sat down. The delegates incorporated a clause giving the presidency to the winning team and making graduates ineligible for office and adopted the constitution. The Hyde Park delegate's demand to exclude their university host from the organization was a typical example of student-adult authority conflict during the 1890s over control of interscholastic sports. After the meet was over, the delegates met again and voted on student officers. In any case, nothing ever came of this state organization, as it rested on a shifting base of student leaders who were here today and gone tomorrow. Such an organization needed the continuity of a regular staff that adult-level institutions could provide.[12]

By 1893 Illinois could boast of two major meets, hosted by the Cook County League and the University of Illinois, as well as various meets by parochial and private schools. Track and field had emerged as one of the principal sports along with baseball and football in Illinois high schools. In terms of athletic governance of the Cook County schools, each sport at this time had a separate league, with a constitution and bylaws. Student delegates would come together usually in a downtown hotel and work out the regulations and schedules for the season.

A typical bylaw in the 1890s was the rule against student ringers, which were common in the 1880s. In the first Cook County League baseball league, for example, there was a provision in the constitution against the use of college players. The ringer problem was raised again in 1891. Several weeks after the formation of the baseball league in January, a letter writer to the *High School Journal* addressed the persistent problem of ringers: "'Outsiders' have always been the bug-bear and bane of the High

4. Hyde Park High baseball team from 1895, by which time the student-run Cook County League for Chicago and suburbs had been well established. Courtesy of the Chicago Public Library, Special Collections and Preservation Division, HYDE 2/5.

School leagues." The writer suggested that, in order to prevent future abuses, each school submit a list of their players to their respective principals to certify that all were students in good standing. The writer noted that in the previous football season, Manual Training was the only "square team of the lot."[13]

At each school, a student manager for each sport would arrange the scheduling and handle the gate and finances. Together the managers would serve as a board of control. Chicago high school teams in the 1890s did not have coaches. In baseball the captain generally did the coaching, and in track and field the teams were led by captains, but only nominally, as the boys were much on their own in terms of devising their practicing and training regimens. Some would confer with college students on training methods and techniques. In football most Cook County schools relied on the team's captain to coach. The students were pleased when teachers as well as "young ladies" attended the games. The students in the early years of the league gave out not only banners and trophies, but cash prizes

5. Englewood High football team practices, 1894, when football teams were coached and managed by the students. Courtesy of the Chicago Public Library, Special Collections and Preservation Division, EHS 1/1.

as well, usually drawn from the league's funds. Evanston High in 1891 won not only the pennant for the baseball championship but also a cash prize of twenty-five dollars. Other awards were given for batting average and base running.[14]

PRIVATE SCHOOL LEAGUE FORMATION IN CHICAGO

In contrast with the East, the Midwest's private schools were slow to form leagues and hold track and field competitions. New York and Boston inaugurated private-school track meets in 1879 and 1885, respectively, but Chicago private and parochial schools did not get involved in track competition until the 1890s, when Northwestern Military Academy in Highland Park and Morgan Park Military Academy both began a field day in 1891. A Roman Catholic school, De La Salle Institute, held its first field day in 1893, the first of its kind ever given in Chicago by a Catholic high school. The following year De La Salle included St. Ignatius College and St. Patrick's Academy in its field day. The first private-school interscholastic meet was not held until 1895, when day schools of the Preparatory League held their first championship. The following year, the boarding schools around Chicago formed the Academic League and conducted a track and field championship.[15]

In the East, the private boarding schools had become engaged in interscholastic activity well before the public schools. They drew upon a middle and upper class that had leisure time for sports and provided more lavish training facilities than did the public schools. In Chicago the public schools, although deficient in facilities, generally preceded the private schools in sports activity and often drew from the same class of students. The city's public schools, unlike those in the East, therefore, generally surpassed their private-school counterparts in athletic achievement. For example, in 1903 the *Chicago Tribune*, reporting on the track season, commented that the public high schools in the Midwest had a "higher class of athletes" than the private schools. In another article on a proposed track and field meet between the private schools of the East and the Midwest, the paper noted that the meet would "undoubtedly be won by the East."[16]

Chicago-area private schools in the 1890s were organized into two conferences—the Academic League and the Preparatory League. They were initially student run and came together as all-inclusive leagues supporting a full sports schedule. The boarding schools in the Chicago area were mainly served by the Academic League, founded in 1896 with a track and field tournament. That first spring, the league also sponsored tennis and baseball competition. In the fall of 1896, football was added to the schedule. The three charter members and mainstays of the league were the boarding academies—Morgan Park Academy, Northwestern Academy (after 1907 Evanston Academy), and Lake Forest Academy. These schools were a product of the midwestern colleges creating their own preparatory departments, as a means to ensure a sufficient number of adequately prepared students. Many midwestern public high schools provided an inadequate preparatory course for college, and sometimes students would enroll for a year in the preparatory department before entering the university. Northwestern Academy started as the preparatory department of Northwestern University, which opened in 1855. Lake Forest Academy was established by Chicago Presbyterians in 1858 as the first phase of the opening of Lake Forest College (which opened in 1860). Morgan Park Academy was founded as an independent military academy for boys in 1873 and became a coed preparatory school in association with the University of Chicago in 1892.[17]

The Academic League was vigorous in its football, track and field, and baseball programs. Compared to developments in the eastern boarding schools, the Academic League had a poor program of minor sports, supporting only tennis. The member institutions competed independently in swimming and golf. The preparatory schools that shared a campus with a college saw an occasional unhealthy intermingling of college and high school students on teams. It was not until 1897 that Northwestern University barred preparatory students from its teams, one reason being that the Northwestern Academy teams were weakened when the top players were removed to play on the university team. And it was not unknown to see a college ringer on a preparatory-school team. Disputes kept the league in turmoil, with some championships not being awarded, and in 1900 the league reorganized with new bylaws, one of them barring collegiate athletes from all league contests.[18]

The Preparatory League was a conference of small private day schools organized in 1895 that were, as the name indicates, secondary-school institutions designed to prepare students for higher education. These schools were usually located in old brownstone residential-type buildings in upper-crust neighborhoods. Most of the member schools in the league had names that reflected their purpose. The mainstays of the league were Harvard School in the Kenwood community; South Side Academy in the Hyde Park area; Princeton-Yale and Oxford, both located in the wealthy Prairie Avenue section on the near South Side; and University School and Chicago Latin, both located on the near North Side. In the spring of 1895, the Preparatory League began sponsoring baseball and track and field competition. The league inaugurated football championship series in the fall of 1895 and later added golf and tennis to the schedule. In the early years, the track meet was held under the auspices of the Chicago Athletic Association (CAA), and league officers often used the facilities of the club for its meetings.[19]

The Preparatory League was generally not as competitive as the Academic League and Cook County League in most sports, with the huge exception of the country-club sports of tennis and golf. In golf the league was by far preeminent, and its schools, particularly Harvard, pioneered the sport in the area. Yet for most of its dozen years of existence, the league was in perilous health. The schools were small and going into decline, as public schools were growing in favor. By 1907 all but Chicago Latin and Harvard School had closed down. The last league competition ended in 1906.[20]

LEAGUE FORMATION IN THE EAST

The league formation was built around a track and field meet in the East, and as in Chicago it was usually preceded for several years by intramural field days in individual schools. The pioneers in the East were the boarding schools, notably St. Paul's of Concord, New Hampshire, which conducted its first field day in 1875. By the 1880s, such schools as Phillips

Exeter Academy, Adelphi Academy of Brooklyn, Berkeley Academy of New York City, and Germantown Academy in Philadelphia were holding field days. Although it seems likely that the eastern boarding schools had the first field days, Shattuck School in Faribault, Minnesota, was conducting field days as early as 1872.[21]

Interscholastic track and field meets in the East were inaugurated on May 17, 1879, when some one hundred boys from New York City's private secondary schools gathered together on the grounds of the Manhattan Athletic Club (Eighth Avenue and Fifty-Sixth Street) to compete for the first time in a track and field meet, which during that era was called "athletics." Although the city had previous experience with such athletic meets by private clubs, this event was the first time secondary schools competed, and the New York Times, aware of this novelty, introduced a new term to their readers, interscholastic, to define the competition. The meet helped the public become aware that there were sports events being conducted by the secondary schools, representing another area of athletic endeavor, and that it had a name—interscholastics.[22]

In 1879 New York City had not yet developed a public high school system, so all the participating schools were private day schools that served the city's upper crust. Competitions included the 100-yard and 220-yard dashes; 100-yard hurdles; quarter-mile, half-mile, and mile runs; mile walk; running high jump; running broad jump; a three-legged race; and tug-of-war contests. There were no throwing events and no relay contests. The Times did not mention the school affiliation of the individual competitors, but the team contests mentioned such schools as Cutler, Wilson and Kellogg, Gibbens and Beach, and Charlier. The paper reported that the meet was viewed by a "very large assemblage of interested and approving spectators." The following year, the meet, formally called the "Interscholastic Athletic Games," featured such new events as the bicycle race and football throw. By 1884 the schoolboys, who were running the meet, awarded a trophy to the champion team and had formed an association, the Interscholastic Association, to conduct the annual competition. The New York Interscholastic track and field meet is the first example of a league originating from and coalescing around the holding of a track and field meet.[23]

Other league championship competitions in the Interscholastic League, however, were added only much later. In 1892, during the winter, Berkeley School conducted the first open indoor track meet for league members, and in the spring the league introduced baseball as a league competition. In the fall of 1893, the league introduced a league championship schedule for football (although some members of the league had played football since at least the fall of 1884). Other sports soon followed, with the adoption of tennis in 1894, ice skating in 1897, ice hockey in 1898, and basketball in 1898. The *New York Times* devoted almost all its coverage of secondary-school sports to the New York Interscholastic League, because its readers went to those schools.[24]

The league was organized by the students, and they represented their schools in league meetings. In the various sports, captains directed and coached the teams, and managers handled the schedules, finances, and overall business of the teams. The schoolboy-run league decided on certain issues such as eligibility requirements and age limits, which in the league was twenty. In 1894 the league voted on a new constitution and formed a board of arbitration to handle disputes. The board was made up of one faculty member from each school, thus establishing a dual league administration of students and faculty. Even prior to that time, the Interscholastic League had worked with adult administrators, forming alliances with such groups as the University Athletic Club and the Knickerbocker Athletic Club, which managed the indoor and outdoor track and field meets in fields and armories. Many of the athletes from the schools belonged to private athletic clubs and regiment armory teams as well, where they received their athletic training.[25]

The Long Island Interscholastic Athletic League was the second significant league established in the New York metropolitan area. The membership was a combination of public and private schools in Brooklyn, Queens, and other areas of Long Island. The league was formed in the fall of 1893, with four schools competing in football—Boys High of Brooklyn, Adelphi Academy, Polytechnic Institute, and Bryant and Stratton Business College. By the time of the league's first track and field meet the following spring, three more schools had entered the league—the Latin School, St. Paul's, and the Pratt Institute. The entrance of the venerable eighteenth-century school Erasmus Hall into the league in 1898 added a second public school to the eight-team league.[26]

Unlike in many other early leagues, track and field did not spur the formation of the Long Island League. The first year, the league sponsored football, track and field, baseball, and tennis, and particularly notable was the league's aggressive adoption of winter sports, having added handball, basketball, ice skating, indoor track, and ice hockey before the end of the decade. The league was begun and administered by the students of the various schools, and by necessity deferred to adult supervision only in establishing sites for the various events, namely, indoor and outdoor track and field sites and indoor arenas for basketball, handball, ice-skating, and hockey competition. As was the nineteenth-century custom, the students at each school formed an athletic association to sponsor and organize competition. Delegates from each school association then met in league meetings to arrange schedules and organize interschool competition. Most of the competition was conducted at a financial loss. The winning school in each sport was usually awarded twenty-five dollars to purchase a trophy.[27]

Near the end of the 1890s, as New York City began opening public high schools, the first league for those schools was formed, called the Public High School League of the Metropolitan District. The "Metropolitan League," as this conference was informally called, was something of a poor cousin to the New York Interscholastic League and the Long Island Interscholastic League. New York City was much slower than Brooklyn in establishing public high schools, and it was not until the school year of 1896–1897 that the schools Manhattan Boys (later named DeWitt Clinton) and Bronx Mixed (later Cooper, then Morris) opened. Brooklyn added a new high school as well that year, Manual Training. The league was formed in the spring of 1899, after four public schools sought admittance into the all-private Interscholastic League and were rejected. Undoubtedly, the members of the Interscholastic League wanted to keep their organization an all-private-school one, and there was more than a hint of class bias involved as well. The four public schools—Manhattan Boys, Bronx Mixed, Jersey City High, and Brooklyn Manual Training— inaugurated the Metropolitan League with a track and field meet and a baseball series. Football, indoor track, handball, and basketball were added to the schedule in subsequent years. In 1900 Commercial High and Flushing High joined the league.[28]

The formation of New York City's Public Schools Athletic League in 1903 supposedly had its genesis in the shabby nature of the high school leagues that preceded it, but the Metropolitan League represented a bit of reformation in high school sports in the New York area in that it was the first local league that was under faculty control, at least in theory. How much the faculty kept the schoolboys under control is unknown. Said a Mr. Vanderpool of Brooklyn Manual:

> The chief idea of this athletic league is that the faculty shall have entire control of all athletics and thus see perfect fairness meted out to all. We wish to adopt the scheme used at present by all the big colleges. If any boy has failed to be promoted and is thus going over his work for the second time, or if he is not up to the mark in his classes, he cannot play upon any team. Thus character is introduced into the subject of athletics and interest in studies is kept up if only that the boy may be allowed to play football or baseball. This plan has been introduced into college athletics and has proven a success; why should it not act in the same way with us? It certainly sounds the death knell of professionalism in school athletics.[29]

In any case, the Metropolitan League and other New York City leagues, such as the Bronx and Queens athletic conferences, would be swept aside with the formation of the PSAL in 1903.

League formation in Boston was one of the earliest, and, as in Chicago, initially separate leagues were established for each sport and only gradually melded into one overarching league. Although there was considerable student initiative in the formation of these leagues, some of the time the leagues were formed as a result of an adult initiative to expand sport into the high schools. Track and field was the first sustained league competition for Boston-area schools. The schools formed an organization called the Interscholastic League, which conducted its first outdoor meet in the spring of 1886. The meet sponsorship was taken over in 1889 by a new organization called the New England Interscholastic Athletic Association, formed by Harvard graduates. The Interscholastic Football League was formed in June 1888 to sponsor football competition among the high schools in Boston and its suburbs, and in the spring of 1889 a baseball league was formed under sponsorship of the Boston Athletic Association (BAA) (there was an earlier baseball league during the 1884 and 1885 seasons). The sportswriters commonly referred to all these organizations collectively as the "Interscholastic League."[30]

Boston-area schools expanded interschool competition for the 1891–1892 season, adding in the winter season ice polo and indoor track. Indoor track was added to the league schedule under the sponsorship of the Boston Athletic Association. The indoor meet was held each March in the Mechanics Building. The BAA meet outlasted the "Interscholastic League," and continued for many years after the schools drifted off into other leagues after the turn of the century. Meanwhile, in 1891, the Harvard Lawn Tennis Association began an annual tennis tournament, which was open to all schools in New England but basically served as the meet for Boston-area schools. The Harvard Interscholastic was considered a regular part of the Interscholastic League's calendar and obviated any need by the league to create its own meet. Rowing was added as a sport in 1898 under BAA sponsorship. Thus, by the end of the 1890s, Boston schoolboys had a full panoply of sports competition across the calendar.[31]

The Philadelphia private schools were organized into a conference early, in 1887, when they came together in the Interacademic Athletic Association. Two initial sports offered by the league were football and track and field. Early members were Germantown Academy, Haverford Grammar, Penn Charter, De Lancey, Friends' Central, Swarthmore, and Episcopal Academy. After the turn of the century, the league featured a full calendar of sports, adding ice hockey, baseball, tennis, and basketball in the first decade after the turn of the century. In the 1890s, there were a sufficient number of Quaker secondary schools in Philadelphia to form the Friends' Interscholastic League. They competed in at least football, basketball, and tennis through a couple a years after the turn of the century. Philadelphia dates the formation of the Philadelphia Interscholastic League to 1901, but in several sports, notably football and basketball, the public and private schools in the area were competing among themselves for several years previously.[32]

The New Jersey Interscholastic Athletic Association, formed in 1896, was the first conference in the state and was student initiated and run. As with most student-run leagues, the students formed an alliance with adult organizations to provide facilities and officials, notably the New Jersey Athletic Club for the track and field meet. The league took in both public and private schools: its public-school members were Newark Central, Montclair, Plainfield, and East Orange, and its private-school members were Newark Academy, Bordentown Military Institute, Stevens Preparatory, Pingry, and Montclair Military Academy. The league began with a track and field contest in 1896 and then expanded with football and tennis competition. The New Jersey Interscholastic Athletic Association would break up into private and public conferences after the turn of the century.[33]

Tennis and Indoor Track Join the Interscholastic Calendar

The leagues formed initially to sponsor baseball, football, and track and field competition soon expanded their offerings through the 1890s to include such sports as speed skating, handball, basketball, golf, tennis, and indoor track. The sports of tennis and indoor track were the most popular new additions to the calendar in the decade, and the high school leagues were highly dependent on alliances with private athletic clubs and universities in providing these sports to their students. Indoor track facilities were not available in most high schools at the time, and neither were tennis courts. The Cook County League in Chicago, along with other big-city leagues in the country, added tennis and indoor track to their sports calendars, and the pattern of how these sports took hold with the schoolboys, and in some cases schoolgirls, proved fairly consistent across the land. The story of the adoption of tennis and indoor track in the newly formed leagues illustrates how high school students needed to form alliances with adult authorities so as to conduct certain sports.

Tennis in Illinois was pioneered in the schools of Cook County as far back as the 1880s, when in the fall of 1884 Lake View High had a tennis club, and students at the school were playing tennis in lieu of football in the fall of 1886. Evanston High in the fall of 1886 was also playing tennis.

As early as 1888, tennis was part of some of the high school intramural field days along with track and field events. The West Division school paper gave this report on the sport in May 1891: "The tennis season has begun. Already, one by taking a short walk in any direction from the high school building, may see the tennis balls flying, and hear the thud of the balls on the racquets. The game has recently become very popular in W.D. A short time ago courts were scarce and players few, but now good courts are abundant and everyone plays tennis."[34]

Unlike other high school sports, the game involved both boys and girls, and, as noted by the West Division reporter, "the exercise is not severe so the game can be played and enjoyed by ladies as well as gentlemen. This is an important feature for the popularity of the game in high school." The school conducted an intramural tennis meet in June 1894, but apparently chose not to compete against other schools, for on June 18, the *Chicago Tribune* reported on the first Cook County high school tournament, held in Oak Park. It included six local high schools, but not West Division.[35]

Although the schoolboys did not reproduce the 1894 tournament in the following years, tennis in the schools was thriving. Early in 1895, student representatives from most of the private and public schools with tennis teams came together to form the University of Chicago Inter-Scholastic Association, to serve as the governing body for the first "Western Interscholastic Tennis Games" to be held at the university in June. Surprisingly, no elite private-school player made the finals, which was won in the singles by a Chicago Manual student and in the doubles by a North Division pair, maybe indicative of the elite nature of the public schools at this time. The student association was not sustained, but the University of Chicago conducted an annual interscholastic meet for all the private and public schools in the Chicago area through the next couple of decades.[36]

Tennis was a privileged sport, and the pattern in most of the country showed greater development in the private schools than in the public schools. The eastern private schools were vigorously involved in the sport throughout the 1890s, competing in league meets and interscholastic events. There were six principal university-sponsored meets—Yale, Harvard, Columbia, Princeton, Pennsylvania, as well as Chicago. Every August, in conjunction with the national tennis championships sponsored by the National Lawn Tennis Association (NLTA), the winners of these meets would compete for the National Interscholastic Tennis Championship, established in 1893, the first national high school tennis tournament of any kind.

The National Interscholastic had its origins in the Harvard Interscholastic, established in 1891. The Harvard tournament was held in early May, and although only eastern secondary schools participated, the winner was from the Chicago area, Robert D. Wrenn, whose home was the Chicago suburb of Highland Park, but who played for Cambridge Latin. In 1893 the Harvard Interscholastic was emulated by other eastern universities, when Yale, Princeton, and Columbia all established tennis interscholastic tournaments. At this point, the NLTA stepped in and inaugurated a national interscholastic tennis championship, in which the winners of each of the interscholastic meets would compete for a national trophy. From 1893 to 1914, the National Interscholastic, held at the Casino Club in Newport, Rhode Island, was the most prestigious tennis event for boys in the country.[37]

Thus, during the 1890s, although high school leagues in the major metropolitan areas did not sponsor tennis meets, they were served by local university meets, Boston by Harvard, Philadelphia by Pennsylvania, New York by Columbia, New Jersey by Princeton, and Connecticut by Yale. In 1906 a native Californian, John C. Donnell, who had developed a stellar reputation playing for the Harvard Military Academy in Los Angeles, won the Columbia Interscholastic playing his last year in high school for a Manhattan private school, Trinity. It was one of the first indications in the East that California was producing outstanding high school tennis players. The state established its first major interscholastic in 1899, when the Ojai Valley Tennis Club sponsored the Southern California Tennis Interscholastic. In 1904 the Los Angeles County League sponsored its first tennis tournament. In northern California, Stanford University during the next decade sponsored an interscholastic, whose representatives went to Newport to compete in the National Interscholastic.[38]

Indoor track, which prospered in the 1890s in the high schools, like outdoor track and tennis, was also dependent on student alliances with adult authorities. The students ran the track and field programs in their respective schools through their captains and managers, but they needed adult authorities to obtain facilities and equipment to conduct competition, and in the winter a large indoor facility was essential. It was a rare high school at this time that had a gymnasium with an indoor oval, and thus high school athletes were dependent on such institutions as National Guard regiments and universities to provide venues and sponsorship for track and field meets.

Chicago-area schools lagged a few years behind compared to schools on the East Coast when it came to developing a program of indoor track competition. The earliest indoor track meets for secondary schools were conducted in New York and Boston. In New York City, the private schools of the Interscholastic Association pioneered indoor track. Barnard School first conducted an intramural indoor meet in 1891, and by 1894 it had evolved into an open meet for all the private schools. The first open meet in the city was established in 1892 and was sponsored by another Interscholastic Association member, Berkeley. In 1896 the Long Island Interscholastic League sponsored its first indoor track meet and opened it to all private and public schools in the Metropolitan area. Most of the meets were conducted at local armories, notably the Eighth Regiment and Twenty-Second Regiment, both in Manhattan.[39]

Madison Square Garden was also used for several large meets. In 1896 the New Manhattan Athletic Club sponsored a huge meet at the venue that drew more than two hundred boys from New York, New Jersey, and Pennsylvania, and the following year the Knickerbocker Athletic Club sponsored a large meet that drew schools from New York, New Jersey, Connecticut, and Massachusetts. In 1903 the Public Schools Athletic League was launched with a huge indoor track and basketball extravaganza at the Garden, involving more than one thousand elementary and high school boys.[40]

Indoor track for high schools was introduced to Boston in 1892, when the Boston Athletic Association sponsored its first meet for local high schools in the famed Mechanics Building. The meet served as a league championship for the local Interscholastic League, the loose confederation of public and private schools. The meet continued for many years even after the schools drifted off into other leagues after the turn of the century. The BAA built the meet up to such a degree that by 1903 it was called the New England Interscholastic Indoor Meet and was one of the highlights of Boston's winter sport schedule. When a league for Boston public schools alone was inaugurated in 1905, it sponsored an annual indoor track meet at the Mechanics Building as well. The following year, the Preparatory League also added an indoor track meet at the Mechanics facility to its schedule.[41]

In the Chicago area, indoor competition for high schools began in 1895. In March of that year, three Cook County schools—Englewood, Hyde Park, and South Division—entered a relay race that was a part of a Chicago Athletic Association meet at the First Regiment Armory (Sixteenth and Michigan) that involved amateur, college, and high school students. During the next twenty years, it was common for public and private secondary schools to participate in such meets, usually involving no more than a relay or two. The First Regiment Armory was the mainstay of indoor track during the 1890s. In April 1895, the CAA sponsored an indoor meet solely for the Cook County League high schools at the First Regiment Armory, which drew seven schools.[42]

The CAA dropped its support after the 1895 meet, and for the 1896 meet sponsorship was jointly taken up ad hoc by the University of Chicago and the First Regiment Armory. The *Tribune* gushed over the event:

> A howling mob of high school enthusiasts saw the purple and white of Englewood crowd all the other colors out of the rainbow at the First Regiment Armory last night. . . . The meet was the best managed one ever held in Chicago, and all honor is due to Prof. Stagg, who had the affair in charge, and the First Battalion of the regiment, under the command of Lieut. Lattan. The genial commander was everywhere at once and took keen delight in "firing" off the floor those who had no business there. Gold medals were awarded as first prizes and silver ones for second; banners were given in the team races, and everyone was suited with what they got.[43]

The Cook County League indoor event, however, expired after 1896, despite the generous sponsorship for the meet and newspaper acclaim of its success. In part filling the void was the University of Chicago, which for the years 1896–1898 sponsored a high school relay in conjunction with their annual indoor meet held at the First Regiment Armory. In the first two years of the meet, the secondary schools were limited to just relay races, but in the third annual (and final) meet, the program was expanded to include jumping, walking, and various running events. Separate team championships were determined for each group of schools, public and private. The secondary-school relays were always one of the more popular events in the meet. The *Tribune*, reporting on the relay race in 1897, said, "The noisiest events of the night were the team races between high schools, for in every part of the hall and in every gallery were 'rooters,' and the girls of Englewood, Hyde Park, and English High, and delegations from Northwestern Academy, Harvard School, University School, Princeton-Yale School, and Morgan Park Academy were urging on their candidates."[44]

Some National Guard units not only supplied their facilities to conduct meets but also formed athletic associations to field teams and to conduct meets that would include high school athletes. The foremost National Guard meet in Chicago was one conducted by the First Regiment Armory Athletic Association, at varying dates from January through March, at its armory. The first meet was held in 1896, and it was continued into the 1920s when the First Regiment had become the 111th Infantry Brigade. These meets would bring together the top amateur teams—notably the squads of the First Regiment, Chicago Athletic Association, and the Central Young Men's Christian Association (YMCA)—university teams, and high school teams.

In a unique feature of indoor track, most of the events would combine all the athletes of different ages and at marked levels of ability, and to equalize the competition officials would handicap each of the contestants. In a 100-yard sprint, for example, each of the runners, based on their previous efforts, would be given a different starting mark—the best runners farthest back and the least-accomplished ones closest to the front. Needless to say, disputes often arose at such meets over officials' judgments in determining each contestant's handicap.[45]

Outside sponsorship of high school indoor track in Chicago attained greater significance in 1899, when the Central Division of the American

Athletic Union (AAU) inaugurated a relay race for secondary schools along with its usual program of track and field events held for university and club teams. The first seven meets were held in Milwaukee, and usually the relay was a competition between Milwaukee and Chicago schools. In 1904 there were a sufficient number of schools to provide separate relay races for public and private schools.[46]

The creation and growth of interscholastic track and tennis competition in the 1890s are highly illustrative of the fact that although the students for the most part ran the athletic leagues, and sponsored the sports, they could not offer such sports as track and tennis without alliances with adult institutions, which had the facilities and administrative support needed for the conduct of such events. At the same time, the students were participating in these sports with virtually no regulation by the private clubs and universities. Such regulation would begin near the end of the decade but would not really come to fruition until after the turn of the century.

What was developing in the high schools in the 1890s in parallel to interscholastic sports—and would have a huge impact on the governance and control of interscholastic athletics—were physical education programs in the schools and the concomitant physical education profession. The physical educators during the first years of the new century would cast their eyes on high school interscholastic sports, see problems with its student-run and student-alliance structure—that they were more character destroying than building—and see that such sports could become a part of the educational curriculum and be brought under faculty control. Thus, the course was set for the search for control over high school sports during the next couple of decades.

3

The Physical Education Movement and the Campaign for Control

From approximately 1880 to 1900, interscholastic sports in America were largely under student initiation and direction. In the next decade, educational reformers brought student athletics under their regulatory control, not only to end reputed abuses in interscholastic sports but also to make them a part of the physical education curriculum.

Physical education reformers in the high schools followed the colleges in taking over sports programs with the catchphrase "Athletics are educational." Their reform was tied to the overall reform in American education and overall reform in American society during the Progressive Era. Reformers of high school sports reflected the era's values in their vision that athletics and games for youth would help ameliorate some of the pathologies of modern industrial society, particularly in the large urban centers. They were at one with the playground movement of the same era that sought to provide youth opportunity to play outdoors in games and sports. The provision of sports in high schools was thus seen by reformers as a means to build good character and citizenship and to lessen juvenile delinquency and social vices and to counter the health-destroying effects of the slums with wholesome activities that promoted health and vigor.[1]

In addition, one of the principal reforms of the educational establishment was the desire to make education available to all. Schooling for all was seen as a means of social reform by bringing the working class and immigrants into the elementary and secondary schools and making the

45

schools broad-based democratic institutions. Such schools would facilitate the Americanization of the population into one melting pot.[2]

To achieve these ends, the educational establishment, from 1898 to 1908, carried out three vital reforms that helped shape the American public high school into the institution that we know today. In the most significant of them, educators moved the public high school from being almost solely a college preparatory institution serving a small sliver of the middle and upper classes to becoming a broader educational institution serving a much larger segment of the student population from all types of backgrounds. At the same time, school administrators were in the process of taking control of the extracurriculum, notably athletics, which students had previously run, and developing student activities into a bonding institution to serve all students. Finally, high school educators, in a long war against secret societies (that is, fraternities and sororities), succeeded during this period in suppressing their activities in the schools and at the same time their domination of the extracurriculum. These three reforms should be viewed as interrelated, and in one city, Chicago, they all came together in the educators' fight for control of high school sports and how the public high school culture was reshaped into the kind of institution that reflected Progressive Era ideals.

As the public high schools in the United States grew in enrollment 711 percent from 1890 to 1918 by bringing in a population increasingly made up of immigrants and working-class students, educators of the day believed that the high school, as a representative of all taxpayers, should embrace all groups in society, be as inclusive as possible, be unified in spirit and action, and bring students into conformity with a common ethos of democratic and American values. Although this objective can be interpreted as intending to educate and Americanize immigrant children in a common "melting pot," that "melting pot" should also be viewed as bringing all children together of diverse social and economic backgrounds. The Chicago Board of Education typified that view when in 1906, while combating secret societies, it wrote: "The American common school system stands for equal opportunities for all pupils to get a preparation for the responsibilities that come with maturity. Any influence that disturbs this equality of opportunity disturbs the spirit and destroys the basic purpose of our common schools."[3]

THE PHYSICAL EDUCATION MOVEMENT

The rise of physical education in the schools paralleled the emergence of sports in the schools during the last two decades of the nineteenth century. These parallel developments remained, well, parallel. As physical educators were entering the schools and creating classes in physical education, at the same time the students were initiating and conducting games and contests both intramurally and interscholastically. There was a level of antagonism between the two realms, with many physical educators finding sports inimical to the educational mission of the school, while students quietly and not so quietly rebelled at performing the boring and repetitive physical exercise routines. At the groundbreaking Physical Training Conference of 1889 that brought together in Boston all the country's leading physical educators, however, the intention of physical educators was to bring high school sports into the physical education program. The great pioneering physical educator and preeminent figure there, Dudley A. Sargent, in his conference statement said, "What America needs is the happy combination which the European nations are trying to effect; the strength-giving qualities of the German gymnasium, the active and energetic properties of English sports, the grace and suppleness acquired from French calisthenics, and the beautiful poise and mechanical precision of the Swedish free movements."[4]

Yet the separation of the two realms was manifest at the conference in which not one representative of the growing sports movement was in attendance. Even though, throughout the 1890s, many physical educators knew that their classes needed something more than calisthenics to animate their students, little was done to bring the sports extracurriculum under the purview of the physical educators. There were exceptions. Physical educators created two new indoor sports as lively alternatives to calisthenics. In 1891 basketball was invented by physical educator James Naismith at the YMCA training school in Springfield, Massachusetts, and in 1895 the YMCAs generated volleyball. A few physical educators at this time were making the argument that athletic games could be beneficial in the educational realm, notably E. L. Richards, who said, "They furnish an exercise not for the body alone, but for the whole man, every part of his nature including his mind, his social nature, and even his moral nature being brought into play."[5]

Only after the turn of the century, however, did physical educators take a serious look at the athletic games that the students were playing. They surmised that football, baseball, track, as well as basketball had value for developing physical vigor in the students and thus needed to be brought into the physical education curriculum and that the extracurriculum of interscholastic sports needed to come under their control. What energized them to take this look and move to take over interscholastic sports was that after more than a decade of rapid growth, interscholastic sports under the prevailing system of partly student and partly adult control, mostly outside the educational system, were in need of drastic reform.[6]

The physical education movement, like the movement of interscholastic sports, took a long time to germinate. Early in the nineteenth century, some prep schools and colleges engaged in some level of formal physical education instruction, but there was no profession and no science of instruction. Early in the nineteenth century, Friedrich Ludwig Jahn in Germany created a system of physical exercise, which came to be called gymnastics, and organized it into Turnverein (Turners) clubs. Some of his followers came to the United States in the 1820s and founded the first gymnasiums at Harvard University and Round Hill School, along with a public one in Boston. The German immigrants' Turner organization not only trained young men and women in gymnastics, but also did much to promote the adoption of physical training in the schools. The Young Men's Christian Associations were first established in the United States in 1851 and also did much to encourage formal physical education training. Dudley A. Sargent developed a system of physical education using exercise machines in 1878, and in 1881 he founded the Sargent School of Physical Education in Cambridge, Massachusetts, followed by his Harvard Summer School of Physical Education in 1887. From the 1860s to the end of the century, thirty-four normal schools of physical education were founded.[7]

In 1885 some sixty physical educators came together at Adelphi Academy in Brooklyn to form the Association for the Advancement of Physical Education; "American" was added to the name the following year to render the group's acronym AAAPE. From 1885 to 1895, the association published an official proceeding, and in 1896, the AAAPE published its first professional journal, the *American Physical Education Review*. Only 49 enrolled as members in the first meeting, but the membership rapidly increased, reaching 1,076 by 1900. Most of the early discussion and research of the AAAPE was related to anthropometry (the study of human body measurements) and to the advocacy and need for gymnastics in the schools (and disputations over the systems to be used—Swedish, German, or Sargent's). The early publications of the AAAPE were virtually devoid of comment on sports.

Boston helped pioneer mandatory exercise in the schools in 1853, and on the state level, California pioneered mandatory physical education in the high and elementary schools in 1866. During the 1890s, five states advanced physical education in the high schools by passing mandatory physical education laws, beginning with Ohio in 1892, but progress was slow in the states and such laws did not become the norm until the 1920s. In calculating the number of organized courses in physical education in American society in 1901, Sargent counted some 270 colleges and universities, 500 YMCAs, and 300 Turners, but he did not try to guess for secondary schools, only saying that "the number is known to be large."[8]

Physical educators looked at the landscape early in the new century and saw that they had succeeded in making physical education a part of the curriculum in many secondary schools and that physical education programs were expanding year by year. But in the other realm of school activity, they saw the fast-growing interscholastic movement still was largely under student initiative and control. In regard to this situation, Sargent asked his physical education colleagues in 1903 a most significant question: "Should school authorities carry the matter of physical training further and undertake to provide instruction for special athletes and assume the direction and management of interscholastic contests and athletic games?" The answer in Sargent's view was yes.[9]

The aim of physical educators to bring interscholastic sports under their purview was nourished no doubt by the educational establishment, which likewise was taking a look at interscholastic sports at this time and coming to nearly the same conclusions. For one, educators were beginning to see sports as being integral to American high school education. A somewhat philosophical essay in the *School Review* reflected this point of view, saying:

> All sound conceptions of school duties now include some attention to the sports and athletic interests of students, but it is doubtful whether their full value and educational significance is generally understood. The real boy, the entire boy, is to be found here with all his natural tendencies, good and evil. Even the scholastic virtues of order, system and, above all, of persistence and industry, are quite as well taught here as in the schoolroom. But beyond this, if a wise control, constant and complete, but friendly and sympathetic, goes into all the sports and games, we will see at once great gains in the higher ranges of morals and manners.

This view, which saw sports as character building, soon gained resonance among a growing number of educators, who soon coalesced into a movement advocating the takeover of interscholastic sports.[10]

Educators Examine Interscholastic Sports

The reformers in education recognized that it was natural that young people (especially boys) had the desire to play and that as educators it would not be wise or correct to suppress play activity and prevent young men and women from organizing games among themselves. They also recognized that problems had arisen with the conduct of young men and women in organizing these games, including the use of ringers, corruption in the conduct of the games and of management, overemphasis on sport above studies, and excessive commercialization. The solution of the reformers was for the faculty to become engaged. Only a few years earlier, in the 1890s and early 1900s, many faculty members considered interscholastic sports outside their purview, and what their charges did during off-school hours was not deemed their concern.

The learning theories of the physical education establishment, best exemplified by Luther Halsey Gulick and Henry S. Curtis (head of the playground movement), were shaped by the progressivism philosophy of John Dewey and the psychological theories of G. Stanley Hall and Edward L. Thorndike. Dewey emphasized that learning should be broadened beyond the focus on the individual to bring in the group and society at large, and sports were seen as fulfilling this educational philosophy. Hall's and Thorndike's theories of child development pointed to the need for play, not only as an educational tool and a means for healthful vigor, but also as a way to redirect children and young people away from juvenile delinquency and sexual preoccupation.[11]

The advocates of reform who contributed to the education journals were largely teachers, principals, and superintendents who were engaged with the students in the schools. Typical was the essay in the journal *Education* by Canton, Ohio, school superintendent J. M. Sarver, who argued that in the development of the child, educators needed to be concerned with both the mind and the body, as they are inseparable. He continued, "In adolescence when there is a new birth of the individual physically, intellectually, and morally, the desire is strongest to indulge in sports requiring motor activity. Such sports are preferred in the ratio of four to one, as appears in child-study reports." But he pointed out that there are "evils of excess" with unsupervised sports activity and recommended that faculty provide the "oversight and management." He warned against the idea that interscholastic sports were not a faculty concern, asserting that if "teachers take the position of neutrality or hostility there is little hope of preventing the evils which they deplore."[12]

What the reformers wanted to do was revealed in various surveys conducted by the educational establishment in the first years of the new century. In 1905 G. S. Lowman of Brookline High in Massachusetts conducted a survey, "The Regulation and Control of Competitive Sport in Secondary Schools of the United States." He sent out 881 survey questionnaires to public and private schools across the country and received 357 replies. Given the less than stellar feedback, the participation rate may not have been the optimum of what Lowman wanted, but it gave him and the readers of the *American Physical Education Review*, in which he published his findings in two reports (public and private), a strong sense of the state of high school faculty regulation in 1905.[13]

The key question Lowman asked was who regulated and controlled student sports in the high school—students, faculty, or both? In 1905, often prior to instituting full faculty control, many schools created boards of controls or athletic associations in which members included both faculty and students. In many other schools, the functions of regulation were divided: whereas the students might handle scheduling and coaching, the faculty might handle finances and eligibility issues. What Lowman found for the public schools was that 61 percent of his respondents reported that regulation and control fell under both faculty and student control, whereas only 12 percent reported faculty control alone and nearly one-fifth (19 percent) reported student control alone. Eight percent responded with "none," which might be construed as default to student control. For the private schools, he found 67 percent under direction of both, 10 percent faculty alone, and 17 percent student control.[14] The nearly 20 percent figure in both public and private schools given for student control alone was cause for concern among many of the educators.

Lowman also asked of his respondents what kind of regulation would be preferred in the schools and found that there was a considerably greater desire for faculty control. In the public schools, nearly 37 percent preferred faculty control, whereas 54 percent opted for combined faculty-student control and only 10 percent preferred student control. In the private schools, the numbers were 35 percent opting for faculty control, 59 percent for faculty-student control, and 6 percent for student control. The list of reasons given by the respondents who wanted faculty control alone was telling: "Better discipline, young men need control, represents final authority, boys too immature, presents irregularities and abuses in athletics, more mature judgment, prevents grafts, maintains scholarship." The advocates for student control cited "better interest, education of self-government, boys should manage their own play." The respondents who preferred combination control emphasized better harmony in the schools and cited "better representation, boys manage and faculty supervise, enthusiasm of students and common sense of faculty, check on student body, and develop co-operative spirit."[15]

High school coaching in 1905 was still in neophyte development. In many schools there were no coaches, in some schools there were graduate coaches (whereby recent student graduates would come to coach the team), and in some schools there were "professional coaches," meaning either they were hired by the students or the school or they were a part of the faculty. Lowman's survey shows a mix of sources for coaching, with 23 percent of the public schools and 29 percent of the private schools opting for graduate coaches.[16]

Lowman found only 20 percent of the public schools and 55 percent of the private schools reporting that they conducted physical examinations. In other areas of faculty control, 100 percent of the public schools and 91 percent of the private schools reported a scholarship rule (requiring a minimum grade point average for participation); 91 percent of the public schools and 37 percent of the private schools banned prizes, scholarships, and other compensation in any form; and 80 percent of the public schools but only 25 percent of the private schools enforced a four-year eligibility rule. Regarding the question of who was responsible for the "conduct of teams," Lowman found that in the public schools, 82 percent gave some form of a "faculty" response, leaving a still hefty 18 percent for student responsibility, but in the private schools 97 percent gave some sort of "faculty" response.[17]

An even higher level of student control was found in the selections of captains (when captains often served as coaches) and managers (when managers were schedulers and handled game finances). In the public schools, 77 percent of the students or teams chose the captains, and 52 percent chose the managers; in the private schools, the figures were 95 percent and 45 percent, respectively. Lowman reported that 40 percent of the public schools and 17 percent of the private schools gave managers full power to schedule games and that one-third of the public schools and one-fifth of the private schools gave managers responsibility for the expenditure of money raised for athletics. He made some of his few editorial asides on these results, saying, "This is not for the best interest of athletes" and "too much power is given the manager."[18]

Another nationwide survey in 1905, involving school superintendents, on the extent of physical education in the schools, was conducted by James Huff McCurdy, a Massachusetts physician who later became editor of the *American Physical Education Review.* He asked a straight up-and-down question as to whether interscholastic sports met with their approval. Of the 128 cities that reported that they hired physical education teachers, nearly 90 percent approved of competitive high school athletics. Of the 427 cities without physical education teachers, 75 percent gave their approval. Besides the strong correlation between the presence of physical education in the schools and the approval of interscholastic sports, there is the eye-opening overall high approval rate for interscholastic sports from the top secondary-school administrators. Despite the well-publicized attendant evils associated with high school athletics, school administrators concluded that their educational value outweighed their negative impact in the schools.[19]

The McCurdy and Lowman surveys appeared in the *American Physical Education Review,* the premier journal of the recently emergent physical education field, with the purpose of building a case for the physical education establishment assuming control of interscholastic athletics. The findings for greater regulation, which undoubtedly did not come as a surprise, reinforced the feelings of many physical educators in the high schools that interscholastic sports must be brought under their control. What was surprising in the surveys was that as late as 1905, there was still a considerable degree of student control of athletics, either wholly or shared with faculty, which made all the more acute from the educators' perspective the need for reform.

Physical educators and educational leaders were animated by the nature of abuses and level of corruption that they found in interscholastic sports. The evils were likewise measured by Lowman, but he found far from unanimity over the issue. Among his public-school respondents, nearly 30 percent of them said there were no evils, and among the private-school educators, half of them said there were no evils. By far the biggest evil named by both public- and private-school educators was "poor scholarship," which was named by roughly one-quarter of both of these educators. As far as other evils, the biggest public-school responses were nearly 15 percent each for "bad conduct and company" and "too excessive and too much time." The private-school responses were spread over too many categories to be of value.[20]

Educator William Orr, in a 1907 *American Physical Education Review* article, decried the lack of institutional control over high school athletics, suggesting that no more than 10 percent of the high schools in the country were under proper direction and supervision. His laundry list of abuses reflected the standard ones of the era. The conduct of high school sports particularly elicited his ire, as he cited the low standards of play, lengthy schedules, use of ringers, and crowd rowdyism. He also noted the fraud in the handling of funds by the student managers and the overemphasis in the schools and the daily press on high school sports. In a particularly fastidious editorial in the *School Journal* from 1901, the writer railed, "In institutions where athletics are in the lead, scholarship appears hardly to be running at all. The proper purpose of the school is not subserved. The type of man who is headstrong, belligerent, and uncouth is preferred to the thinker, the scholar, and the gentleman."[21]

Critics of interscholastic sports also found that educational institutions were increasingly being evaluated on the basis of games won or lost. Comments by George L. Meylan of Columbia University in 1905 were typical, pointing out that as a result of excessive interest in athletics, high school sport was suffuse with corruption and commercialism. He noted that the desire to win at any cost had resulted in the hiring of coaches and trainers and cited with alarm that a secondary school near Boston was paying its football coach fifty dollars a day. He noted that pressure on a professional coach to keep his job can encourage "tricks and deceit to gain victory." Under the pressure to win, there is also the tendency of the coaches and captains to use athletes who are injured or not in shape to compete, thus risking permanent injury to participants. He added that there were instances of some colleges and universities offering inducements—tuition, board, room, laundry, and pocket money—to stellar prep and high school athletics to attend their institutions to play sports, along with the practice among many secondary schools of enticing talented athletics from other schools to attend their institutions.[22]

Dudley A. Sargent in his 1903 largely favorable assessment of student athletics voiced some qualms, citing physical problems from overtraining

and the overemphasis on sports that creates abuses like gambling, unsports-
manlike play, the use of ringers, and the use of athletics to promote the
school. He also noted with displeasure that sports involved the few rather
than the many. The solution, in his view, was that school authorities
needed to step in and take control.[23]

Although educators recognized that abuses and evils existed in interscholastic sports, they were overwhelmingly supportive of them in the
schools and saw value in terms of the educational mission of the schools.
Physical educators saw their value in terms of their mission to ensure the
health and physical fitness of their students. The Lowman survey also
produced another set of responses on what educators found to be of value
in interscholastic sports. In the two separate surveys conducted—one of
public schools and one of private schools—the questions asked of each
institution were not the same or did not require uniform answers. Among
the public schools, the five most mentioned benefits in sports were
school spirit, health, scholarship, moral and manly character, and self-
control. Unaccountably using slightly different descriptors for the private
schools, Lowman found the five highest benefits mentioned were school
spirit, general physical development, "increased interest" (in school, one
assumes), better scholarship, and self-control. By assuming the "health"
response in the public schools and the "general physical development"
response in the private schools to be roughly the same, there was a fair
correlation of what educators valued in interscholastic sports in the first
years of the new century.[24]

The pages of the *American Physical Education Review* were replete
with articles advocating the need for physical education classes in the
schools, as would be expected, but there were also many articles noting
the rise of interscholastic sports, seeing their value in the physical well-
being of students, and urging that they be incorporated into the physical
education curriculum. Meylan of Columbia commented, "The first benefit derived from athletic sports is health and vitality to the participants.
This is a real benefit, for nothing can take the place of athletic sports to
develop strong, vigorous bodies in boys and young men. Formal gymnastics have their corrective and educational value, but they can never
take the place of out-door sports to develop organic vigor." St. Louis High

School principal W. J. S. Bryan argued, "Both in individual events and team playing, the powers of observation are called into the keenest activity, as upon the accurate noting of conditions and circumstances successes of failure depend. The alertness, the quick perception, and prompt action of a pupil on the athletic field are often in strong contrast to the dreamy indifference of the same pupil in the recitation room."[25]

Sargent argued that physical education and athletic games went hand in hand. Physical education with its formal exercises provided the developmental foundation by which athletes could "train, strengthen and develop the different parts and organs of the body" and "furnish[ed] the best kind of preparatory training for the various kinds of athletic contests." He looked favorably on such contests, pointing out that they helped build character, developing not only better physical powers but better moral and mental qualities as well.[26]

Many educators lauded high school athletics in fostering school spirit. Meylan mentioned the "spirit of loyalty," which can bond the students together and with their teachers in common loyalty to the school. At the Principals' Conference, at the 1902 National Education Association (NEA) conference, W. J. S. Bryan said, "But a more obvious effect is the creation of school spirit, or a sense of loyalty to the institution whose colors are defended on the gridiron or the diamond, on the track or the rowing course," but cautioned against "excessive jubilation and noise demonstration."[27] Nebraska high school principal Earl Cline noted:

> Inter-high-school contests in athletics add to the interest in athletics. Good athletics cannot exist without such contests. The interest depreciates. Man by nature is adventurous. He likes to run risks. The chance or possibility of losing spurs him to exert dormant strength. It is so with athletics. The very fact that the boys knows that he must match his strength and skill with the strength and skill of a foreign opponent causes him to strive harder, to practice more, and to do better. . . . [C]ompetitive contests in athletics with other schools will assist in stirring up a high school spirit, a spirit that, if well controlled—an enthusiastic spirit not a rampant one—can not help but redound for the good of the school. It will be a spirit of fellowship, that will keep the eyes of the community on the school.[28]

Physical educators of the day almost universally saw the value of high school sports in terms of social control, as being both an inhibitor toward schoolboy vices, high jinks, and other antisocial behavior and a force to guide the schoolboy into the norms of society under standards of good citizenship. Meylan said, "We have strong testimony from many college presidents and school masters whose experience runs back thirty years that there is much less vice and debauchery among students since the advent of athletics, because the practice of sports affords a natural outlet for superfluous animal spirits." The most violent and aggressive was football, and educators saw particular social-control virtues in the game precisely because of its brutal nature. Henry S. Curtis noted, "Football . . . seizes upon a boy, without any large interest, and gives him a great controlling one. It rouses him to think. It impels him to act. It keeps him from committing depredations to ease off the strain of supercharged muscles and nerve cells. It keeps him from social temptations." Colonel Charles W. Larned of the United States Military Academy focused his concern over the raging hormones of young men: "They afford a fine objective for physical energy which, in the young needs an outlet, guidance, and control; and which, if not thus occupied, finds vent in mischief and dissipation. . . . [T]hey keep a man sexually clean and healthy, free from morbid emotions and a too highly developed subjectivity."[29]

Larned's comments were echoed by a host of educators valuing sports as a means of controlling adolescent sexuality. Such observations in this regard were usually more indirect than Larned's, and typical was the comment of school superintendent Frank Herbert Beede, in the pages of the *School Journal*, who said, "Athletics . . . substitute an interest in things wholesome and legitimate [in place of] interests that might be harmful and demoralizing." E. H. Nichols of Harvard University wrote, "Another point, which I hesitate to elaborate is often made an important point, and that is the effect that athletics have in inducing boys to avoid the ordinary vulgar temptations."[30]

In most regards, "social control" in the American high school merely involved having students behave in socially accepted ways so that they could be good and productive students and ultimately good citizens. Educators emphasized the importance of sports in teaching students to get in the habit of accepting and obeying authority. Not only would interscho-lastic sports free the twentieth-century schoolboy from everyday vice and even thoughts of vice; the educators of the day also saw great value in their being used to tame rambunctious youths both to accept authority and to value authority. W. J. S. Bryan at the NEA conference in 1902 reflected the views of his colleagues when he said, "Athletics unregulated have been harmful; regulated, they may be made to exert a wholesome disciplinary influence," adding that "one of the most striking effects of athletics is the prompt and unquestioning recognition of authority as vested in coach or captain, which results in absolute and immediate obedience to the one temporarily clothed with the right to command. . . . [A]t least it is a very effective analogy for the teacher to draw, and discloses the falseness of the position of the pupil who fails to yield a like cheerful obedience to school authority."[31]

Sargent, who was running his summer school at Harvard in 1903 when he wrote on interscholastic sports, was particularly taken with the argument that team sports helped in molding character and submission to authority of an individual player. He wrote that the player "learns, too, the higher lesson of unity, or co-operation as the basis of complete suc-cess. Victory results from the combined efforts of thoroughly trained indi-viduals who are working heartily for the accomplishment of a common purpose. Playing games governed by well defined rules trains character by developing a spirit of hearty submission to law." Harvard's Nichols noted the very value of athletic organization in the development of young men, commenting, "Another very valuable gain from competitive athletics is the training in the control and management of men. This training of course comes chiefly to the captains and managers." These observations on how sports can inculcate authority in high school youth may be seen as something more global in social-control intentions, in that school authori-ties may have seen their role in producing good productive workers for the modern industrial state, a point developed by certain historians, notably Timothy Patrick O'Hanlon.[32]

Nichols's comments hark back to Curtis's point concerning the value of football, who saw that it could develop loyal citizens of the state. Curtis noted that all team sports "are conventional dramatization of the game of

war" and that the team game represents the earliest form of the organization of society and "is one of nature's own methods of leading the youth
into patriotism." What raises most eyebrows today, and maybe a few in his
day, is his fatuous remark, "What does it matter if a leg is broken now and
then? Broken legs are soon mended. It is worth a dozen broken legs, if you
can teach a boy to be a hero and a patriot."[33]

Curtis saw football as molding patriotic warriors, as did the American
military establishment, notably as represented in the Larned address. In
listing the virtues of athletics at schools and colleges, he had the future
needs of the military in mind when he asserted, "Athletics on a high ethical basis are a splendid training in self-restraint, in chivalric bearing, in
decision of character, in quickness of judgment and in resource in emer-
gency." Larned spent some time in his talk on the program of New York's
PSAL and noted with hearty approval the league's yearly mottoes—Duty,
Thoroughness, Patriotism, Honor, and Obedience—noting that three of
them constituted the motto of West Point and served as basic principles.
His talk directly addressed the value of physical education in the schools in
creating a strong and healthy American people, but the barely stated corollary was this benefit in also building strong armed forces for the country.[34]

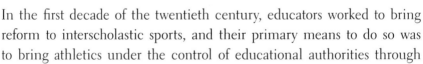

In the first decade of the twentieth century, educators worked to bring
reform to interscholastic sports, and their primary means to do so was
to bring athletics under the control of educational authorities through
the physical education departments of the schools. The physical educators had successfully accomplished a number of objectives during this
era, notably fully establishing physical education as a profession, bringing physical education into the high schools as a legitimate part of the
curriculum, establishing the necessity of reform of interscholastic sports,
and taking over control of the sports from the students. Physical educators not only began running the school sports programs but also took over
the coaching and management of the teams from the student leaders. In
doing so, they argued that they were eliminating vices and abuses and at
the same time building in their young athletes good character and health,
physical vitality, and morality.

To these reformers, it was evident that control of interscholastic sports could not be effectively accomplished unless it was done collectively, within a larger framework of athletic conferences or state associations. An individual school could impose scholastic standards, age limits, and other controls on their students, but such controls would break down as long as the school's competitors had older students and less rigorous grade requirements. New overarching institutions of control were needed. Thus, control of interscholastic sports and the new faculty-imposed regulation would in this era take place through two primary mechanisms—local high school athletic leagues and state high school athletic associations.

PART TWO

Establishment of Institutional Control, 1900–1920

4

Educators Impose
Institutional Control

The establishment of leagues and state associations by educators in the years after 1900 bringing about institutional control over interscholastic sports was neither seamless nor uniform across the nation. In most areas of the country, educator-sponsored high school leagues were formed in most big cities and in many rural areas, usually two ways, from whole cloth or by taking over existing student-run or joint student-faculty-run leagues. In many areas, especially rural areas, there were few leagues, and only gradually did league formation spread nationwide. What league formation that did take place in rural areas was for the purpose of supporting county-wide track and field meets and basketball tournaments. On the state level, the formation of high school associations was originally focused in the Midwest, but then it spread slowly across the country over a period of more than two decades. Most state associations initially focused on only one or two sports—usually basketball and sometimes track and field—with little interest in regulating any other sport. The growth of state associations would gradually gain strength in the next two decades and eventually form the basis for national governance.

League Formation

Not long after the turn of the century, educators had already begun their debates and arguments over how large a role adult authorities should have in high school leagues, and in some cities, such as Chicago and Boston, adult oversight was gradually imposed over a number of years. Many of the early advocates of faculty control initially argued for a halfway measure whereby students and faculty shared management and control of the sports. Some included student alumni in the mix of authority, at a time when many secondary schools regularly had their alumni coach their athletic teams. At a presentation given to a gathering of principals at the National Education Association in 1902, W. J. S. Bryan of St. Louis argued for the need for leagues in the following manner:

> When more than one school is involved, concerted action is required, and the conscious cultivation of the true sportsman's spirit. In school organizations and interscholastic leagues, faculty, pupils, and alumni should act in conjunction, if the best results are secured. The desire of school authorities must be to contribute to maturity of judgment and knowledge of affairs, which pupils may not possess on account of inexperience. . . . They must be made to feel that, while the management of athletics is laid largely upon them, the very existence of school organizations is dependent on the favor and approval of the principal.[1]

Dudley A. Sargent envisioned a similarly modest program of how physical education could bring sports contests, both intramural and interschool, under its direction and control. At this early stage, many of the physical educators, including Sargent, saw the management of sports to be a cooperative relationship between the students and faculty. Sargent even said that "pupils of the higher schools should be encouraged to try and manage their own sports and athletic contests." He added, however, that overall administration should be in the hands of an athletic committee, consisting of students, student grads, and faculty members (essentially including the physical education director). In his view, such an athletic committee should, with athletic committees of other schools, form an athletic association, or league, to regulate interscholastic contests.[2]

Another typical halfway advocate was a school superintendent in Canton, Ohio, J. M. Sarver, who in 1902 laid out a plan for faculty involvement in terms of establishing a structural organization, first with a school athletic association, which he saw as student managed but "under supervision of a committee of teachers." He saw one of the valued roles of the committee to be in assisting with the financial management of the association. He envisioned the next step in athletic organization as an "inter-school athletic association," or league, which would devise uniform regulations and eligibility standards. A 1903 report on Central High School of Philadelphia described favorably the school's athletic association: "The entire management of all athletic exercises is under the control of an athletic council, consisting of three members of the faculty, four alumni, and seven undergraduates, five being captains of the most important school teams, and two elected at large annually from the entire student body." These views received affirmation in the April 1903 meeting of the North Central Association of Colleges and Secondary Schools, which served the Midwest.[3]

The members of the North Central Association at the meeting adopted the report of the Committee on Athletics, which laid out the areas of reform needed in the colleges and secondary schools. The very first specification of the report was that each school needed to establish an athletic association to be in charge of athletics, with at least two members being faculty members. The committee should also be responsible for all receipts and expenditures of money, "pass upon and ratify" all contracts for contests with other schools, and be responsible for all intramural contests. Other standards included rules on eligibility and a requirement that a faculty member attend all contests. The North Central Association did not specify the need for leagues per se. However, it did call for a certain level of interschool organization, requiring that in cities where there were several schools of the same class there be a board of review, which the committee called a senate, consisting of two faculty members from each school, to arbitrate disputes.[4]

The sense among most educators was that a large part of the reform of interscholastic sports could be achieved by the formation of leagues. Of course, leagues had been rapidly growing since the early 1890s, but what the educators had in mind was a new type of league that either had complete faculty control or was shared by faculty and students. What they did not want were exclusively student-controlled leagues. E. V. Robinson, a principal from Central High in St. Paul, Minnesota, cited his experience with a local league, saying: "There is the Northwestern Athletic Association, which has a very high-sounding title, though it really includes only the schools of Minneapolis, St. Paul, and Stillwater; and that thing is a stealing thing from start to finish. It is a notorious fact that in various ways hundreds of dollars have disappeared. And it's, so far, entirely out of the control of the faculty of any of the schools."[5]

The desire of these educators to reform high school athletics by means of forming leagues reached its fruition with the formation in New York City of the Public Schools Athletic League in late 1903. Subsequently, when educators looked at reform models for the creation of interscholastic leagues, they invariably pointed to the PSAL. It was the largest school league in North America and became a model for educators not only across the continent, but overseas as well. The PSAL reflected the Progressive Era ethos of the need to ameliorate urban ills and to Americanize and uplift the impoverished and largely immigrant populations of the big cities. Its philosophy of providing athletic competition for both elite athletes in the high schools and broadly across the entire school population and deep into the elementary schools helped not only to raise the physical fitness and improve the health of the city's youth but also to bring many youngsters the opportunity for play and sports.[6]

The genesis of the PSAL came from the appointment in early 1903 of famed physical educator Dr. Luther Halsey Gulick as director of physical training for the New York public school system. Compared to other major cities, the athletic programs for the New York boroughs were backward, underdeveloped, and rife with corruption. Gulick reported: "I discovered baseball teams, not a single member of which belonged to the school which his team represented. The athlete and hero of the small boys was too often a semi-truant, while honesty and good sportsmanship were not greatly admired virtues. Low moral standards obtained generally." He also decried that only a small percentage of students participated in athletics. Gulick saw a serious need for reform and devised a grandiose plan to form a new league—the PSAL—that would involve most of the student population, from grade school to high school. He founded the league along with two other influential New Yorkers—General George W. Wingate (a member of the New York City Board of Education) and James E. Sullivan (secretary of the Amateur Athletic Union).[7]

Although the PSAL received sanction by the board of education, it was originally set up as a private corporation that would not receive public tax money. The founders of the league recruited local businessmen to serve on the league's board of directors and become paying members of the league, while soliciting contributions from prominent benefactors. The PSAL began with an athletic extravaganza held at Madison Square Garden on December 26, 1903. It involved 1,040 boys, mostly elementary school students, in basketball and track and field events. In the spring, the league held its first outdoor high school track and field championship. In the school year of 1906–1907 cross country and soccer were added, and the 1907–1908 school year saw the addition of rifle marksmanship, swimming, tennis, and baseball. The addition of rifle marksmanship was due to the advocacy of General Wingate, and the PSAL created the most extensive rifle-marksmanship program in the nation.[8] Under the goal of "sports for all," the PSAL in the elementary schools created "class athletics," by which each class in a school would compete in a collective competition in each event that was scored by the class average, and "athletic badge tests," by which all schoolboys competed to earn an athletic badge by attaining certain standards in jumps, pull-ups, and runs.[9]

The formation of the PSAL generated considerable coverage, not only in the popular press, but also in educational and physical education journals nationwide, and influenced the development of similar leagues across the country. In one report, from 1917, seventeen other cities in the United States formed athletic leagues modeled after the PSAL. It is not clear how many of these cities actually emulated New York City in every respect, that is, to build an organization based on private donations and to provide athletic training broadly across the student population deep into the grammar schools.[10]

Philadelphia was one of the major cities that emulated the PSAL and carried out an athletic awards program in an organization that included both secondary and elementary schools. The city dates the formation of its public high school league back to the Philadelphia Interscholastic League, organized in 1901 among both public and private schools. In several sports, notably football and basketball, the public and private schools in the area had been competing among themselves for several years in a schoolboy-run league. Basketball and track and field were recognized as the first sports, but football, though not formally on the schedule, engaged all the same teams, and newspapers usually recognized the school with the best record as the "interscholastic champion." In 1902 baseball and crew were added to the schedule. The public-school members included Central, Central Manual, and Northeast. There were at least twelve different private schools that were members—secular, Quaker, and Catholic—the most notable being Brown Preparatory, Roman Catholic, and Friends' Central Select. The Interscholastic League in some of the sports evolved into a virtually all-public league, such as in basketball in 1911 when Roman Catholic was the only private school. Some Philadelphia educational authorities expressed concerns at the time that there was too much independence by the students, there were too many abuses, and the league was in need of reform and greater adult supervision.[11]

The Philadelphia school system responded by forming the Philadelphia Public High School League in the 1911–1912 school year, when Central, Central Manual, and Northeast Manual withdrew from the Interscholastic League to join with Southern and West Highs to form a five-school league. Germantown, a private school, joined a few years later. Football, basketball, rifle, and outdoor track were offered the first year, baseball and crew the following year. Soccer and cross country were added just before World War I. The league was brought under closer supervision of the board of education in May 1912, when the board moved the league from under control of the principals to control of the Supervisory Committee on Athletics, appointed by the superintendent of schools. The decision brought even greater control of athletics under the purview of educational authorities by also removing alumni involvement in the league. The alumni associations of various Philadelphia high schools had been so involved as to have purchased and maintained athletic fields on which the local high schools could compete. High school fraternities were also abolished.[12]

Philadelphia, following the New York model, created a giant annual field day in which both grade school and high school students, girls and boys, competed in various games and athletic contests. High school competition in the field day was limited to freshman and sophomore classes, however, and the Philadelphia authorities had the students compete as part of teams organized by age groups, rather than under their individual schools. Athletic events included standing broad jump, basketball throw, and shuttle relay, and games included dodgeball and captain ball. The Philadelphia public schools also sponsored interschool contests for grammar school boys competing for their schools in both track and field and soccer.[13]

The road to reform of interscholastic athletics in Boston was like the experience in Philadelphia, one taken in gradual steps. The Boston-area secondary schools in the first years of the new century belonged to a variety of leagues, which included a loose confederation of leagues by sport called the Interscholastic League. Some leagues were almost wholly student run, some part-student and part-faculty run, and some student and alumni run. Regarding the latter, the Preparatory League, founded in 1900, was administered by a combination of student, alumni, and Harvard captains. The Boston city schools belonged to a variety of private, public, and suburban leagues, and in 1905 city educators decided to form a new league, the Boston High School League, with two aims in mind. One was to bring all the city schools into one organization and the other to ultimately reform student athletics and bring them under greater control of school authorities. The initial meeting to form the league included captains, managers, and faculty representatives, reflecting the traditional collaboration between students and faculty. The new league thus came under a board of control that consisted of undergraduate, alumni, and faculty members from each school. The formation of the Boston High School League (BHSL) inspired educators in the Boston suburbs to reorganize the Suburban League in 1907 along the same lines.[14]

The formation of the BHSL in 1905, while rationalizing the city schools into one organization, had not yet taken the next step toward reform, namely, the complete assumption of control of interscholastic sports by administrators. Back in 1903, James B. Fitzgerald, the director of physical training of the Boston schools, voiced concern over the state of athletics in the schools and urged each of the headmasters of the schools to create a code of regulations. By 1905 most headmasters had done so, but students still had too much control over athletics. Thus, the Boston school superintendent that year asked the state legislature to authorize the School Committee to bring high school athletics under its control. In

1906 the state legislature invested the School Committee with the authority to "supervise and control all athletic organizations composed of pupils of the public schools and bearing the name of the schools." The following year, the School Committee directed that it would thenceforth appoint all high school athletic coaches. By 1911 the director of physical training had been renamed the director of physical training and athletics, and all athletics revenues and expenses were regulated by the School Committee, ending the last vestiges of student management of high school athletics in the Boston schools. The new regime required that a teacher of the school serve as treasurer and responsible manager of the athletic organizations of the school.[15]

The Boston school system also tried to broaden athletic training across its population, in obvious emulation of New York's PSAL. In 1910 school authorities created a physical training program in which all students—boys and girls—were required to meet certain standards of achievement each of their four years in high school. For a boy to obtain a point for physical training, he had to set certain marks in running, jumping, chinning, putting the shot, and swimming. Each girl had to play a certain number of running games, throwing games, and striking games; set marks in running, jumping, and swimming; and show skill and practice in rhythmic exercises, folk dances, balancing, and song games.[16]

In Washington, DC, Edwin Bancroft Henderson, a pioneering black educator, in 1910 organized the African American high schools and grammar schools into the Public Schools Athletic League with programs and a Progressive educational philosophy modeled after the guiding principles of the New York PSAL.[17]

The original PSAL model of financing a school sports program through private charity was not adopted by other cities, and neither was it sustained for long in the PSAL. By 1911 the board of education was funding many parts of the PSAL program, and three years later the board brought the organization fully under its control. Over the next several decades, as voluntary funding gradually withered away, the bulk of the PSAL program was financed by the city budget. Although not all the original aims of the PSAL were sustained, the vision of its founders on how interscholastic sports should serve American youth remained the ideal for educators and reformers for decades afterward.[18]

THE CHICAGO PATH TO REFORM

In Chicago educational authorities gradually took control of interscholastic sports over a number of years and had to face considerable student opposition. The Chicago metropolitan area near the end of the nineteenth century included the fastest-growing city in the nation, at more than 1.1 million inhabitants and 185 square miles, surrounded by such prestigious suburbs as Evanston, Oak Park, and LaGrange. The city, plus these collar communities, were all located within one huge county, Cook County. During the late 1880s and early 1890s, the students in the local public high schools got together to engage in interscholastic athletic competition. Around the sports of football, baseball, and track and field, the Cook County schools formed a loose organization, generally called the Cook County League. Typically, as they were nationwide, these contests originally were largely student initiated, student run, and student controlled.[19]

During the years 1898–1908, school authorities in Chicago and its suburbs gradually took control of the interscholastic program from the students. Near the end of the 1890s, the "Cook County League" was well in place with a fully panoply of sports. But with haphazard growth came abuses, principally involving the use of ringers, and it was obvious that some overarching governing body was needed. This demand led school authorities to form the "Cook County High School Athletic League" in February 1898 and adopt a constitution for the league. The provisions of this constitution represented the first attempt by Cook County school authorities to take control of athletics from the students. However, the delegates to the meeting on the constitution consisted of equal parts faculty members and student representatives, and the final document was a compromise of each group's power interests.[20]

The constitution placed management of athletics in equal parts with a board of control, consisting of one delegate from the faculty of each school, and with a board of managers for each branch of sports, consisting of students from their respective schools. The initial provision proposed for the constitution was that the board of control would be in charge of the collection of all funds—dues, initiation fees, and game receipts—and would have the power to determine rules for all contests. However, student opposition reduced the board of control's powers to the collection of dues and initiation fees, determining eligibility, and hearing protests. The board of managers retained considerable power for the students, as it was still the primary rule-making body, decided the schedules, and retained control of money receipts from the athletic games. The constitution, while solving some problems of athletic governance, laid the groundwork for unfinished business as far as the faculty were concerned and ensured future conflict between the students and the school authorities.[21]

The prevailing system of athletic control in the Cook County schools apparently produced highly successful sports programs in track and field, baseball, and especially football. In 1902 and 1903, Hyde Park and North Division, in a pair of extraordinary intersectional games with Brooklyn schools for the "national championships," swamped them 105–0 and 75–0, respectively. After the second defeat, New York lost its enthusiasm for intersectional contests against Chicago public-school teams, and the series was terminated.[22]

Edwin G. Cooley became superintendent of the Chicago school system in 1900 and began working to take control of interscholastic sports, which, despite the reforms of 1898, continued to be plagued by dissension and rampant abuses. For example, in the fall of 1901, South Division's football team was expelled from the league for using ineligible players. Then, the next spring, Hyde Park's baseball and track and field teams were barred for the use of ineligible players. Hyde Park was considered the strongest track team in the state, and its students launched a revolt by trying to establish a rival league independent of the board of control. This attempt to restore student control over athletics was bound to fail, as none of the other schools that spring had been barred.[23]

An ongoing concern of Chicago school authorities was that schoolboy managers retained far too many responsibilities and powers. They began chipping away at them as early as January 1901, when they drafted a new set of rules and bylaws and took the power of selecting referees

6. Pioneering high school intersectional football game in 1902, which saw the student-coached Chicago Hyde Park defeat the faculty-coached Brooklyn Polytechnic team 105–0 with a superior western-style open game. Courtesy of the Chicago History Museum.

and umpires from the managers and placed it in the hands of the board of control. Another conflict arose over the power to determine student eligibility for participation, something that theoretically the constitution of 1898 put in the hands of the school authorities. However, abuses by the high school teams forced the board of control to impose new eligibility standards that required football players to have been enrolled as students within two weeks after the opening of school and that members of the baseball and basketball teams must be enrolled in school at least one month before the first game of the season. A scholarship standard was imposed as well, requiring players to carry at least fifteen hours a week (a full course load) and to maintain a general average of passing. The new rules apparently were so lenient that they elicited no student opposition. That would not be the case the following year. In the fall of 1902, the board of control, under pressure from Cooley, imposed a more rigid scholarship rule that required student athletes to maintain a passing average in every course.[24]

The scholarship rule in the fall 1902 season forced North Division to disband its football team, as some team members left to enter private schools. Other schools also lost key players. In reaction the students rebelled over the immediate issue of the new scholarship rule, as well as the long-festering issue of erosion of their control of the game. The students contended, reported the *Chicago Tribune*, that "their teams cannot play under the present conditions, but if the board will go back to its rules of two years ago and annul Superintendent Cooley's rules the trouble will end."[25]

The center of the student rebellion was in the one area where they still had some powers, the board of managers. The high school managers got together in early October with the intention of forming a new league. One student said, "We are simply going to organize a new high school athletic association which will be under the management of the students and not the teachers, many of whom never saw a football or baseball game and are opposed to the sport." He asserted that the students had "put up with the Board of Control and their rules long enough," and they would withdraw if the rules were not modified, as they were "simply ruining the athletes." The student finally pointed out that "two years ago there were big mass meetings in every school just before a game, but it is not so now, for the teams are not representative of the schools, as some of the best men are out of the game, and the board of control does not seem to care. The boys used to manage the affairs and I guess they can do it again." The student managers prepared a plan to set up a new board of control, which would consist of a student delegate from each school, and also a faculty and alumni representative from each school chosen by the students. In essence, this plan was designed to return the game to full control by the students.[26]

The board of managers was all set to launch a new league when Superintendent Cooley suddenly caved in to the threat and granted concessions to the students, by easing the scholarship rule to require only an overall passing average for a full course load. Cooley and the board of control also partially met the student demands to have a student representative from each school on the board by permitting two student managers to be represented on the governing body.[27]

Minor instances of rebellion over faculty supervision broke out on all levels during the 1902–1903 school year. In late September, the managers tried to book a meeting in a downtown hotel, but were thwarted by a board of education member who got wind of the meeting and had the hotel bar the "outlaw affair." There was also an example of rebellion on the field in November, when Hyde Park captain Walter Eckersall found his role of coaching the team—which he had been doing all season from years of custom—being contested by a faculty coach. Reported the *Chicago Tribune*, "Capt. Eckersall and Coach Lee Grennan of Hyde Park became involved over a matter of authority last Thursday night, and as a result Eckersall refused to go out for practice last night, claiming his power had been taken from him, but he was finally persuaded to take his place at quarterback."[28]

Educators also showed heightened concern over the still powerful student managers and their control of the finances in athletic contests, derived primarily from football contests. In 1903 an article by Englewood High teacher Harry Keeler in the *School Review* cited a number of triumphs by the Chicago school authorities in governing eligibility of players, adjudicating protests, and requiring students to obtain certification of good health from a physician.[29] What remained, he said, was that the faculty must take control of game finances from the student managers. He laid out the situation:

> Many of these boys, who are elected to their position by the members of the teams, or by the athletic association, not because of any special fitness for the position, and who are untrained in affairs of such an important nature, are often called upon to handle and control sums varying from $300 to $1,000, and sometimes even more. Do we realize what burdens are placed upon the shoulders of these managers? Their longest term of office is seldom over three months, during which period they are obliged to meet expense bills of all sorts—equipment of players, traveling expenses of teams, tickets, advertising, use of grounds or halls, police protection, telegraphing, telephoning, postage, etc., and occasionally to report and place in the care of the high-school treasurer (who is not infrequently a student) any surplus.[30]

Keeler further explained the pitfalls of such a system, resulting from incompetence and malfeasance of the student managers, citing particular games involving Chicago high schools. He recommended that teachers assume control of the game finances and that the school systems institute rules to give the teachers that control.[31]

In March 1904, Superintendent Cooley imposed a new set of rules on the Cook County League, taking back what he had conceded under pressure from the student revolt in the fall of 1902. The two student-manager representatives were booted off the board of control, and eligible students were required to have passing grades in all four core courses. Answering the criticism of Keeler, the rules required that in addition to the student manager there be a teacher manager who would oversee all arrangements for games and be in charge of ticket sales, seriously eroding the one area of student control. Finally, the superintendent would be given power to suspend a student at any time, a rule the *Tribune* surmised was intended to give the superintendent the tools to suppress a student rebellion. An important change in the governance of the league was the assumption of power by the principals, who demanded the authority to make all rules on eligibility and certain rules on the conduct of games. The board of control became more of an executive body, enforcing rules made by the Principals' Association.[32]

The triumphant Chicago school authorities would soon find that their 1904 regulatory reform was insufficient. Underlying and providing the backbone to student resistance was a far more insidious element, the secret Greek-letter societies, which had taken hold in the schools and come to dominate the extracurriculum in many Chicago high schools. Most of the football players were fraternity members, and it was the fraternities that were most resistant to the imposition of control from school authorities. The battle over the scholarship rule was in reality a proxy battle with the secret societies, the opening salvo in a long war for control of student athletics in Chicago.

Conflict also arose in 1904 over the use of paid coaches. Some of the smaller schools objected to this development, saying they were unable to pay a coach and compete on an equal level with other teams. A proposed new rule to ban paid coaches was defeated by a narrow margin, the feeling being that paid coaches added a measure of adult supervision over the athletics. That decision was soon reversed, however, because the 1906 Cook County League's constitution banned paid coaches. In 1908 the Cook County League again permitted "pro" coaches, citing that it was a better system than "depending on alumni to turn out teams." The revocation of the ban may have been more in acquiescence of practices that had already developed. Most of the schools by this time were employing faculty coaches (who under the ban were working on their own time) rather than using alumni.[33]

In 1904 the new governance of mostly adult supervision allowed the Cook County League through its board of control to develop more formal alliances with private and university organizations. In indoor track, for example, this idea came to fruition through a committee headed by an Oak Park teacher, Albert L. Clark, to "arrange a systematized series of meets." Under Clark's guidance, the committee submitted a proposal to schedule five meets—three preliminary, a semifinal, and a final. Points would be accumulated from one meet to the next, and the winner would be declared at the end of the final meet. The board of control approved the plan on January 16, 1904, but the key hitch was to obtain the newly constructed Bartlett Gymnasium as a facility and to get the University of Chicago to act as sponsor. Clark wrote to Amos Alonzo Stagg and diffidently asked him for university sponsorship: "The suggestion has been made that it might be possible to induce you to take hold of these meets and run them; i.e., supplying gymnasium, ribbons, officials, medals, etc. The Committee is desirous of making this a yearly event and consequently having a medal that is distinctive and of such design that it shall be adopted as a permanent medal."[34]

Stagg was sold on the idea and scheduled each of the meets as part of dual indoor meets with Western Conference schools. The cost was not inconsiderable. The university had to provide expensive medals to the first three contestants, which at $13 per set was not cheap in 1904. They were ordered from a New York jewelry firm. The total cost for the medals, team banner, and other awards came to around $150. The admission to each of the early meets was 25 cents and to the final meet 50 cents. The board of control would collect one-quarter of the proceeds, and no rent for the facility would be charged to the league. Five meets were held from January through March, in which teams cumulated points leading to a championship.[35]

Meanwhile, in December 1903, New York's Public Schools Athletic League had been launched with a huge indoor track and field meet for high schools and grammar schools, and educators across the country hailed the program as the best and most ambitious of any in the country.[36] Yet Chicago boosters thought they offered an impressive alternative, as an *Inter Ocean* scribe noted: "A better system of conducting a championship, where so many schools are involved, does not exist in the country. To begin with the place of holding the meets is ideal. The main room of Bartlett gymnasium is spacious, beautiful, and airy. It has a straightaway of fifty yards, a perfectly constructed track thirteen and a half laps to the mile, and a seating capacity for 1,500 persons. Besides, every accommodation known to modern athletic science is afforded the athletes in the way of lockers, rubbing rooms, baths, etc."[37]

Stagg undoubtedly thought the system was good, as he could make use of all of the university's assets to lure potential recruits, and using frat men to beguile high school boys was one such technique, as noted in his personal notes after one season of competition: "A pleasant and beneficial feature was promoted by our university undergraduates in entertaining the high school men. On the evening of the preliminary meets the various fraternities entertained all the competitors at supper." The University of Chicago's new sponsorship of high school indoor track was deemed to have an immediate impact on building the sport in the high schools. The *Inter Ocean* reported on the 1905 season: "The final meet of the Cook County High School Athletic league, held at Bartlett Gymnasium Saturday night, brought to a close the most successful indoor season for high school athletics ever known in Chicago."[38]

In rural areas, particularly in the midwestern states, league formation of a sort took place with the establishment of county-wide track and field meets and basketball tournaments. In Michigan one-third to one-half of the counties in the state held track and field meets. Track and field meets were also flourishing in Ohio counties in the early 1890s and included girls' competition as well as boys' competition.[39]

Emergence of State Associations

The large metropolitan areas were the focal point of most reformers of interscholastic sports, partly because many of the abuses in high school sports centered on football, which largely was the providence of big-city high schools. Outside the big cities, however, many small secondary schools were entering into interscholastic sports through track and field and baseball. In many states, by the 1890s, such as Ohio and Illinois, schools would compete in the emerging meets sponsored by universities. After the turn of the century, basketball, because of the small number of players needed to field a team, swept through the rural sections of the country. State high school athletic associations arose and grew powerful in response to the growing interscholastic basketball movement that was spreading to every corner of their states. The earliest associations were from the Midwest, where basketball exploded in popularity throughout the region, notably in Wisconsin (1897), Illinois (1900), Indiana (1903), and Ohio (1907).[40]

Wisconsin established the first state high school athletic association in the nation. Its genesis came when, following a successful promotion of a statewide track and field meet by the University of Wisconsin in May 1895, a group of students from various high schools proposed the formation of a statewide league. As a result, a meeting of students was held in December 1895, and another in March 1896, to advance the formation of such a league. In December 1896, the City Superintendents and High School Section of the State Teachers' Association at their annual meeting appointed a committee to draw up a set of rules to govern high school athletic contests. The proposed rules drafted by the committee were debated a year later at the section meeting and finally adopted. One rule debated by section attendees was the recommendation by the committee that schools having fewer than fifty students be allowed to play three nonstudents on a team. The section voted against that suggestion, feeling it merely endorsed the ringer problems of the past. The acceptance of the rules in 1897 constituted the beginning of the Wisconsin Interscholastic Athletic Association.[41]

The Illinois High School Athletic Association dates its formation to 1900 out of a meeting of high school principals held in conjunction with the annual meeting of the Illinois State Teachers' Association in Springfield. In 1905 the IHSAA had only twenty-one members, none from Chicago, and the organization was soon seen as serving the state outside of the large metropolitan areas.[42]

Indiana dates the formation of its athletic association to 1903, when the Northern Indiana Teachers' Association held a meeting at Richmond. In conjunction with the meeting was a conference of high school principals, who decided on the need for statewide regulation of high school athletics and concluded with a suggested body of rules and regulations, called the Richmond Agreement. Two follow-up conferences in December by the principals created a constitution and the formation of the Indiana High School Athletic Association.[43]

Many of the early interscholastic state-level competitions were sponsored by state universities, such as track and field meets sponsored by the University of Illinois and University of Wisconsin. Such track and field sponsorship led to the distinctive organization of the Texas state association, the University Interscholastic League, which was formed as part of the University of Texas. The first high school activity sponsored by the University of Texas was debating, when the University of Texas Extension Bureau formed the Debating League of Texas in 1910. In 1905 the university formed the Texas Interscholastic Athletic Association to sponsor a track and field meet. The two organizations came together in 1912 as the University Interscholastic League.[44]

From the formation of the Wisconsin state association in 1897 to 1917, state high school athletic or activity organizations were formed in thirty-three states. In the second decade, the formation of state associations spread nationwide from the Midwest. The East formed state associations in Pennsylvania (1913), Maryland (1914), Vermont (1915), and Massachusetts (1916), and the South saw the organization of such associations in Virginia (1913), South Carolina (1913), Kentucky (1916), and Alabama (1916). Early state associations in the West included ones in Utah (1910), Wyoming (1912), Kansas (1913), Oregon (1914), and California (1914).[45]

The vast majority of state associations were formed by state-level secondary-school educational establishments. Notable exceptions included Texas, with its university-sponsored association, and Maryland, whose association was controlled by a playground group. By the 1920s, twenty-two of the associations held their annual meetings at the same time of their respective state teachers' associations and six in conjunction with their annual high school principals' association. The formation of state high school associations thus brought with it the emergence of control of interscholastic sports by the educational establishment.[46]

The creation of leagues and state associations under control of the educational establishment successfully imposed faculty guidance and regulation over interscholastic sports, but this new era of institutional control did not immediately bring about a transformative new era of reformed high school sports. By the end of the first decade of the new century, many educators felt that the change of governance merely represented the beginnings of a long, hard road in their search for reform. A lack of regulation and control still plagued many of the sports, in that leagues and state associations were still not fully established nationwide. The leagues and state associations also had to contend with continued abuses and persistence resistance from students, stiffened by the existence in many places in the country of flourishing Greek-letter societies in the schools. The vision of educators of a system of interscholastic sports under their control that built character and appreciation for the democratic values of American society remained incomplete for some time.

5

STUDENT RESISTANCE
TO CONTROL AND REFORM

The nationwide reform of governance in interscholastic sports with the imposition of adult-sponsored leagues and state associations saw students in most areas acquiesce to the new faculty control and passively accept the new order of things. In many areas, however, educators faced persistent student resistance, stiffened by rebellious high school Greek-letter societies and continued abuses in the decade leading up to World War I. In Chicago student resistance to control and reform was especially acute. Educators saw the deleterious influence of Greek-letter societies and persistent student misbehavior as undeniable evidence that only teacher-directed and -regulated high school sport could build character.

The standard story on how sports have evolved in the high schools is that students generally accepted and appreciated the imposition of faculty coaching and administrative control, with a minimum of conflict. Historians' accounts of reform of interscholastic sports in Michigan, Boston, and New York mostly seem to confirm this belief. Regarding Boston, Steve Hardy said, "Only after continued prodding and complaining (sometimes by the students themselves) of the growing evidence of abuses and cheating did the administration enact reform and regulation from above." With regard to the formation of the Public Schools Athletic League designed to reform interscholastic athletics in New York City, J. Thomas Jable explained that teacher involvement in the new league "certainly enhanced teacher-pupil relations." Jeffrey Mirel, writing about Michigan high schools and the student reaction to faculty takeover of their leagues, said, "What is important to note is that in no student publication was the end of the student-run athletic associations lamented or denounced." Thomas W. Gutowski said of the Chicago schools, "For the most part, students welcomed growing faculty control. . . . [S]tudents went along because faculty involvement gave them things they needed: assistance in raising money, places to hold meetings and contests, offices for school papers, the expertise of teachers who acted as coaches and orchestra leaders, and smoother running leagues."[1]

SECRET SOCIETIES RETARD REFORM

Student reaction to reform, however, should be considered a mixed one, especially if one considers the existence of fraternities and sororities in the public schools as part of the battle over control of the extracurriculum. Though seemingly separate issues, in Chicago they became intertwined, and what took place was a decade-long struggle between the students and the faculty, fought tooth and nail in the courts, involving decisions that went all the way to the state supreme court. This vigorous student opposition arose from the attempts by school authorities to suppress "secret societies," a battle that rested on who in the school controlled sports and other areas of the extracurriculum, but ultimately rested on how a public high school should be defined. The fraternities dominated the sports teams, and control of the sport activities was intimately tied into their ability to function in the high schools. An early historian of Michigan interscholastic sports, Lewis L. Forsythe, likewise found a mixed student reaction. He particularly noted that the student-run athletic associations in big-city high schools were often dominated by fraternities and that "these groups often made it difficult for the principal to make new standards and procedures effective."[2]

High school authorities found the extracurriculum dominated by the secret societies because the students viewed their institutions as junior versions of the elite-dominated colleges, where fraternities and sororities defined themselves in terms of their achievements not in the classroom but in the club room and on the athletic field. The secret societies created a powerful and intoxicating culture that dominated college life, with football and the attendant social whirl that surrounded the game as the preeminent activities that shaped this culture. Thus—to the younger brothers and sisters in the high schools—the colleges of the Progressive Era, whose life was shaped by the Greek-letter societies, served as the model of what an educational institution should be.[3]

The Chicago school administration apparently thought that it had won the battle for control of high school athletics after its adoption of new regulations in March 1904, which was achieved without any visible student resistance. The administration was therefore unprepared for the much more difficult conflict that emerged soon afterward in May, when the board of education launched a campaign to suppress fraternities and sororities in the high schools. On June 22, the board formally adopted a rule that attacked membership in these secret societies, touching off a battle that would be waged furiously for five years, as the fraternities and sororities went to the courts repeatedly to obtain injunctions against any enforcement of "antifrat" rules. The secret societies, made up of the sons and daughters of Chicago's elite, had the support of some of the captains of industry and some of the most influential citizens in Chicago society, and they had plenty of friendly judges who would support their cause. The collateral damage from the war was to degrade severely the football program in the Cook County schools, as many top athletes in the league found themselves on the sidelines.[4]

Secret societies first emerged in the 1880s in Chicago high schools, but it was not until the mid-1890s that the schools, in imitation of the colleges at the time, first formed the Greek-letter secret societies that we are so familiar with today. More than fifty of these groups were formed in Chicago high schools from 1880 to 1915. Hyde Park alone had eighteen, and another high school had at least sixteen.[5] The fraternities and sororities were established in imitation of the college groups, carrying out rush parties to attract students and using secret ballots to choose members (which explains why educators called them "secret societies"). Their purpose was purely social, and they selected like-minded students whose social status was presumed equal to their own. The social status of these Greek-letter groups was clearly upper-middle- to upper-class, and the groups tended to flourish in the more elite Chicago public schools, such as Hyde Park, Phillips, and Lake View. The secret societies held parties, dances, and dinners;

published journals; and preened their presumably "elite" status around the school by waving Greek insignia pennants and wearing rings, pins, buttons, and sweaters bearing their fraternity's or sorority's Greek-letter insignia. Some groups even maintained chapter houses off the school campus.[6]

The Chicago high schools of the 1890s and the early part of the next century were considered among the elite institutions of the city. Whereas in the East, the upper-middle-class or upper-class youngster of high school age was sent to one of the elite boarding schools (such as Lawrenceville, Exeter, or Andover), or attended one of the elite day schools (such as Trinity, Cutler, or Berkeley), in the Chicago area there was just as good a chance that the boy or girl would be sent to a Chicago or a suburban public school, such as Hyde Park in Chicago or New Trier in Winnetka. The Chicago high schools in the mid-1890s were truly for the elite, serving only 6,681 students, or 4 percent of the high school–age population of 174,811. The high school population grew to 9,661 students in 1900 and to 11,208 students in 1904. The Child Labor Law of 1903, which forbade employment of children younger than fourteen years of age and regulated employment of children fourteen through sixteen, only mildly affected the high school enrollment in the law's initial years. Thus, such high schools as Hyde Park and Phillips had the same class of people who established the fraternities and sororities in the colleges. The administrators of private schools, particularly eastern boarding schools, generally accepted fraternities, as they fitted in with the away-from-home college model.[7]

In the East, likewise, some public-school systems were more accommodating to the existence of high school fraternities and sororities. In Massachusetts and New York, "some of the older schools" were reported to have found secret societies helpful in running the schools (such as Boston Latin and Brooklyn's Erasmus Hall). In New York City, the public schools reported minimal involvement of students in secret societies, or if there was involvement, there was considerable support and sponsorship by the faculty. There was, it appears, little conflict in New York City over the issue of high school secret societies.[8]

That the eastern experience was so different can be attributed in part to the large number of private schools that siphoned off "secret society" types from the public schools. Chicago and other midwestern cities also had a plethora of private secondary schools, but relative to the East—for example, where New York City developed no public high schools until 1897—the public high schools were valued more highly in the Midwest by the middle and upper classes, which often preferred them to the private academies and day schools in the area. In many of Chicago's suburbs, the public willingly paid higher taxes to build schools of elite standards, notably New Trier and Lake Forest Highs.[9]

In Chicago's public high schools, as well as most American public-school systems, the emergence of fraternities and sororities was met with alarm. Beyond alarm, Chicago high school educators were outright hostile at this imitative collegiate world created by their students. Cook County school superintendent Augustus Nightingale insisted that high schools should not ape colleges and said that to "call these pupils freshmen, sophomores, juniors, and seniors, to encourage class yells and class colors, to espouse the brutality of football, or even to permit the existence of secret fraternities and sororities, are each and all detrimental to the better interests of the growing, adolescent child." He further proclaimed, "These institutions in colleges are an inspiration; in high schools, a menace. . . . [T]hey should be eradicated."[10]

On the national level, the "frat question" first attracted national attention in 1895, when the subject was discussed at the National Education Association, but only after the turn of the century did the issue fully engage the educational establishment. A book on high school culture, *Student Life and Customs*, which appeared in 1901, barely touched on secret societies, but noted that in a survey, nine respondents condemned them and in six of the respondents' schools they were permitted to exist. In the following years, the *School Review, Education, NEA Proceedings*, and other publications of the education establishment all would become fully engaged with the issue.[11]

The NEA dealt with the problem of secret societies at its forty-third national meeting in St. Louis, Missouri, in July 1904. There, Gilbert B. Morrison of McKinley High of St. Louis addressed the conclave on the subject, after which the organization appointed a committee to examine the issue and report back to the organization the following year. Morrison gathered survey results, testimony, and other findings collected locally in

Chicago, Washington State, and other locales. The Morrison-authored committee report detailed universal condemnation by school authorities against the existence of secret societies in high schools. Based on the report, the NEA in 1905 passed a resolution condemning secret societies.[12]

The *School Review*, the educational establishment's journal on secondary education, was particularly involved with the issue, publishing letters, reports, court decisions, and research papers. Notably, a committee of the conference (appointed in 1902) issued an influential report in 1904 based on a survey of 306 schools. The report, authored by Chicago principal Spencer C. Smith of Phillips High (which had a large number of secret societies), found an almost universal agreement from secondary-school authorities that secret societies were a damaging presence in high schools. The *Review* followed this coverage with condemnatory essays by Gilbert B. Morrison and William Bishop Owen and in December 1906 published the Washington Supreme Court decision that ruled that school authorities had the right to regulate against membership in fraternities and sororities. Other professional journals joined in attacking secret societies at this time, notably *Education* and the *Elementary School Teacher*.[13]

As Chicago was one of the hotbeds in the development of high school secret societies, its school system's experience with the issue both exemplified and reflected national developments. Its objections to secret societies mirrored the complaints of education authorities nationwide. They were based on assumptions of what a public school education represented, that is, a socially democratic institution. Thus, one of the most frequent objections was the "undemocratic nature" of secret societies. A 1904 report from Chicago principals and teachers to Superintendent Edwin G. Cooley, which helped launch the school system's campaign against secret societies, made exactly these points: "We believe these organizations are undemocratic in nature, demoralizing in their tendencies and subversive to good citizenship." Furthermore, "Since the public school is an institution supported by public tax, all classes, without distinction of wealth or social standing, are entitled to an equal share in its benefits. Anything that divides the school community into exclusive groups, as these societies do, mitigates against the liberalizing influence that has made one people out of a multitude."[14]

Another frequently observed objection was that members of fraternities and sororities, despite their native intelligence and upbringing in cultivated homes, tended to neglect their studies to engage in secret-society frivolities. The 1904 Chicago report said, "Our experience shows that the scholarly attainments of the majority of students belonging to these secret societies are far below the average, and we have reason to believe that this is due to the influence of such organizations." A 1907 board of education report backed up this observation with some hard statistics. At one high school, of the eighty-seven sorority girls in eleven societies, thirty were below passing grade, and of the thirty-four boys in five societies, nineteen were below passing average. Thus, the 1902 conflict over the scholarship rule can be seen to represent the first attack in the war against what was deemed the pernicious influence of secret societies.[15]

Secret societies were also faulted for being character destroying, because they introduced immature high schoolers into a world of adult behavior and mores—encouraging them to engage in adult social habits and class snobbery, and in their vices as well. The 1904 principals and teachers report alluded to this appeal by saying, "They offer temptations to imitate the amusements and relaxations of adult life, while their members have not acquired the power of guiding their actions by mature judgment." A 1907 board of education report spelled it out: "Idleness, expense, trivial conversation, indulgence, love of display, and the spread of gossip all go with the fraternity; and that, in the case of some special boys's [sic] organizations, we may add to these keeping of late hours, ribald language, obscene songs, smoking, drunkenness, gambling, and social vice."[16]

The criticism of fraternities and sororities by the principals and teachers that particularly hit home was that they saw these groups as destructive of the community of interest in the high school and subversive to the authority of the faculty. The 1904 report said, "The effect of secret societies is to divide the school into cliques, to destroy unity and harmony of action and sentiment, and to render it more difficult to sustain the helpful relations which should exist between pupils and teachers." A 1906 report was more explicit on their subversiveness: "They are centers of rebellion against school regulation. They are a self-appointed, irresponsible power in the school, interfering with the free initiative of other students and with the authority of the faculty."[17]

Almost as frequently observed was that secret societies tended to dominate the social organization of the school, take a disproportionate share of the students' offices, and command the athletic teams. The 1906 report noted, "These secret aggressive groups take an unfair share of the school advantages, and treat the rest of the students as 'barbarians.'" For example, Cooley reported on one Chicago high school where fraternity or sorority members held twenty of the twenty-five elective positions in the school.[18]

The popular press nationwide echoed these same charges against secret societies, voicing roughly four main concerns: they were inimical to the spirit of democracy and shared community in the high school, dividing the school into cliques; they encouraged immature students to imitate the worst behavior of adults in their shabby snobbishness and frivolities by the girls and the taking up of vices by the boys; they were inimical to scholarship; and they encouraged disrespect for and rebellion against school authorities. The most notable of the articles was William Hard's long essay in *Everybody's Magazine*, in 1909. A *Chicago Tribune* editorialist, Hard, along with all the other local editorial writers, had attacked secret societies in high schools for years, and he laid out the entire case against them in this popular general-interest magazine, using many examples from the Chicago Board of Education experience. Sororities in high schools were also attacked in the pages of the *Ladies' Home Journal*.[19]

The Chicago Board of Education "antifrat" rule of 1904 did not attempt to abolish fraternities and sororities outright. The intention of the rule was to bar any public recognition for all members of fraternities and sororities—by denying them the use of schoolrooms for meetings, the use of the school name, and the ability to represent the school in athletic and literary contests or in any other "public capacity." The participation in extracurricular activities by secret-society members was made contingent on their renunciation of membership in their Greek-letter group and their discarding of articles of clothing or jewelry with Greek-letter insignia. While educators gave the condemnatory name "secret societies" to fraternities and sororities because of their secret initiations, paradoxically, the educators by their actions were forcing the Greek-letter societies to become more secretive.[20]

The antifrat rule made its most immediate and dramatic impact on the football programs in the schools. Early in the 1904 football season, several of the Cook County League schools lost their best players to the antifrat rule, and Hyde Park was the school most affected by the rule, but Phillips was affected as well. Both teams lost games to schools that were less impacted by the ban. Four Hyde Park students, among them star player Calvin Favorite, filed suit and obtained a court injunction in mid-October that restored players to the Hyde Park and Phillips teams, considerably strengthening their programs. The court reasoned that if athletic teams or literary societies of the schools were allowed to hold meetings on the school premises and use the school name, then school authorities could not discriminate against secret societies and they should be legally entitled to the same privileges. The suit would wend its way through the courts for the next four years. With the help from the courts, Hyde Park increased its veteran players from one to six. Throughout the remainder of the school year, the injunction remained in place and was in effect when the board published its annual report in June 1905.[21]

The Chicago Board of Education throughout the 1905–1906 school year attempted repeatedly to enforce its antifrat rule and was repeatedly thwarted when parents of fraternity members went to the courts to impose injunctions. In late November 1906, the board of education was finally able to restore the ban. Whereas in the previous year, perennial athletic power Hyde Park was able to hold off the board the entire season through court injunctions, its 1906 football team in the last two scheduled games was hard hit with the loss of key players—particularly captain Eberle L. Wilson. The Hyde Park parents filed a suit, *Eberle L. Wilson v. Board of Education of the City of Chicago*, to prevent the board from enforcing its 1904 antifrat rule. The suit would eventually be taken up by the Illinois Supreme Court and would ultimately represent the final defeat of the supporters of secret societies.[22]

During the 1906 and 1907 seasons of football competition, the football league was in disarray and reverted back to the days of essentially student control. In June 1906, a joint committee of the board of control and the high school principals voted not to award a championship for the coming football season. The constant struggle against the fraternities had worn on the administrators' resolve, and there was an overall sense of "let's wash our hands of this mess," as reflected by the fact that although there was no injunction in effect, the 1904 ban on secret societies was not being enforced.[23]

In September 1906, the principals allowed the students to form teams. The *Inter Ocean* reported that the principals were "willing to let the boys play if they wish to," indicating the degree by which students were still making decisions beyond faculty control. The only area of faculty control was in their retention of determining eligibility. As the students began to organize teams, the newspapers continued to recognize the existence of a "Cook County" championship series, and the ad hoc league—called the High School Association—worked out a round-robin weekly schedule of competition. The essentially student-run league was not fully respected, though, and the season was somewhat in disarray, as the scheduling became ad hoc. Some schools formed "outlaw" teams against faculty wishes, such as Crane playing under its old name of "English High" and McKinley playing under its old name of "West Division."[24]

The level of football apparently did not suffer from the league's disarray. The 1906 season saw the introduction of a new open game of football as a result of the rules reform implemented by the colleges following the 1905 season to make the game less brutal. Despite the battle raging between the students and the school authorities, the students and coaches were attuned to the changes in the football rules and adapted with remarkable facility. The *Chicago Tribune* reported on a University High–Hyde Park game: "The new game was played brilliantly by both teams. Forward passes, onside kicks, long punts, and wide end runs made the contest spectacular in the extreme. There was little semblance to the old style game even among the high school boys." Regarding an Oak Park–North Division game, the *Inter Ocean* remarked, "The schoolboys demonstrated that they had applied themselves to a thorough study of the new rules. The forward pass, the onside kick, quarterback runs, and the end runs were tried and executed with remarkable ability." In the East, in contrast, the high schools were slow to adopt the forward pass, and game reports showed no enthusiasm for and little ability to adapt to the open game that the forward pass offered.[25]

When the 1907 season began with the formation of a "new league," several newspapers commented negatively on the previous season. The *Chicago Record-Herald* explained, "The new league closes a chapter of high school football management that the lads are not proud of. Last season, as an experiment, the board of control decided to let the Principals' Association run the sport. The association paid little if any attention to the teams, letting the managers do about as they pleased." The *Inter Ocean* said, "The action of the Board of Control last year in refusing to allow the formation of the usual league had a dampening effect on the spirits of the majority of football enthusiasts." Clearly, the 1906 by default schoolboy-run league did not succeed in the eyes of many, who believed that a faculty-run league would be superior.[26]

Football in the 1907 season again saw no league competition sponsored by the board of control, and the league continued in disarray, with the problem of dealing with exclusion of fraternity members on several teams. Hyde Park and Phillips each presented teams with virtually no football experience, as all their players from the previous year were barred from participating. The circuit court before the season had given the board the green light to enforce its 1904 antifrat rule. The extent to which fraternities dominated athletic competition in these years is most revealing from the Hyde Park situation. In a preseason football report, the *Inter Ocean* commented, "The anti-fraternity rule will be noticed at Hyde Park, and it is possible that the school will not be represented by a team. The prominent athletes at Hyde Park are nearly all fraternity men, but the past year has developed many promising performers among the 'barbarians.'"[27]

The 1907 season was initiated when the head of the Principals' Association, Dr. Charles Edgar Boynton, called on the team managers to come together in late September to form a league and draw up a schedule. Five schools answered his call—Hyde Park, Englewood, Phillips, Crane Tech, and North Division. Boynton appointed an advisory board for what was largely a league run by the student managers. The organization was called the "Cook County High School Football League." Oak Park chose not to compete against the city schools, contending that it would not participate in the "outlaw" league.[28]

In November 1907, the Illinois Appellate Court affirmed the decision of the Superior Court of Cook County in the *Eberle L. Wilson* suit, filed by the parents of four Hyde Park students. What was at issue was the board's right to bar fraternities and sororities from representing the school and using school facilities. The court ruled against the parents and said that the school board had the power to bar secret societies from using the school name or the school building and to prohibit fraternity members from representing their school in any literary or athletic contest. The *Chicago Tribune* wryly observed in supporting the court's decision, "The public schools were not instituted primarily for the purpose of engaging in interscholastic athletic contests" and scathingly denounced fraternities as "potent factors for evil."[29]

Emboldened by the appellate decision in the *Wilson* case, Chicago school authorities in January 1908 stepped up their antifrat campaign. The president of the board of education, Otto C. Schneider, and the superintendent, Edwin G. Cooley, declared a "war of extermination" against fraternities and sororities. They believed they were free to pass even more stringent rules against secret societies by banning membership altogether and promising to "make membership grounds for expulsion." The board's position was strengthened even more on March 5 when the Illinois Appellate Court upheld the board position in the *Calvin Favorite* suit filed by parents of four Hyde Park students in the fall of 1904. Finally, on April 23, 1908, in the most decisive case in the board's long struggle against secret societies, the Illinois Supreme Court ruled in favor of the board in *Eberle L. Wilson v. Board of Education of the City of Chicago*, affirming the lower-court decisions.[30]

When the schools opened in early September 1908, school authorities moved to get signed statements from some eight hundred secret-society members in the schools (out of a total high school population of thirteen thousand), renouncing their memberships under threat of expulsion. On September 11, at Hyde Park High, fifty-one defiant students were expelled, and when they tried to enter the school on September 14, they were escorted out of the building. The same day, some twenty-five representatives of eighteen fraternities and sororities met with alumni to plan their strategy and form the Inter-Fraternity Protective Association. A defense fund of one thousand dollars was started, with the intention of increasing the amount to twenty-five thousand. Their lawyer, John C. Wilson (the father of Eberle L. Wilson), went to court to file a suit against the board on behalf of Hyde Park student Edward M. McDonald. The *Chicago Record-Herald* reported that "the sons and daughters of several millionaires were among those suspended yesterday from the Hyde Park High School," and the *Inter Ocean* noted that the combined wealth of those parents was fifteen million dollars.[31]

There would be no more injunctions. On October 3, in the circuit court, Judge Windes, after hearing the *McDonald* case, ruled that the board had the power to ban secret societies under their right to impose regulations and that there were no rights in the state or federal constitution violated by the regulation banning secret societies. The board attorney announced, "This ends fraternities and sororities. They lost in the other fight and they lost this one."[32]

The victory of the Chicago Board of Education over the secret societies, following favorable court decisions, paralleled similar antifrat victories across the country around this time. The states of Minnesota, Indiana, Michigan, Ohio, and Kansas all enacted laws that banned high school fraternities, and a myriad of school boards across the country—notably in Seattle, Washington; Springfield, Massachusetts; Meriden, Connecticut; Brooklyn, New York; Indianapolis, Indiana; and Louisville, Kentucky—successfully put bans into effect. Reflecting the experience of Illinois, school-board bans in Washington and Minnesota were upheld by the state supreme courts.[33]

Despite the aggressive opposition mounted by the profraternity forces, the 1908 football season was conducted under a successful ban on fraternities. School authorities now felt comfortable in restoring institutional control over the football program, with the board of control reimposing control over the Cook County League. The 1909 football season was the first peaceful one in years. Opening day of the school year was a remarkably quiet one, signaling the end of open resistance by the fraternities and sororities. Freed by the courts to make regulations, the board of educa-tion's subsequent campaign against the secret societies was reduced to a guerrilla conflict, the enemy appearing and disappearing, seeking to evade direct confrontation but continuing to skirmish and undermine authority. The board thus revisited the secret-society ban annually, stiffening the rules each time. In January 1913, the board suspended some two hundred students in a clampdown on secret societies. By January 1915, the board had in place its most stringent rule ever, requiring permanent expulsion of secret-society members from the school system.[34]

Although fraternities and sororities were not completely abolished in Chicago-area high schools, by 1909 they had ceased to be a disruptive force, stripped of their power to dominate the extracurriculum. Within a few more years, school authorities with successive regulation succeeded in forcing them completely underground. The administrators had won the war, as they effectively destroyed the power and cachet of secret societies so that they no longer had the ability to parade their reputed "in-group" social superiority before their fellow students. Chicago high schools no longer had a secret-society problem.[35]

High school fraternities and sororities remained a persistent and mostly minor issue for decades afterward. A 1931 questionnaire of 171 school systems nationwide found that in 101 of them, fraternities and sororities were specifically forbidden by state or local rules. By the 1940s, secret societies were again flourishing across the country, but educators mounted a campaign similar to the Progressive Era campaign and largely eradicated the problem.[36]

PERSISTENCE OF STUDENT-FACULTY CONFLICT

As long as there are rambunctious, rebellious high school students, there will always be conflict with the faculty in the secondary schools. Besides the conflict over secret societies, student rebellion manifested itself in several other areas during the Progressive Era, notably in disputes over long-distance travel, student rowdiness at games, and the issue of profes-sionalism. Ever since the two famous Chicago–New York intersectional football contests in 1902 and 1903, Chicago-area schools, often under student initiative, had been crisscrossing the country in search of worthy opponents. With the completion of control by school administrators in the Chicago school system, this kind of travel was becoming more heavily scrutinized and meeting with objections.

The administration faced conflict with the students in 1908, after Englewood had won the league championship and the Englewood boys arranged a late-December trip to the Far West. The trip caused considerable controversy with the board of education because the team left before classes had shut down for the Christmas break. The board was outraged and wanted to know who had given the students permission to go. Not far from their minds was the scandalous postseason trip the North Division team made to Seattle the previous year, when the team members broke into the University of Washington lockers and made off with "a large collection of running shoes, boxing gloves, sweaters, and tennis rackets." But institutional control over high school athletics had not yet been fully imposed in 1908, judging by the conflicting signals that the Englewood players received from different authorities. Englewood principal James E. Armstrong thought the decision to make the trip did not rest with him, saying, "It made no difference whether I granted or refused to grant the boys permission to go west, so long as their parents favored their being taken out of school in order that they might go."[37]

During the three-week visit, Englewood played two games with top teams in the Pacific Northwest (Butte, Montana, and Longmont, in Denver, Colorado). The following year, Englewood repeated as champion and again arranged a western trip, and as before, the holiday intersectional matchups were opposed by the board and by the new superintendent, Ellen Flagg Young. This time the board prevailed, and the boys did not go. The board's disposition was not helped by the league's title game, which had erupted into fisticuffs on the field and rioting and fighting in the stands between the partisan fans.[38]

The Chicago Board of Education ban on intersectional travel was not sustained beyond 1909, as city and area public and parochial high schools continued to make ambitious postseason trips. Suburban Oak Park made a Pacific Northwest trip in 1910 and then traveled to Boston in 1912 to introduce the forward pass to the East and claim a "national championship" (a year before Notre Dame played Army in New York and supposedly exhibited the virtues of the forward pass to the East). Historically, Chicago high schools played a more open football game than did schools in the East, and after the forward pass was legalized for the 1906 season, it flourished in Chicago and suburban schools. Among the many other intersectional trips, Phillips High in 1912 went to the Pacific Northwest to play two games, and DePaul Academy traveled to Boston in 1915. Intersectional football matches were obviously considered acceptable by some high school authorities during this era.[39]

Whereas football was only occasionally disrupted by fighting, the Chicago Public High School League basketball program was plagued throughout its existence with dissension and fights at games. The hothouse atmosphere of basketball courts with their continuous action and fans in close proximity to the players and officials seemed to generate a lot of heat. Conflict came to a boil in 1908 and put the existence of the league in peril. Early in the season, in January, four teams lodged protests with the basketball committee that were forwarded to the board of control. The protests included charges of professionalism, slugging, and unfair and incompetent officiating. President of the board of control and principal at North Division High Charles Edgar Boynton threatened that "dissension among the teams in the Cook County High School Athletic League must cease, or eventually athletics in the Chicago high schools will be done away with."[40]

High school baseball also became a major problem in the league. During the first decades of the twentieth century, the population's engagement in sports was not only in the major professional leagues, but also in countless pro, semipro, and amateur organizations and teams sponsoring every kind of sport activity. Sponsors included YMCAs, ethnic groups, church organizations, small businesses, large corporations, and athletic clubs. Teams playing for these organizations ranged from the honest amateur and the corrupted amateur to the semipro and the professional. These teams recruited players and participants not only from the general population but also from the secondary schools and colleges. The situation was thus ripe for the development of a major problem of professionalism, pitting the educational establishment, with their newfound responsibilities for the sports extracurriculum, against their students, whose opportunities to play elsewhere, sometimes for cash, were great and enticing.

Of all the sports competition in the high schools, baseball was by far the most corrupt. Baseball had produced the most extensive level of amateur and semipro competition, including church leagues, club leagues, and industrial leagues. The natural gravitation of talented high school boys toward these leagues was a persistent problem. Periodically, league authorities engaged in campaigns to root pros out of the prep game. *Pros* in the newspaper lingo of the day had a broad meaning, covering both amateur and semipro teams where the players may or may not have been paid.

Other sports were by no means exempt from charges of corruption. Football, though less extensively developed in the amateur and semipro fields, had a number of so-called prairie-football leagues—semipro organizations that usually played on Sundays. In the fall of 1910, for example, Hyde Park's star quarterback, Leslie Hart, was expelled from the prep league for professionalism. He was initially charged with playing on a semipro football team, the Barefoot Eleven, in the previous season. Hart contended he had never received any payment and was unaware that the Barefoot Eleven was a professional team. Then he was charged with playing for a semipro baseball team in the summer of 1910, getting paid five dollars for each game. The Leslie Hart case proved to be the impetus for the Cook County League to deal with a long-festering problem with "professionalism." The *Chicago Tribune* commented that the Hart case could only mean "a big crusade against professionalism."[41]

The professionalism problem was most persistent in baseball. Back in 1908, Phillips was expelled from the baseball league, because its star pitcher, Lindquist, was also playing for the Gunthers, a famed semipro team. In 1910, in the high school indoor baseball league, with freshman George Halas (of future pro-football fame) at right short and Walter Halas as the pitcher, Crane swept through the regular season undefeated. Then, just prior to the semifinals, in mid-March, Crane's prospects of repeating as champion were severely damaged when Walter was barred from the league by the board of control as a professional.[42]

In 1911 the professionalism issue came to a boil, with league authorities out for blood. They had no trouble finding evidence, turning the league season into a disaster when seven of the eight teams in the major division of the league were disqualified for "violations for using 'pros.'" Lake View, which ended in last place, was deemed the only "clean" team. The league found that Phillips, the putative champion, had five players playing for outside teams. No pennant was awarded that year. Regarding the continuing scandals, the *Tribune* said, "Frequently pupils who have graduated from Chicago high schools have been thrown out of athletics in the University of Illinois because of their professionalism while taking part in Chicago high school sports."[43]

The suppression of Greek-letter societies immensely helped school authorities prevail in their control of high school sports by World War I, and the American public high school, although not representing the ideal institution as envisioned by the early-twentieth-century educators, was much the better for the absence of Greek-letter societies and the end of student-run athletic games. Interscholastic games were now being conducted under the understanding of the most idealistic aims of educators, supporting the educational mission in helping to build student unity, good character, and good citizenship. In accordance with the Progressive Era understanding that school reform leads to broader social reform, American society was much better as well.

Yet the search for control was not at an end. At the same time national interscholastic sports were undergoing reform, they were also experiencing an explosion of new sports, and now largely under the initiative of school administrators, often in alliance with outside sports agencies. The sports of cross country, soccer, basketball, swimming, indoor baseball, speed skating, ice hockey, marksmanship, golf, rowing, and lacrosse became part of the athletic calendar. These new sports, while providing students with new opportunities, presented school officials with new challenges as well with regard to control of athletics, as the world of interscholastic sports expanded far beyond its original boundaries of the early twentieth century.

6

WINTER INDOOR SPORTS
FILL THE VOID

The construction of gymnasiums in the high schools during the 1890s laid the foundation for the development of indoor sports, particularly basketball. Educators by this time saw physical education as intrinsic to the development of American high school youth. Gymnasiums were originally designed for gymnastics and calisthenics instruction, but games soon took more and more time on the floor space, as educators saw that they had value in their educational mission. Although indoor baseball was played in some high school gymnasiums, participants usually searched for larger facilities, such as armories. Eventually, most colleges and many high schools built gymnasiums with running tracks often circling above around the basketball courts. Some universities had indoor facilities that were sufficiently large to host interscholastic indoor track meets, and these venues were often used for league and other big interscholastic events. Swimming was also adopted by many high schools, but its adoption was not initially contingent on the schools having swimming pools. Most early high school swimming competition was sponsored by private athletic clubs, which had their own pools, and most high school swim teams trained in the local YMCAs. The support of outside institutions, such as armories and athletic clubs, brought to the forefront issues of control as well.

BASKETBALL: THE IDEAL INDOOR GAME

During the winter seasons of the early 1890s, there was little interscholastic activity. In the Northeast, there was some indoor track, and in Chicago indoor baseball, but by and large there was a huge void, students finding themselves engaged only in dreary callisthenic drills. Basketball was invented in December 1891 by Dr. James Naismith at the YMCA's International School for Christian Workers (Springfield College) in Springfield, Massachusetts, a result of an entreaty by the school's physical education head, Luther Halsey Gulick, to Naismith to devise an indoor game that could engage students during the winter months. After some experimentation, Naismith devised a completely new game that met with immediate enthusiastic response. Within a couple of months, basketball was rapidly spreading across the country through a network of YMCAs. By May 1892, the YMCAs in the Chicago area were eagerly taking up the "infectious" game, and in 1893 they were in regular competition with one another and with outside teams, notably the University of Chicago's affiliate school, Morgan Park Academy.[1]

Basketball on the collegiate level in Chicago was likewise organized early, with a pipeline to Chicago from Springfield College, Amos Alonzo Stagg, who had been one of the members of the teachers' team that competed against a students' team in the first public basketball contest. He left Springfield for the University of Chicago in the summer of 1892 to become the school's coach. Intramural basketball games began at the university in March 1893, but only one outside game was played, against Morgan Park Academy. The following year, Stagg commenced regular competition in the YMCA league. At this time, basketball filled the gym with many bodies, as nine men played per side. The first intercollegiate contest involving five-man squads was between the University of Chicago and the University of Iowa in January 1896.[2]

The earliest schoolboy basketball in Illinois thus was played by Morgan Park Academy in 1893 and 1894, but it competed only against its parent school and YMCAs. The school appears to have been the first secondary school in the country to have taken up the sport, but its enthusiasm did not last. When the Morgan Park Academy helped form the Academic League in 1896, basketball was not on the schedule.[3]

In December 1895, student delegates of the Cook County high schools got together to form a league around a winter sport. The question was whether they wanted the sport to be basketball or indoor baseball.

Both sports were fast growing in popularity at the time, but indoor baseball was growing faster and the delegates chose that sport by a vote of seven to two. North Division, one of the two votes in the minority, opted out of the indoor baseball league and instead joined the YMCA basketball league, becoming the first public school in the area to adopt basketball for boys, but lasting just one year. Meanwhile, the game flourished among the girls in the local high schools, with the girls forming a league and getting notices from the newspapers and educators.[4]

With boys' basketball flourishing in the YMCAs, however, it was not long before boys in junior YMCA programs were bringing the game to their high schools. In Chicago the first boys high school teams formed on a permanent basis occurred in 1900, and on March 2 the first interscholastic game in Illinois was played between Englewood and Elgin. The game mushroomed so much that by the following year, a league of eight schools was formed. The first league season was short, with games played from mid-January to mid-March. However, four league teams played a passel of extra games in early March in a tournament held at the Coliseum at the first annual show of the International Forest, Fish, and Game Association. The opening day of the show included the first day of high school basketball competition, and fifteen thousand people flocked to the Coliseum, which promoted public interest in high school basketball and possibly encouraged its development.[5]

The Cook County basketball league grew rapidly, and the season became progressively longer, with twelve teams in the league in 1902 and the title game being played on March 29 and with fifteen teams in 1903 and the season ending on April 26. By this time, boys' basketball had surpassed girls' basketball in popularity and had transcended the idea that the game was essentially a "girls' game." While the Cook County League ostensibly served all schools in the county, not all the schools chose to join. Whereas such schools in the western suburbs as Oak Park and LaGrange were active members in the league, most of the schools north of the city along the North Shore played informally against each. However, in a basketball dispute, Evanston, a founding Cook County member, withdrew permanently in 1907. Evanston immediately helped organize among the northern suburban high schools a new conference, the North Shore

League, to play not only basketball but a full schedule of sports. This same year, the Academic League belatedly added basketball to its schedule. Boys' basketball had thus spread throughout the Chicago area.[6]

The number of schools in the Cook County League steadily increased each year so that by the 1910–1911 season, there were seventeen schools competing. The league that year introduced a lightweight program. Players in the lightweight program could not weigh more than 130 pounds individually or more than an average of 125 pounds per team. By the 1912–1913 season, the Cook County League was becoming unwieldy— particularly in basketball, with thirty-three lightweight and heavyweight teams—and in the spring of 1913, the Chicago schools decided to break

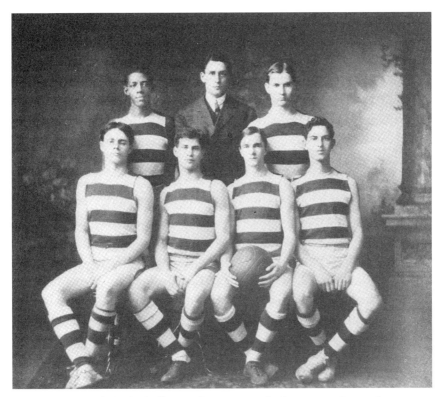

7. Hyde Park High basketball team from 1903, which gives evidence that among the earliest basketball teams, faculty coaches were already present. The African American player on the team is Sam Ransom. Courtesy of the Chicago History Museum.

apart the league and create a conference that would have only Chicago public high schools as members. The suburban schools with University High then formed their own league.[7]

Meanwhile, basketball across the state was also growing rapidly. In 1908 Illinois became the second state after Wisconsin to adopt a state tournament. The first year of the tournament was an invitational conducted in late March by Oak Park High at both the school and the Oak Park YMCA. The school's athletic director, Lewis Omer, invited all of the reputed top schools in the state to participate and received sanction from the Illinois High School Athletic Association. The first tournament drew only an eleven-team field, but at each session the bleachers and gallery were filled with enthusiastic fans. The IHSAA, which had feared that the tournament would not pay for itself, was pleased with the gate receipts and the overall reception for the event and so made the tournament an annual event and assumed direct sponsorship. It changed the tournament from an invitational affair to embrace all members of the association. The IHSAA divided the state into districts, and district champions would meet in the finals. The organization had some two hundred schools at the time, but no members from Chicago and only a few from the surrounding suburbs.[8]

Boys' basketball elsewhere around the country grew with the same speed. As early as 1896, a suburban school of New York, Yonkers High, participated in a league with YMCAs. The two schoolboy leagues serving the New York area soon added basketball to their winter calendars, the Long Island League in 1897 and the Interscholastic League in 1899. In 1900 the Metropolitan High School League, made up of newly established public high schools in Manhattan and the Bronx, adopted basketball. When the Public Schools Athletic League was formed in late 1903, basketball and track were the two initial sports that launched the league. At the Olympic Games in St. Louis, Flushing High, the PSAL inaugural league champion, took the Olympic Inter-City Bowl, one of the many contests conducted in conjunction with the Olympic Games.[9]

As in Chicago, basketball in Boston and Massachusetts started out mainly as a girls' game during the late 1890s. However, a few early boys teams were formed, notably Holyoke High near Springfield, which formed a team in 1897. By the time of Boston's huge Sportsman's Show in March 1900, there were enough high schools in the state to sponsor a tournament, which included mostly public and private schools in the Boston area. In 1901 Holyoke High went to the Pan-American Exposition in Buffalo and competed for the "national" interscholastic basketball championship. It was not much; only two other schools competed, the Pratt Institute of Brooklyn and Mt. Vernon High of New York. In 1903 a number of Boston suburban schools in East Boston and Roxbury formed a basketball league, and by 1904 the boys' game was prospering, surpassing the girls' game in interest. Boston proper began league competition for its city schools in 1905.[10]

Boys' basketball in the Philadelphia secondary schools was pioneered by a private school, the Drexel Institute, in 1897. The following year, the school was joined by a public school, Central High, playing each other as well as local colleges and amateur clubs. In 1899 Drexel and Central were joined by several other public and private schools, and a basketball league was formed, with Central being joined by the two other public schools (Manual and Northeast) and Drexel being joined by four other private schools (Brown Preparatory, Spring Garden, Eastburn, and Roman Catholic). The league was generically called the "Interscholastic League." In 1900 a second high school conference in the city was formed by five private schools—Friends' Select, Abington Friends School, Friends' Central, Eastburn, and Swarthmore Preparatory. When a number of private schools and public schools in Philadelphia came together in the 1900–1901 season to form the Philadelphia Interscholastic League, basketball was among the first year's offerings.[11]

Besides its tremendous growth in the big cities, high school basketball also grew in rural America. The small number of players required for the game and its low expense made it possible for even the smallest of schools to form a team. Once the game was established in a rural high school, the basketball team became virtually the only local team that a small town had to rally around to build their civic pride. The game spread rapidly throughout the farmlands and across the nation. Rural organization of basketball centered not so much around a league, as in the big cities, but in the state tournament, helping to precipitate the formation of state high school athletic associations in many states to sponsor such tournaments. Many of the earliest state tournaments were initially sponsored by colleges and universities before a high school association assumed sponsorship.[12]

Wisconsin has been credited as the first state to conduct a state championship in basketball, when in 1905 Lawrence College of Appleton inaugurated a tournament. In 1916 the Wisconsin Interscholastic Athletic Association assumed control. Other states quickly followed Wisconsin's lead—Illinois in 1908; Montana and Ohio in 1909; Indiana and Nebraska in 1911; Kansas, Iowa, and South Dakota in 1912; Minnesota in 1913; and Utah in 1914. All these early pioneering states were in the Midwest and West. The earliest states in the East and South were West Virginia in 1914 and Virginia and North Carolina in 1915. Within a few years after World War I, most all states had adopted a state basketball tournament.[13]

By World War I, basketball had become the most popular sport for boys after football. The game seemed destined to triumph in its popularity, as it filled a sports vacuum in the winter and unlike football could be played by a school of any size, plus it could be played a couple of times a day if need be, lending itself to exciting tournaments. The game's growth was greatly facilitated by the spread of compulsory physical education across the country into every little hamlet, with the requisite building of gymnasiums, thus providing an almost universal venue for basketball games. Growth was especially strong in rural areas. Whereas in the cities basketball was considered a part of a sports program that could redirect young men into wholesome activity, in the rural areas basketball became an expression of small-town boosterism and the only sports entertainment for many rural people.[14]

SWIMMING EMERGES AS AN INTERSCHOLASTIC SPORT

Competitive swimming in the country's high schools goes back to the 1890s, but there was not much of it. The sport did not truly take off until the 1920s, when high school conferences and state associations began adding the sport to the winter program. Prior to that time, it was mainly nurtured in the major metropolitan areas in the private athletic clubs, a few universities, and a few big-city leagues, mainly located in the northeastern section of the country and Southern California. In Chicago the groundwork for competitive high school swimming was established in the late 1890s when the Chicago Athletic Association began its youth programs and sponsorship of swimming in the high schools. Most colleges and secondary schools of the day did not have swimming pools, and few ever attempted to organize teams during the 1890s. The CAA knew that for swimming to grow as a sport, it must work to develop interest in it among the younger generation. At the 1897 national outdoor meet, for example, the club sponsored a 100-yard schoolboy race, with representatives from South Division and English high schools. In the winter of 1898, the CAA inaugurated its junior swimming and water-polo squad for swimmers of grade school and high school age.[15]

In July 1898, the Chicago Swimming Club organized a competition called the "First Annual Amateur Swimming Carnival." The meet featured a variety of adult and youth events. In an 80-yard race for "schoolboys," representatives came from both public and private secondary schools—English High, Manual Training, North Division, Hyde Park, and Armour Academy. A water-polo match at the carnival pitted the CAA juniors against a team representing Hyde Park High. The interscholastic competition at the Chicago Swimming Club did not lead to more competition. No high school swimming races in Chicago appeared for the next three years. Instead, several Cook County public and private schools competed in water-polo matches. The CAA saw the fostering of water polo as a way of developing new strong young swimmers. The year 1901 saw the formation of the Interscholastic Water Polo League, which adopted a schedule for March and April that included teams representing both secondary schools and amateur clubs.[16]

Raising the visibility of interscholastic swimming as well as swimming competition in general in the Chicago area was the Sportsman's Show, a large extravaganza conducted by the International Forest, Fish, and Game Association and held in Chicago for only two years, 1901 and 1902, at the newly completed Coliseum. It combined an exhibition of fish and game sports with various athletic contests—such as basketball games, mentioned earlier—and was instrumental in the promotion of aquatic sports in the

Chicago area. These aquatic sports were water-polo games and racing contests for amateur clubs, high schools, and YMCA teams, plus exhibits of fancy diving. High schools involved in the Sportsman's Show swim races and water-polo events were Hyde Park, English High, North Division, Armour Academy, and Lewis Institute. Interscholastic aquatic sports were not sustained after 1902, and only North Division felt compelled to field water-polo and relay teams, competing regularly for the next two years against university and club teams.[17]

The modern era in American swimming emerged in 1905 with the advent of the fast and efficient crawl stroke. As it was adopted across the country, competitive swimming was energized with a flowering of meets in the high schools, colleges, and clubs. In Chicago the University of Chicago had completed its new field house, Bartlett Gymnasium, which housed a swimming pool, and proceeded to build an ambitious swimming program. The university developed a competitive schedule with its midwestern rivals and began sponsoring high school competition, hosting several high school meets in the winter of 1905, one of which was billed as the "Cook County Championship." Six schools participated, two private and four public. The Cook County meet, however, was conducted only one more year, in 1906.[18]

The Illinois Athletic Club (IAC), founded in 1904, would play a major role in the coming years in fostering high school swimming. After opening its clubhouse on Michigan Avenue with its beautiful, classically designed swimming pool in 1907, the IAC began ascendancy in the swim world that would supersede all other private and public swim organizations in the Chicago area. Well aware that the future of swim competition lay with the youth, the IAC inaugurated an annual interscholastic meet in 1908, attracting eight schools, three of them private. That year Perry McGillivray, then a sophomore at Crane Tech, set a national high school record in the 40-yard backstroke with a new "push-off" technique (which was soon universally adopted).[19]

The work of the Chicago schoolboys in particular in 1908 set off signals in the swimming world that prep swimming had arrived. In a wrap-up of the year in the *Chicago Tribune*, Frank Sullivan noted:

Most notable of all has been the remarkable development of school-boy swimming that has multiplied by six or eight the total number of America's registered swimmers and has given us scholastic records equal to the country's best of a few seasons ago. Swimming always has been a young game, supported best by youthful physique, but never has this point been so well illustrated as by the 16 year wonders of 1908. In every large city, high school leagues have been formed; the Illinois Athletic Club interscholastic has been initiated as an annual feature, and New York has had a schoolboy meet which listed over 200 entries in a single event.[20]

By the second decade of the century, high schools had become almost equal partners with the athletic clubs in sponsoring swim competition. In 1913, when the Cook County League split into separate suburban and city leagues, both adopted swimming as a sponsored sport. The IAC coach, William Bachrach, particularly hailed the Suburban League, home of swim powers Evanston, New Trier, and Oak Park. Related Chester A. Foust of the *Record Herald*, "Coach Bachrach of the IAC believes the swimming league organized by the suburban high school officials to be the biggest boost the splashing game has been given in a long time. He says that the league will develop some more stars for his team."[21]

An *Intercollegiate Swimming Guide* published in the midst of World War I contained an illuminating report on the 1916 season from one of the pioneer high school swimming coaches, Chauncey A. Hyatt, of New Trier, the first high school in the Chicago area to have a pool:

In the Middle West there has been a steady development of swimming in the secondary schools. Each succeeding year more swimmers have been developing and previous performances bettered. The develop-ment is due to several reasons, but probably the most important one is the fact that boards of education are beginning to consider natatoriums just as essential as gymnasiums and nearly every new high school has been included in its plans. Several schools built several years ago have added swimming pools and are recognizing aquatics as part of the high school curriculum.[22]

Hyatt listed fourteen schools in Illinois and Indiana with swimming pools. The *Swimming Guide* listed eleven high school national records, of which Chicago schools held five; New York schools, one; New Jersey schools, one; and Massachusetts schools, four.[23]

As in Chicago, high school swimming in New York City benefited from a combination of support from private clubs and educational institutions. New York's annual Sportsman's Show sponsored an interscholastic relay as early as 1900, and the local AAU in its swim meets was sponsoring interscholastic relays as early as 1902. The New York Athletic Club (NYAC), which was a dominant power in amateur swimming during this era, unlike the Chicago clubs, however, did little to support high school competition. From approximately 1913 to 1917, the athletic club held a meet, which it billed as a "national interscholastic," but it never amounted to much, attracting Massachusetts powerhouse Brookline High and few local private and public high schools. Among the universities, the most prestigious meet was the University of Pennsylvania Interscholastic, begun in 1903. It attracted about a dozen public and private schools each year from Pennsylvania, New Jersey, and New York. Not until Princeton began sponsoring a swim meet in 1913 did New York metropolitan universities enter the interscholastic swim arena.[24]

League competition in Boston and Philadelphia would not exist until the 1920s, but in New York the PSAL began an extensive program of swimming competition in 1907. The PSAL conducted both a dual meet series as well as a tournament championship, and the meets were normally held in local private-club and college pools. There was an occasional water-polo match between two league schools as well, but the sport soon died out.[25]

In Southern California, the land of sun, sand, surf, and sea, swimming likewise emerged early as a thriving interscholastic sport. High school swimming in California was an outdoor sport, and meets were usually held in the late spring. A Southern California championship meet was inaugurated in June 1910, attracting six high schools—Los Angeles High, Los Angeles Polytechnic, Long Beach, Santa Barbara, Santa Monica, and Harvard Military School. In 1914 sponsorship of the Southern California Swimming Interscholastic was assumed by the High

School Athletic Council that regulated high school sports in the southern part of the state. By 1916 a state championship meet was held between the champions of the southern and northern sections. California high schools early on were producing world-quality swimmers, notably Ludy Langer, from Redondo High.[26]

Unlike New York and Chicago, which saw a brief interest in water polo in the high schools, in California the sport flourished, sustained with regular competition into the 1920s and later. In 1913 three Los Angeles–area high schools—Los Angeles, Long Beach, and Los Angeles Polytechnic—formed the Los Angeles County Interscholastic Water Polo League. By 1918 a Southern California Interscholastic championship was being held for the sport.[27]

Swimming made its way onto the high school sports calendar before World War I, but it was limited to a few sectors of the country and only in a few large cities, namely, New York, Chicago, and Los Angeles. That high school swimming arose as an urban activity was because it benefited from the early promotion and sponsorship from the private clubs and universities in those cities. Although students swam for their schools, they received their coaching and training elsewhere. That kind of support by the second decade of the new century kick-started the schools themselves to organize swimming contests and add the sport to their league schedules, install coaches, and even add swimming pools to their facilities.

Indoor Baseball: The Chicago Game

Before there was the game of softball, Illinois high schools played a similar game called indoor baseball. It was a cramped little game in which the rules were preeminently designed to facilitate play inside armories, gymnasiums, and similarly confined venues. It may be hard for the modern sports fan to imagine high school students playing baseball in gymnasiums, yet throughout the 1890s and during the first decade of the next century, indoor baseball was one of the most popular winter games in the Chicago area, engaging each week thousands of youngsters, young men and women, and adults. Private-club teams, college teams, and as well as high school teams flourished and prospered in competition with one another, drawing big and enthusiastic crowds of rooters, and Chicago newspapers each winter were alive with news of league contests. The game was what basketball is today, the preeminent winter sport activity for Illinoisans.[28]

The basic equipment of an indoor baseball team was a huge seventeen-inch ball and a sticklike bat. No gloves were worn, and the catcher wore no mask. The ball was truly soft—the rules called for it to be made of a "yielding substance," far from the hardness of the softball of today. The distance between bases was greatly reduced from baseball, only twenty-seven feet apart. The pitcher was a mere twenty-two feet from home plate. Sandbags served as bases, and players were allowed to slide into them and push them along in the slide. The game was played by nine men, with two shortstops, left and right, and only two outfielders, left and right.

Indoor baseball was invented by George Hancock in 1887 at the Farragut Boat Club on Chicago's South Side. About twenty members were gathered in the gymnasium of the clubhouse on Thanksgiving Day to follow via telegram the progress of the annual Harvard-Yale game. A combination of good spirits and empty time on their hands resulted in one of the young members picking up a stray boxing glove and tossing it to another member, who with a stick batted at it. Hancock, watching what was transpiring, was inspired to make a formal game of the high jinks. In the next several years, the game spread like wildfire throughout the Chicago area, and by the winter of 1891–1892, there were flourishing amateur leagues involving more than one hundred teams. In an 1892 city guide, the editor said that indoor baseball attracts "thousands of spectators of the best classes. In fact, indoor ball is particularly the sport of gentlemen, and especially among club members." And in the early 1890s, the gentlemen who had the leisure time to play indoor baseball were also enrolling their sons and daughters in the public high schools.[29]

West Division, a school centered in an upper- and upper-middle-class area around the West Side neighborhood of Union Park, was the first high school to adopt the sport for boys, and in the winter of 1891–1892, it played a variety of amateur teams, plus one other secondary team, Chicago Manual Training. On November 21, 1891, in the first interscholastic game on record, Chicago Manual met West Division. It was not until December

1895, however, that delegates of the Cook County high schools decided to form a league to play the sport. The delegates drew up a constitution and formally named the conference the Cook County High School Indoor Base Ball League. At this time, the league was completely student run. Curiously, early on in the meeting, it was evident that indoor baseball was not the automatic choice of the delegates. A new winter sport was also growing in the area, basketball. The delegates thus were presented with two options regarding adoption of a winter sport—basketball or indoor baseball—and by a vote of seven to two, indoor baseball got the nod.[30]

The decision to adopt indoor baseball not only helped make the sport prosper but also helped retard the growth of boys' basketball in metropolitan Chicago. (Basketball was spreading rapidly throughout the area, but in the high schools it was a girls' game.) Only five schools participated in indoor baseball the first year because of the difficulty in obtaining halls. The city's newspapers regularly reported on the league, which played a double round-robin schedule from January to mid-March. Beside the tangible award for winning the conference, the champion also received the balance of the treasury, seven dollars. The following year, typical of amateur and semipro leagues during that time, there was a large turnover of league members. By the third year of competition, seven teams made up the league, and by 1900 ten schools chose to field teams. The 1900 season was capped off by a championship game between West Division and Lake View witnessed, according to the *Inter Ocean*, by "probably the largest crowd ever at an indoor game."[31]

The most successful school in the league, Crane Technical (formerly English High), another West Side school, emerged as a power in 1906. Its team that year featured pitcher and outfielder Walter Halas, an older brother of George Halas, the future owner of the Chicago Bears. In 1907 West Division, renamed McKinley, ruled the roost for its last banner. But the competition against its nearest West Side rival was most fierce, as exemplified by a *Chicago Record-Herald* report:

> Rivalry between adherents of the McKinley and Crane High School indoor baseball teams culminated yesterday in the arrest of four members of the Crane School. Excluded from the McKinley High School

gymnasium where a contest between the opposing teams was in progress, the Crane rooters are declared to have indulged in a demonstration, which was halted abruptly by the arrival of the police. . . . Only the players, officials, and a few instructors witnessed the game. All other spectators were barred by order of the Principal George M. Clayburg on account of outbursts of enthusiasm at previous games which were asserted to have verged upon the disorderly.[32]

One peculiarity of the indoor baseball competition in Chicago was how the West Side high schools—West Division, Crane, Medill, and Austin—dominated the league. An educator at Crane, fighting to save the sport in 1914, told the *Tribune* that the school "depended upon indoor baseball to help the technical school financially. He also pointed out that all West Side schools are deeply interested in the game." There may have been something demographically or socially conducive on the West Side

8. Crane Tech High School indoor baseball team from 1913, with future owner of the Chicago Bears pro football team George Halas (*top row, third from left*). Courtesy of David Riddell and Elizabeth Krasemichener.

to cause that area to do well in indoor baseball. It appears that indoor baseball, despite its gentlemanly origins, had by the first decade of the century become a blue-collar sport, at least among high school players, and it thrived in working-class schools. At Crane Tech, the game drew many Czech kids, such as the Halases, and other players named Kleka, Napratek, Vovesny, and Kubat. Demographically, the West Side had changed its makeup since the 1890s, as the upper classes moved north and farther west, leaving a more working-class and immigrant population.[33]

After the Cook County League broke up in the summer of 1913, two new leagues were formed in its stead, the Chicago Public High School League and the Suburban League. None of the new Suburban League members played the sport, and the Public League played for just one more season. High school indoor baseball subsequently thrived mostly in the more working-class, immigrant-heavy Catholic League, formed in 1912, which adopted indoor baseball and annually up to 1915 conducted a round-robin schedule. After that time, some schools continued competition for a few more years, but by the early 1920s, the sport was dead. The tremendous growth of and enthusiasm for basketball at this time undoubtedly was the greatest contributor to killing interest in indoor baseball.[34]

Few high schools in the rest of the country played indoor baseball. In New York, the PSAL conducted a boys' tournament in the grade schools during 1911–1912, and the sport was listed as an intramural activity for girls. San Diego conducted a county tournament for high school girls around the time of World War I. Minnesota sponsored a high school boys' league, and some high schools in Michigan and Ohio took up the sport. The sport apparently was not taken up by high school boys outside the Midwest.[35]

Meanwhile, indoor baseball informally moved outdoors, around 1906–1907. Boys of all ages were taking it outside onto the streets, sandlots, and playgrounds. Charles Phelps Cushing, writing in *Collier's* in 1911, noted the phenomenon:

> Give all due credit, then, to those unsung adventurers among the boys
> of Chicago who first dared to disregard a label and play indoor baseball
> outdoors. In gymnasiums for a good many years the indoor game has

been popular because it is so well adapted to a small area of floor space; but it was only three or four years ago that Chicago boys began to adopt this form of play for street use. So fast has the idea spread that today nearly every small boy in the city has at one time or another practiced the modified style. In the thickly populated sections particularly, it is rapidly becoming one of the most popular boys' games.[36]

The game rapidly became a staple of the city's playgrounds by all age groups, from grade school students in schools around the city to office workers in the Loop who took afternoons off to play games in Grant Park. The term *playground ball* arose to describe this outdoor version of indoor baseball. In the spring of 1907, delegates from the South Park playground system, Cook County high schools, Chicago grammar schools, parochial schools, and the Cook County Bible Association got together and formally established the game of "playground ball," launching the sport on a trial basis during the spring of 1907. The new game was deemed a success, and in December the delegates reconvened, formulated rules, and founded the National Playground Ball Association, a name chosen to reflect their intention to make the organization national. For outdoor play, the baselines were lengthened to thirty-five feet, and the distance of the pitcher's mound to home plate was lengthened to thirty feet. Two ball sizes were chosen, twelve inch and fourteen inch, the larger to be used in smaller playing areas.[37]

Chicago also established an outdoor game from the indoor game using a sixteen-inch ball, and that version of softball gradually gained ascendancy over the twelve-inch and fourteen-inch versions of the game in Chicago proper, while elsewhere in the country softball with the smaller balls prevailed. Indoor baseball went into steep decline in the second decade of the century, and by the mid-1920s indoor baseball was a dead sport. Eventually, softball's origin from indoor baseball was forgotten.

ICE SPORTS

Ice skating and ice hockey were both developed as interscholastic sports, but primarily in the East. Ice skating in New York had been around since the Dutch established the colony of New Holland. The activity first became a rage during the 1860s, when the middle and upper classes avidly took up ice skating, but after the fad blew over, it faded for a couple of decades, only to reemerge in the 1890s. But skating on outdoor sites at such parks as Central in Manhattan and Prospect in Brooklyn provided limited days for skating activity because of the area's moderate winters (compared to New England and the Midwest). By the mid-1890s, Metropolitan New York had built a number of indoor ice rinks, notably the St. Nicholas Rink, the Ice Palace, and the Clermont Avenue Rink, and these venues made possible the adoption of ice skating as an indoor sport.[38]

New York high schools began taking up ice skating in the 1890s, and in 1897 the two leagues in the area, the Interscholastic Association and the Long Island Interscholastic Athletic League, both initiated ice-skating racing. In January the Interscholastic Association launched a meet at the St. Nicholas Rink of four events—220-yard, 440-yard, 880-yard (for juniors), and mile races. The first year's meet drew five schools, but the sport did not prosper, and the league did not continue with speed skating after 1900. The Long Island League, made up of public and private schools in primarily Brooklyn, held its first meet at the Clermont Avenue Rink in March with four events—220-yard for seniors, 220-yard for juniors, 880-yard, and 5-mile races. The following year, the number of events was expanded to include a 440-yard race and a mile race. The Long Island League sponsored competition up to March 1903.[39]

Precipitating the end of ice skating in the Long Island League was the move of the Brooklyn public schools into the newly formed PSAL in the 1903–1904 season. The Long Island Interscholastic League discontinued ice-skating contests after 1903, because the Brooklyn schools in the 1903–1904 season had joined the newly formed PSAL, which took in all the public schools of the five boroughs. The PSAL did not immediately adopt ice skating, and schools that continued the sport found only occasional contests against each other in the next few years. The PSAL introduced ice-skating races in March 1907, holding its meet at the St. Nicholas Rink with three events—440 yards, 880 yards, and 1 mile. The league, however, to the distress of the schools, did not sustain the sport and called off a scheduled 1908 meet. Thereafter, speed skating continued in the New

York schools, as some of the schools conducted borough championships and some competed in amateur contests.

Chicago, however, mysteriously failed to support interscholastic ice skating in these early years, despite having a thriving speed-skating culture. Chicago eventually established high school speed skating in the 1920s.[40]

In the East, ice hockey developed first in Boston, which became a hotbed for the sport during the first decades of interscholastic sport. It actually began as a rambunctious, less scientific game called ice polo, using a ball instead of a more controllable puck. Ice polo had its origins in roller polo, an eastern sports craze during the 1880s that took the new game of polo and put it on roller skates. The ice-polo variety of this game developed on ice during the same decade and in the next decade took root in the area's colleges and secondary schools. In metropolitan Boston, the suburban schools of Cambridge High and Latin, Melrose, Medford, and others formed the Suburban High School Ice Polo League in the 1891–1892 season. This league continued through the decade, but by the late 1890s, the game had to compete for appeal with ice hockey, a new import from Canada.[41]

By 1900 ice polo had been swept aside, as schools throughout Massachusetts rushed to adopt ice hockey, notably the schools of the Boston-area Interscholastic League. Ice polo remained only in the Merrimac Valley, where certain suburban schools such as Amesbury, Haverhill, and Dummer Academy continued league competition in the sport for a few more years.[42]

The adoption of ice hockey by New York schools took place only a year or so after the adoption of ice skating. The Interscholastic League sponsored the sport from 1898 to the league's virtual demise in 1905, and the Long Island Interscholastic League sponsored the sport from 1899 to the league's collapse in 1904. Ice hockey was not among the initial sports sponsored by the PSAL, and thus in 1906 the former schools of both the Interscholastic and the Long Island Leagues created a conference just for ice hockey, called the Interscholastic Hockey League of Greater New York. At least three PSAL schools participated in the league as well. This hockey league thrived until 1915, by which time many of the Manhattan private schools that made up the bulk of the league's membership were in decline and disappearing.[43]

The years of World War I saw a new growth of interest in ice hockey in New York, as well as in the public schools. The *New York Times* reported that at the end of 1917, ice hockey had emerged as "one of the leading winter sports" and discussed the growing interest in the amateur leagues, the colleges, and the high schools. A new high school hockey conference, the Long Island Interscholastic Hockey League, was formed with nine members, seven public and two private schools. This league met its demise after only one year, because the PSAL responded to the new interest in hockey by taking over the league in the 1918 season. The PSAL strangely dropped sponsorship of hockey after just two seasons, and the league disbanded after the 1919 season. A few public schools continued playing an independent schedule, until the PSAL finally established a sustainable ice-hockey program in the 1923–1924 season.[44]

Ice hockey arose in many other places in the East and Midwest. In western Pennsylvania, secondary schools formed a hockey league by the 1901–1902 season, and in Minnesota, the secondary schools, which, like Boston, had begun playing ice polo in the early 1890s, switched to ice hockey after the turn of the century. Philadelphia private schools competed in ice hockey as early as 1899, when Haverford of Philadelphia and Cutler of New York met in an intercity game that year. In 1901 all-star high school teams representing each city competed against each other. By 1903 ice hockey had been adopted by many of the boarding schools of the East, notably Pomfort (Connecticut), St. Paul's (New Hampshire), and Phillips Andover (Massachusetts). While ice-hockey competition was far from universal in the high schools, by World War I it had become firmly established in a few locales, chiefly Boston.[45]

In Chicago ice hockey, like ice skating, was virtually nonexistent in the first decades of interscholastic competition. In late 1915, Hyde Park High formed a team and managed to recruit Lane Tech and Phillips into forming a league, but after Hyde Park beat them, the two schools lost their enthusiasm for the game and dropped the sport. Chicago had virtually no indoor rinks for ice hockey, which inhibited its development in the city. The sport would not return to Chicago-area schools for many decades.[46]

RIFLE MARKSMANSHIP

Rifle competition in the high schools emerged in the first decade of the century in the East, particularly New York City, where rifle shooting was promoted vigorously by the PSAL from its founding in 1903, and Washington, DC, the headquarters of the National Rifle Association, which regularly sponsored national rifle shooting beginning in 1909.

Rifle shooting for the high schools in New York City was initially sponsored by private organizations, such as sportsmen's organizations. The most notable of these shows was the New York Sportsman's Show, a three-week extravaganza held in February and March each year in Madison Square Garden. The first show opened in 1894, and by 1903 the extravaganza was attracting 75,000 people. The show's organizers in 1902 added shooting contests for boys, representing high schools from the city and upstate New York. The Sportsman's Show extravagantly dubbed its contest the "Schoolboy Shooting Championship of the United States." A Dwight student, Charles M. Daniels, who later built an extraordinary amateur career as America's preeminent swimmer, won the first championship.[47] The 1908 show, now called the Motor Boat and Sportsman's Show, attracted some 500 boy shooters, most from the New York area. The same year, another sportsman's group, the Forest, Fish, and Game Society of America, also sponsored schoolboy contests, involving 250 boys from New Jersey, Connecticut, and New York. The large number of boys participating in these sports shows at this time was due in part to the formation of the PSAL five years earlier and its adoption of a strong rifle-shooting program that brought many more schoolboys to the sport.[48]

When the PSAL was founded in 1903, General George W. Wingate was elected the organization's first president. Wingate was a Civil War veteran and picked up his general title as a member of the National Guard in the 1870s. He had a long interest in military preparedness and in training high school youth in drilling and marksmanship. He had earlier introduced into the schools a military training program called the American Guard, which trained high school boys in calisthenics, marching drill, and rifle marksmanship. As one of the founders of the PSAL, his special interest was in building an extensive rifle-shooting program. In the first years of the rifle competition, beginning in 1907, the PSAL worked with the annual sportsmen's shows and offered competition for various cups. The first step in the rifle-shooting competition was training on the sub-target gun machine, a machine that simulated a shot on a target without using actual bullets. The students would graduate to other competition conducted with live ammunition using a 22-caliber rifle, on both outside and indoor ranges.[49]

The National Rifle Association (NRA), a longtime sportsmen's organization but even then concerned about national defense issues, was one of the biggest sponsors of high school competition. The NRA initiated its first national contest in 1909, a telegraph championship whereby the schools would send in their results to NRA headquarters in Washington, DC. Each school would conduct its shooting under direction of an official (usually a school faculty member) appointed by the NRA. Each team member, using a 22-caliber rifle, would fire ten shots standing and ten shots prone at a bull's-eye target fifty feet away. The school reporting the highest team score would win the national championship. The NRA usually announced the winning school in late April or early May. In the first year of the contest, more than thirty schools participated from all over the country. The winning team was awarded the Astor Cup, presented by Colonel John Jacob Astor.[50]

The NRA began a "league" competition in 1911, called the Interscholastic League of School Rifle Clubs. This national championship was also a telegraph meet, usually during March and April. The league's season extended from early January to early April, when the NRA would report the winners, that is, the schools with the best round-robin records. The NRA began with one league, but then expanded the league to separate ones for high schools and military academies. Each league was further broken down into classes—A, B, and C for high schools and A and B for military academies.[51]

The strong presence of the NRA in Washington, DC, had a big impact on the local high schools, which became particularly strong in rifle marksmanship, forming both boys and girls teams and conducting league competition beginning in 1910. Central High became a nationally recognized power in rifle. Rifle marksmanship was virtually unknown in most secondary schools across the nation, but had become a thriving sport in some locales, especially New York City and Washington, DC.[52]

Chicago was far behind the East in support of high school rifle competition. Unlike New York's PSAL, which made rifle-marksmanship competition a huge part of the extracurriculum, the Chicago public-schools administration had no interest in developing such a program prior to World War I. The impetus for rifle competition came from individual schools and outside groups, notably the Illinois State Rifle Association, the First Regiment Armory, and the Sportsman's Club of America. A small number of Chicago's public and private secondary schools began adopting rifle shooting around 1909 and 1910. Some of the pioneering schools in the area were Crane Tech, Lake View, Englewood, and Morgan Park Academy. In response to this burgeoning interest, the Illinois State Rifle Association added in 1910 an interscholastic state championship section to its sections on regimental rifle shoots and revolver-team matches for police departments. The state meet sponsored by the Illinois State Rifle Association does not appear to have lasted beyond 1916.[53]

HANDBALL: THE NEW YORK GAME

Handball represents a sport typical of one locale, arising in Brooklyn in the 1870s and remaining concentrated in the New York metropolitan area decades later. Irish immigrants in Brooklyn introduced the sport to the United States in the 1870s, building the first handball courts and spreading interest in the game by conducting contests between their top professional players. Handball soon spread throughout the population as a formal indoor sport and also as an outdoor pastime, seeping down to the children of New York and becoming a popular street game. By the mid-1890s, handball was adopted in some secondary schools of the New York metropolitan area. The first high school league to sponsor handball was the Long Island Interscholastic League, which featured the sport in its winter calendar from 1895 up to at least 1903. The league consisted of public schools such as Erasmus Hall and Brooklyn Boys and private schools such as Polytechnic Prep and Adelphi. There was some interscholastic girls competition after the turn of the century, when in 1902, for example, Erasmus Hall and Eastern District High met for a match.[54]

After the formation of the PSAL in 1903, some public high schools, mostly on Long Island, continued to compete in handball, but it was not an official league sport. There was some discussion by the PSAL to add the sport, but it was rejected by league authorities, who cited the lack of available handball courts. Finally, in the fall of 1926, the PSAL added handball to its offerings and switched the sport to the spring in 1927.[55]

Indoor sports emerged in the nation's high schools because they filled a vacuum in the sports calendar. The routine of calisthenics developed by physical education departments had little appeal for high school students, whose natural inclination was to play athletic games. Indoor sports were highly dependent on institutional support for their spread into the secondary schools. What animated all this support was the desire of the older participants to develop and train the younger generation in their sport not only to sustain the sport but also to bring better-trained and better-conditioned athletes into their sport as a means of gaining a competitive edge. Educators looked favorably on the new wintertime competitions, as the challenge of games, besides being more engaging to the students, was thought to do more than calisthenics in building strength of character. Yet outside support of YMCAs, athletic clubs, and universities in providing facilities would become an increasingly disquieting development for educators, who found that high school competition out of their purview eroded their control.

Elsewhere on the calendar, league administrators worked to add more sports, especially in the fall, a season when football was the only sport. The most notable new fall sports were soccer and cross-country, but there were also golf (originally a spring sport, but often scheduled in the fall) and a plethora of other outdoors sports as interscholastic sports exploded in the first decades of the new century.

7

New Outdoor Sports Advance the Educational Mission

Whereas indoor sports were introduced primarily to provide game competition in lieu of the dull routines of physical exercise, new outdoor sports were introduced for a variety of reasons. Sometimes the students chose the sport, as in golf, but the sport's nature meant that outside organizations, namely, private golf clubs, played a huge role in helping disseminate the sport among secondary-school students. In the case of soccer, the impetus came from the faculty, who introduced the sport as a less brutal alternative to American-style football. Cross-country in Chicago was developed by the high school faculty, but in the East outside organizations, notably universities, were most instrumental in the sport's development. Rowing in particular was dependent on boat-club support, both financial and institutional, whereas lacrosse in the high schools received outside support from lacrosse clubs and universities. The broadening of the athletic extracurriculum was thought to expand the benefits of sports to more of the school population, benefits that included physical and character development and thereby filling the educational mission of the high school and the aspirations of Progressives to uplift society as a whole.

Golf Emerges Out of the Country Clubs

Golf is more than four hundred years old, and while the Dutch claim to have originated the sport, the Scots developed the game as we know it. In the United States, golf made its appearance in the late eighteenth century, making inroads in Charleston and Savannah, but disappearing from the scene around 1820. Golf reemerged in the 1880s in various locales, notably Oakhurst, West Virginia (ca. 1884); Troy, New York (1886); and western Pennsylvania (1885–1887). The traditional launch of golf in the United States, however, dates to 1888, when transplanted Scotsman John Reid laid out the first course, St. Andrew's Golf Club, on Long Island. The seed that Reid had planted took root and grew rapidly. By the mid-1890s, golf had exploded as the new sports rage among the upper middle and upper classes, primarily in metropolitan New York, Boston, and Chicago.[1]

The first Chicago-area golf course was built in 1892, when Charles B. MacDonald, Chicago golf evangelist and preeminent player in America, with the help and sponsorship from his friend Hobart C. Chatfield-Taylor, laid out a seven-hole course for the Lake Forest Golf Club. The following year, MacDonald formed a club and built a nine-hole course in the western suburb of Belmont. MacDonald in 1895 helped form the Chicago Golf Club, which opened an eighteen-hole course he designed in Wheaton. The building of other clubs so rapidly followed that there were twenty-six by 1900. In 1899 the completion of the Jackson Park Public Links on Chicago's South Side was important for the development of golf in the public schools. It was the first public golf course built in the Midwest and the only one in the Chicago area until 1907. The opening of the Jackson Park course was seen as an opportunity for the masses to enjoy the game of golf. Most of the early public-school matches were held at Jackson Park.[2]

Chicago's place in the golf world was solidified in 1897 when the Chicago Golf Club hosted both the United States Open and the United States Amateur. In 1899 the leading Chicago golf clubs formed the Western Golf Association (WGA), with membership open to clubs within five hundred miles of Chicago. The WGA the same year inaugurated both an open and an amateur tournament.[3]

Golf in Chicago-area secondary schools arose only after the turn of the century after nearly a decade of flourishing growth and course building. The development of interscholastic golf in the Chicago area closely paralleled similar developments in Boston and New York, where it first emerged among its elite students from the private schools and then spread downward into the middle and even in some cases the working classes in the public schools. And it is in the East where the first interscholastic golf arose. The first interscholastic golf tournament in the United States was the Lakewood Interscholastic, held on April 30, 1898, in a New York suburb. The Golf Club of Lakewood sponsored the eighteen-hole medal-play event. Seventeen schoolboy golfers participated, hailing from the schools of Lakewood Heights, Blake's School, Cutler School (all in New York), Lawrenceville (New Jersey), and Hamilton (Philadelphia).[4]

The following year, the Cutler School of the Interscholastic Association established the New York Interscholastic Tournament, which was played at St. Andrew's Golf Club in the first week of April. The event attracted seven schools. The *New York Times* lauded these developments, saying, "It is of good aid to college teams to obtain new and experienced material year after year. A number of school team matches will be held this season. The Cutler School is arranging several games with other schools and clubs." In October 1899, the *Chicago Tribune* likewise reported on this phenomenon in a story on collegiate golf: "Perhaps one of the greatest aids to college golf, both for the male and female students, is the fact that the private and preparatory schools as a general thing have provided golf links as the exercise for the boys and girls attending these schools. . . . Already these schools have placed players in the field."[5]

The Cutler-sponsored New York Interscholastic was the precipitating factor that led to similar interscholastic tourneys in other cities. In March 1900, the *Chicago Tribune* delineated the growth of golf and reported on the importance and influence of the New York Interscholastic, noting that as a result, many schools had taken up the game, in New York, Boston, and Philadelphia. The sportswriter saw this development as good for the game, as this early play would produce better golfers.[6]

By the turn of the century, everything was in place in Chicago for the emergence of interscholastic golf competition. Besides the availability of courses and the inspiration of East Coast developments, there was the evangelistic spirit of such clubs as Onwentsia that avidly sponsored interscholastic events and sought to encourage the spread of the game into the prep-school ranks. Also laying the groundwork was the existence of flourishing prep leagues, notably the Preparatory and the Academic, where one might expect to find young athletes whose fathers belonged to golf clubs and played golf. Prep-school players were invariably members of junior teams and even senior teams of the local golf clubs, and many of the young players were "much better than their older brothers and parents." Young players from the Preparatory League and Academic League schools competed with the adult players at the various area clubs, notably Onwentsia, Exmoor, Glen View, and Midlothian.[7]

The earliest record of any Chicago-area school participation in golf dates from June 1899, when Harvard School played University School for the inaugural Preparatory League championship. The league by 1901 was featuring many golfers who would go on to much greater fame, notably Mason Phelps and Warren K. Wood (from Harvard School), H. Chandler Egan (Rugby School), and Walter Egan (University School). As early as 1899, Evanston, a public school, had formed a golf team, led by a junior, William Holabird Jr., who had already developed a national reputation on the links. Holabird was one of the few early public-school players of note.[8]

Until 1902 all the amateur champions of the United States Golf Association (USGA) had been older transplanted Scots and Englishmen. That year the golf world was stunned when a young nineteen-year-old from Glen View Golf Club, Louis N. James, came from last place in the qualifying round of sixty-four golfers to take the championship from Eben M. Byers. This performance was the first explosive evidence that the Chicago area was producing extraordinary golfers and significantly reshaping the game from a predominantly immigrant avocation to an American one. James was born on the West Side and later moved to the North Shore with his family. Like so many of the upper-class youth in those days, he was sent east to prep school, namely, Hill in Pottstown, Pennsylvania. After two years, however, he returned to the Chicago area and attended Northwestern Academy, a school in the Academic League.[9]

What truly helped to break golf out of the confines of a few country clubs was the image the sport presented to the American public, of clean-cut wholesome and healthy-looking college kids, such as H. Chandler Egan and Mason Phelps. This perception helped immeasurably to erase the image from the 1890s of cigar-smoking, bearded, somewhat-soused Scotsmen. That the sport was played on elegant and beautiful landscaped courses in front of imposing clubhouses stamped the sport as not only elite but also genteel and civilized. It was a sport that even some of the nonelite could relate to, and soon an ever-greater number of golfers of more modest means were taking up golf. The Olympic Games in St. Louis in 1904 demonstrated that Chicago was exploding with young golf talent. The three competing teams were all American, and each represented a club. The winning club was the Western Golf Association, stocked by the best young golfers in the Chicago area, most of whom had recently competed in prep schools in the Chicago area.[10]

The growing activity in Chicago of golf in the secondary schools culminated in 1903 with the establishment of the Western Interscholastic Golf Tournament, sponsored by the Western Golf Association. The inaugural Western Interscholastic showed the extent of high school activity in the sport in 1903, in the public as well as in the private schools. Participating public-school players included boys from Oak Park, Wheaton, Jefferson, and Hyde Park. The interscholastic immediately became the state's most prestigious high school golf competition, and local papers would devote a full column and large headlines to covering it. The Western Interscholastic was the equivalent of a similar tourney on the East Coast called the Eastern Interscholastic, which began in 1910.[11]

Meanwhile, in 1908, schoolboys in Chicago-area public and private secondary institutions under the leadership of future great Chick Evans formed the Western Interscholastic Golf Association (WIGA) to provide a high school team championship competition. The Western Golf Association had sponsored an individual interscholastic championship since 1903, but no team competition. Evans became the league's first president. By this time, certain suburban public schools, such as New Trier and LaGrange, were as competitive as the private schools.[12]

In 1911 the Cook County League began offering team competition, and its dual-meet series gradually subsumed the WIGA dual-meet series. In the fall of 1913, the Cook County League was superseded by the Chicago Public High School and Suburban Leagues, and both offered golf team competition in the spring of 1914. The replacement of the WIGA team championship by Cook County League competition both ended schoolboy sponsorship and signaled the emergence of public-school golf

9. Golfer Charles "Chick" Evans at the tee, 1908, competing for Evanston Academy in an interscholastic tournament, when most high school competitors in golf came from private schools. Courtesy of the Chicago History Museum.

dominance. The Western Interscholastic individual competition demonstrated this trend—in the first six years of the tournament (1903–1908), five winners were from private schools; in the last eight years, all were public-school winners (1909–1916).[13]

The 1909 USGA national amateur, held at the Chicago Golf Club, in Wheaton, in September, stunned the golf world when seven of the eight quarterfinalists were young Chicago products. The extraordinary achievements of Chicago's young golf talents at this time were the subject of considerable comment. Tom Bendelow, writing a feature called "Golf around Chicago" for the *Spalding Official Golf Guide*, reported in 1911, "The quality of golf displayed during the past year was the best we have seen yet. Records were broken at almost every open tournament, and the principal star in the golfing tournament was none other than the redoubtable 'Chick' Evans. . . . Altogether the young players around Chicago are about the best that can be got together in the United States, no section barred." But this world of Chicago prep golf would not continue. On the horizon was junior golf.[14]

New York was the center of the interscholastic golf world in the first decade of the new century, mainly because of the prestige of the New York Interscholastic begun in 1899. The tournament recognized a team championship determined in the qualifying round, a medalist who scored the lowest stroke total in the qualifying round, and an individual championship determined by match play by the final qualifiers. This format became standard for most interscholastic tournaments. The tournament usually attracted about twenty-five golfers from mostly private schools in the New York and New Jersey areas. Only about two or three schools usually competed for the team title. By 1904 the meet was generally referred to as the "metropolitan interscholastic." The most notable golfer to win the interscholastic was 1904 champion Jerome D. Travers. The last meet was held in 1907.[15]

The other significant eastern tournament was the Greater Boston Interscholastic. It was inaugurated in 1902 by students who formed the Greater Boston Interscholastic Golf Association to run the tournament. The golfers represented both private academies and public high schools in Boston and the suburbs. The association scheduled dual matches through May and June, ending with a tournament in mid-June. Awards were given to the tournament winner, the winning team, the consolation winner, and the medalist (lowest score for a round). In later years, the tournament was moved forward to July.[16]

The most famous golfer to win the Boston Interscholastic was Francis Ouimet, who helped introduce golf to Brookline High and won the tournament his junior year, in 1909. His modest working-class background was noticed as a trend in interscholastic golf by the golfing establishment during the 1910 tournament. The *American Golfer* commented: "This year's championship . . . gave further evidence of the change which has come over the meetings since they were held in earlier days of golf. Then only players who belonged to clubs and were well known as good golfers had much to do with the meetings, but now the championship is taken part in by caddie boys and grammar school boys, as well as those from private preparatory schools and the high schools. The championship this year was the most democratic yet held, and did not suffer on that account, but was all the more interesting."[17]

The celebrated victory of Francis Ouimet in the United States Open at the famous Country Club in Brookline, Massachusetts, in 1913 was an iconic event for the democratization of golf in the United States. The penetration of golf into the public schools with league competition played a huge role in spreading the sport to all classes of students. Whereas Chicago had established golf in its public-school league as early as 1911, it took another decade for other major city school systems to adopt the sport. New York's Public Schools Athletic League, for example, adopted golf only in 1920, and the Philadelphia public schools adopted it as late as the 1922–1923 school year.

The schoolboys did a commendable job in the first decade of the twentieth century in establishing golf in the secondary schools, but the golf establishment was soon developing a new program for high school–age golfers, called junior golf. *Golf Illustrated* reported in 1914 that junior golf tournaments were replacing interscholastic tournaments. In Chicago the Cook County League took over the Western Interscholastic team competition in 1910, and the WGA terminated individual competition after the 1916 tournament. The WGA had begun a junior tournament in 1914, not only duplicating the interscholastic but also doing a much better job than the schoolboy tourney in drawing players from the entire Midwest. Another factor in the termination could have been that WGA organizers felt that the University of Illinois individual state championship inaugurated in 1916 was broader in scope in taking in the entire state and thus superseded its efforts.[18]

In Boston a notice in the *American Golfer* in early 1911 by the executive committee of the Massachusetts Golf Association sent out ominous signals that the Boston Interscholastic would face changes. The report noted that the interscholastic tournament had been loosely organized and that the committee desired to take over the competition. What transpired was that the interscholastic was terminated after the 1912 season, and in 1914 the association introduced a Massachusetts junior championship. Similarly, in New York, the Metropolitan Junior Golf Tournament was inaugurated in 1912. By World War I, as the nation followed the lead of Chicago, Boston, and New York, junior golf was firmly established across the nation. Although the era of major interscholastic golf tournaments had come to an end, these tournaments had established golf in the secondary schools and helped bring the sport into the public schools, besides forming the basis of junior golf.[19]

Soccer as an Alternative to Football

Soccer is the American name for what the rest of the world calls football. The word *soccer* began as a slang derivative of the name that the sport was originally called, association football—the kicking-style game that was played under the rules of the Football Association, formed in England in 1863. Soccer was introduced into the United States by British immigrant clubs in the last two decades of the nineteenth century. By the late 1880s, English, Scottish, and Irish residents in Chicago had formed association-football clubs and were competing against each other. But the impetus for soccer's introduction into Illinois high schools would come not from these immigrant clubs, but from the universities and colleges.[20]

The breakthrough year for soccer in the universities was 1905, a direct result of the concern about the mounting number of deaths and injuries produced by football, the most dangerous and violent college sport of the day. There was a rising clamor among the public either to reform football or to abolish it altogether. Because of this growing disfavor with football, many colleges around this time were dropping the sport, and soccer appeared to be a more palatable diversion (although on the West Coast, rugby emerged as the alternative). The *Inter Ocean* in March 1905 reported on the increased interest in soccer:

Many things have come about to increase the public interest in the association or kicking game of football, and indications in various parts of
the country indicate that this will be the most successful year in the
history of the sport in the United States. About thirty clubs play the
"socker" game in Philadelphia. New York is taking it up, and St. Louis
had two leagues of four clubs each playing in autumn and spring. The
most salient point, however, is that some of the colleges have become
interested in the sport, which will undoubtedly do more to bring it to
the attention of the American public than any other method that could
be devised.[21]

Such colleges as Harvard, Haverford, Pennsylvania, and Columbia were
starting up teams. They along with Cornell formed the Inter-University
Association Football League, and the following spring league competition
was begun.[22]

The injuries and deaths produced by football in the high schools likewise encouraged some educators to turn to soccer. A slew of physical educators as well as champions of soccer argued that soccer was not only less
dangerous than football, but a more democratic sport that allowed many
more students to enjoy the benefits of open-air physical exercise in a non-
brutal sport. This point was argued by physical educator Henry S. Curtis
in "A Plea for Association Football," in the influential *American Physical
Education Review*, in 1906. Ernest Cecil Cochrane, writing for one of the
annual advocacy articles on soccer for the *Spalding Guide*, noted the brutality of football in discussing how secondary schools were helping to advance
the game. He argued, "Probably the greatest factor in the development of
the game is its adoption by the big private and public schools. Many of the
preparatory institutions and smaller colleges are supporting elevens owing
to the absence of rough or brutal plays, and it is these that the future development of the game must be, in large measure, looked for."[23]

In Illinois the high schools were swept by the same winds as the colleges, where it was the violence of football that directly precipitated soccer's first inroads. Chicago's Englewood High had experienced a serious
football accident in the fall of 1905, which motivated an English teacher,
Archibald Patterson, to establish in the fall of 1906 a soccer team as a

safer alternative. Englewood was unable to schedule other high schools, its inaugural game being with the Wanderers, an amateur Anglo-American cricket club, and the University of Chicago. Englewood remained the one area high school playing the sport, but in the fall of 1908, Oak Park High School adopted soccer. Like Englewood, the school had experienced a fatal football accident in the fall of 1905. Oak Park played a schedule of colleges and club teams and did not meet Englewood until the spring of 1909, when the two schools played two games. The first game was perceptively recognized by the *Chicago Tribune* as groundbreaking, seeing the match as the advent of high school soccer in the area. Soccer was finally adopted by the Cook County League in the spring of 1912. The league added a fall series the following autumn.[24]

The Cook County League broke up in the spring of 1913 to form two new leagues, the Chicago Public High School League and the Suburban League. The sport thrived in the Chicago schools, as by 1914 eight schools were participating. In the summer of 1915 at the Sportsmen's Club Carnival, a soccer tournament was held by the Chicago high schools, along with competition in track, fencing, and indoor baseball; in the fall, the league added lightweight competition.[25]

Unlike many other sports that arose in the high schools, soccer did not start appreciably earlier in the East. When New York City's PSAL adopted a full athletic schedule in the fall of 1906, it included soccer but not football (city schools continued to play football, but not under direct PSAL supervision). The league's initial soccer program attracted seven schools. The PSAL not only sponsored high school competition, but promoted an extensive soccer program in the grade schools as well. Most school systems were slower in adopting soccer as an interscholastic sport, although many quickly adopted soccer as an interschool and intramural sport for grade school youngsters. Baltimore began a high school tournament in 1913, along with an extensive grade school program in 1909. In Philadelphia the public high school league first sponsored soccer in 1914; in Los Angeles, interschool soccer competition began in the middle schools in 1911 and in the high schools in 1913.[26]

Soccer was largely established prior to America's entrance in World War I, and the impetus was the 1905 football crisis, motivating many educators in the secondary schools, as well as in the universities and colleges, to adopt the sport. Compared to most of the sports that preceded it, soccer entered the high schools not as a result of student initiative, but because the faculty and league officials introduced the sport.

CROSS-COUNTRY

Cross-country began as the English sport of hares and hounds, which engaged public-school youngsters as far back as the eighteenth century. The rules of the sport replicated the chase of hares and hounds, in which two runners, the hares, would take a head start, and then be chased by about five runners, the hounds. The hares would drop slips of paper to indicate their scent, and often sportswriters would describe the race as a "paper chase." The first cross-country racing club started in the United States was the Westchester Hares and Hounds Club started in 1878. By the mid-1880s, the sport was beginning to adopt the term *cross-country*.[27]

Chicago began developing a big interest in hares and hounds in the late 1880s, when the Chicago Amateur Athletic Association took up the sport. It flourished throughout the 1890s and evolved into the sport of cross-country. In the mid-1890s, Northwestern University formed a cross-country club, but engaged in intramural competition until it met the University of Chicago in 1902. When the eastern schools conducted their first intercollegiate meet in 1899, cross-country in the form we know it had supplanted hares and hounds.[28]

Although Chicago-area institutions of higher learning had taken up cross-country, none chose to sponsor interscholastic competition. Oak Park High thus took the lead in pioneering the sport in the Chicago area in the fall of 1904. One member of the school's faculty, Albert L. Clark, was especially instrumental in launching the sport. He was the school's representative on the board of control of the Cook County League, chairman of the track committee, and responsible the previous spring for establishing the league's indoor track program. Clark went to Oak Park's athletic director, Lewis Omer, to advocate the adoption of cross-country running.[29]

Omer, persuaded by Clark's entreaties, held the school's first intramural meet on December 18, 1904, on a three-and-a-half-mile course. In the fall of 1905, Oak Park conducted its second annual intramural run. Like many indoor track and field meets of the day, the race was a handicapped affair, so the winner was not necessarily the best runner. The *Chicago Tribune* noted that Oak Park intended to bring in other schools. Oak Park's proselytizing finally bore fruit with a breakthrough event in the fall of 1907, when Crane Tech inaugurated a meet involving Oak Park and five West Side schools—McKinley, Crane, Northwest Division, Austin, and Medill—holding it on the first Saturday of November. The *Tribune* noted the race's significance, saying, "The run, which was the first open run held by a high school, was a great success, and it is expected other schools will follow suit next spring."[30]

League authorities took notice and conducted the Cook County League meet in the fall of 1908, awarding both team and individual championships. In its third year, the event, in a blinding snowstorm, was witnessed by five thousand spectators, but the meet attracted only three schools—Oak Park, Englewood, and Crane. Cross-country was not fated to be established in Chicago schools at this time. The 1908 run was the last, as interest in the sport went into decline. Cross-country would not be reestablished in the high schools until the mid-1920s.[31]

In contrast to cross-country's failure to sustain itself in Chicago, the sport prospered in the East. The first secondary schools in the country to conduct cross-country meets were the private schools of New York City's Interscholastic League. In 1898 Trinity School sponsored an intramural meet, and the following year both Trinity and Cutler sponsored open meets against fellow league member Berkeley. Cross-country was not sustained in the Interscholastic League, however, but the sport experienced a resurgence in New York's public schools in the fall of 1906, when the sport was adopted by the PSAL. The first year, three schools participated, and by 1910 the meet attracted eleven schools. The sport thus exploded in both the high schools and the colleges, with Princeton University inaugurating an interscholastic in 1906 and Columbia University beginning its interscholastic in 1911.[32]

Philadelphia, in particular, was a hotbed for the new sport of cross-country running. During the century's first decade, its newspapers every fall were filled with reports of cross-country meets, by colleges, YMCAs, private clubs, Catholic organizations, and even the Schuylkill Navy (Philadelphia's famed organization of rowing clubs). The University of Pennsylvania began sponsoring an intercollegiate meet on Thanksgiving Day as early as 1895. Thanksgiving Day in the city was always the biggest day for cross-country competition, when scores of organizations sponsored meets, and the local papers provided a couple of columns reporting on the results. The upshot of all this activity encouraged the University of Pennsylvania to establish a meet for high schools in 1903. The meet at first attracted only local public and private schools, but beginning in 1905 Lawrenceville Academy of New Jersey was the first nonlocal school to enter, followed in 1906 by Mercersburg Academy of Pennsylvania. By 1908 the University of Pennsylvania was billing its meets as the "American Interscholastic" and taking on national championship pretensions, although only schools from the mid-Atlantic states participated.[33]

Rowing

Rowing was one of the earliest sports to take hold in the United States, arising primarily in Philadelphia, New York, and Boston. Boat clubs in Philadelphia by the early 1830s had set themselves up along the Schuylkill River and reputedly organized the country's first regatta in 1835. In New York City, boat clubs established themselves along the Hudson River as early as 1834. In Boston the rowing clubs organized themselves along the Charles River, and the first Boston City Regatta was held in 1854. Collegiate rowing began after Yale formed a team in 1843 and Harvard in 1844. The two finally competed in 1852, racing in the first intercollegiate contest held in any sport in the United States.[34]

The eastern high schools, primarily private academies, were the first secondary schools to adopt the sport, usually schools located near amateur boat clubs in New York, Boston, and Philadelphia and near universities that sponsored rowing. Phillips Exeter Academy took up rowing in 1872, but competed only against Harvard and dropped the sport in 1883. The other notable prep school, St. Paul's of Concord, New Hampshire, formed an intramural program in 1871. Both Harvard and Yale relied heavily on Exeter's and St. Paul's graduates to man their rowing teams. These scattered activities show that rowing in the secondary schools failed to take root and thrive during the nineteenth century.[35]

The sport's failure in the secondary schools rests on the nature of crew itself. The sport was expensive. A shell cost nearly $400, at a time when a year's college tuition was $150. There was also the expense of shipping the shells to the regatta sites. In 1878, for example, to support a crew, the Harvard freshman team had to raise $1,500 by drawing subscriptions of $25 from each "wealthy man in the class." On top of expense, the season was short, usually May and June, and limited to only a couple of regattas, with generally no interest or support from a ticket-paying public. If one takes into account that prep schools drew on smaller groups of wealthy students, the difficulties in establishing crew in the secondary schools become even more magnified.[36]

Not until the late 1890s do we see widespread adoption of crew by the secondary schools with the encouragement and financial and material support of boat clubs. In Philadelphia the students at Central High, Penn Charter, and several other schools, with the assistance of the Schuylkill boathouses, took up rowing and formed the Interscholastic Rowing League in 1897. In Boston the Boston Athletic Association began sponsoring a secondary-school rowing league in 1898, lending assistance by supplying boats and coaching. Nine Boston-area schools participated the first year, about half public (such as Boston English and Boston Latin) and half private (notably Volkmann School and Stone School). The competition was held in May in a regatta staged over several days.[37]

In 1903 the National Association of Amateur Oarsmen granted Philadelphia the right to host the first national rowing championship, called the American Henley Regatta, which would be equivalent to the annual Henley Regatta in the United Kingdom. The city's eleven boat clubs formed a new national organization, the American Rowing Association, to run the regatta, the first of which was held in July 1903. Thereafter, the regatta was held annually in May. One event, beginning in 1904, was an interscholastic eight-oar competition. Though touted as a national championship event, the interscholastic race usually included a couple of Philadelphia public schools, notably Central and West High Schools, and a few out-of-state teams, among them Cascadilla Prep (New York),

Stone School (Boston), Georgetown Prep (DC), and Baltimore City College high school.[38]

In New York City, a number of public high schools adopted crew under the encouragement of the Harlem Regatta Association, which had been sponsoring regattas on Decoration Day since 1873. In March 1907, the association chose to add to its program an eight-oar boat race for high schools. The various rowing clubs involved in the regatta made available their boathouses and instructors to the high school teams, and within a few weeks some two hundred schoolboys formed teams, obtained shells, and began practicing at the various crew racing clubs. The regatta's first interscholastic contest attracted five crews—from Morris, Townsend Harris, Stuyvesant, DeWitt Clinton, and Commerce.[39]

In 1907 the PSAL recognized crew as a league sport, but because of its expense the league withdrew its support in 1908. Without PSAL sponsorship, several schools dropped the sport, but a few chose to continue to support their crews and participate in the Harlem Regatta. But with only two or three schools participating each year, the sport was failing. In 1914 the Harlem Regatta came under the purview of the newly formed New York Rowing Association, and the association introduced a "Junior Four Gigs for High Schools" contest. The event attracted six schools in New York City, New Jersey, and suburbs, notably New Rochelle, home of the powerful New Rochelle Rowing Club. New Rochelle High dominated the Harlem Regatta for most of its years. The New York Rowing Association continued to sponsor an interscholastic eight-oar contest up through 1925. Occasionally, such schools as Stuyvesant, Washington, and Commerce would form crew teams and compete, but their participation in the sport remained haphazard. In 1926, after a Washington rower drowned, the PSAL banned the sport.[40]

LACROSSE ARISES IN THE EAST

Lacrosse originated among the Native Americans. Early in the nineteenth century, middle-class Englishmen around Montreal learned to play the ball-and-stick game that the local Mohawk Tribe had been playing. The French called the game *lacrosse*, a term that they used for any Indian game involving a curved stick. The first formal rules and instructions for the games were published in 1860 by William George Beers, recognized as the "father of modern lacrosse," and the game spread throughout Quebec and Ontario, primarily through private clubs. During the 1870s and 1880s, Canadian immigrants to the United States brought the game to cities in the Northeast, primarily around Boston, New York, and Baltimore. It is these areas where lacrosse was largely established for most of its history in the United States.[41]

The first intercollegiate lacrosse organization was formed in 1888, when Princeton, Johns Hopkins, and Stevens joined together in the Intercollegiate Lacrosse Association. The next college rowing group, the United States Inter-University Lacrosse League, was formed in 1894 and brought together Harvard, Columbia, and Cornell. Both of these organizations came together in 1905 to form the United States Intercollegiate Lacrosse League. The colleges, in turn, sought to build feeder systems by promoting the sport in the secondary schools in their vicinity.[42]

Lacrosse became a game for the affluent in the elite colleges and subsequently among the more prosperous students in the high schools and prep academies. Johns Hopkins University promoted the sport to Baltimore's two elite public secondary schools, Baltimore City College and Baltimore Polytechnic Institute. Baltimore City College had a team from 1879 to 1891, dropped the game for a few years, and resumed for a season in 1896. By 1902, however, with the aggressive proselytizing from Johns Hopkins students, lacrosse took hold permanently at Baltimore City College, and by 1912 Polytechnic Institute took up the sport.[43]

In the New York area, lacrosse took root in the secondary schools primarily on Long Island, and the genesis for its development there was the Crescent Athletic Club, located in the Bay Ridge section of Brooklyn. Lacrosse was the showcase activity of the club's eighteen sports. The borough's high schools became involved in lacrosse in 1905, and when the Crescent AC opened its club facility, it celebrated the event with a golf tournament and two lacrosse matches.[44]

Lacrosse in Long Island schools prospered after World War I. Under the aegis of the Crescent Athletic Club, a league was formed in 1917 called the Metropolitan Interscholastic Lacrosse League. Initial members were Manual, Boys' High, Erasmus Hall, St. John's Prep, Flushing—all from Long Island—and Stevens Prep, in Hoboken, New Jersey. Matches were conducted in Brooklyn's Prospect Park and at the Crescent Athletic Club. The school with the best record in round-robin play would win the league title, with medals for the first- and second-place team members being donated by the Crescent AC. In addition, school matches among PSAL schools—Manual, Boys', Erasmus Hall, and Flushing—doubled as competition for the PSAL title.[45]

In the Boston area, the private clubs and universities were responsible for promoting lacrosse among the secondary schools. The sport made virtually no inroads among the public high schools, however, and its schoolboy development in New England was primarily in the elite academies, notably Phillips Academy, in Andover, Massachusetts, where it was first played in 1881, and Phillips Exeter Academy, in Exeter, New Hampshire, where it was adopted in 1882.[46]

The development of the various new outdoor sports in the secondary schools each followed their own distinctive trajectories, but what they all had in common was that there was no opposition raised by educators to this expansion, as each new sport was thought to add to the educational mission of the schools. In many cases, it was the educators who took the lead in introducing new sports and encouraged their students to take them up. In the case of soccer, the motivation was to find a less brutal alternative to football, a sport that was too often seen as going against the ethos of gentlemanly sport, as being character destroying rather than character developing, as football's most ardent defenders argued. The country-club sport of golf befitted the image in America of upper-crust young gentlemen with both money and character.

In the East, the elite universities lent cultural cachet to rowing and lacrosse and were likewise thought to be suitable character-building activities for young gentlemen of high school age. Yet the spread of outside sponsorship for many of these new sports would emerge as a major issue of governance and control in the 1920s. During this same Progressive Era, the girl students were likewise taking up a variety of new sports, but this experience for the American high school girls would turn out much differently than it did for the boys, where athletic competition for girls became a highly contentious issue and whereby the search for control led to far more constrictive outcomes.

8

THE NEW ATHLETIC GIRL AND INTERSCHOLASTIC SPORTS

The first decade of the twentieth century represented a bold new experiment for American womanhood. The country was experiencing an unprecedented interest in sports and leisure, as football, baseball, boxing, and track and field flourished as never before. A plethora of other sports also emerged as popular pastimes and drew considerable spectator interest, notably basketball, golf, tennis, bowling, and swimming. At the same time, women were growing in numbers in all levels of the workforce— from blue-collar factory to white-collar office—and were especially prominent in education, and becoming more visible in politics and in the social issues of the day. This emerging presence of women in so many areas of American life generated a national debate over women's role in society. That debate focused in part on the emergence of modern women playing sports. Sport historian Susan K. Cahn rightly sees the "popular interest in sport and concern over women's changing status converg[ing] in the growing attention paid to the 'athletic girl,' a striking symbol of modern womanhood."[1]

After the turn of the century, the country saw an explosion of sports activity in all walks of life, from the elites to the working classes, with the formation of private athletic clubs, industrial teams, church leagues, settlement-house programs, as well as in the public and private schools, particularly the secondary schools. At the same time, many people in the medical and educational establishments had come to the realization that not only men but also women needed physical exercise for health. In the colleges, guided by new scientific theories that saw the need for exercise in both men and women, physical education departments were formed to bring exercise to both groups. The bicycle craze of the 1890s, which saw women joining men in healthy outdoor excursion, helped encourage the idea that moderate physical exercise in the healthful outdoors was invigorating for modern American women. Among the upper classes—with a centuries-long tradition of leisure pursuit—women and girls were increasingly participating in outdoor recreations, notably croquet, horseback riding, archery, swimming, golf, and tennis.[2]

Educators and urban reformers of the Progressive Era thus demanded that playtime and exercise were needed for the modern girl, who was often hyperbolically described as direly unhealthy looking, particularly among the working class. A reporter for the *Chicago Tribune* in 1910 saw the modern work regimen producing a result of "thin chested, anemic looking girls, with dull eyes and lifeless hair, pasty skinned, indifferent, with that pathetic what's-the-use-of-caring-about-anything-anyway expression that fairly eats at your heart when you see it." The lack of playgrounds and organized sport activities for young girls in the city, where the girls could experience normal play and recreation, was thought by reformers to produce unwholesome girls, according to Elizabeth Burchenal, the executive director of New York's Girls' Branch of the Public Schools Athletic League. She said, "We are building up a type of girls here which ought to make us shudder. How often do we see its representatives? Hatchet-faced, sharp, but not intelligent looking, powdered, wearing enormous hats decorated, probably with 'willow plumes,' often without the slightest glint of youth in their poor eyes even at an age as early as sixteen or even fifteen."[3]

In response to such entreaties as Burchenal's, in 1906 the Playground Association of America was formed to provide healthful exercise for children of urban centers, and it campaigned relentlessly and effectively to get municipalities to provide more parks and park programs. Soon New York, Chicago, Boston, and other major cities were dotted with public parks providing recreational programs. By 1909 more than two hundred cities offered playground programs, most notably in Chicago and New York, which together invested fifteen million dollars in them. YMCAs and YWCAs also contributed mightily to bringing sports to young girls. Businesses and industrial concerns began sponsoring sports and leisure activities and building gymnasiums to ensure their employees got their healthful exercise.[4]

The nation's high schools joined these organizations in providing more sports and exercise for young women. They were fast growing into more inclusive institutions that brought more working-class students into the educational system as well as into the extracurriculum. Thus, they took the lead in energetically involving girls in physical activity. Not only did they engage the "new athletic girl" in calisthenics and gymnastics exercises, but they also had them participating in sports activities, notably indoor baseball, basketball, and track and field events. Although intramural activities were most common, interscholastic competitions were considerable and growing. At this juncture, the educators had to face the tensions of the era, in which the programs they were providing for their "athletic girls" were exhilarating to some as representing modern womanhood, but deeply disturbing to others who associated athleticism with masculinity and lack of feminine restraint. For much of the educational establishment, the search for control with regard to high school sports for girls was based on the proposition that the new athletic girl had to be reined in.[5]

A cacophony of voices in the popular press and in the academic sphere was being heard on both sides about the virtues of exercise and sports for women. Champions of sports for women emphasized their value in developing female health and beauty, and participants and fans alike enjoyed the competition against other schools. Skeptics of female athleticism did not outright disapprove of exercise and sports for women, but voiced concerns about competition and the physical stressfulness of certain sports. Golf and tennis were deemed more acceptable than basketball and track and field.

A watchword of concern was *masculinization*, not only in physical attributes and muscular development but also in the excesses of emotion and excitement that male-type competition engendered. On top of this worry was the belief that women were prone to loss of emotional control and neurosis, challenging their good character. The commentary relating to frenzied adolescent girls driven by "powerful impulses" and "overindulgence" is rightly suggested by Cahn as "thinly veiled" concerns about female sexuality. Some Progressive Era doctors were voicing objections that strenuous sport would endanger a woman's reproductive capabilities, an argument that had resonance with the Victorian view that the role of young ladies was to prepare themselves to become childbearing wives. The "athletic girl," in the eyes of many observers, was clearly not the demure and feminine future wife of the American male.[6]

The critics of competitive athletics for girls largely came from the ranks of collegiate physical education instructors, mostly female. They promoted the belief that there should be sports for girls, but only in "moderation." Competition between schools, with attendant loud crowds urging girls to go all out, was considered too much excitement and stress on the female psyche. Thus, interschool competition should be abolished in favor of intramural competition only. Certain sports, such as basketball and track and field, were considered too physically taxing for young girls, and if such sports were played, the rules needed to be modified and adapted to the presumed capabilities of young ladies. Sports such as archery, golf, and tennis were acceptable, but even though they were quiet and pastoral, they came under the ban on interscholastic competition.[7]

In Chicago, and across the country, a tremendous fight was waged during the first decade of the century over the "new athletic girl." Girls were enthusiastically joining and participating in interscholastic athletic contests on teams organized by mostly male educators. These interscholastic contests, mostly basketball, were encouraged and promoted in the nation's newspapers, which ran photos of high school teams, wrote enthusiastically about the contests, and in general treated the girl athletes as though they were boys. That was the rub. What transpired in Chicago was echoed in many places across the country and provides a rich portrait of a daring experiment for high school girls, which was killed off in one city after another roughly between 1910 and 1920. Much of the debate centered on basketball, but other sports were also involved, albeit on a lesser scale.

BASKETBALL

In Chicago, during the first decade of the century, schoolgirls were competing in basketball, indoor baseball, tennis, and track and field. Basketball was by far the most popular sport. The standard history of women's basketball tells us that not long after basketball was invented in 1891, physical educators adopted less strenuous forms of the game for women that soon spread nationwide. The most famous pioneer of women's basketball is Senda Berenson, who at Smith College devised a modified game for her charges in 1892, one that reflected her views of the female constitution as being less athletic and robust than it was for boys. She drew lines to divide the court into three parts and did not allow players in those sections to move out of them. In this line game, her rules barred snatching the ball, holding the ball for more than three seconds, or dribbling more than three times. After her rules were published in a *Spalding Guide* in 1899, the game thrived. In the South, another pioneer of women's basketball, Clara Gregory Baer, devised an even more restrictive line game, which she called Basquette, in which the court was divided into seven sections, with no movement allowed between them, and which completely barred dribbling, snatching, and guarding. She introduced this game at Newcomb College in New Orleans in 1893. After she published her rules in 1895, Basquette spread throughout the South.[8]

Despite the evident popularity of these line games in women's colleges, they were not the prevalent forms in the early days of girls' basketball in the high schools. What the young ladies mainly played was the five-player boys' game, often called the "YMCA game." The girls played it in two variations, one variation using "interference rules," which was the boys' game that permitted snatching of the ball, and the other variation using "noninterference rules," a slightly modified game barring the snatching of the ball. From approximately 1895 to about 1910, girls in high schools in most sections of the nation played under boys' rules, most using interference rules and a minority using noninterference rules. Only a small minority of high schools initially played line basketball. Girls' basketball using boys' rules predominated in the New York area, Boston, the Midwest, and the upper South.

The Chicago area in the early days of girls' basketball was particularly a hotbed of boys' rules. Basketball in the city's high schools did not take hold in Cook County until 1895, and then curiously only as a girls' sport. Basketball for women had been introduced in Illinois in 1893 by Delmar

Darrah, who organized a team at Illinois Wesleyan College, in Bloomington. In the fall of 1895, Austin High of Chicago started a team and played against squads from the University of Chicago, Lake Forest University (now Lake Forest College), and Hull House. Then the following fall, Oak Park High organized a team, and the first interscholastic girls' game in Illinois (or perhaps the country) was played on December 18, 1896, between Oak Park and Austin. These two schools shortly afterward were joined by Englewood and Evanston in interscholastic competition. The girls took to the game avidly and with the spirit of the new athletic girl. When a teacher introduced basketball to the West Division High girls in October 1899, the school-newspaper reporter for girls' athletics exclaimed, "He has promised us an exceptionally fine time, and what girl would not be inspired and feel herself two inches higher in her boots, when told that she was going to learn 'boys games.'"[9]

The 1898 Cook County League constitution recognized girls' basketball as one of the league's sports, but it was not until February 1900 that league competition leading to a championship was established. The occasion of its formation elicited a long article by Frances A. Kellor, a graduate sociology student at the University of Chicago and a future social reformer of some note. She told her readers that there had been tremendous growth in basketball in the previous five years and that it had grown so much in women's organizations that basketball was now often viewed as a woman's game. She noted that the local high schools had shown the "most systematic work" in development of the game. At this stage of development, Kellor described three kinds of games that were then prevalent—interference, noninterference, and line basketball.[10]

Although Kellor deplored some of the roughness of the game, particularly for high school girls, she thought the benefits of basketball were great, saying that the girls "learn to control the body, to avoid injuries, to coordinate the physical actions," and noted, "Basket ball develops grace of movement by reason of the freedom of movement which it necessitates." And to appeal to critics who cautioned that physical activity for girls might affect their role as future mothers, Kellor said, "The game keeps alive the play instinct as essential to continued inspirational or original work and so essential in the home with children." Kellor made no mention about the

issue of girls playing before the public, but some authorities in the Chicago high schools had qualms about girls playing basketball before audiences, as evidenced by the experiences of the Hyde Park girls' team in the
1901 season. The team was scheduled to play the Englewood girls as part
of the sports program at a giant fish and wildlife exhibition being held in
the Coliseum. The Hyde Park principal barred his girls from playing the
game, saying that "it was a too public a place for the young women, who
are of the best families in the communities." The reporter noted that the
girls were "charmed by silver medals and a banner" offered by the exhibit
officials and that the Englewood team had met no opposition from school
authorities.[11]

Kellor overlooked another benefit to the Chicago high school girls:
their empowerment to take on the responsibilities of organizing and man-
aging a league. The students had to bring together teams throughout the
vast Cook County area, find a coach (usually a faculty member), determine rules, draw up schedules, rent halls for contests, make travel arrangements, collect admission fees, purchase uniforms, and be responsible for a
treasury and general administration of the league. Even after the assumption of faculty control of the league by 1904, the student managers still had
considerable responsibilities with scheduling and travel arrangements.[12]

Generally, the girls managed the basketball league smoothly, but the
game suffered two years of disarray during the 1902 and 1903 seasons with
disputes over the kind of rules the girls would play under. The league split
into two factions—those schools that favored playing under interference
rules and schools that favored noninterference rules. There was no league
in 1902, but the schools playing under the interference rules formed a
conference in 1903. The schools playing noninterference rules made
arrangements to play each other informally and to play out-of-town teams.
The Cook County girls' league reunited all the schools under interference
rules for the 1904 season, but this time it came in dispute with school
authorities. Superintendent Edwin G. Cooley, not a fan of girls playing
interscholastic basketball, wanted the girls to play under noninterference
rules. Following Cooley's wishes, school authorities in the league tried
to impose noninterference rules, but, according to the *Chicago Tribune*,
"the plan failed, as the members from the schools which have teams in

the league protested, and stated that their teams would probably refuse to play according to the milder rules. A motion to lay the matter on the table was carried, and the girls will be permitted to play by their favorite rules."[13]

The 1905 season saw the largest participation in girls' basketball, with eleven teams in the league. The girl managers arranged a round-robin schedule in two divisions. When a champion was finally crowned on April 19, it ended one of the longest seasons in the league, one that began in early December. Conflict continued into subsequent seasons between the girls and school authorities. In 1906 some girl teams from schools headed by principals who opposed the league were forced to disband, but the managers after a month of fighting school officials finally launched a league in mid-February. Only five schools participated, and the schedule was completed in one month.[14]

Whereas the much-shortened season might have assuaged some concerns, the girls' habit of extending the league season with pre- and post-season games and long road trips was hardly gratifying. For example, the Hyde Park 1905 champs traveled to Dwight to play a game, and the 1906 Oak Park champions went all the way down to Springfield and St. Louis to play games. Although the traveling was hardly endearing, the fact that the Oak Park girls played twenty games despite the shortened season was something that raised concerns.[15]

Girls' basketball, on the other hand, met with a great deal of acceptance in their communities and in the press. The big-city newspapers reported on the girls' games as regular sports events, which was dramatically different from their approach when girls' basketball first started and was then something of a novelty. There were none of the qualifying remarks to remind readers they were reading about female players. The only difference in their treatment was that the papers referred to each player with the title "Miss." The newspapers regularly presented photos of the girl teams and write-ups. Local community newspapers, such as Oak Park's *Oak Leaves*, treated their champion girls' teams as hometown heroines, writing extensive profiles on the girls and their successes. At the end of the 1906 season, the *Oak Leaves* traditional front-page photo, which covered the entire page, was given to the championship girls' team.[16]

10. Joliet High School girls' basketball team of 1907, when Illinois girls' teams competed interscholastically and claimed state championships. The educational establishment would soon suppress such activity. Courtesy of the Howard and Lois Adelmann Regional History Collection, Lewis University.

The 1907 season was severely shortened by the Cook County League Board of Control. Each school was limited to just four opposing competitors during the season. But a school could play their opponent more than once, so the schedules were larger than four games. No league championship schedule was allowed. The girls' game by this time was under threat.[17]

Girls' high school competition flourished in the pre–World War I era, replicating the Chicago experience in such areas as Boston, New York–New Jersey, Ohio, and California. Interschool sporting events involving girls experienced rousing interest by the press, coaches, fans, and especially the female athletes themselves. Basketball was the most popular, but as in Chicago, indoor baseball, tennis, and track and field also engaged the girls.

Girls in the New York–New Jersey area began playing basketball at least as early as 1896. At first games were purely intramural. Typical of the day, the newspapers treated the subject as a novelty that focused more on the girls' dress and behavior than on the game itself. In 1897 the *New York Times* reported on a match game between Montclair High of New Jersey and Horace Mann of New York City, and what comes through in the report is the overall positive attitude expressed toward female participation in the sport. The paper also stressed that the game was not too exhausting for the girls, quoting the gym director: "There is no better exercise for them. It makes them cool, quick, active, alert, and above all things, teaches them to keep their tempers. . . . And you see, though they are tired, they are not exhausted." The reporter noted, "Judging from the way they went jumping around, exchanging compliments with their friends and enjoying themselves generally, they were not."[18]

By the winter of 1899–1900, interest in girls' basketball had grown so rapidly that a league was formed, the Girls Interscholastic Athletic League (later called the Metropolitan Girls Athletic League). Although centered on basketball (using boys' rules), the league also sponsored tennis and gymnastics. The league drew schools from a wide swath of schools in New York and New Jersey, namely, Manual Training, Erasmus Hall, and Eastern District from Brooklyn; Newtown and Flushing from Queens; Port Richmond and Stapleton from Staten Island; and Jersey City from New Jersey. No schools were involved from Manhattan or the Bronx, where public high schools were just emerging.[19]

By the winter of 1903–1904, boys-rule basketball for girls was also thriving in New Jersey, where East Orange, Englewood, and Montclair were playing regularly. Plus, New York private girls' schools were also getting engaged in the game, notably Madison Academy, Staten Island Academy, Sachs Academy, and Ethical Culture High. As elsewhere in the country where the girls played by boys' rules, the game tended to get physically rough. A game in 1905 between Madison Academy and Staten Island Academy produced numerous injuries and was described in the *New York Times* as such: "The contest was one of the liveliest that any girl basket ball teams have played in this city in a long while. Roughness was prevalent from the first toss of the ball, and before it had been in progress five minutes time was called while the girls rearranged their hair and made needed repairs to their gymnasium costumes." The janitor was quoted as saying, "It was a terror of a game, the fiercest I ever saw here."[20]

Yet the exercise that the girls gained from playing basketball was not overlooked by the game's defenders. The *New York Times* in a 1904 feature on the girls' game commented, "Physically basket ball develops not only the muscles, but the heart and lungs, strengthens them in every way, and thus promotes the health and longevity of the player. . . . Anything that tends to assist the healthful development and the control of the nerves in women is in this age a thing to be greatly encouraged." This encouragement would not withstand the forces of reaction, however.[21]

In Boston the pattern of girls' basketball competition was highly similar to the model of New York–New Jersey. Girls were playing outside contests in Boston as early as 1899, at least at one private school—Cushing Academy of Ashburnham. By 1902 public schools, particularly in the Boston suburbs, were avidly playing interscholastic contests with one another. Schools fielding teams included Stoneham, Lynn English, Lowell, and Newton. Sportsmanship was virtually unknown, and severe mismatches were common, such as when Lowell beat Dedham, 83–4, and Norwood beat Sharon, 71–2.[22]

The girls in Boston were playing by boys' rules, but there was a bit of modification in the game—for example, with shortened halves. Often doubleheaders were arranged, with a boys' game followed by a girls' game. The games drew anywhere from 125 spectators to 800. About 200 spectators seemed to be the norm, which was about the same for the boys' games. The *Boston Globe* gave generous coverage to the girls' contests, and as with the boys often featured prominent photos of the teams and minor write-ups on the players and how their season was going. The schools sponsoring girls' basketball appear to have been largely private, suburban, and rural schools, as the schools in Cambridge and Boston are absent from the reports.[23]

Basketball developed as a girls sport in California more rapidly than it did in the rest of the country. As early as November 1892, the University of California in Berkeley played a game against Miss Head's School, a private preparatory school. By 1898 UC Berkeley was playing practice games against two private (Miss West's and Miss Lake's) and one public high school (Lowell). The next year, Bay Area high schools, notably San Francisco and Oakland Highs, were competing against each other. High school basketball emerged in Southern California in the late 1890s, when three Pasadena schools (Marlborough, Throop Pasadena Institute, and Pasadena High) and Los Angeles High formed teams for interschool competition. Pasadena High garnered the most headlines, forming in 1900 an unbeatable team with three Sutton sisters—center Violet and forwards Florence and May (all three developed considerable reputations at tennis, and the youngest, May, later emerged as an international tennis star).[24]

In 1903 the growing enthusiasm for girls' basketball generated the formation of the Girls Basketball League of Southern California, consisting originally of five secondary schools (Girls' Collegiate, Marlborough, Monrovia, Ontario, and Pasadena High Schools) and three college institutions (Pomona College, Throop Institute, and Normal School). The following year, the Los Angeles County High School Athletic League added girls' basketball to its program, bringing such schools as Los Angeles, Santa Monica, Alhambra, Whittier, El Monte, and Polytechnic into competition. By 1907 there were seven leagues competing in Southern California, and at the end of each season, playoffs were held to determine the champion of Southern California.[25]

Unlike in Chicago and the East Coast, the Los Angeles girls played the line game, probably because early California leagues included both colleges and high schools. Yet the California variety of the line game is described as extremely physical, where newspapers of the day described one roughhouse scrape after another, with fisticuffs, hair-pulling, hard elbows, tumbling, and other aggressive and illegal tactics as the norm. A reporter at one game in 1907 noted, "There was something disquieting in the grim and murderous determination with which the young ladies chased each other over the court." The rowdy tactics of the California girls' games suggests that although the girls were playing the line game, they must have used interference rules.[26]

As in Chicago and on the East Coast, most of the girls' teams were coached by men, and women played not just for the social enjoyment but also out of fierce competitiveness with rival schools. True to the pattern of those other areas, California schools played in front of mixed audiences and traveled far and wide for competition. The girls were competing just like boys' teams, and the physical education establishment in the state was concerned. A reaction against the girls' game in California was about to set in.

INDOOR BASEBALL: THE CHICAGO GAME

Indoor baseball was a huge winter game in Chicago, and as high school boys throughout the city were spreading the joys of the sport in the late 1890s, it was taking root among the girls as well. As early as 1895, West Division had an intramural girls' team, sponsored and coached by a teacher, Milo S. Walker, who made himself a national advocate for women's participation in the game in various publications, such as the *Spalding* guides. He argued that the sport was a better alternative than basketball, as it was not as violent as girls' basketball, and that "high exertion" would be required only "at intervals."[27] In 1899 West Division found competition with other schools, and in 1901 a formal indoor baseball league was organized. The *Tribune* reported on the girl managers forming a new league on the West Side, naming Marshall, Medill, and West Division as members. The teams played a round-robin schedule, and they played the game unmodified, using regular boys' rules and equipment. Walker, however, thought the game would have more appeal with the girls if the rules and equipment were modified. He suggested using a lighter, softer, and more elastic ball, even more so than the already squishy seventeen-inch ball, and mentioned that Spalding supplied such a ball and that it met with much success.[28]

The year 1901 would be the only season that there would be a girls' indoor baseball league. For the 1902 season, West Division talked up resumption of the league, and in the school newspaper a reporter cited its benefits: "Indoor baseball is certainly a suitable game for the majority of girls. It is not rough and unlike basketball, it does not require very great strength and endurance. Instead of these it requires quickness and self-control. For these reasons it would certainly be beneficial to any who became interested in it." The other schools were unmoved, and the league died, but indoor baseball for girls continued to revive itself every few years thereafter.[29]

Whereas Chicago was the hotbed of indoor baseball, the game succeeded in taking root in pockets across the country. In 1909 two women educators, Gertrude Dudley and Frances Kellor, in their book *Athletic Games in the Education of Women*, proposed that indoor baseball was an ideal game for girls and women, more preferable than baseball, primarily because the balls were soft, the bat light, the length of throws required short, and exertion required only at intervals. Few high schools in the country adopted the sport as an interschool activity, but one of the areas where competition arose was in Southern California. Schools such as San Diego, National City, Coronado, and Long Beach competed against each other and in leagues.[30]

Track and Field

Early high school track activity for Chicago girls came from a couple of annual field meets at two Chicago schools, Lake View and Phillips. In 1900 Lake View High on the North Side began experimenting with girls' track and field contests when it started up a field day. At most high schools, field days were a fading institution, but at Lake View one particular teacher, Emil Groener, conceived the field day and promoted it as a huge spectacle—with track events for both boys and girls, mass callisthenic drills, and relay races. The field day was held around the last week of May. In the initial field day, the *Chicago Tribune* found girls' participation to be such a novelty that it focused its coverage on the girls, often in a condescending manner. Reporting on the 25-yard dash for girls, the paper wrote, "At the start they were bunched, but some friend of Aleca Bosselman cried out, 'A mouse,' and Aleca doubled her pace and won in a walk."[31]

By 1902 the field meet was attracting five thousand spectators, described by the *Chicago Tribune* as "friends and parents of the pupils." Boys participated in the 100-, 220-, and 440-yard dashes and the half-mile and mile run. Girls participated in the 25-, 50-, and 100-yard dashes and the high jump. Lake View held its last field day in 1906. The school was not only a pioneer in intramural track and field for girls, but also conducted an annual track and field contest with McKinley High during these years.[32]

Phillips High began conducting an outdoor field day in 1905, bringing hundreds of boys and girls together to participate in mass callisthenic and track and field events. Besides the decorous calisthenics, these "new athletic girls" competed in dashes and hurdle races, beanbag throws, and broad and high jumps. The *Chicago Tribune*, as with the Lake View field day, gave extensive coverage to the events, illustrating them with large photos of the girls hurdling, tossing, and jumping.[33]

Elsewhere in the country, track and field for girls found particular favor in Ohio, which pioneered interscholastic girls' track and field in 1894 at the Lorain County annual field day, which decided to include some girls' events along with the usual boys' contests. Other Ohio counties within a few years also added girls' events to their annual field days. Eventually,

11. Phillips High girls racing in the school's annual field day, 1907, an activity that would soon be ended by Chicago educators who feared medical and emotional effects of vigorous competition for teenage girls. Courtesy of the Chicago History Museum.

an unofficial state meet was sponsored by Mt. Union College in Alliance, Ohio, beginning in 1917. Ohio was virtually alone, however, in providing outside track competition for girls. In New Jersey, the Montclair High girls in 1903 were competing in dual meets with amateur clubs, but there were no other high school teams. The Philadelphia public schools in 1908 introduced a few token high school events for girls to their annual field day for both secondary and elementary schools, but the competition never prospered. Clearly, track and field for girls in the high schools existed only in isolated pockets in the country and provided little opportunity for the new athletic girl.[34]

TENNIS

Although tennis was considered acceptable as a competitive sport for girls, Chicago-area high schools were slow in formally adopting the sport. As early as 1891, girls were competing in tennis on an intramural level, notably at West Division High School, but not until the school year of 1909–1910 did local schools form girls' tennis teams for the purpose of interscholastic competition. Waller (which also went by its old name, North Division) was a pioneer in girls' tennis, forming a team in 1910 and arranging a contest with Northwest Division. By the following year, interest in the sport had so swelled that the Cook County League conducted its first girls' league schedule with eight schools.[35]

Girls' high school tennis flourished most in California, where during the first two decades of the century, the state fast developed a reputation as a generator of extraordinary tennis talent. Schoolgirl May Sutton of Pasadena High amazed the world when at the age of fifteen she won the US national tennis championship in 1905 and in 1906 and 1907 when she won Wimbledon. Her tennis activities during her school years reveal an extraordinarily rich interscholastic competition for girls in the sport in California. Sutton won a high school tournament conducted by the Thatcher School in Ojai four consecutive years, 1902–1905, as well as secondary-school tournaments in Alhambra, Ocean Park, San Diego, South Pasadena, and Venice. Her school sponsored boys' and girls' tennis teams that competed in the Los Angeles County High School Athletic League, which conducted an annual tournament that included both boys and girls and provided singles, doubles, and mixed-doubles championships.[36]

HIGH SCHOOLS TAME THE NEW ATHLETIC GIRL

The women leaders of the physical educational establishment looked across America during the first decade of the last century at the "new athletic girl," and what they saw appalled them. In most sections of the country, girl basketball players were gallivanting around their states playing other teams, often hundreds of miles away, before unruly mixed crowds, generally playing for male coaches, and playing a brand of basketball that involved a degree of roughness and exertion that was considered thoroughly unsuitable and even unhealthy for young ladies. Reformers ramped up their campaign in earnest around 1907–1908 to domesticate the game, believing that only through action could basketball for girls be saved. A 1908 report of the Second Annual Congress of the Playground Association of America said, "The noteworthy thing about this special conference was that the consensus of opinion was almost entirely toward the side of differentiating the sport of girls and boys. . . . The paper on the subject, advocating the Women's Rules for girls when played with strict supervision under the direction of women coaches, met with unanimous approval." This quote laid out exactly what they wanted: to put boys and girls sports into separate spheres and to modify drastically the game the girls were playing.[37]

Frances A. Kellor and Gertrude Dudley in their earlier-mentioned 1909 book, *Athletic Games in the Education of Women,* discussed both the state of women's athletics and the professional opinion about the subject. Dudley and Kellor described a situation where in many parts of the country, the girls organized the teams, formed leagues, set up schedules, and obtained the coaches, and noted that in many school districts, the authorities were indifferent to this lack of faculty control. The authors' criticism of the girls' game begins with an allusion to the baneful influence of a sugar high:

A typical list of refreshments eaten between the halves of a hard game or immediately afterwards includes pie, cream puffs, chocolate éclairs or charlotte russe, varied with peanuts and popcorn; and a championship contest is often followed immediately by hours of dancing. High school contests are also conspicuous for the bad spirit shown. Attacks upon officials, wrangling of teams, calling of names, bitter denunciatory remarks about opponents, intentional roughness, fault-finding, "rattling of players," by school girl or boy audiences, and personal characterizations are common in games where players alone are in control.[38]

A great issue with many educators regarding girls playing by boys' rules was that they believed biological and emotional differences between men and women required different approaches to each gender in establishing appropriate physical activity. On a most basic level, educators believed that because girls possessed smaller hearts and lungs and were weaker physically, they did not possess the endurance to play basketball by men's rules. They also had concerns regarding stressful physical activity on their role as future mothers and worried that basketball could weaken their "vital force" needed to produce babies. For this reason, the men's game was deemed to go against women's essential nature. Whereas competition was considered a male trait, women were deemed more attuned to the spirit of cooperation and sensitivity to the feelings of others. The preface to the 1908 *Spalding's Official Women's Basket Ball Guide* warned how competitive basketball would adversely affect a girl: "She cannot go into competitive games in the same spirit with men without developing dangerous nervous tendencies and losing the grace and poise and dignity and self-respect we would all have her foster." What some observers today might dismiss as mere scrappiness, the Victorian attitudes of the educators saw as "dangerous nervous tendencies," exhibiting bad character.[39]

To be fair to the physical educators, there were many reports of girls' games that simply got out of hand, such as the report of a game between two Connecticut schools in 1903:

The girl teams in a basketball contest between the Waterbury High school and the Boardman Training school of New Haven engaged in a real fight in the second half of a game in New Haven. The girls struck each other in the face, pulled hair, tripped, and threw one another on the floor, and lost all control of themselves. Coaches and spectators tried to stop the fight, but failed. The girls were oblivious to all else and they reached at each other with true ferocity. Time was sounded before the game was over and the players had to be almost dragged apart.[40]

Here in one game we have the poster child of everything that physical educators deplored about girls' basketball—the lack of ladylike decorum, the roughness, and the loss of control. Although Dudley and Kellor were strong advocates of the healthful and social benefits of girls' participation in competitive team sports, they generally sided with their colleagues regarding the criticisms of interscholastic competition, but at the same time they believed that opponents tended to exaggerate the dangers of such competition. The authors objected to the strain on the girls in traveling and playing away games at distant schools, concomitant with the occasional lack of supervision and safeguarding of the teams, plus the emphasis on winning to the detriment of teaching educational values and the character of the audiences.[41]

Reformers saw the purpose of basketball for girls as merely one of simple enjoyment of participation and benefit of recreation. The line game played intramurally was seen as fostering such aims. Dudley and Kellor, however, departed from the physical education establishment in their disfavor of the line game. They felt the line game inhibited teamwork and that it was a "less open and attractive game." They were dismissive of health concerns: "At one university where supervision and training are of a high standard, an annual average of one hundred girls have played the game by Rules for Men for the past nine years, and during that time not one serious accident, not one broken bone, and not one collapse from overplaying have resulted." They also asserted that the testimony that they received from girls was that they preferred playing under boys' rules, but, more important, they wanted to play regardless of the rules. Dudley and Kellor recommended use of men's rules only in conjunction with a non-interference rule, which they felt would do much to prevent injury and avoid rough play. The two educators were clearly a minority on this issue, as the line game supplanted the boys'-rule game across the country during the next decade.[42]

Another key concern was that men were often coaching girls. Edward B. DeGroot, a California educator, in his article "Should Girls' Teams Be Coached or Managed by Men?" in the 1908 *Guide*, answered his question with an emphatic no. He said, "Teams coached and managed by men almost invariably defeat teams coached by women. . . . [I]n one case there is a group of players representing girls' ideals and practices in athletics and in the other case there is a group representing boys' ideals and practices in athletics." He demanded that the situation be changed. Dudley and Kellor shared their colleague's concern over the use of male instructors and coaches: "Men instructors train primarily for contests, are interested in developing teams and have little patience with weak girls." They recognized, however, that men at that time tended to possess the superior knowledge of the game and that women instructors of the day lacked this understanding and tended to "baby" players.[43] Basketball was the centerpiece and the focus on participation in interscholastic sports by the "new athletic girl." Most debate regarding girls' sports activities revolved largely around basketball, and that debate had catastrophic effects on interscholastic sports for girls in high schools across the country.

The downfall of girls' basketball in Illinois seemed to come partly from the girls' adherence to the more athletic boys' game. In November 1907, the Illinois High School Athletic Association banned girls' basketball, saying, "The game is altogether too masculine and has met with much opposition on the part of parents . . . and that the exercise in public is immodest and not altogether ladylike." To add insult to injury, in the very same article, there was a notice that the association planned a state tournament for boys the following March. With some three hundred schools affected, the chilling effect of the ban put an end to competition even in schools that were not members of the association.

For the next several years, a number of schools continued interscholastic competition for girls' basketball, but by 1911 almost all interscholastic activity had ceased in Illinois schools. The yearbooks at this time show an increasing direction toward intramural contests, usually between class-year teams. At the same time, there was a widespread changeover to the adoption of girls' rules.[44]

In basketball elsewhere in the country, the end to interscholastic competition replicated the Chicago experience. In the New York–New Jersey area, where the girls' game played under boys' rules was particularly popular, reports in the papers show that by 1906, some New Jersey high schools, notably Newark High, had switched to women's rules. The director of physical education at the school, Augusta Lane Patrick, contributed an essay to the 1905–1906 *Spalding's Official Women's Basket Ball Guide* lauding the benefits of the decision of Newark to abandon boys' rules in favor of the line game. She felt that the no-grabbing rule of the girls' game helped minimize roughness and that line play alleviated exhaustion and strain. Patrick presented herself as being a convert from the boys' rules and recommended that other schools make the switch. Her proselytizing and the advocacy of others bore fruit. After 1905 there were few reports in the press of girls' games, and the few that were reported were played under the line rules. The end of boys' rules in the New York–New Jersey area came with the founding of the Girls' Branch of the PSAL, with a philosophy that girls' sports should minimize competition and physical stress.[45]

The Girls' Branch of the PSAL was formed in November 1905 for the purpose of sponsoring physical exercise, dance, and games for girls. It was headed by leading female physical educators, and the board consisted of public-spirited women of the city. Like the parent PSAL, it was a separate entity from the school system and initially a wholly voluntary organization. Although the Girls' Branch received official recognition by the board of education in 1909, there was no financial support, and the organization was forced to constantly plea for money from wealthy donors. The driving force in the Girls' Branch was Elizabeth Burchenal, who became its first executive secretary. She was assisted by Julia Richmond, the first director, and Catherine S. Leverich, the president, in setting up the girls' program. Their design for the league reflected the view of Gulick and Sargent that girls needed healthful outdoor activities but also that they should not participate in interschool and physically stressful sports.[46]

In the late spring of 1906, the Girls' Branch sponsored a demonstration day in baseball, basketball, and field hockey to show what they had in mind for girls' sports. The *New York Times*'s headline and subhead bluntly laid out the issue: "New Kind of Athletics for City Schoolgirls; They Won't Try to Play Like the Boys Any More." And they did not. Rather, the girls from several high schools and elementary schools were mixed into red and yellow teams for noncompetitive games. The basketball game was not even played to the finish. These kind of games anticipated the "play days" that were promoted during the 1920s.[47] The Girls' Branch specified that high school girls could participate in intramural relay races, hurdle relays, baseball throw, and basketball throw, and team games included indoor baseball, field hockey, basketball, and volleyball. The organization also sanctioned intramural participation in golf, tennis, swimming, and gymnastics, as well as folk dance. The launch of the Girls' Branch effectively terminated the Metropolitan Girls Athletic League, which conducted its last basketball championship in the winter of 1905.[48]

Meanwhile, in Boston, the girls by 1910 were still engaged in interscholastic contests—indeed prospering—but the games had been modified to girls' rules. At this time, some teams were adopting a six-player game, although the five-player version continued to be popular with the majority of schools. As elsewhere in the country, the girls by World War I were being circumscribed by what they could do. In 1912, when the girls' game was near the height of popularity, a number of Boston suburban schools formed a league for competition. Although league contests continued into the early 1920s, the sport declined considerably after World War I so that only a handful of schools were competing by 1923.[49]

In Southern California, moderation of the girls' games began in 1907. In June of that year, the Los Angeles County League Executive Board, concerned with the strenuousness and the "rough and tumble tactics" of the girls' game, modified the game in several respects, notably banning "wrestling with the ball" and imposing noninterference rules. The authorities also changed the number of players from five to six, bringing the game into congruence with the line game as played elsewhere in the country. The prevailing two fifteen-minute halves were considered too taxing on the girls, contributing to the breakdown of order in the games, so the board imposed rules stipulating three ten-minute periods separated by ten-minute rest periods.[50]

By 1910, however, moderating the game was not enough for some critics of girls' basketball. Interscholastic competition itself was coming under fire. The *Los Angeles Times* reported on critics who were decrying the "dangerousness" of the sport. High school and college yearbooks in the state during 1910, 1911, and 1912 showed a trend toward abandonment of interscholastic play for interclass play. School newspapers changed their tone to focus less on basketball and more on recreational sports, such as hiking and wall scaling, and by World War I interschool basketball had come to an end in California.[51]

The suppression of interschool basketball across the country was replicated in the sports of indoor baseball, track and field, and golf. After the indoor baseball league in Cook County came to an end in 1901, interschool contests were sporadic in subsequent years. In 1912 there was a flurry of interscholastic activity, when the Phillips girls arranged a series of matches with other city schools, notably Marshall and Hyde Park. By 1917 all interschool competition had ended. In the spotted areas in the rest of the country where girls played interschool indoor baseball, notably in New Orleans and Southern California, by World War I the sport quickly faded to be replaced by line basketball.[52]

In Chicago the groundbreaking field days for track and field at Lake View and Phillips came to an end well before World War I. In 1911, the last year of the field day, Phillips High had eliminated the jumping contests and added ethnic dancing. Moderation had set in. A *Chicago Tribune* sportswriter lauded the Phillips field-day concept, editorializing, "Instead of being confined to a few of the physical experts the contests were participated in by hundreds, both boys and girls. This is the proper conception of athletics for scholars, whether in the schools or the colleges. Other institutions might well follow Wendell Phillips' example." His points would be echoed by women physical educators in their movement to suppress interscholastic sports for girls. The field days disappeared, but they were a laudable early example of educators in the Cook County League seeing no reason to exclude their young female charges from track and field competition, even of the intramural variety.[53]

12. Marshall High School girls' indoor baseball team of 1912, when Chicago high school girls' teams were competing against each other. This early incarnation of softball was considered suitable for girls and was enormously popular in Chicago. Courtesy of the Chicago Public Library, Special Collections and Preservation Division, EGP 6/11.

Tennis saw a similar trajectory downward after a promising start. In Chicago, following the breakup of the Cook County League in 1913, the new Chicago Public High School League continued to offer girls' competition. The tennis series generated one star, Marian Leighton, who was the subject of a feature article in the *Chicago Tribune* in 1916. She headed the Girls Athletic Association at Hyde Park High and participated in basketball and swimming, as well as tennis. In 1915 and 1917, she won the league's singles tennis title. The Public League, however, did not sustain its support in girls' tennis, choosing to make the October 1917 tournament its last. The Chicago Public High School League would revisit tennis for girls in the 1920s. Elsewhere, notably in California, girls' tennis competition likewise went into decline. Where there was a rich level of league competition in the first decade of the century, in the next decade interschool competition was gradually done away with in the state, as evidenced by high school yearbooks in San Diego that tell the story of girls lamenting the inability to compete against other schools.[54]

The Progressive Era was an exhilarating time for the new athletic girl, and for a few short years she prospered in the secondary schools across the land. That prosperity did not last, however, as the physical educators who had controlled sports activities for women in the colleges found that interscholastic competition for girls was not only inappropriate but too physically stressful and potentially physically harmful to their young womanhood. And the emotional stress and overexcitement in the girl, often in public exhibition, were deemed damaging to their character. These educators prevailed in the cultural war down into the high schools so that by World War I, girls' athletic programs had been moderated in most areas to eliminate interschool competition and to domesticate basketball to almost universal adoption of the line game. Competition in basketball, indoor baseball, track and field, and tennis all initially prospered and then were eventually moderated or suppressed.

Although the educators' aim to control sports for girls in the Progressive Era succeeded far better than it did for the boys, the issue of control would be revisited during the 1920s, when educational authorities once again were forced to engage in a suppression campaign, as interscholastic sports for girls prospered, once more challenging educators on their conception of competitive sports on the physical development and character development of the American high school girl.

PART THREE

Triumph of National Governance, 1920–1930

9

INTERSCHOLASTICS AND THE GOLDEN AGE OF SPORTS

The 1920s is considered the golden age of sport, an era that gave us an unprecedented number of sports titans—Babe Ruth and Lou Gehrig in baseball, Red Grange in football, Jack Dempsey and Gene Tunney in boxing, Bobby Jones and Walter Hagen in golf, Helen Wills and Bill Tilden in tennis, and Paavo Nurmi in track and field. At all levels of competition—high school, college, amateur, minor league, and major league—there was an increased level of interest and great commercial expansion. Interscholastic sports, along with their counterparts on the college and professional levels, grew in scope and scale, as the high schools supported ever-greater numbers of student athletes and provided more sports in larger and more expansive competitions.

The growth in interscholastic sports was in part based on far-greater numbers of students participating in sports. Fueling the growth in the number of students was the broadening of the student population beyond college preparatory, leading to the development of the comprehensive high school. By 1918 the comprehensive high school, with its variety of vocational, homemaking, and college-prep courses designed to serve all kinds of students, was deemed the standard organization for secondary education. The growth in the number and variety of students was a result of the advent of compulsory-attendance laws that after 1900 spread to the majority of states and in many cases increased the age of attendance up through high school. Much anti–child labor legislation in the states also fueled this growth. Influential educator Ellwood P. Cubberley saw these developments as deleterious to the public schools in that they now had to educate those students who presumably did not come to learn, the "truant and the incorrigible," "children of inferior mental ability," and other "misfits," in his unfortunate language.[1]

The National Education Association in its policy-shaping 1918 report, *Cardinal Principles of Secondary Education*, saw one of the roles of the comprehensive high school as instilling "ethical character" and common social values in the students. The educational establishment strongly believed interscholastic sports brought students together in shared social values and kept the marginally interested students in school and therefore encouraged their development. Cubberley typified their views in his remarks on faculty-directed sports: "Few other things do so much to transform the yard bully into a useful school citizen, bring out the timid and backward pupils, limit accidents, create good feeling, reduce discipline, teach pupil self-control, train the muscles and eye to coordination in games involving learned skills, or awaken the best spirit of the pupils." Cubberley and other educators throughout the 1920s extolled high school sports for their character-building impact on the secondary-school student.[2]

The number of sport offerings increased, largely in the big cities, which had a large number of comprehensive schools with huge student populations, conducive to sports expansion in a variety of sports, appealing to their diverse populations. For example, New York City's PSAL offered fourteen sports, which included programs unknown in most other parts of the country, such as lacrosse, handball, and ice hockey. Philadelphia offered eleven sports, which included a couple of uncommon sports, bowling and gymnastics. Not all schools in these big-city leagues would adopt every sport. Whereas almost all the schools in such large systems would adopt major sports such as football, basketball, baseball, and track and field, many fewer high schools in these leagues would take up the minor sports, typically offering about ten to twelve sports. The growth of wealthy suburban school districts with extensive athletic facilities and campuses also encouraged the adoption of more sports.

In many high schools during the 1920s, the educators expanded not only their offerings but also the scope of competition. They had their institutions competing beyond their state borders and in other sections of the country. There was a greater level of competition for state championships, as many more state athletic associations came into being and more began offering state championship competitions. At the same time, universities and colleges were enlarging their sponsored high school competitions, building them from local and sectional contests to national contests and becoming fully commercialized endeavors.

HIGH SCHOOLS STRIVE FOR INTERSECTIONAL GLORY

Football was a highly visible manifestation of high school sports aggrandizement, in imitation of the college and pro sports world. The 1920s saw college football reach the height of popularity, and across the country universities built stadiums seating eighty to one hundred thousand for Saturday-game extravaganzas. In the universities and colleges, intersectional games became a regular part of collegiate football, most notably California and Ohio State (1921), Princeton and Chicago (1921 and 1922), and Notre Dame and Southern California (1926). The intersectional contests helped fuel media and fan interest—generating reams of copy on titular national champions—and thus transforming the sport from one built on sectional interest to one national in scope.[3]

High school football likewise saw a rage for intersectional and intrasectional games and the crowning of sectional and national champions by the media. The nation's newspapers heralded certain intersectional matchups as national championship games. In my survey of Illinois secondary-school football programs, I found that the state's high schools competed in forty-two intersectional contests from 1919 to 1929, mostly against eastern schools. Prior to the 1920s, there were only seven intersectional contests from 1900 to 1910 and fifteen contests from 1911 to 1917.[4]

Ohio emerged as a preeminent football center, and schools from Dayton and Toledo in particular would travel across the country, contending for national recognition. The 1923 team from Scott High in Toledo, for example, in garnering a 9-0 record and national honors, played four out-of-state teams—from Massachusetts, Illinois, Washington, and Iowa. The final game against Washington High of Cedar Rapids, Iowa, was played before thirteen thousand fans in Scott High's newly constructed stadium.

Scott High was said to have offered Washington High the largest high school guarantee up to that time, seventy-five hundred dollars. The following year, another Toledo team, Waite High, in achieving a perfect 10–0 record and earning press recognition as the national champion, played just three schools in Ohio, along with two in neighboring Michigan and one each in Indiana, Illinois, Louisiana, Tennessee, and Massachusetts. The Massachusetts opponent was Everett High, and Waite's postseason matchup with that school was publicized as being for the national championship. These titular national championship games would get coverage not only in the home states of the competitors, but also in large metropolitan newspapers in Chicago, New York, and Los Angeles.[5]

In Illinois the schools most engaged in intersectional and out-of-state contests were Chicago's Englewood, Lindblom, and Phillips; Proviso of suburban Maywood; and DePaul Academy of the Chicago Catholic League. They sought such games not to achieve sectional or even national championships, but to achieve recognition for their programs and to expand the horizons of the school beyond their own communities. By 1921 the Chicago press took notice of the rapid growth of intersectional contests across the nation and in Illinois, notably in a *Chicago Tribune* article, titled "Eastern Trips Boost School Football," which opened with the assertion that "coaches of the teams that went east are unanimous in their belief that intersectional games are of great benefit to both the players and the schools they represent." Besides the obvious educational and cultural benefit of expanding their students' understanding of the world, the reporter contended, such trips also helped expand football knowledge by exposing the coaches and players to different and unfamiliar styles of play, and the often lavish receptions and closing dinners given by host teams encouraged sportsmanship.[6]

Englewood, a Chicago Public League power through the mid-1920s, surpassed all the city schools in the length and number of its intersectional and sectional trips, which totaled seven, their purpose to sustain the school's long winning legacy in football. This effort was only partially successful, as the school managed to win only three intersectional contests, losing big against Ohio and Pennsylvania schools. One Public League school with a winning intersectional record was Lindblom, with its most impressive win against City College High School of Baltimore in 1925, romping over its opponent 96–0. Said the *Tribune,* "Never before has this city seen such a clever scholastic football team in action. And never before has a City College football team been forced to suffer such an ignominious defeat. . . . [I]t met a superscholastic team which ranks with the best." Lindblom used intersectional games to establish its growing reputation as a football power.[7]

Proviso, under a succession of administrations and coaches, was committed to running a top-notch football program, and as part of that program its intersectional schedule for the next two decades was the most ambitious in Illinois. Proviso in annual trips during 1919–1924 played two sectional games against Ohio schools and seven intersectional games, six of them against teams in Massachusetts. Proviso considered intersectional contests as something of a cultural broadening for its students. In most cases, the trips to the East by midwestern and western schools were expanded to include touring other cultural sites, and on more than one occasion the high school teams visited the White House and met with the president.[8]

Catholic high schools from Illinois also competed in intersectional contests, usually against other strong Catholic football powers, as in 1920, when DePaul Academy traveled to St. James, in Haverhill, Massachusetts. DePaul, having been the city's preeminent Catholic League power in the previous decade, continued to engage in intersectional contests throughout the 1920s, even though the school won only two league titles. DePaul surely did not succeed in adding glory to its program, losing all five of the intersectional contests. The school authorities at DePaul most likely saw these contests as merely spreading the name of their institution and giving the boys some travel experience.[9]

High schools from the South began entering the intersectional high school gridiron wars in the second half of the 1920s. During the last three seasons of the decade, all eleven of the intersectional games played by Illinois schools involved southern opponents. Of the eighteen southern contests during the decade, seven of them pitted a predominantly black Chicago school, Wendell Phillips, against segregated black schools from the South.[10]

The intersectional football games involving Illinois schools in previous decades were instrumental in spreading the superior midwestern game to the East. But by the 1920s, Illinois was no longer a preeminent high school football state, and Ohio and Pennsylvania played a better brand of football. In the twenty-eight games played between Illinois and Ohio schools during the 1920s, Illinois schools won only six. Most intersectional games were played by schools that had rich and winning football traditions, but there were many nationally recognized football powers that rarely if ever played an intersectional contest. Thus, in this era of significant expansion of football intersectional and sectional contests, the obvious motivation to showcase a winning program was not the only or even the primary reason high schools played these matches. Rather, because of the varying cultures of these schools, long-distance travel for their football teams was considered desirable and educational and part of the character building they saw in sports.

Chicago Public High School League Leads

The Chicago Public High School League in the 1920s exemplified the experiences of a big-city American high school league, exploding with new sports—namely, indoor golf, wrestling, gymnastics, ice skating (speed skating), rifle, and fencing. By the end of the decade, it would sponsor sixteen sports for boys, more than any other major city. The league was one of the leading advocates of intersectional competition, notably promoting baseball and ice skating in competition against New York City. The following discussion on the Chicago Public High School League covers much of the league activities, with the exception of rifle and fencing (which are covered in the following chapter).

Indoor Golf

Typical of its expansion into exotic sports was the league's sponsorship of a wintertime sport called "indoor golf," which was a putting game. The sport was popular in several major cities, both as a competitive game and as recreation, and in 1924 a league board of control member and head of a local golf association persuaded the Chicago Public High School League to adopt the sport. The first year's meet was limited to boys and attracted ten school teams, of four golfers each. In 1925 Schurz and Lake View Highs inaugurated competition for girls. Lake View was particularly vigorous in encouraging and training its students in golf. Its golf club, with more than seventy members, was the largest in the league, and the school brought in a notable golf pro to give weekly instruction on Fridays to a special gym class of the golf-club members. The class, in which students received regular physical education grades, received national attention. Indoor golf proved to be a fad, however, and it soon faded, the last Public League meet being held in 1930. Indoor golf never caught on in the high schools in other states and never caught on outside the Chicago public high schools.[11]

13. Senn High indoor golf team from 1927, a sport known only in Chicago high schools, and its inclusion in the Chicago Public High School League schedule helped the city lead the nation in the number of sports offered in the high schools. Courtesy of the Ray Schmidt Collection.

Wrestling

Wrestling was a late bloomer in interscholastic sports, and it was not until the mid-1920s that Chicago high schools began taking up the sport, around the same time that other midwestern states began adopting the sport. Iowa was the first state to conduct a high school state championship, in 1921. Indiana was another early pioneer, when in 1922 Indiana University began sponsorship of a state high school meet. In the Southwest, Oklahoma became another early hotbed of the sport, launching its state tournament in 1922.[12]

The Chicago Public High School League adopted wrestling in 1926, but the sport had many years of incubation outside the schools in playground and amateur competition. As early as 1910, grammar school and high school boys were participating in city playground and park-district tournaments, plus amateur club meets. In 1911 a team of Lane Tech wrestlers competed under their school's name in the local Amateur Athletic Federation meet. In 1916 Hyde Park, Harrison, and St. Cyril all organized teams and competed against one another, but the competition was not sustained after that year. In 1923 Tilden Tech and Bowen conducted a wrestling exhibition between halves of a basketball game. Finally, the league conducted its first championship tournament in April 1926, with twelve schools and 166 wrestlers participating. By 1929 the Chicago Public League had twenty-three schools competing, organized into three sections, but there was little wrestling competition in the state outside Chicago. In such cities as New York, Philadelphia, Washington, Atlanta, and Los Angeles, wrestling was virtually unknown in the public schools.[13]

Wrestling, as true of just about every interscholastic sport during the 1920s, found a university to sponsor a national tournament or one that aspired to be a national tournament. Northwestern University added a wrestling interscholastic to its national tournament program of indoor track (held since 1910) and swimming (1914). The meet was held in the third week of March and attracted national high school powers from the two hotbeds of wrestling, Iowa and Oklahoma.[14]

In October 1927, when the physical education director of the Columbus Public Schools, B. E. Wiggins, wrote an article for the *American*

14. Harrison High wrestling team from 1926, which was one of the new sports adopted by high schools in Chicago, and most notably in Iowa and Oklahoma. Courtesy of the Chicago History Museum.

Physical Education Review, he named the following states as having either "sectional" or state wrestling meets sanctioned for high schools: Massachusetts, New Jersey, Ohio, Michigan, Indiana, Illinois, Minnesota, and California. What he inexplicably omitted were two states in the central part of the country with some of the earliest and most accomplished wrestling programs, namely, Iowa and Oklahoma. With these two states included in the total, six of the ten states with "sectional" or state meets were from the Midwest and one was from the Southwest.[15]

Gymnastics

Long before competitive gymnastics developed in Chicago schools, the city had a vigorous gymnastics program that had been developed by its sizable immigrant populations of Germans and Czechs in the nineteenth century. The Germans pioneered gymnastics in the city through their Turners, and the Czechs followed with their Sokols.

Chicago schools had adopted light gymnastics, or calisthenics, for their physical education classes as early as 1866, but under the heavy German and Turner influence in the city, the Chicago Board of Education formally adopted the Turner system of heavy gymnastics in 1889. A formal course of exercises on apparatus to go along with the established callisthenic program was instituted, and the board hired a German Turner, Henry Sudor, to supervise the new program. In 1891 Northwest Division High opened with a gymnasium, recognized as the first indoor public high school gym in the nation. The building of gymnasiums in other schools, in Chicago and nationwide, rapidly followed, so that by 1914 all of the city's twenty-two high schools had at least one gymnasium. Gymnastics at first was taught only as a routine exercise and not as a competitive sport.[16]

Despite Chicago's rich background in gymnastics, the city was not the first major metropolitan area to develop a secondary-school competitive program. Some New York schools adopted gymnastics earlier, notably Trinity School, a private school in Manhattan, which began intramural gymnastic contests by 1899. After the turn of the century, Trinity was joined by more than a half-dozen schools in New York and New Jersey, both public (DeWitt Clinton and Commerce) and private (Horace Mann and Newark Academy). Columbia University sponsored a gymnastics interscholastic meet for three years, 1901–1903, which apparently expired from lack of sufficient interest.[17]

Gymnastics remained largely moribund in the New York–New Jersey area until it was revived in the mid-1920s. In New York City, such schools as DeWitt Clinton, Stuyvesant, and Brooklyn Manual took up the sport, but they lagged competitively behind their New Jersey counterparts—notably Dickinson, Newark Central, and Emerson. The University of Pennsylvania began sponsoring a gymnastics interscholastic in 1924 and attracted such schools from New Jersey as Dickinson and Newark Academy, along with such Pennsylvania schools as Germantown, Philadelphia Northeast, and Haverford. The Philadelphia Interscholastic League also sponsored a gymnastics championship.[18]

The area's high schools also flocked to the Metropolitan AAU Interscholastic Gymnastics Championships, launched in 1926 by Roy R. Moore, the US gymnastics coach at the 1920 and 1924 Olympic Games. The first meet drew twelve public and private schools from the New York–New Jersey area. The first six places were held by New Jersey schools. In the first year, the meet was held in the gymnasium of the City College of New York, but in subsequent years the meet was held at Jersey City's Dickinson High, the center of gymnastics in the metropolitan area. The Swiss Turn Verein of Hudson County (where Dickinson and other New Jersey gymnastic powers were located) was particularly prominent, winning national AAU team championships in 1926 and from 1928 to 1939. New Jersey was a pioneering state in gymnastics, as it presented its first state competition in the sport in 1926, decades before any other state sponsored a tournament.[19]

About the same time as competitive gymnastics revived in the eastern schools, Chicago high schools also began adopting the sport. Competitive gymnastics in the city schools was the product of some farsighted hardworking individuals who came through the rich tradition of gymnastics in the city's Turner halls and Sokols. Thus, it was a Czech American from the West Side and a Sokol all-around national champion, Henry J. Smidl, who almost single-handedly introduced the sport in Illinois. While teaching at Englewood High in 1924, Smidl persuaded the Public League to sponsor a team championship in the sport and recruited two other schools to form teams and participate, Harrison High and Lane Tech. Harrison was located in a West Side Czech neighborhood, where many Harrison students belonged to the Sokol where Smidl also instructed in gymnastics. The following year, Smidl moved to Lindblom High and there created a dynasty that won twenty-four senior titles. Beginning in 1940, Smidl was challenged by another gymnastics power, Senn, whose team was coached by Alfred E. Bergman, a nationally recognized coach at the Lincoln Park Turners. Lindblom and Senn would produce practically all of the city's high school team titles and graduate a host of gymnasts into national and international competition. As in New Jersey, these programs were built by people who came out of European gymnastics and had a draw from immigrant populations familiar with the sport.[20]

Baseball

High school baseball, which today is an also-ran for the attention of sports enthusiasts, was a golden-era beneficiary of America's fascination and interest in sports. Throughout the 1920s, extensive columns of ink and banner headlines in the nation's newspapers were devoted to high school baseball games. Of particular public interest to New York and Chicago fans of high school baseball was the annual New York–Chicago intercity game held each year from 1920 to 1926 between each of the cities' league champions. For a few short years, each city's annual playoffs for the league title followed by the championship contests between New York and Chicago high schools were some of the biggest stories in interscholastic sports, garnering great attention in the newspapers and attracting crowds in the tens of thousands.

The New York–Chicago intercity series was kick-started by the *Chicago Tribune* on May 23, 1920, when the paper's baseball writer, James Crusinberry, traveled to New York and reported excitingly on the High School of Commerce baseball team. He was highly impressed with their play—their hitting and their intelligent fielding—and was particularly impressed with a player by the name of Lou Gehrig. He noted the disadvantages and poverty of the team, describing how the Commerce players were poorly dressed and equipped. Two days later, he wrote another dispatch from New York reporting on Commerce's challenge to Chicago. The wheels quickly turned to get an intersectional game organized, with extensive encouragement and promotion by the *Chicago Tribune*. Hugh L. Ray, president of the Faculty Board of Athletic Control, got behind the *Tribune* proposal, raising two thousand dollars from "leading citizens and firms" to underwrite the costs of bringing the Commerce team to Chicago.[21]

Lane Tech won the Chicago schools' playoffs and met Commerce in Cubs Park before 6,600 fans, on June 26. The game was a blowout by the players of Commerce, who won 12–6. The high point of the game was a home run hit by Lou Gehrig in the top of the ninth, a mighty blast that flew over Cubs Park's right-field wall.[22] In the years following, the *Chicago Tribune* provided the most extensive coverage of the annual game, always leading with an inch-high banner headline across its sports page.

The *New York Times* treated the annual series with far more modest coverage. Early in the series, Chicago fans tended to outdraw New York fans for the game, which alternated yearly between each city. The 1921 game in New York drew only 5,000 fans, but the 1922 game at Cubs Park attracted 10,000 fans. But as the series went on, the games played in New

York began to significantly outdraw Chicago's games. The 1923 contest between Washington and Lindblom was held at the Polo Grounds before 40,000 spectators. The following year, in Chicago, only 6,500 fans were in the stands. In 1925 Lane Tech and Flushing High of Queens played before 57,178 spectators at Yankee Stadium, the largest crowd ever to see a high school baseball game, a figure that may still stand.[23]

The 1926 intercity game was between Lane of Chicago and Evander Childs of New York. Upon arriving in Chicago, the Evander Childs players were treated to a parade through the Loop on the way to their near-north hotel. Chicago got its biggest crowd of the series, when 18,000 fans attended the game. Among the spectators were Cubs president William L. Veeck and baseball commissioner Kenesaw Mountain Landis. The 1926 game was the last of the New York–Chicago series. The New York Board of Education canceled the 1927 game, citing their belief that the series was excessive for high school boys. The Chicago Public High School League and *Chicago Tribune* tried to prevail on the New York authorities to relent and hold the game, but were repeatedly rebuffed. Chicago made offers for an intercity game to Omaha and St. Louis, but was rejected by both.[24]

The Chicago experience in the 1920s was replicated in a number of other big cities, as their public high school leagues expanded their sports offerings. But educators by the middle of the decade were beginning to have qualms about long-distance high school contests and began to withdraw their support for such endeavors. In 1925 Chicago's director of physical education in the public schools, Edward C. Delaporte, found he had to defend the New York–Chicago baseball series before critics at the annual conference of the American Physical Education Association. What happened to the New York–Chicago baseball series was an intimation of things to come, whereby almost all national and sectional contests would be increasingly resisted by the secondary educational establishment and terminated.[25]

Speed Skating

At the beginning of the 1920s, speed skating had been flourishing in Chicago for more than two decades, with formal competition among men and women, boys and girls, organized in teams sponsored by private clubs, playgrounds, and parks. The youths of the city were active in speed skating to a degree unknown in any other city in the United States. Chicago skaters were destined during the 1920s to have great success in North American speed skating. That success would be owing to climatic factors, demographic factors, and cultural factors.

In terms of climate, Chicago had a decided advantage over most large cities. Taking an average of the January temperature, the key month for speed skating, only Milwaukee (21.8 degrees) and Minneapolis–St. Paul (10.8 degrees) had colder climates than Chicago (27 degrees). With regard to demographics, in 1920 Chicago produced more young boys aged ten to nineteen (210,000) than any other city next to New York (470,000), meaning more youthful athletes and more skaters. New York's advantage in youthful population was offset by the city's disadvantage in climate. New York City did not have the abundance of outdoor rinks in the parks and playgrounds, in part because there was not the number of freezing days to make them useful facilities. Also, having a sizable Norwegian population proved critical in the early years to producing top-notch skaters. Only three US cities had a sizable number of Norwegians—New York, Chicago, and Minneapolis–St. Paul (treating the latter as one metropolis), which in the 1920 census showed populations of 40,000, 45,000, and 52,000, respectively. Olympian and Hall of Fame skater Eddie Schroeder, who competed in the 1920s and 1930s, pointedly asserted, "The origin of competitive speed skating in Chicago came from the Norwegians, who lived around the Humboldt Park area—that's where it all started."[26]

By 1905 a whole array of skating clubs had been formed in Chicago, usually based in the city parks. In 1917 the *Chicago Tribune* began sponsorship of the Silver Skates competition. The Silver Skates proved to be a watershed event, as the *Tribune* not only almost daily promoted the competition but also reported on every other meet, high and low, in the city, thus generating a huge interest and growth in speed skating. By 1923 the Chicago area in the wintertime was dotted with more than six hundred outdoor rinks (more than any other city), and thousands of boys and girls of all national origins were skating.[27]

The progress of Chicago in speed skating was spectacularly mani-fested in 1921 and 1922 in a series of schoolboy competitions among the major cities of the Northeast. They involved considerable hoopla, with banner newspaper headlines, parades, coaching by national champion skaters, and festive parties. These contests were initiated and promoted by Chicago's mayor, "Big Bill" Thompson, whose governing approach was to give Chicagoans bread and circuses as he allowed corruption and sleaze to spread through city hall. Tryouts pared down 176 candidates to a team of 18, further divided into three teams of 6—grammar school, junior high (first two years), and senior high (last two years). This group included two future Olympians and Hall of Fame skaters, O'Neil Farrell of Austin and Eddie Murphy of St. Ignatius. The meet organizers rapidly built up the scope of the enterprise so that the Chicago schoolboys' itinerary grew to include competitions along the way in Cleveland, Pittsburgh, and Phila-delphia before the big race in New York. At each stop, the contests were held in indoor rinks, which supposedly put the Chicago boys at a disad-vantage. Nonetheless, in every city the Chicago schoolboys beat the com-petition by one-sided scores.[28]

In 1922 Chicago chose to serve as host for a national meet. Four cities responded to invitations: Milwaukee, Detroit, Cleveland, and New York. Again the competition was divided into three divisions—grammar school, junior high, and senior high. Unlike the previous year, when all the com-petition was held in indoor skating rinks, the competition in Chicago would be held in the Chicago manner, outdoors on the lagoon at Garfield Park. To help celebrate the skating championships, the Chicago organiz-ers gave the city a big parade two days before the big meet, led by a long array of fire trucks carrying each of the visiting teams, followed by Chicago team and meet officials, and twelve thousand Reserve Officers' Training Corps (ROTC) marchers from the city high schools. As expected, Chi-cago dominated the meet on February 25, winning first place with forty points, followed by Cleveland (thirty points), Milwaukee (nineteen points), Detroit (four points), and New York (two points).[29]

The intercity competition of 1921–1922 energized Chicago school authorities to belatedly add a high school tournament in 1923, thus finally bringing high school competition into the rich array of skating competition already available for the city's youth. The first meet was held in mid-January. Laudable as it was to add speed skating to the Chicago Public High School League program, no plans were made to include a competition for girls. The girls in the city were highly active in club, playground, and Silver Skates competition, and in some high schools had formed teams, but school authorities were blind to the possibility.[30]

By the winter of 1928, Chicago once again was eager to prove its worth in schoolboy skating with the rest of the country. Particularly avid was Mayor Big Bill Thompson through his ice-skating committee, which found an event in upstate New York called the Adirondack Gold Cup meet, where competition was held at Lake Placid and Saranac Lake. The Gold Cup meet would feature many local schoolboys who were long engaged in high school and amateur competition, and the feeling was that Chicago schoolboys would surely meet worthy competition. Chicago sent sixteen schoolboys, which included Eddie Schroeder of Tilden Tech and future Silver Skates winner Edwin Stundl of Harrison High. The board of education provided twelve hundred dollars for trip expenses. The triumphant Chicago schoolboys garnered more than the combined totals of all the other cities, mostly Lake Placid and Saranac Lake, the only vital region in the East for schoolboy skating. The big Lake Placid High star in the meet was future Olympian Jack Shea.[31]

Interscholastic speed skating never grew elsewhere in the country, and in fact receded in the few pockets it did exist. Wisconsin and Michigan had the only state high school associations that regulated speed skating, although they did not sponsor state tournaments. In New York, the speed-skating state meet ended in 1932, when all state title competition was terminated. Chicago, virtually alone in the country, continued with a high school speed-skating program.[32]

The Chicago Public League led the nation in the expansion and promotion of intersectional competition. Indicative of its leadership, in 1922 as a result of the growing popularity of such football games, as well as the recent intercity schoolboy contests in speed skating and baseball, the league encouraged Chicago to meet with representatives from New York, Milwaukee, Detroit, and Cleveland to further intercity competition, but nothing ever came of the meeting. For one, New York's PSAL had a policy of not playing postseason football games.[33]

Befitting the golden age of sports, the nation's universities and colleges built up their sponsorship of high school competitions as much as they did their own athletic programs. More and more universities took up sponsorship of tournaments, and commercialization increased as they built up these competitions into first sectional championships and then national championships. The most predominant sports sponsored by the universities were basketball and track and field, but becoming increasingly common and growing in the 1920s were such competitions as cross-country, swimming, and tennis.

Cross-Country

The sport of cross-country had been steadily growing in the interscholastic ranks since its origins out of the hare-and-hounds contests in the late 1880s. The first notable cross-country meet in the East was that of the University of Pennsylvania, established in the fall of 1903, on Thanksgiving Day. By the early 1920s, the *New York Times* was giving the meet several paragraphs and hailing it as a national contest. In 1921 the meet attracted 150 runners and twenty-five schools, with individual runners coming all the way from Iowa and teams as far away as Buffalo. The University of Pennsylvania terminated its cross-country extravaganza after the 1923 meet.[34]

Columbia University entered into high school cross-country sponsorship in 1911. Columbia generally sponsored its run in mid-November and initially attracted schools from only the New York metropolitan area. Within five years, the meet was attracting 165 individuals representing around fifteen teams and by the early 1920s more than 400 runners and more than twenty teams. The meet attracted such nationally ranked powers as Mercersburg Academy, Newark Central, and Schenectady High, and by the 1920s the Columbia meet dwarfed the Pennsylvania meet. In

1924, with the termination of the Pennsylvania meet, the *New York Times* deemed Columbia's meet as being for the eastern scholastic championship. Schenectady High dominated throughout the 1920s, in a meet that had grown to include thirty schools and 350 to 400 runners each year.[35]

Newark, New Jersey, had long been a center of cross-country excellence, primarily through the achievements of Newark Central, and thus in 1926 crosstown rival Newark Preparatory launched a meet. But despite sending out 500 entry blanks, Newark Prep hosted only a modest field in its first year. The next year, however, the *New York Times* hailed the meet as being for the "national scholastic championship." Among the 189 runners from some twenty schools were representatives from among the top cross-country powers in the East. By the end of the decade, the meet attracted about twenty representative schools from New England down to Virginia and was still hailed in the East as a "national championship" meet. The middle states section of the United States did more than any other area to make cross-country a high school sports spectacle, sponsoring virtually all the major meets in the country for secondary schools.[36]

Swimming

Swimming involved much less competitive excess, but in the East and Chicago, the sport during the 1920s reached levels of expansion that were disquieting to educators, particularly as the sport was so heavily sponsored by private clubs and universities, to the exclusion of the secondary-school educational establishment. Illinois was a center of swimming in the 1920s, mostly because of the training its high school boys received at the private athletic clubs, notably the Illinois Athletic Club, which, under the coaching of William Bachrach, had one of the best teams in the nation during that decade. The IAC recruited many of its swimmers from the local high schools, and one way to find the talent was to sponsor high school swimming meets. From 1908 to 1919, the IAC schoolboy meet was simply called the Illinois Athletic Club Interscholastic and was usually held in December. In 1920, however, the IAC introduced a second meet for high schools, to be held in March. The IAC called its winter meet a "national" interscholastic. There was little "national" about the meet, though, which attracted about ten local schools and one team from New York. As with its inaugural meet, the IAC's subsequent national tournaments never amounted to much, and in 1927 the IAC wisely dropped the word *national* from the tournament's name.[37]

Northwestern University established a swim meet that was more genuinely national. In 1914 athletic director Lewis Omer added a swimming interscholastic to be held the same day as the indoor track and field meet. During the first years of the swimming tourney, the competition involved mostly local schools. In 1923, however, the event for the first time advertised itself as being "national," when it attracted a sizable sixteen schools, of which three were from out of state, two from Detroit and one from Minneapolis. The Northwestern swim meet was able to make a better claim to national status when true national powers from Atlantic City, New Jersey, and Wilmington, Delaware, began annually participating in 1924.[38]

In the East, a plethora of university-sponsored interscholastic swimming meets had emerged, mostly after World War I, the most notable being the ones held at Yale, Rutgers, Columbia, and Pennsylvania. The

15. Englewood High yearbook swimming graphic from 1928, showing how private clubs (as well as universities) sponsored swimming during the decade. Courtesy of the Chicago History Museum.

eastern universities in 1922 also established an individual national championship swim meet, which rotated among host institutions. The earliest and most prestigious national swimming meet for secondary schools was the National Interscholastic conducted by the University of Pennsylvania, founded in 1903 and asserting "national status" beginning in 1923. Most of the schools came from the Eastern Seaboard, but with such national swim powers as Mercersburg, Atlantic City, and Wilmington participating, along with nationally ranked individuals from the Midwest, the meet regularly produced record-breaking performances and somewhat earned its "national" tag.[39]

Swimming in the high schools was a highly publicized sport during the 1920s, its high visibility owed in part to the tremendous coverage of amateur swimming in the sports pages of the day, which made such swimmers as Johnny Weissmuller and Gertrude Ederle household names. Swimming lent itself to national coverage because it was a sport built on records, and anywhere in the country a swimmer could achieve national success by merely breaking a record. Several college institutions generated extensive newspaper coverage with their national interscholastics and in turn fueled the drive for high school teams and individuals to make long trips to compete for athletic glory.

Tennis

Since its inception in the secondary schools during the 1890s, tennis had been extensively sponsored by universities and colleges. The National Interscholastic, which thrived at Newport, Rhode Island, from 1891 to 1915, was briefly revived during 1923 and 1924 by the United States Lawn Tennis Association (USLTA). The revived national, however, came into conflict with the USLTA's expanded junior tennis program after two years and was thus terminated, but the interscholastic meets sponsored by Yale, Harvard, Princeton, and Pennsylvania not only thrived but grew in popularity as the decade wore on.[40]

The university meets during the decade were augmented by many more tournaments sponsored by high school leagues and state associations. For example, New York's PSAL introduced tennis competition in

1908, the Atlanta Prep School Athletic Association in 1915, and the Philadelphia Public League in 1920. State associations introduced tennis competition as early as 1920 in Ohio, 1922 in Florida, 1924 in Virginia, and 1925 in Wisconsin. In California, where tennis was huge, the Southern California Interscholastic had been the highlight tournament in the state since 1914.[41]

In Illinois the University of Chicago and the University of Illinois both sponsored tennis tournaments. The University of Chicago had sponsored a midwestern interscholastic tennis tournament from 1895 to 1917, but when it resumed in 1924 it was limited to local schools. The University of Illinois Interscholastic began in 1912, and it eventually supplanted the University of Chicago Interscholastic in sending winners to the National Interscholastic. The Illinois and Chicago meets typified university-sponsored tourneys during the 1920s, as neither made claims for national or sectional championships. Instead, Illinois served as the state championship event and Chicago as the metropolitan championship event. As such, they, along with other university-sponsored, locally focused tennis tournaments around the country, did not come under attack during the decade.[42]

Basketball

In the 1920s, basketball was played by more high schools than any other sport, and it was often the genesis of many state high school associations, many of which were formed to regulate basketball. Basketball, unlike football, did not have a long history of intersectional competition prior to the 1920s. However, it soon surpassed football in intersectional interest, mostly as a result of the National Interscholastic Basketball Tournament played in Chicago from 1917 to 1930. In March 1917, the athletic director and football coach at the University of Chicago, Amos Alonzo Stagg, launched a high school tournament that would be played in the school's Bartlett Gymnasium. Because the tourney involved schools throughout the Midwest in its first year, it was designated as being for the central-states championship after an earlier tournament of the same name. The tourney had twenty-three schools, twelve from Illinois, both public and private.[43]

World War I interrupted the Chicago tournament, but it returned in 1920 with little press attention. The University of Chicago treated the tournament title game as a "curtain raiser" for the Chicago-Pennsylvania game, which was deemed to be for the national collegiate basketball title. The following year, Stagg designated his meet as a "national tournament," although most teams were from the Midwest. Seven of the twenty-six team entries came from the East, although there were no entries from the South and only one entry from the West. A problem in attracting teams was its date, the second week in March, which conflicted with many state tournaments. Passaic High of New Jersey, for example, fast garnering a national reputation that would put its "wonder teams" in the Basketball Hall of Fame, wanted to test itself in the national tourney, but the dates for its state tournament conflicted. In 1922 Stagg wisely moved his tournament to the first week in April, which allowed for invitations to state championship teams. The tournament featured thirty-two entries, including eleven state champs. Press coverage grew more extensive, the championship game garnering banner headlines and considerably more ink in the *Chicago Tribune*.[44]

The 1923 tournament achieved Stagg's objective of being truly national in scope. The meet featured forty teams from thirty-one states—nine western, eight southern, four southwestern, six midwestern, and four eastern. Stagg managed to get this level of participation, despite barring for the first time Catholic and private schools. The *Chicago Tribune* celebrated this achievement by publishing a huge map of the United States, showing lines leading from the entry locations to Chicago and captioning the image "All Basketball Paths Lead to Chicago." The game results of the five-day tournament were reported over the new medium of radio, and certain games were filmed by "movie men." Newspapers across the country gave coverage to the tournament, most remarkably even in states and cities that had no entries, such as New York and Los Angeles. Stagg's National Interscholastic in significance had become the equivalent of the NCAA Tournament of a half century later. However, prohibitions by high school athletic associations in certain states meant the tournament could never be all-inclusive. The basketball hotbed of Indiana, for example, after

1922 barred its teams from participating, and Rhode Island and California never sent representatives.[45]

Each year the tournament received more and more coverage in the newspapers, so that by the late 1920s, the five-day event was garnering inch-high banner headlines across the tops of sport pages almost daily. In 1924 Stagg began promoting the tournament as "the World's Greatest Basketball Interscholastic." The 1927 tournament reached an all-time high of participation with forty-three entrants, thirty-three of which were state champions. The following year, a compelling narrative emerged that stoked interest in the tournament nationwide—the success of teams from small, impoverished rural hamlets overcoming great odds to beat powerful schools from the rich suburbs and big cities. Carr Creek, Kentucky, which practiced on a pounded-earth outdoor court, made it to the quarterfinals in 1928 and got national publicity in the *Literary Digest* and *St. Nicholas*. This "little school" narrative was repeated in every subsequent tournament.[46]

For most of its history, the National Interscholastic Basketball Tournament excluded parochial and private schools and never invited any black schools to participate. Thus excluded from the mainstream of interscholastic competition, these schools went on to create parallel tournaments that could showcase their high school athletes in a national forum, namely, the National Catholic Interscholastic Basketball Tournament, National Academy Interscholastic Basketball Tournament, and National Interscholastic Basketball Tournament (which the African American sponsors gave the same name as the Stagg tournament). Besides these national extravaganzas, there were many sectional tournaments mostly sponsored by universities, notably the Eastern States Scholastic (in Glens Falls, New York), University of Pennsylvania Interscholastic, Cotton States Interscholastic (at Alabama Polytechnic Institute, in Auburn, Alabama), New England Interscholastic (at Tufts College, in Medford, Massachusetts), and Rocky Mountain Interscholastic (in Denver, Colorado).[47]

During the 1920s, the nation was awash with not only state basketball championships in nearly every state, but also championship tournaments in every section of the country, plus a passel of national tournaments.

Because tournaments were the largest moneymaking contests in high school sports, received extravagant coverage in the newspapers, and required long-distance travel and time away from school for the schoolboys to participate, these basketball events soon became the focal point of educators' concerns about excess in interscholastic sports, damaging to the educational and character-development mission of the high schools.

Track and Field

National meets in track also grew enormously during the decade, both indoor and outdoor meets. One of the most prestigious of the East Coast indoor meets was conducted by Newark Central High of New Jersey, which inaugurated what it called its "national interscholastic" in 1918, holding it in a local armory. Despite its claim as being national in scope, the Newark meet never drew secondary schools outside the East. Most of the participating teams were New York City and New Jersey public and private schools, plus a few perennial East Coast track powers, notably the Mercersburg and Hill schools from Pennsylvania. The meet drew capacity crowds, in which national records were usually set, and was subject to considerable media attention.[48]

The Newark National Interscholastic was challenged for prestige and national importance in the Midwest by Northwestern University's national interscholastic, inaugurated in 1910. In the first few years of the meet, which was always held the last weekend in March, the competition mainly involved Illinois schools. A swimming meet was added to the program in 1914. When Northwestern resumed its interscholastic after World War I, in 1920, the indoor meet was expanded to include teams from throughout the Midwest. By the 1924 meet, Northwestern was touting its indoor contest as a "national interscholastic." The schools participating in the track meet, however, were all drawn from midwestern states, particularly Detroit schools. The number of entries by this time numbered more than three hundred athletes. By 1929 more than six hundred contestants annually participated in Northwestern's indoor meet and its attendant swim and wrestling meets. Other midwestern indoor meets with a large sectional or national scope during the 1920s and '30s were the University of

Michigan meet held in Ann Arbor (1927–1932) and the National Academy meet held in Madison, Wisconsin (1928–1932).[49]

The greatest level of university sponsorship in interscholastic sports in the 1920s was in outdoor track and field. The East Coast had a plethora of university interscholastic meets, namely, at Harvard (1886), Princeton (1897), Columbia (1907), Yale (1902), and Pennsylvania (1902). Some university meets were essentially sectional championships, notably the Harvard Interscholastic, which was the equivalent of the New England championship. Since its inception, Pennsylvania's interscholastic was specifically designated as the "Middle States Championship."[50]

What most caught the nation's interest during the decade, however, was the national tournament sponsored by the University of Chicago, begun in 1902 by Stagg. The meet was usually scheduled during the first weekend of June. Stagg intended from the beginning to make it national in scope. Because of the exigencies created by World War I, the tournament was suspended after the 1917 meet. The tournament resumed in 1921 with a broader national scope. That year Stagg created a separate division for private academies, so that the meet included nearly 50 public schools and a dozen private schools. Most of the entries were one or two individuals from a school, not whole teams. Only schools with elite programs received team (although truncated) invitations. Stagg regularly invited individual state champions to compete in his meet. The following year, the meet was designated as a "national Interscholastic."[51]

By 1923 Stagg's Meet, as the interscholastic was popularly known, was rightly reported by the local newspapers as attracting the "cream of American high school track and field stardom." The meet drew seven hundred contestants, representing more than 150 high schools and academies, and generated big stories across the country. The *Los Angeles Times* heavily covered the thirty-two athletes from a dozen California cities who participated in the meet. Nearly half the points generated in the public-school meet came from California schools. The breaking of national high school records, usually called "world records" by the tournament, became a regular occurrence. Stagg relocated the meet to the much-larger Soldier Field in 1926 and 1927, but returned to Stagg Field for the 1928 meet. The 1929 meet drew more than nine hundred athletes and represented thirty-three states, and by this time, along with its sister basketball meet, it represented the apex of high school national championship extravaganzas.[52]

Wagenhorst Survey of High School Sports

This profile of high school sports in the 1920s needs to be set in the context of the sports offerings of the vast majority of secondary schools in the country. Lewis Hoch Wagenhorst in his 1924 survey of 366 high schools nationwide found that only four sports were sponsored by more than 10 percent of the schools—namely, basketball (98 percent), football (91 percent), baseball (64 percent), and track and field (44 percent). The country-club sports saw much lower sponsorship percentages, with swimming (9 percent), tennis (7 percent), and golf (1 percent). The results for other school sports were as follows: soccer (4 percent), hockey (3 percent), wrestling (2 percent), skating (1 percent), and rowing (0.5 percent). His survey mentioned only two girls' sports: basketball (6 percent) and volleyball (2 percent). There were no mentions of indoor golf, gymnastics, cross-country, rifle marksmanship, fencing, handball, or lacrosse. Wagenhorst's small sample of 366 schools constituted only about 2 percent of the roughly 20,000 high schools in the country in the early 1920s, so that may possibly explain the invisible or nearly invisible results he received for some sports.[53]

The growth in the number of sports offerings in the high schools and the great expansion of interscholastic sports into a national scope during the 1920s were exhilarating to many fans of sports and helped immensely to build the role of high school sports in the entertainment and sports culture in communities across America. The ensuing commercialism, the inordinate attention paid to high school sports heroes, and the cross-country travel to play games weeks beyond the season were inherently at odds against the positive value that educators saw in high school sports, namely, the development of character. Few educators voiced concerns about the growth in the number of sports, but they could see no good in sending basketball players across the country to engage in national championships, seeing it as undermining the educational purpose of the schools and exposing high school students to high-pressure commercialized environments, inflating their egos, and helping them lose their sense of purpose in playing sports.

Other school-age groups not served or fully served by the public-school establishment—namely, private-school students, Catholics, girls, and African Americans—wanted some of this same high school sports experience. School authorities for these groups valued sports not only as character building but also as bringing them into mainstream American society. These groups in many cases were trying to catch up with the public schools with programs in basketball, football, baseball, and track, but also successfully worked to increase the number of sports offerings and to add competitions on league, state, sectional, and national levels. The same sort of tensions between the character-building aims of the educators and the presumed overemphasis on sports was experienced by these groups as well, whose sports programs especially flourished in the 1920s, as their narratives will reveal.

Often, high school students who engaged in military sports were also made to be seen as outsiders from the mainstream. One of the legacies of World War I was the large growth in the military sports of rifle and fencing, and the rise of marching drills and review, which were often used in place of physical education. The first "outsiders" chapter will thus deal with military sports.

10

CREATION OF MILITARY SPORTS
IN THE SECONDARY SCHOOLS

Military sports in the secondary schools substantially emerged after America's entrance into World War I, when the country awoke to the need for military preparedness. During the war, high schools, as well as universities and colleges, began to train students not only in rifle marksmanship and physical conditioning but also in drill (marching and handling rifles with precision) and review (standing at attention with precision). These exercises were designed to instill discipline and obedience in future soldiers. In most of the secondary schools where military training was introduced during the war, it was sustained into the 1920s, but as a whole in the nation's high schools it remained far from universal. Military training survived in a paradoxical environment where its advocates saw the need for military preparedness in an era of increasing isolationism, disarmament, and pacifism, growing out of a sense of disillusionment with World War I and foreign entanglements.

Under Republican administrations, there was international engagement, but it took the form of trade agreements, naval disarmament treaties in 1922 and 1930 that reduced US military strength, and the Kellogg-Briand Pact of 1928 that committed the country as one of the thirty-one signatories to the renunciation of war as "an instrument of national policy." The latter reflected a national public mood of disillusionment with World War I and war in general. On the home front, the US Army went from a high of 2.8 million during World War I down to 117,000 men by the late 1920s. While the Republicans were strong advocates of disarmament, as well as their allies in business, they were strong advocates of army and navy appropriation bills and military preparedness.[1]

In this context, military training received considerable approval from educators and the public, but also met considerable opposition, especially when it came to the involvement of high school girls. Many educators also looked at school sports, and particularly football, as well as conventional physical education as valuable military preparation for the nation's young men, and in part football's growth during the twenties reflected this rationale. Some educators thought physical education should be the only form of military training in the high schools.[2]

Most of the same high schools that developed drill and review also included in their extracurriculum the military or quasi-military sports of fencing, rifle shooting, and, in some rare institutions, polo. While becoming skilled in such sports probably made American students perfectly prepared for the Polish cavalry of the 1930s, the finest in the world at the time, these martial skills were not of much use for modern warfare. What advocates of such sports stressed, however, was that these activities would help instill a fighting spirit in young men, imbue them with the desire for victory, create a common bond, and help turn them into future officer-worthy leaders.[3]

Military sports had a pedigree in American schools prior to World War I, emerging in the late nineteenth century with the establishment of military academies. These academies provided preparatory-school training, but in a learning environment shaped by a regimen of military-style discipline and organization. These schools very soon became highly popular with upper-class and upper-middle-class families with problem children, who rebelled at conventional private-school education. In such schools, drill and review were frequent, and the sports of fencing and rifle marksmanship were encouraged. In the 1890s, some educators argued for the value of drill and review for public high school students. Such training was taking place in several public-school systems in the United States, notably in the Boston public schools after Reconstruction. Nationwide, some seventy-four hundred high school students were already taking drill as early as 1890. The Boston Physical Education Society—the physical education establishment in that city—took notice of this fact and issued a report in 1896 adamantly opposing such drill as not only useless but physically harmful, objecting to the repetitive handling of heavy muskets by still growing young men. The tone was of an adamant distaste for guns in schools. The well-known leader in physical education Dudley A. Sargent also weighed in with a scathing essay denouncing drill and the claims of its supporters as being of value in physical development. Regarding the recent interest in military drill, Sargent sniffed, "Undoubtedly the wave of patriotism that periodically sweeps over the country is partly responsible for this revival of military spirit." As one of Chicago's high school cadet commanders much later commented, "Before [World War I], universal military training in the public schools were frowned upon as tending towards militarism."[4]

The United States historically was not what might be called a "militaristic" nation, and as a consequence there was little or no military training offered before World War I in the schools. In 1910, for example, only 34 public high schools out of 2,392 schools responding to a Bureau of Education survey reported that they offered military drill. The secondary schools at the time simply were not thought of as institutions designed to prepare young people for the military, and as a consequence few public schools included in their extracurriculum the military sports of fencing and rifle marksmanship. A notable exception in the public-school arena was the Public Schools Athletic League that served New York City. Since its inception in 1903, the PSAL had as one of its aims the preparation of its male students in rifle marksmanship and boasted the largest high school program in the nation. The chief architect of the rifle marksmanship program was the PSAL head, General George W. Wingate, who argued that America needed to be militarily prepared, and said that the "only way this country will ever become prepared for war is to have the people in mass trained in the use of the rifle."[5]

WORLD WAR I SPURS MILITARY TRAINING

With the outbreak of the war in Europe in 1914, the drumbeat gradually increased in the United States for greater military preparedness as the country became increasingly drawn into the conflict. Various influential

Americans came together to work for greater American military strength and a vastly expanded army. A leading voice in this movement was army chief of staff Leonard Wood, who advocated universal military training and founded a military training camp, Plattsburgh Barracks, in upstate New York, in 1913, for the training of civilians, university students, and high school students. Initially, Wood involved many eastern prep schools in adopting military training and soon brought in public schools. As of 1915, one survey showed that just 113 schools, reaching an estimated total of 14,500 boys, offered military drill. In 1916 Congress passed the National Defense Act, which under Section 40 called for the establishment of ROTC in both institutions of higher learning and secondary schools.[6]

Even before the passage of the law, many secondary-school systems under the influence of the Preparedness Movement had begun instituting drill and review and thinking in quite martial terms, and some argued for universal military training in the schools. Dudley A. Sargent was having none of it and published in 1915 an article as scathing as his 1896 article, condemning the physical harm that drill did to young men, pointing out that in the militaristic countries of Europe, there was no schoolboy drill and that gymnastics was the foundation for physical training for the military. His sentiments were shared by many leading figures in the physical education establishment, notably Edward B. DeGroot, director of physical education in the San Francisco schools, whose essay condemning universal military training was published in April 1917, the same month that the United States entered the war against Germany. He exclaimed, "Woe betide school men, our common school system and much of democracy if the military mind, rather than the pedagogical and social mind, is given the leadership in the solution of educational problems and the training of our schoolboys of tender age."[7]

Critics of the rush toward military training would not see their views prevail, as across the nation high schools swept up in patriotic fervor began adopting various forms of military training, usually involving drill and marching. A system of military training, called the "Wyoming Plan," became increasingly popular in high schools across the nation. An inspector-instructor from Wyoming, Lieutenant Edgar Z. Steever, designed the program in 1911 based on the formation of a division of student cadets, who would be divided into units that would remain constant throughout the school year. In a year-round program, these units would engage in competition—beginning with wall scaling and calisthenics in the fall, followed by drill, troop leadership, and field firing in the winter and early spring, finishing the school year with interschool contests in May. In the summer, the boys would attend fourteen days of summer camp. The idea of this year-round program was to give the students a sense of military life.[8]

Steever promoted his plan as an alternative to the standard military-drill programs in the schools, arguing that his plan was modeled on competitive sports. He said, "It is high school against high school; we get all the dash and all the efficiency of the football team in our national-defense games." The Wyoming Plan thus found acceptance from some educators who had opposed military drill in the schools, it being only one component of a full-year program of activities. National publications, namely, *Everybody's* and *Outlook*, even lauded the plan under the idea that it avoided militarism. The Wyoming Plan spread beyond its state of origin, after it was promoted in *Everybody's* in late 1916, and subsequently received approval from the federal government, namely, the US Army War College, a number of congressmen, and Secretary of War Newton Baker. The upshot was that schools that put together cadet brigades of one hundred or more students were supplied with an instructor and equipment by the federal government.[9]

The Chicago school system brought in Steever for the 1916–1917 school year to initiate a Wyoming Plan–type military-training program in its high schools. Chicago school authorities had been developing a plan for an optional course in military training as early as August 1916. The spring 1917 program was modest, in which participation was voluntary and the number admitted to the cadet corps was limited to three thousand. Within a year, the military training was made compulsory. The idea of turning public high schools into a feeder system for the armed forces might seem to some as perhaps un-American—reminiscent of Kaiser Germany or some other European state where militarism was more politically and socially accepted—but the Chicago school authorities argued that military training was advancing the American way. Said the superintendent's report, "One of the main ideas underlying the introduction of military training in the high schools was to make them a real democracy by putting every boy in the same sort of clothes and requiring of each exactly the same duties."[10]

Military training in the Chicago schools in its first year for the general student body involved a program of two-armed semaphore signaling, making dummy Mills bombs and dummy grenades, and war games; for the cadets, the program entailed wall scaling, drill, and review. For the general student body, competition was held in signaling, but the grenade throwing was canceled because of inclement weather. Competition was held for the cadets in one giant extravaganza at Grant Park on Chicago's lakefront. Each high school was represented by one company. In the late spring, the first rifles arrived from the Rock Island Arsenal, numbering only 750. Some instruction was given in nomenclature, care, and handling of the rifles, but no target shooting was done.[11]

The Armistice in November 1918 did not end military training. The Chicago public schools put military training on a permanent basis with the formation of Junior ROTC in the schools in early 1919. The system had twenty-one high schools that served male students at the time, and every one of them formed ROTC units. A two-year elective course, ROTC required three hours a week of training time. The War Department each year assigned to the school system a certain number of officers and noncommissioned officers to conduct the training. In April 1919, twelve thousand ROTC enrollees—six thousand on the North Side and six thousand on the South Side—were inspected for review by a representative of the War Department. That summer the first military camp (Camp Roosevelt) was held near Muskegon, Michigan, for some thirteen hundred students. This camp continued throughout the 1920s. Within a couple of years, most of the schools also sponsored bands organized on a military model, with the students wearing army brown uniforms and subject to military-style direction. The school orchestras were considered the "civilian" ensembles, whereas bands were considered "military" ensembles. Besides the usual drill and review competitions of the ROTC units, the school bands likewise competed for league championships. Rifle marksmanship was now included in the training at ranges in the schools and at the armories, although formal competition had yet to be introduced into the schools.[12]

The sports of rifle marksmanship and fencing in the Chicago high schools arose directly out of the American experience in World War I. Although rifle marksmanship was engaged by some schools prior to the war, it never attracted more than a handful of schools, and the Chicago Public High School League had not sponsored competition in the sport. Fencing was virtually unknown, although a few schools had experimented with it.

RIFLE MARKSMANSHIP

Rifle marksmanship gradually became a part of the Chicago schools' interscholastic program during the 1920s through ROTC programs. An ROTC program at a school involved organizing the boys into a company or several companies, depending upon the number of boys participating. A school that had several companies would often form a battalion. Military training included close-order drill, instilling the knowledge and technique of handling firearms, first-aid training, signaling, and rifle marksmanship. Schools in short order formed rifle-shooting teams, but their competitions were not initially league sponsored, but rather outside-sponsored midwestern competitions, notably the Sixth Corps Area tournaments.[13]

In 1925 the Chicago Public High School League finally inaugurated a city championship in rifle marksmanship. The competition involved a regular season of dual-meet matches that winnowed out four teams that competed in the league championship tournament, usually held in the late fall. The high school competitors used 22-caliber rifles, and shooting was done at targets fifty feet away from four positions—prone, standing, kneeling, and sitting. This tournament involved direct competition at shooting galleries, usually in the basements of the schools. The annual city tournament was held at an outside range, notably the Hamilton Club Rifle Range. The schools also engaged in outside competition, many conducted in the spring term. Boys' and girls' teams sometimes competed in the same meet, as when the Chicago schools entered competitions for both boys' and girls' titles at the National Outdoor Life Exposition held at the Coliseum. Other important competitions were the National Rifle Association national championship, Winchester National

High School Championship, and Hearst Trophy. Outside contests were conducted two ways: by actually meeting the school at a shooting gallery and tallying the scores (the National Outdoor Life) and by shooting at a designated range with a designated observer and telegraphing the score to the meet officials (Hearst, NRA, and Winchester). Telegraphic meets were also held between schools, competing on their home ranges. In 1923, for example, Evanston High competed against Lawrenceville Prep in a telegraphic meet.[14]

The preeminent Chicago public school in rifle marksmanship was Lake View, which by the standards of other public schools in the city was heavily "militarized," if that is the right word. The school had the city's largest ROTC chapter, with four large companies, and its ROTC chapter won all the city's drill competitions in the 1920s. Of the 6,000 students enrolled in ROTC in approximately twenty Chicago high schools, 425 of them were from Lake View. The school's military band, one of twenty in the Public League, won more than its share of league titles, and the school's boys' rifle team won the city league championships annually. Although the league did not provide a title competition for girls' rifle, the Lake View girls' squad dominated outside competition. An interesting twist to the Lake View rifle teams was that their shooting coach was a woman, Mary Monahan, described in the yearbook as "the only woman rifle coach in the country [for boys]."[15]

In the Chicago suburbs, the schools with the most advanced marksmanship programs were located mostly on the North Shore, mainly Evanston, Waukegan, and Deerfield-Shields (in Highland Park). In the early 1920s, Evanston emerged as a rifle power and won at least two "national championships" conducted by the Winchester Junior Rifle Corps. John Damer of Evanston High won the Great Western individual high school championship in 1922. Later in the decade, Deerfield-Shields and Waukegan emerged with nationally recognized programs.[16]

Chicago was a baby in rifle marksmanship in comparison to New York City's PSAL, which had the most dynamic program in the nation. Whereas before World War I, many of the shooting competitions engaged by the schoolboys in New York were sponsored by national outdoor shows and private entities, by the end of the war the PSAL had taken over sole

16. Englewood High boys' rifle team from 1924, in an era when Chicago high schools as a result of the Preparedness Movement during World War I engaged in military sports and training. Courtesy of the Chicago Public Library, Special Collections and Preservation Division, EHS 2/2.

sponsorship of the rifle competition and conducted meets year-round. During October and November, the league held a series of meets leading up to the fall championship in December, called the Standard Bearer Trophy, "emblematic of the city championship," while the winter and spring months were reserved for various cup competitions, notably the Peters, Du Pont, and Winchester. In the spring, an individual competition was held for the Remington Trophy.[17]

There were also a variety of national competitions that engaged high school rifle teams across the nation, most notably the one held by the NRA. After a lapse in the competition during World War I, the NRA competition was resumed in 1920. The organization did away with various class competition and focused on just two categories of competition: high school and military academy.[18]

Another national competition was the William Randolph Hearst annual trophy competition, usually held in May of each year. The trophy was given not to high school rifle teams per se, but to ROTC rifle teams. By 1927 there were 111 schools participating in the annual contest. Army officers served as official referees at the ranges where the competitions were held. All the teams nationwide were annually ranked. For example, Chicago's Fenger High bragged that its team went from fifty-seventh place in the country in 1924 to eleventh place in the country in 1925 and then to fourth in the country and first in Chicago in 1926. The Winchester Junior Rifle Corps competition, sponsored by the Winchester Rifle Corporation, was another notable national rifle tournament of the 1920s and was usually held in March and April of each year. High school competition included a national boys' competition and a national girls' competition, the latter usually won by Crosby High of Waterbury, Connecticut. Other divisions of the competition were for YMCAs, Boy Scout troops, and miscellaneous groups, such as church teams and messenger-boy teams, grouped in an open division.[19]

FENCING

Although fencing had been a part of many eastern secondary-school programs from before World War I, the sport did not begin to gain supporters in the Chicago schools until the early 1920s. Fencing was not considered a sport essential for military preparedness in twentieth-century America, but for decades it was found in the nation's military academies, partly because of the legacy of the sport as part of a proper officer's training and partly because it was considered valuable for instilling a martial spirit. At that time, there were a number of tournaments sponsored by Amateur Fencers' League of America (AFLA) clubs, Turner halls, and the University of Chicago that offered competition to high school–age students, both boys and girls. As the sport grew, a few teachers in the schools finally got together and persuaded the Chicago Public High School League to sponsor its first fencing tournament in late-May 1924, attracting seven schools. Chicago high schools during the decade produced many of the captains and top fencers for the intercollegiate Big Ten fencing teams. In the late 1920s, one Chicago school, Senn, saw its graduates win four out of five Big Ten individual championships. The school conducted a daily credit-earning class in the sport.[20]

Within a couple of years, the Chicago Public League conducted two meets and a team championship, followed a week later by individual championship competition, which was held in conjunction with the gymnastics meet. Competition was usually held in one of the high schools. The sport tended to attract first- and second-generation immigrant boys from such countries as Italy and Hungary, many of them of Jewish background. These groups were historically attracted to the sport in Europe and retained their allegiance for fencing in America. Most Chicago schools that had notable success in fencing had sizable Jewish American populations, such as Roosevelt, Senn, and Hyde Park. By the late 1920s and early 1930s, about ten schools participated in the annual city meets. Chicago high schools also competed in a Cook County meet sponsored by the Foil Club of Chicago; it also drew a few suburban schools, notably Morton High of Cicero. Some Chicago high schools competed with prep schools in the Midwest, such as St. John's Military Academy, in Delevan, Wisconsin. The sport continued to thrive through World War II, after which it went into decline.[21]

In 1926 the Amateur Fencers' League of America inaugurated the first state tournament for Illinois high school fencers; each team comprised three men. Most of the competitors came from Chicago schools. Competition was held in foils only. In most years, the state championship meet was held in April and conducted in Bartlett Gymnasium at the University of Chicago. The winning team was awarded the Kraft Cup, symbolic of the state championship.[22]

While state chapters of the AFLA worked to develop fencing in the high schools at the local level, having notable success in Illinois, the national headquarters in New York City during World War I inaugurated a national championship in foils. The National Scholastic Foils Competition was held each year in New York City at the Fencers Club, the oldest fencing organization in the United States, having been founded in 1882. During the 1920s, the Fencers Club was located at 155 East Fifty-Fourth

17. Lindblom High boys' fencing team from 1926, when fencing was a popular military sport in Chicago high schools. Only New York high schools developed a comparable fencing program. Courtesy of the Chicago Public Library, Special Collections and Preservation Division, ECC 3/10.

Street, and in the 1930s it was located at 320 East Fifty-Third Street. The AFLA in the early years had a difficult time building interest in high school fencing. Invitations for the meet were sent out in 1916, but only one entrant responded and the meet was called off. The first meet, conducted in 1917, was exceedingly modest, as only four entrants showed up (all from the New York Military Academy). The next two years saw participation again only from the New York MA, but the organizers conducted a meet nonetheless. In 1920 the meet featured two schools, New York MA and Paterson High, and eight competitors. The following year, with the participation up to ten competitors and four schools, the AFLA designated the meet a national competition. No New York public schools were involved, but besides New York MA and Paterson High, the meet included St. Francis Xavier and the Braden School.[23]

Throughout its history, the AFLA meet featured mostly competitors from the New York metropolitan area. In 1926 the city's Private Schools Athletic Association introduced fencing to its program, and increasingly thereafter schools from that league, notably McBurney Prep and Polytechnic Prep, participated in the national tournament. The first New York public school, Townsend Harris, participated in 1926. By the end of the decade, a Metropolitan interscholastic championship was conducted, attracting twenty-seven fencers from eleven public and private high schools, six of which were New York public schools.[24] In 1931 the PSAL added fencing to its schedule, thereby boosting interest in the sport, and by the early 1930s the AFLA meet (no longer claiming itself a national competition) had become much larger—more than thirty competitors representing fourteen schools from the New York metropolitan area and two schools from New England. By the late 1930s, as the PSAL developed a strong fencing program, the New York public schools dominated the AFLA competition. In 1939 the AFLA asked the PSAL to take over sponsorship of the meet.[25]

POLO

Polo was a sport popular with cavalry officers, but owning horses is an expensive proposition, and thus the sport made only minimal inroads into interscholastic competition. No more than a handful of schools, all private academies and predominantly military academies, ever competed any one year in the sport during its prime in the 1930s. The principal championship was the national interscholastic, begun in 1929 and held in various New York City armories. The United States Indoor Polo Association sponsored the event, which it conducted in late March and early April along with its other sponsored events, the intercollegiate and open competitions. All the schools were private academies, and there were only about two to four schools competing each year. The first year of competition saw "Berkshire–New England" win, which was a team consisting of two players from St. Paul's and one from Berkshire. Thereafter, all the competing teams represented just one school. The schools competed for the George C. Sherman Cup, named for the avid indoor polo promoter and the president of the United States Indoor Polo Association. His son was a member of the winning Berkshire–New England team of 1929.[26]

Throughout most of the history of the tournament, the competition was dominated by Lawrenceville, which introduced its first team in 1930. Lawrenceville often competed against Culver Military Academy for the championship. The United States Indoor Polo Association suspended its various competitions after Pearl Harbor in December 1941 and did not resume them until 1946. The interscholastic competition, however, was not resumed, but the organization established a junior competition in 1947, essentially replacing the preparatory-school contests.[27]

Chicago Disarms the Military Girl

In Chicago military sports and military drill and review were well established in the city's secondary schools by the 1920s, but school authorities found an unanticipated opposition to its schoolgirls being engaged in such activities. Girls wielding weapons during the early 1920s did not face opposition, but another facet of military training, drill and review, proved to be the precipitating factor that generated opposition to girls bearing arms. The girls' version of a ROTC drill team was called Girls Military Training Corps, or GMTC, and like a ROTC unit was trained by a US Army officer. Austin High pioneered drill and review for girls in 1920 and for several years was the only school in the country with a GMTC unit. By 1926 there were at least five highs schools in the city league that featured drill units for girls, notably Calumet High, which had one of the city's most vigorous GMTC programs. In June 1926, the GMTC units of both Austin High and Calumet High participated in exhibitions at a huge mass drill tournament of all Chicago ROTC units.[28]

The adoption of the military extracurriculum for girls in most of the schools was initiated by the female students, animated by the liberating trends of the 1920s. Said Major Frank L. Beals, the supervisor of military training in the Chicago schools, "Groups of girls in the various schools petitioned their principals to permit them to take military training, or merely to form rifle clubs. The principals in turn called in the military-training instructors and asked them to help out in this."[29]

By 1926 military sports and drill and review for girls had become far too visible to the public. In January of that year, school authorities found themselves facing an uproar over girls' participation in these activities. Lake View High, being the most aggressive school in the league for military training, sponsored not only a girls' rifle team and a girls' fencing team, but also a girls' drill team, a photo of which was displayed in the *Chicago Tribune* in January 1926. The publication of this photo added fuel to the flames.[30]

At a January 1926 school board finance committee meeting, a member of the board of education and aspiring candidate for mayor, Johanna Gregg, opened up the meeting with what she considered shocking information, that girls in the city high schools were taking military training. Not only were young girls handling rifles, but they were also shooting them. She had found five high schools engaged in drill and review, from eighty girls at Austin High to nineteen girls at Fenger High, and found seven high schools sponsoring rifle teams. She proposed an official investigation. Gregg, aware that she was addressing a finance committee, also objected to the expense involved for activities—notably paying the salaries of nine military instructors—that were "not proper and legitimate features of . . . girls' education."[31]

Another board member, James Mullenbach, spoke out in agreement, saying, "I saw, in Germany, military training at its best and worst, But even the Germans never resorted to training their women. . . . Some of the instructions—how to get the other fellow in war—hardly can be read before a mixed group of students. Are we encouraging this sort of militarism and brutality in the schools?"[32] The *Chicago Tribune*'s highly conservative editorial board attributed the opposition to overall pacifist sentiments of opponents who did not even approve of military training of boys. The paper saw no reason at all that "women and girls shouldn't enjoy the thrill of marching in a well drilled group or of plugging away at a tantalizing black bullseye. . . . Why spoil their fun?" The paper in its "Inquiring Reporter" column, which asked persons on the streets questions on controversial issues in the news, asked, "Would you approve of military training for girls?" The responses from five presumably randomly selected individuals, male and female, were positive. One of the respondents, a housewife, commented, "I wish I could have had that training when I was in school." A school official also made light of the criticism, saying, "The girls have simply chosen this form of exercise in lieu of basketball or hockey. It is optional with them and their parents whether they take it."[33]

The Lake View High student newspaper in March 1926 vociferously defended the rifle team: "Rifle practice, as taught at Lake View, is a sport, pure and simple. Some of the critics cannot seem to grasp the idea of anyone taking up a sport just for the love of the sport. . . . [T]hey do not understand how a girl can aim and hit a target for pleasure." The Lake View paper went on to explain how safely the sport was conducted and how it benefited the girls in developing coordination and control of muscles and eyes.[34]

Yet the critics won the cultural war. There was a huge retrenchment of all girls' sports activities in Chicago schools in 1926, including the abolition of league-sponsored golf, tennis, and swimming competition and a clampdown on basketball and track and field competition. Military sports for girls likewise were eliminated. Chicago school authorities were responding to the ideology of the physical educators of the day that disapproved of interschool competition for girls. A budget crunch in the school system contributed as well to the termination of girls' sports and military training. Thus, after the annual mass drill tournament of ROTC units in 1926, participation of girl units was terminated.[35]

The highly visible Lake View program saw its girls' drill and rifle teams terminated after 1926, but that defeat did not stop the school's star shooter, Mary Ward, who achieved national fame as "Sure Shot Mary" for her perfect scores in both high school and national contests. Ward helped coach and competed on the boys' team, helping them take the 1927 league title in February by scoring five hundred out of five hundred bull's-eyes. For this achievement, she was written up in *Ripley's Believe It or Not*. Fencing remained an acceptable sport for girls. The schools of Lake View and Lindblom sponsored girls' fencing teams into the 1930s, but they were prevented from competing interscholastically.[36]

18. Lake View High girls' rifle team from 1926 at the height of the controversy over girls engaged in military sports and training in Chicago schools. Lake View, along with other Chicago schools, disbanded their girls' rifle and drill teams. Courtesy of the Chicago Public Library, Sulzer Regional Library, Lake View High School Collection 5/4.

The dispute over the girls' participation in military training was in part a proxy battle by many opponents in the school system toward all military training in the schools. The *Chicago Tribune* quoted a spokesperson for the teachers, who said that most of them "deplore, oppose, and would prevent military training in the schools." These opponents scored an easy victory on the girls, but the boys' program was too popular and too well entrenched for its opponents to terminate.[37]

By the mid-1920s, military training nationwide was offered in sixty-three high schools and thirty-nine military academies. Of this number, the Chicago Public Schools Athletic League sponsored ROTC units in about twenty high schools, rifle marksmanship in nearly the same number, and fencing in about ten schools. In the summer, there were nationwide twenty-three military training camps for high school students, and the Chicago schools participated in one, Camp Roosevelt, in Michigan. New York City, with many more high schools, had a similarly thriving program, and students in Washington, DC, also excelled at rifle marksmanship. Unlike in Chicago, Washington, DC, had the largest girls' rifle-marksmanship program in the nation (where one school, Central High, had 250 girls come out for the sport in one year) that not only was not suppressed but prospered into the 1930s.[38]

That military training in the schools found acceptance in the nation's school system—at least for boys—was a triumph over many American traditions that viewed the country as a democracy and not at all militaristic and at odds with many countries in the rest of the world, with their dictatorships, their monarchies, and their strutting, goose-stepping soldiers. That these countries' armies brought them into the great destructive conflagration of World War I only heightened these differences. Many Americans thus viewed with alarm the idea of military training as too close to the militarism of the Old World. Yet the World War I experience and the fears the war engendered produced a dramatic acceptance of military preparedness in the nation's high schools. In most places, military sports thus took root only after World War I. With the triumph of the Preparedness Movement in the high schools, the bulk of the American population came to see not only the value and necessity in military training but also that it had become normalized and thoroughly American in spirit. Military sports were imbued with the broader appreciation of sports as character building and a builder of democratic values, and often as an element of control. The view of military training and military sports as serving an essential educational value thus became a verity held by many educators for several decades, at least until the Vietnam War era, when ROTC and rifle marksmanship in the secondary schools were severely challenged.

11

The Private and Catholic Schools' Parallel World of Interscholastic Sports

In the 1920s, as the public schools built and expanded their interscholastic sports programs, they established the models by which the private secular and religious schools built their sports programs. Private secular schools were popularly called prep schools, as they were virtually all college-preparatory institutions. They predominated largely in the East, many of them boarding schools that took in students nationwide. By far the largest religious private-school program was run by the Roman Catholic Church, and its schools were often called parochial schools, because most of them were founded in parishes. A number of Episcopalian, Quaker, Lutheran, Jewish, Christian Reform, and Ethical Culture schools also began to prosper in the 1920s and built sports programs, but their number was usually one or two per major city, and the schools tended to find homes in preparatory-school leagues. The private schools during the decade sought to build the same sort of sports experience for their students as the public schools in their creation of leagues and invitational meets and tournaments, many of them national in scope. As with their public-school counterparts, private- and parochial-school educators viewed sports as beneficial to their students' moral development, but with a special emphasis on what they brought from their religious or cultural sphere.

PREPARATORY SCHOOLS

Eastern Preparatory Schools

Although not sizable, preparatory schools compared to their public-school counterparts tended to prosper in interscholastic sports with a large amount of athletic talent. They were schools without boundaries and could roam far afield in recruiting top athletes. The most elite of the prep schools were in the East—notably Phillips Andover, Phillips Exeter, Lawrenceville, Hill, and Mercersburg—and they had their choice of athletes from across the nation. This fact was demonstrated in their success in the biggest interscholastic meets of the 1920s. For example, in track and field, Mercersburg dominated the University of Pennsylvania's Middle States Interscholastic and Andover the Harvard Interscholastic. The leading swimming meets at Columbia, Yale, and Rutgers frequently showed Mercersburg and Lawrenceville as champions.

Certain sports were especially dominated by prep schools, notably the country-club sports—golf and tennis—which young persons born of privilege learned at their parents' country clubs, and the prep schools' traditional sport of rowing, in which the cost and maintenance of shells were beyond most public-school and Catholic-school programs. Private schools in particular coalesced into their own competitions in golf and rowing, which were highly prominent during the 1920s, paralleling the similar aggrandizement of interscholastic sports by the public and Catholic schools.

Rowing was one of the most flourishing prep-school sports during the 1920s, primarily among the private secondary schools of the middle states and New England. The premier secondary-school rowing race in the country was the interscholastic eight-oar competition held at the American Henley Regatta in Philadelphia beginning in 1904, which in its early years saw many of its winners come from Philadelphia public schools. When the American Henley resumed an interscholastic eight-oar competition after the war in 1921, its champions reflected the shift in strength from public to private schools. The Philadelphia Interscholastic League dropped crew in 1919, and thereafter preparatory and Catholic schools took the rowing championships. A separate regatta was established in 1927 for local Philadelphia schools, the Stotesbury Cup Race.[1]

The American Henley Regatta ended its interscholastic event after the 1932 competition, leaving a void for a national title, which was soon filled. In 1934 Edward T. Stotesbury announced that his Stotesbury regatta would expand its local Philadelphia field and go national. That plan did not take form until the 1935 regatta, when not only a national eight-oar was contested, but so were four-oar and single sculls. The Stotesbury Cup Race was always conducted on the Schuylkill River, which tended to keep the field narrowed largely to the Eastern Seaboard. The same year saw the formation of the Schoolboy Rowing Association of America (SRAA). The first national regatta sponsored by the SRAA was held at Worcester, Massachusetts, in 1935. The SRAA would rotate the site for the national interscholastic annually and tended to draw a more geographically dispersed field than did the Stotesbury.[2]

American schoolboy crews by the late 1920s were also competing internationally, at the venerable Henley Regatta, in London, England. The Kent School of Connecticut was the first American secondary school to row in the Henley in 1927, when it competed for the Thames Challenge Cup, an event for crews that are "less senior in their makeup." The Kent School returned to the Henley in 1930 and 1934. Browne and Nichols School of Cambridge, Massachusetts, was the next American prep school to participate, winning the Thames Cup in 1929, followed by the Tabor School of Marion, Massachusetts, in 1931 and 1934.[3]

Golf through much of its early history was largely a special preserve of the prep schools. In early 1910, several schoolboys from a variety of private preparatory schools in the Philadelphia–New Jersey–New York section of the country came together and formed the Eastern Interscholastic Golf Association. The model for the organization was the Greater Boston Interscholastic Golf Association and the student organization that sponsored the New York Interscholastic. The Eastern Interscholastic was open to teams from the New England states (although few participated), the middle states, and Maryland and Virginia. The organization sponsored both an individual championship and a team championship, plus it gave awards for medalist, the driving-contest winner, and the putting and approaching contest.[4]

The Eastern Interscholastic was a step backward in the democratization of schoolboy golf, as most of the participants represented elite private academies. The organization limited participation to schools "having a four-year preparatory course for college." Three schools that regularly participated in the tournament—Pawling (NY), Lawrenceville (NJ), and Hotchkiss (CT)—had built their own golf courses. A telling example of these schools' elitist values was what happened to Edward Cleary of Roman Catholic High, in Philadelphia, following the 1911 tournament. He was stripped of his medalist award "on the ground that he was a caddie," deemed a violation of the golfer's amateur standing. In contrast, a good percentage of the participants in the Boston tourney probably at one time or another worked as caddies, notably Francis Ouimet (who famously won the US Open in 1913).[5]

The Eastern Interscholastic golf tournament seemed to falter after its first few years, and by 1916 it attracted only eight entries from two schools, Pawling and Lawrenceville. The following year, however, found an upsurge of twenty-two entries with schools participating from as far apart as Sweetser Academy in Massachusetts and the Tome School in Maryland. Growth continued apace, and by 1922 the tournament attracted more than forty entries. Within a few years, the number would more than double. The Eastern Interscholastic golf championship continued to thrive through the Depression years and decades after.[6]

There were never enough private schools in most states for them to come together and hold a meaningful state championship, and no statewide private-school associations emerged during the 1920s. State private-school championships were generally of the titular kind, whereby a school might claim to be state champion by virtue of its victory over another highly regarded school. Some exceptions were in New Jersey and Virginia, where the state associations sponsored private-school competition.[7]

In most areas of the country, the organization of prep schools into leagues lagged considerably behind their establishment in the public schools during the 1920s. In two cities in the East, however, New York and

Philadelphia, there were separate leagues for prep schools. In New York, they joined together as the Private Schools Athletic Association (PSAA) in 1916, holding championships in most sports except for football. The Philadelphia prep schools were organized into a conference early, in 1887, when they came together in the Interacademic Athletic Association (IAA). By the 1920s, the IAA had the strongest program of any preparatory-school league in the country.[8]

Midwest Preparatory Schools

In contrast to their eastern counterparts, the preparatory schools in the Midwest did not organize themselves into leagues and larger associations until the end of the 1920s. In Illinois, for example, the principal prep schools were Morgan Park Academy, Lake Forest Academy, Wheaton Academy, Elgin Academy, St. Albans, and Onarga Military Academy, and although they regularly competed among themselves, they had no league organization for much of the decade. Many of their contests were against out-of-state opponents—usually Wisconsin (which included St. John's Military Academy of Delevan and Wayland Academy of Beaver Dam) and Indiana (which included Howe Academy and Culver Military Academy). Besides a lack of league competition, there were never any formal contests for state or sectional titles, and any "championships" that were reported were of a titular or mythical variety. Newspapers often referred to such matchups between, say, Lake Forest Academy and St. John's as being for the midwestern championship.[9]

In the mid-1920s, the University of Wisconsin began sponsoring "national" competitions in track and field, basketball, and swimming that provided opportunities for more formal crowning of championships for midwestern prep schools. Like most of the state universities, Wisconsin had long sponsored a state high school track and field meet for Wisconsin's public schools. However, this sponsorship ended in 1924, when the state's high school association took over the state meet. Wisconsin converted its state meet to a midwestern meet, but began to look for other secondary-school competitions to sponsor. The university, one can surmise, looked around at the great variety of national championship meets being sponsored by other universities and could not help but notice the tremendous success of the National Interscholastic Basketball Tournament and the National Catholic Basketball Interscholastic, both in nearby Chicago—which brought reflected glory on their sponsoring institutions, the University of Chicago and Loyola University, respectively. Plus, Northwestern had its national indoor track and swimming championships.[10]

Wisconsin obviously asked itself what secondary-school constituency was underserved by national championships and concluded that it was preparatory schools. The eastern preparatory schools had their sectional tournaments, but none was legitimately national in scope. Wisconsin thus plunged into the national sweepstakes in 1926, providing a basketball and indoor track meet for the private academies and boarding schools, holding the meet the third weekend in March. In 1928 the university also added a national swimming meet to the program.[11]

The first year's National Academy Basketball Tournament attracted eight prep schools from Wisconsin, Minnesota, Illinois, and Indiana. The 1927 tournament was again a modest eight-team event with only midwestern representation, but newspaper reports described the tournament as a national meet. The 1928 tournament became what its organizers had hoped it would become, growing to sixteen teams and adding a bit of true national flavor with the addition of the Tabor Academy from Massachusetts, Castle Heights from Tennessee, and Manlius Academy from New York. By 1930 the meet attracted only eleven schools, only two outside the Midwest.[12]

Wisconsin had less success with its National Academy Indoor Track and Field Meet. The first year's event in 1926 was a small affair, attracting only four academies from the Midwest, but the following year the meet was able to attract nine schools, all from the Midwest. In 1928 Wisconsin added a national swimming meet, which augmented the prestige of the meet, and the number of schools participating in the track meet increased to twelve. The swimming meets were likewise midwestern affairs, attracting only four or five schools each year. In 1930 the track meet attracted only eight schools. Unlike the basketball meet, the indoor track and swimming meets were far less successful in expanding the participation beyond the Midwest, drawing only one non-Midwest representative in the entire history of the meets.[13]

Midwestern private schools began forming leagues in the late 1920s. Four Illinois schools and one Wisconsin school—Morgan Park Military Academy, Onarga Military Academy, St. Albans Academy, Elgin Academy, and Wayland Academy—came together to form the Midwest Preparatory Athletic Conference in 1927. Then in 1930, five private religious and secular schools in the Chicago metropolitan area—Chicago Christian (Dutch Reform), Luther Institute (Lutheran), Wheaton Academy (Evangelical), YMCA Central, and the Pullman Free School of Manual Training—came together to form the Chicago Private School League. These moves were propelled by the sense among private-school administrators that they were missing out on some of the benefits of league competition, notably the tangible award of a league championship. This point was made clear by the *Chicago Daily News* report on the formation of the Chicago Private School League: "It was the logical thing to do, to give these private school athletes a chance to compete for championships the same as the city and Catholic league players. For many years they have gone through their seasons, in many cases undefeated, with no reward whatsoever. And they had really good players." Thus, by the end of the 1920s, the secular and religious private schools of Illinois had conferences that were equivalent in organization to the Chicago Catholic League and the numerous public-school leagues.[14]

THE CATHOLIC SCHOOLS

For much of their history in America, Catholics were set apart or set themselves apart as a group and were not fully assimilated into American culture. They created a vast array of parallel institutions—hospitals, schools, businessmen's clubs, athletic organizations, academic societies, and fraternal groups—that mirrored institutions of the Protestant majority in American society. This network of Catholic institutions has been likened to a "ministate" within the larger culture and fully blossomed through the 1950s, shaping attitudes between the Catholic minority and mainstream America. During the period of the creation of interscholastic sports from the late nineteenth century up to the 1930s, these attitudes included anti-Catholic prejudices and distrust from the majority population and the sense of grievance and estrangement, buffered by cultural pride from the Catholic minority. Between the two groups, a metaphorical "religious war" was waged, and it found its expression in part on the athletic field.[15]

The public-school system, of all the mainstream cultural institutions, as it emerged in the nineteenth century, was unacceptable to Catholics for the education of their children for many reasons, but most notably because it was officially secular and paradoxically also unofficially influenced by the ethos of the Protestant majority population. Many public schools, for example, had Bible readings taken from a Protestant translation, the *King James Bible*. Catholics wanted their children educated in schools that could inculcate them with a Catholic-imbued education.[16]

In another paradox, the Catholic minority created a secondary educational school system in the early part of the nineteenth century that was heavily influenced by developments in the Protestant-dominated mainstream society. The emergence of Catholic high schools paralleled in many ways American schools as a whole. Early secondary schools were initially all academies—separate for boys and girls—designed to accommodate the more elite population. Most of the early Catholic universities and colleges in their provision of secondary-school departments followed this elite academy model. However, as public high schools grew, the Catholic population built more and more independent high schools on the public-school model.

At the time of the first Provincial Council meeting in Baltimore in 1829, the Catholic population was only 4 percent of the national total, numbering five hundred thousand out of a population of twelve million. But following massive emigration into the country by Irish and German Catholics during the next several decades, by 1884, when the Third Plenary Council was held, the percentage of Catholic population had risen to 16 percent, numbering more than eight million out of a total of fifty million. The decisions of this council formed the basis for the Catholic educational system in the United States. The First and Second Plenary Councils, held in 1852 and 1866, respectively, had merely urged and encouraged the erection of parochial schools, but the Third Plenary

Council specifically decreed that every parish should establish an elementary school within two years and bound all Catholic parents to send their children to such schools. Rapid development in the number of elementary schools thus followed, which in turn fueled the growth in the number of Catholic secondary schools.[17]

In terms of growth, the number of new Catholic secondary schools in the late nineteenth and early twentieth centuries paralleled on a smaller scale the growth in public secondary schools. However, all across the United States, the adoption of interscholastic sports in the Catholic secondary schools trailed the public schools by up to several decades. One reason for this lag was that many Catholic high schools were supported by just one parish each, and consequently were too small and too poor to offer a full extracurriculum. Most of the Catholic high schools that were engaged in interscholastic sports were supported by either a diocese or a religious order. Religious orders had founded the first Catholic high schools in America during the nineteenth century, but in 1890 the Philadelphia Diocese pioneered the "central" or diocesan school, when it founded Roman Catholic High that drew students from all the city's parishes.

Another reason for the lag in athletic programs was that the Catholic model of the secondary school in a few respects initially differed from the prevailing model of the American high school. Many Catholic secondary schools were organized in conjunction with either two-year or four-year college departments, and some were organized as six-year schools. As a result, their athletic teams contained many older and bigger students, thus erecting a barrier to finding competition with four-year public high schools. Finally, the schools were dominated by immigrant populations from southern and eastern Europe, where the tradition of athletic contests was much weaker than in the English-speaking world. Also, the Catholic population in the early twentieth century was more working class than the Protestant majority, and students tended to be needed by their families for employment in the workforce after eighth grade or, if they were attending school, during after-school hours.[18]

In 1915 the Catholic Church in America could boast of having some 1,275 secondary schools, almost equally divided into boys' and girls' schools. The total number of students it served was 74,500, representing an increase of 40 percent from the previous three years, producing an average total per institution of fewer than 60 students. These telling figures demonstrate an acute reason for the slowness by Catholic high schools in establishing a strong program of interscholastic sports. The public high schools and the prep schools at this time were rapidly developing an extensive program of interscholastic sports with league and state championships, but the interscholastic meets sponsored by the major universities show practically no participation by Catholic schools. During the 1890s, in both New York and Chicago, two or three Catholic schools at most participated in competition, usually against public and private secular schools because of the absence of sufficient Catholic competition. De La Salle in New York was forced to join the Interscholastic Association, an organization of elite private day schools, and even then its first application was rejected, precisely because the school was Catholic.[19]

Catholic Schools in Chicago

Chicago in the early twentieth century was the most Catholic of America's major cities, with Catholics constituting more than one-third of the inhabitants by the 1930s. In the realm of high school sports, Catholic schools in Chicago reflected the dominant social arrangements in Chicago, which were Protestant and reflected mainstream American society. Thus, Catholic schools in building their interscholastic programs largely patterned themselves after the public schools, but a climate of pervasive anti-Catholicism accentuated their separate development.

Catholic schools in Chicago, as elsewhere, had to await the development of a sufficient number of secondary schools of ample size before a strong program of interscholastic sports could be developed. That expansion did not occur until the second decade of the twentieth century, thereby bypassing the formative years in the development of American interscholastic athletics (1890–1910). The city's Catholic population was not sufficiently large prior to 1890 to develop well-attended secondary schools, but then in the next three decades the city experienced a dramatic increase in immigrant population, one that came largely from mostly Catholic eastern (Poland, Bohemia) and central and southern

Europe (Austria-Hungary, Italy) as opposed to largely Protestant northern and western Europe. Between 1891 and 1910, 425,000 immigrants moved into the city, and the Catholic Church raced to keep up by building new parish churches and schools for such mushrooming groups as the Poles, Slovaks, Croatians, Slovenes, and Italians.[20]

As in the rest of the country, Chicago Catholics established a large number of secondary schools, but the vast majority were parish schools of sometimes no more than a dozen or so secondary students. The period 1855–1916 saw the foundation of sixty-four parish schools, of which nine were for boys alone and thirty-five were coeducational. Practically none of these schools fielded secondary-school athletic teams. Most of the city's Catholic secondary schools that succeeded in establishing interscholastic programs were not on the parish level. Typical was St. Patrick Academy on the near West Side, founded by the Christian Brothers in 1861. Although originally designed to serve one parish, it eventually grew to serve the entire West Side. The Jesuits followed in 1870, when they opened St. Ignatius College, which had a secondary-school department. The Christian Brothers opened their second high school, De La Salle Institute, in 1891. It was designed to be a "central" high school, serving the entire South Side, but also included a college department. These institutions were the only Catholic secondary schools in Chicago of any size in the 1890s, but their activities in sports were negligible at this time. The St. Ignatius boys competed in a variety of sports, but through the college program. De La Salle introduced an annual field day in 1893, while St. Patrick and St. Ignatius sent representatives to compete in public-school open events.[21]

An early Catholic school that later played a role in the development of interscholastic sports was St. Stanislaus College. Its history was typical of the Catholic experience in America, and its example is instructive on why the Catholic schools lagged in interscholastic sports. The school was founded in 1890 by the Resurrectionist Fathers and St. Stanislaus Kosta Parish to serve the emerging Polish immigrant community on the Northwest Side. The first year, the school drew only twelve students in two classrooms. St. Stanislaus was originally founded as a six-year school, and in the arch language of the school history it "partook of the nature of a university," a phrasing designed to suggest that it was essentially a high school. Throughout the 1890s, the parish struggled to draw students, most who came from poor, working-class families. The parents felt they needed their boys to work and did not see the value of secondary education. It took more than twenty years for St. Stanislaus to grow to sufficient size whereby it could field athletic teams, by which time it had reorganized into a conventional four-year institution on the American model. Even then many of the boys could not participate in sports, as they were needed to work after school.[22]

The number of nonparish Catholic schools in Chicago was quickly augmented by DePaul in 1898 (originally founded as St. Vincent's College High) and then St. Cyril in 1900, St. Philip in 1904, St. Rita in 1906, Loyola Academy in 1909, and Holy Trinity in 1910. Many of these schools began small and struggled. The Catholic schools that managed to field athletic teams during the first decade all competed in independent schedules, arranging contests with public and private schools, other Catholic institutions, and private clubs. In such institutions as St. Cyril, De La Salle, and St. Ignatius that had college departments, the boys often competed with college classmates against both colleges and high schools. For example, in 1907 St. Cyril fielded a basketball team composed of both high school and college boys, found no Catholic competition, and proceeded to garner a 7-0 record in crushing contests against five public high schools, one private school, and one amateur team. That such schools tended to field teams bigger and older than their public-school counterparts helped keep the Catholic schools out of the mainstream of Chicago high school sports. Eventually, these schools either dropped or separated from their college departments and became conventional four-year institutions—De La Salle in 1900, St. Ignatius in 1909, and St. Cyril in 1918.[23]

A West Side Catholic school, St. Philip, found league affiliation in the fall of 1911, when it joined the Cook County League, primarily to compete in baseball. The following spring, the school won the league baseball championship. St. Philip's admittance into the league was a bit controversial. There was considerable resistance, as there was only one other nonpublic school in the conference, University High, a member only because of its status as a "lab" school of the University of Chicago's school of education. The Cook County League at first voted against St.

Philip's joining, but after another plea by the school, they relented and agreed to let the school in as an "experiment." They announced that if the membership of St. Philip should prove to be a "success," then they would consider adding more Catholic schools. However, in the early fall of 1912, when St. Ignatius and DePaul Academy applied to join the league, they found their applications to be subject to "delay." The Catholic schools could smell a whiff of anti-Catholicism in the league's rejection, and so a movement began in early October to form a football league. Eight schools attended the groundbreaking meeting, but could not get together on the particulars to form a football league.[24]

Finally, in the third week of November, the schools managed to form the Chicago Catholic High School Athletic League and drew up a schedule of games in basketball and indoor baseball. The founding members were St. Stanislaus, De La Salle, DePaul, St. Ignatius, St. Cyril, St. Philip, Loyola, and Cathedral. By the spring, when a baseball schedule was drawn up, Holy Trinity had joined the league, but Cathedral had dropped out. In the fall of 1913, the league introduced football. By the following year, league champion DePaul felt feisty enough to invite St. John's Preparatory from Danvers, Massachusetts, to Chicago to engage in an intersectional contest. DePaul narrowly lost the game, but it demonstrated that Catholic-league football was thriving. The school booked two more intersectional games in the next two years—a match against Beverly High in Massachusetts and a rematch against St. John's in Chicago, winning both.[25]

Because the Catholic-school population relative to the mainstream public secondary schools and the private schools was composed of students from more immigrant and working-class populations, the sports the league initially sponsored reflected this demographic makeup. For example, during the first four years of the league's existence, only baseball, basketball, indoor baseball, and football were offered, sports that had long engaged the working-class populations. Basketball was the most popular sport, as the league not only provided for heavyweight and lightweight schedules, but also bantamweight (added in 1919) and flyweight competition (added in the early 1920s). The Chicago Public High School League and the Suburban League offered basketball only in the heavyweight and lightweight classes, after experimenting only a few years with a bantamweight class.

19. De La Salle High indoor baseball team, 1913, in the first year of the Chicago Catholic High School Athletic League, its formation driven by the public schools' exclusion from their league. Courtesy of the Chicago History Museum.

The Catholic League added track and field in 1917, but it was not until 1924 that three "country club" sports were added to the league's schedule—golf, tennis, and swimming. The addition of these sports brought the league up to the level of offerings by the Chicago and Suburban public leagues, which helped confirm, in Catholic minds anyway, that they were fully American and fully worthy of being treated as equals.[26]

The Catholic league did not include any girls' schools and did not sponsor any interscholastic sports contests for female students, as all its members were all-boys schools. The girls' schools had a separate development. Catholic education for girls began earlier than it did for boys in Illinois, with the opening of the Academy of the Visitation in southern Illinois, in Kaskaskia, in 1833. That school did not last beyond 1844, but in 1846 St. Francis Xavier Academy opened in Chicago. By 1900 there were seventeen academies and high schools for Catholic schoolgirls in the Chicago area, and in the next several decades, as Catholic immigrants flooded the city, the number grew to more than thirty. Catholic schools were excluded from the Illinois High School Athletic Association and thus were not subject to its restrictions on female competition. However, interscholastic competition did not emerge in the girls' schools until the 1920s, and almost all the contests were limited to basketball. In 1927 the Catholic girls' teams joined together to form a league.[27]

The Catholic schools infrequently competed against public schools in the first decades of interscholastic competition, but early on there was a

20. St. Philip High baseball team, 1924, when the Catholic schools in Chicago and nationwide were building a parallel structure of high school sports to the public schools. Courtesy of the Chicago History Museum.

desire to show mainstream society that Catholic athletes belonged equally in the sporting arena with public-school athletes. The demonstration of that equality would occur in the sport of football, which next to boxing was the most paradigmatic for testing one's manly worthiness in society. This opportunity came with the advent of the Prep Bowl in 1927.

CHICAGO CATHOLICS PROVE THEMSELVES IN THE PREP BOWL

The separated worlds of the Catholic schools and public schools, each competing in their own leagues and tournaments, could not last for long. Indeed, this separation only intensified the idea of competition between the two. By the early 1920s, all the Catholic schools had progressed into the conventional high school model, dropping their college departments and providing their students a full panoply of sports that fully reflected the American sporting tradition. So the stage was set for competition with the public schools.

Another powerful influence that helped draw the public and Catholic schools into competition was the success of Notre Dame, which under Knute Rockne had emerged in the forefront of the college football world. Its success against mainstream American colleges only heightened the sense of athletic competitiveness between the Catholic population and the public-school population. When in 1927 the *Chicago Herald and Examiner* proposed a championship contest between the winners of the Catholic and public leagues of Chicago, it found a rich, fertile soil for the idea to take root and grow.[28]

Under the *Herald and Examiner*'s proposal, the contest would be a charity game, the proceeds going to the paper's Christmas Basket Fund. Ticket sales were conducted at all the city's high schools and at downtown and sporting-goods stores. Students were charged fifty cents and the general public one dollar. By the end of November, Schurz had won the public-school playoffs and Mt. Carmel had won the Catholic-league playoffs. Each school in their football play reflected their separate traditions. The Schurz coach, Bob Koehler, was a product of both the public league and Northwestern University, where his pass-heavy game was honed. The paper reported that Koehler used "Warner formations," a reference to college coach Glenn "Pop" Warner, who used double wings and unbalanced lines. The Mt. Carmel coach, Tom Riordan, was a product of Catholic schooling and was a Notre Dame alumnus. He drilled his team in the "Rockne system" and the intricacies of the famed Notre Dame shift and the single-wing formation. The game drew fifty thousand fans to Soldier Field and was broadcast over local station WJJD by Warren Brown, the renowned *Herald and Examiner* sportswriter.[29]

The early Prep Bowls were not unqualified successes. The *Herald and Examiner,* expecting a turnout of at least seventy-five thousand for the 1927 game, reported fifty thousand, and likely that number was a bit inflated. The next year, there was an even smaller turnout, when only thirty thousand came out to see the game. The match between Tilden Tech and DePaul Academy was preceded by weeks of bickering between the two camps over a couple of issues that divided them. DePaul insisted on Catholic representation in the officiating crew and eventually got it. Differing eligibility rules had long been a subject of dispute, and a resolution came when DePaul agreed to withhold its twenty-year-old center from the game and Tilden stepped back from insisting that its overage player be made eligible. Tilden defeated DePaul, but the *New World* Catholic newspaper that was distributed all over the metropolitan area affected a blasé attitude over the outcome, saying, "In the last two years the Catholic league has won nine of fifteen interleague games . . . so why worry?"[30]

In 1929 and 1930, the Catholic league approached the public league each year, requesting the continuation of the Prep Bowl series, but in both years the public league rejected the overtures, saying it would not participate unless the Catholic schools came more in line with its standards on player eligibility. The Prep Bowl finally resumed in 1931, after Catholic-league rules had come into closer compliance with the rules of the public league and because the deepening Depression called for charity events. The public-league representative, Harrison High, had one of the most extraordinary high school teams ever to suit up in Chicago. The Catholic opponent was Mt. Carmel, which drew its players from the South Side Irish American community. One press report, ever mindful of Notre Dame as the iconic representative of Catholic football, billed the contest as between the "Irish" of Mt. Carmel (with its many Irish-surnamed play-ers) and the "world" of Harrison High (its lineup comprised "many nation-alities"). Harrison High, ironically, led by future Notre Dame players Andy Pilney and Andy Puplis, overwhelmed the overmatched Mt. Carmel team, 44–6. Only thirty-five thousand fans showed up for the Prep Bowl, how-ever. A few weeks later, Harrison went on to beat Miami High in Miami, Florida, 18–7, in a highly prestigious intersectional football series.[31]

In 1932 Catholic champion Mt. Carmel could not arrange a Prep Bowl contest with public-league champion Morgan Park, whose parents refused to allow the game, objecting to the potentially frozen field and excessive length of the season. One Morgan Park parent, a teacher in the school system, William R. Bowlin, cited these issues in the *Chicago Tribune*, but more broadly stressed the overemphasis and commercialization of the high school game: "Football is being stressed all out of proportion to its proper values. It is becoming the reason for attending school. The tail is wagging the dog. Expansive newspaper publicity has elevated the game to major importance, thereby dwarfing every other school activity." He saw potential physical danger to the players by the intensity that would be demanded of them in the game, an intensity heightened by religious affiliation, but cautioned that religion was not "a proper division for rough athletic games."[32]

The sense of proportion that the Morgan Park parents thought they had brought to the game did not survive after the 1932 season. Voices stressing moderation could not overcome the appeal of such a contest in a big city with largely divided Catholic- and public-school populations. The Prep Bowl resumed in 1933, and it came under firm footing when new mayor Edward Kelly began sponsoring the contest in 1934. He used it as a fund-raiser for destitute children, who received "shoes and warm clothes." The adoption of the game by the political establishment ensured its future success, and there were no further interruptions in the series. Using hun-dreds of city workers to push tickets on the public, the mayor's sponsor-ship brought 50,000 fans into Soldier Field to see public-league champion Lindblom play Leo. The numbers increased significantly each year so that by the 1937 game, when public-league champion Austin played Leo, an estimated 120,000 fans packed into Soldier Field.[33]

Catholic Basketball Tournaments

Catholics established basketball tournaments to give their parochial schools suitable participation beyond the conference level, equivalent to what was being provided in public high schools and private academies. The Catholic schools in Illinois and most states did not belong to public-school associations and thus were shut out of most state tournaments. In Illinois two notable tournaments developed—the National Catholic Inter-scholastic Basketball Tournament (NCIBT), sponsored by Loyola University, and the Illinois Catholic State Basketball Tournament.

The premier national tournament in the country in the 1920s was the National Interscholastic Basketball Tournament, conducted by Amos Alonzo Stagg and sponsored by the University of Chicago. The tournament existed, in part, as an avenue by which Stagg could recruit basketball talent. In 1923 Loyola Academy asked Stagg to include Catholic and private schools in the tournament, but was rebuffed. Stagg never made his reasons clear, but one could assume that he did not see the Catholic schools as potential feeders into the university's athletic program. In addition, as state associations were growing more and more powerful, Stagg needed to court them to get their sanction for his tournament. In 1924 his tournament limited most of its entries to winners of state association–sanctioned tournaments.[34]

The administration at Loyola believed that Stagg's rejection of its application to his tournament was based on anti-Catholic sentiment, asserting that Stagg "use[d] every means to keep Catholic schools out of his tournament." Director of athletics Rev. Joseph Thorning, SJ, then proposed to Loyola University that it establish a national Catholic tournament patterned after the one sponsored by the University of Chicago. Thorning immediately received tremendous support for his plan for the tournament from the entire Chicago community. Joining in the effort in establishing the tournament were the Chicago Catholic High School Athletic League, Knights of Columbus Basketball League, and sports editors at the various newspapers. Tournament organizers created a policy-making board of directors drawn from the Catholic league, with Thorning serving as chair. At a public banquet in 1923 that included Knute Rockne,

St. Ignatius coach Ed Daley, Loyola Academy coach Lenny Sachs, and the city's leading sportswriters, the inauguration of the National Catholic Interscholastic Basketball Tournament was announced.[35]

The first year's tournament was held in the third week of March 1924, a week before Stagg's tourney, with an initial field of twenty-six schools. Invitees had to have won a state, county, sectional, or city championship, but schools with a simply outstanding record were also chosen, often second-place tournament winners. Loyola's recently completed Alumni Gymnasium served as the site for all the games. Players were housed at the nearby Edgewater Beach Hotel—at a cost to the university of $175 per squad—which surely proved a memorable experience for many a poor Catholic boy. The winning team was awarded the Cardinal Mundelein Trophy, named after the head of the Chicago Archdiocese. The program of the initial tournament alluded to the organizers' perception of anti-Catholicism, saying that the tournament presented "a spectacle of Catholic harmony and solidarity on a national scale that it [*sic*] has been well said to combat bigotry . . . more efficiently than any propaganda yet devised."[36]

By 1926 the *Loyola News* could boast how the university's national tournament served a valued need for Catholic schools, saying, "Catholic schools have long since been barred from state tournaments and in many localities even from competition of any sort with the public high schools. But, thanks to the tournament, while in many cases these latter restrictions have been lately removed, yet no Catholic school is particularly worried about them any more. They have their own rivalries." Tournament officials at this time claimed total ticket sales for the tournament were between thirty-five and forty thousand.[37]

In 1928 tourney sponsors expanded the tournament field to thirty-two teams, and the schedule increased from four to five days so that no team would play more than one game a day. The number of states sending teams increased from thirteen in 1924 to twenty-two in 1928. The growth of fan interest in the game soon forced the finals to be moved from Loyola's gym to the Chicago Coliseum. As in previous years, thousands of potential ticket buyers were turned away at the championship finals.[38]

While the Catholic National Tourney was thriving in the late 1920s, Stagg's tournament was coming under fire from public-school educators and the National Federation of State High School Athletic Associations, which saw national tournaments as excessive and inimical to high school education. A number of public state associations had started banning their champion teams from accepting invitations to the Stagg tourney. In an attempt to save the tournament, Stagg in 1929 opened the event field to include Catholic and private schools. The NCIBT board was ready to respond and launched a public campaign against Catholic-school participation—an ironic twist when one considers why the Catholic tourney was founded—but then in 1930, the University of Chicago canceled the tournament.[39]

Also in 1930, the North Central Association of Colleges and Secondary Schools (NCAC) in concert with the National Federation of State High School Athletic Associations at its annual meeting came out against

21. The National Catholic Interscholastic Basketball Tournament, 1926, sponsored by Loyola University of Chicago, was established in response to the barring of private and Catholic schools from the University of Chicago's national tournament. Courtesy of the Chicago History Museum.

university-supported interscholastic meets. In response to this possible threat to its membership in the NCAC, Loyola University switched sponsorship to its affiliate, Loyola Academy. This move satisfied the NCAC, although in reality the academy's sponsorship was something of a fig leaf, as the university continued to run the tournament.[40]

When the Loyola Catholic tournament began in 1924, there were barely a handful of states that had even city or sectional championships, let alone a state championship, for Catholic schools. The founders of the tournament realized that for the tournament to thrive and to build credibility as being national in scope, there needed to be many more teams representing sectional and state championships. The tournament thus became a stimulus for cities and states to create Catholic-school playoffs to determine representatives. The university recognized this influence of its tournament and said, "The tournament has built up Catholic athletics to an unprecedented extent." The *Chicago Tribune* reported that the existence of the Loyola tournament was an incentive for Catholic high schools in many states to hold tournaments and form leagues to supply representative champions. In Illinois, for example, a number of downstate Catholic schools outside of Chicago were in a league with Iowa schools when the tournament began, but in 1928 they split off to conduct a "state tournament," and this group by 1934 had morphed into the Illinois State Catholic High School Athletic Association.[41]

In both neighboring Wisconsin and Indiana, the Catholic schools got together for the first time in 1928 to sponsor state tournaments. Much of the push for the formation of state organizations came through the National Catholic High School Association, whose representatives met annually at the Loyola tournament and who by 1934 represented more than seven hundred Catholic secondary schools. Gradually, in more states, and in more and more state sections and cities, Catholic schools conducted formal championship competitions.[42]

This growth in Catholic state high school associations coming roughly a decade after the establishment of public high school state athletic associations was telling evidence of the emergence of the Catholic-school interscholastic athletic programs into a level of relative equality with the public schools. Yet in most states where Catholic state associations were formed, the desire was eventually full integration with the public schools into their athletic associations.

Throughout the Depression, the NCIBT continued to thrive, reportedly drawing more than fifty thousand fans each year, despite moving the finals back to Loyola's gym in 1931. For the finals, the *Chicago Tribune* reported five thousand spectators in 1931, four thousand in 1932, thirty-seven hundred in 1937, and thirty-five hundred in 1941. Even given the usual shaky estimates provided by newspaper reporters, these figures suggest a decline in interest. In 1934 the tournament added a consolation bracket for the first-round losing teams, which undoubtedly helped to sustain attendance figures.[43]

One of the most popular teams at the tournament was the St. Francis Mission, from South Dakota, a Jesuit secondary school whose teams were composed of full-blooded Sioux. The St. Francis Mission team attended the 1925 and 1926 tournaments and returned in 1934, appearing in most of the subsequent competitions. Tournament officials encouraged the St. Francis Mission to attend and helped allay transportation costs. Not only were the Native Americans a draw, but officials also wanted to show the type of work Catholics were doing in educating the Native American population. The St. Francis Mission became the "darling of the tournament," with such colorful player names as Williard Iron Wing, Leonard Quick Bear, and Emil Red Fish and a distinctive fast-paced, rapid-fire style of play developed on the reservation. However, sportswriters and fans could not resist racist comments. The tournament program referred to the team seeking a "scalping knife," and the *Chicago Tribune* reporter stated that the team would "whoop it up" against a first-round opponent.[44]

After the United States entered World War II, the 1942 tournament was canceled. In January 1943, the Reverend F. Maher, SJ, the tournament director, announced the permanent termination of the national tourney. Loyola University was providing its facilities to the US Navy to train cadets, and the tournament was canceled as part of the cooperative effort to win the war. Another reason stemmed from tougher policies of the North Central Association, which in the early 1930s had successfully suppressed interstate tournaments conducted by colleges and universities for public high schools, notably Stagg's tourney. Loyola University had avoided the wrath of the North Central Association in 1930—even though the organization was casting a wary eye at the Catholic tournament back then—but the school understood that it could not continue the tournament any longer.[45]

Catholic Schools in New York

In New York City, the Catholic high schools were further behind than their counterparts in Chicago and Philadelphia in developing a full interscholastic program, remaining largely unorganized up to near the end of the 1920s. In 1906 several New York City schools formed an anemic conference called the Catholic Schools Athletic League (CSAL). The organization was originally formed to provide competition for both grammar and high schools in track and field only. Later baseball competition was added, and at times there was formal basketball competition. The league sponsored no football program and for most years did not sponsor baseball or basketball. De La Salle Institute hosted an annual indoor track meet from 1913 through the 1920s, and at the meet the CSAL would conduct a couple of relay events. By 1923 there was no formal competition for Catholic high schools in the city, with the CSAL mostly focusing on the grammar schools. Some Catholic secondary schools joined the Private Schools Athletic Association that developed in the early 1920s, but only track and field and cross-country competitions were initially offered in that league.[46]

Catholic educators in New York looked around them and saw the city's public schools and private schools with leagues of their own and determined that there was a pressing need to organize their Catholic high schools into a league so that their boys (but, alas, not girls) could enjoy the full fruits of the American secondary-school experience. In March 1926, representatives of ten Catholic high schools got together to form the New York State Catholic High School Athletic Association, which excluded the Catholic schools in metropolitan New York and grouped the remaining Catholic schools into four geographic sections. The following year, however, New York's Catholic schools organized a "Southern Branch" and were let into the statewide association. City league formation came when the Southern Branch schools were organized into the Catholic High

School Athletic Association (CHSAA) in March 1927. The charter members were Fordham Prep, All Hallows, LaSalle Academy, Regis, St. Ann's, and Xavier High, all in Manhattan, and Brooklyn Prep, Bishop Loughlin, Brooklyn Cathedral, St. John's Prep, St. Francis Prep, and Holy Trinity, all in Brooklyn.[47]

In 1928 the CHSAA introduced indoor track, basketball, and baseball to the program, and in 1929 it added cross-country and ice hockey. In 1930 swimming was added to the program. The basketball winner would compete with the three other sectional winners in the state for the right to compete in the Loyola National Catholic Interscholastic Basketball Tournament in Chicago. A. G. Spalding and Company contributed two silver loving cups for the baseball and football competitions. The first team winning the league title in baseball or football three times would receive permanent possession of the cup. Although the New York schools were late in organizing a league, within a few short years they built a league and a program that fully realized the American high school sporting experience.[48]

The rise of high school sports in the Catholic schools, especially in the big cities of Chicago and New York, was driven in part by the growth in the size and number of the individual schools. By 1930 the Catholic population could boast of supporting some 2,125 secondary schools, serving 242,000 students, nearly doubling the per-school average from 58 in 1915 to 114 in 1930. The increase in average reflected the growth in diocesan- and religious-supported schools, with sizable student populations that could support an athletic program, and by the 1930s the church was able to create a fully blossomed program of interscholastic sports.[49]

Private schools during much of the 1920s in many parts of the country lacked the league and higher level of organization that was found in the public schools. On the other hand, the relative wealth of the preparatory schools and the ability to draw from the elite population allowed them not only to surpass the public and parochial schools in their success in such sports as rowing and golf but also to create their own competitions. On the other hand, the largest private-school group, the Catholic schools, with a large proportion of their students being working-class immigrants, built their programs around a few major sports, notably football, but as with most other private schools, they lagged behind the public schools in the creation of leagues, state associations, and tournaments (from local to national). But as the 1920s progressed, private schools of all kinds worked to give their students the interscholastic sports experience of the public schools. The Catholic schools' adoption of interscholastic sports distinctively reflected a desire for Americanization, but institutionally Catholic sports program remained separate and constituted something of a "ministate" in the larger American world of high school sports. Thus, by the 1930s, the private schools, secular and religious, had created a realm of organization and competition that very much resembled and paralleled the mainstream culture, with the same understandings of what competitive athletics could do for their young high school students.

12

GIRLS' INTERSCHOLASTIC SPORTS AND THE EXUBERANCE TO COMPETE

The role of competitive interscholastic sports for girls was one of the most contentious societal issues of the 1920s. Across the country, local boards of education and state-level high school athletic associations were influenced by two national developments in women's athletics that pulled them in opposite directions over the suitability of girls participating in interscholastic sports. In one direction, the explosion of women athletes who attained national distinction in the Olympics and in national highly competitive contests could not help but exert an influence on attitudes concerning the acceptability of girls performing in interschool athletic contests. The examples are legion. In swimming Ethelda Bleibtry, Gertrude Ederle, and such Chicago-based notables as Sybil Bauer and Ethel Lackie became national and international stars. In tennis Helen Wills and Molla Bjurstedt Mallory set the example of extraordinary achievement, while in golf Glenna Collett dominated. Track and field produced two national stars from Chicago, Helen Filkey and Betty Robinson.[1] The newspapers of the day were replete with stories on local club basketball teams and tournaments, local tennis and golf stars, and amateur swimming and track meets, all engaged in activities whose social acceptance was assumed by both newswriters and their readers. With countless stories, images, and positive presentations of female athletic activities presented in the press, the popular pressure to open up sports for their girls could not help but weigh on school administrators.

On the other hand, there was tremendous pressure exerted during the 1920s in the opposite direction, to limit competitive activities for girls from the women's physical educational establishment. The professional organizations for women athletics were specifically formed to provide governance for collegiate women's sport, and their philosophy was completely at variance to what was occurring outside the colleges, where girls and women were happily competing vigorously against each other in immodest dress and in strenuous athletic endeavors, and moreover under male coaches. They believed this growth in popular sport posed a serious danger to girls and women and sought to eliminate these presumed abuses in the colleges and in American society overall. Their foes, invariably male, were the Amateur Athletic Union and other athletic leaders, coaches, business sponsors, and community boosters.[2] This conflict ultimately came down to what each side envisioned to be the modern American high school girl and their competing notions of athletics as builders of physical well-being and moral character.

Two principal women organizations sought to contain female athletics—the Committee on Women's Athletics (CWA) of the American Physical Education Association, formed in 1917 (reorganized as the Section on Women's Athletics [SWA] in 1927), and the Women's Division of the National Amateur Athletic Federation, formed in 1923. Upon the formation of the Women's Division, the new organization issued sixteen resolutions, which became known as the Platform, which in various permutations was the guiding document for its movement in defining its aims, notably to end interscholastic competition for girls, which was considered damaging to their physical health and moral character, and instead to provide noncompetitive intramurals that emphasized participation and sportsmanship. The CWA was more directed at setting standards for college and secondary-school athletics, whereas the Women's Division was designed to campaign beyond the campus in the sports world at large. The Women's Division was thus more active in pressuring educational administrators, athletic clubs and organizations, park and playground officials, and civic officials to eliminate tournaments and athletic meets deemed damaging to women's sport and damaging to the character of American girls and women. Both the Women's Division and the CWA/

SWA helped high school educators organize statewide Girls' Athletic Associations (GAAs) and relentlessly worked with the state leaders to substitute intramural sports for interscholastic contests. Both organizations developed and distributed instructional films, produced pamphlets, and encouraged state GAA leaders to deliver the message on the evils of interscholastic competition to the print and broadcast media.[3]

The objections by physical educators to women's competitive sports were largely the same hoary ones presented for the previous quarter century. They still believed that girls, unlike boys, were emotionally unsuited to perform in the highly competitive environments of interschool contests in public. Sarah Addington in the pages of the *Ladies' Home Journal* in 1923 expressed this concern regarding the college girl, a concern just as applicable to the high school girl: "The wild excitement of the meet itself, the girl's loyalty to the college, the applause of the multitude, the intoxication of outstripping her competitors, all these cause many a girl to sacrifice what seems a problematical future evil to the present hour of triumph. She is swept away by the enthusiasm of the moment. The nervous strain in such contests is tremendous and uses up more vital energy then most girls have to give. . . . The same strenuous objection cannot be made for interclass contests."[4]

The physical educators were still raising the biological issue of the female's presumed inability to handle strenuous physical activity, but they could not point to any medical evidence. Conceded Addington, "There are no statistics, and probably never will be, on the exact harm done to women, or to men, for that matter, by, say, high jumping or distance running, or too strenuous basket-ball playing, or merely too much exercise of any sort. . . . Yet in spite of the absence of these data, our experts are firmly of the opinion that harm does come of unlimited jumping and hurdling to break records, of hot and heavy basket-ball for the 'honor of the school.'"[5]

An objection that developed great currency in the 1920s, which had much to commend itself, was that interschool sports tended to limit the benefits of sport to a few exceptional athletes while ignoring the many. The reform movement had two catchphrases, one of which captured their hostility to interschool contests ("They're not good for the girls who participate in them, and they're not good for the girls who don't") and the other their advocacy of intramural sports ("A game for every girl and every girl in a game"). The latter was surely one of the reformers' more laudable aims. Strong intramural programs did indeed benefit many more girls, and the reformers' campaign in building the Girls' Athletic Associations in the schools was one of their great achievements of the 1920s. In their advocacy of broadening the benefits of athletics for every girl, the reformers were influenced by John Dewey, whose *Democracy and Education* (1916) presented a philosophy of education that emphasized the importance of benefiting not just individuals but the whole social group.[6]

Reformers decried the commercial aspects of sports resulting in many female athletes being sexually and economically exploited by male coaches, businessmen, and town and school boosters. A huge contributing factor to this exploitation was newspapers and journalists who contributed to the so-called winning and losing frenzy of female sports. The Women's Division objected to "exhibitionist type of performances" and of "putting sex into sports," citing risqué uniforms. On the high school level, basketball games were faulted for becoming "spectacles" for local townsmen and civic boosters.[7]

The alternative model offered by the physical educators to the commercialized and overemphasized female sports was based on a separatist philosophy. The Women's Division stated that "the welfare, health, and education of women depends upon the women experts on girls and women's athletics organizing themselves as a deliberating and administrative body to deal with the special problems of athletics for girls and women." The belief was that women could ensure the female athlete would be protected with modestly designed athletic uniforms, distinct sets of women's rules and standards, and audiences that were predominantly female. The critics of interscholastic competition for girls saw the essential value of sports as promoting sportsmanship, loyalty, citizenship, initiative, and good conduct in sport, but believed that such character building that sports provided was undermined in an interscholastic setting, one critic noting that "all thoughts of sportsmanship, loyalty, and health thrown to the four winds in the winning or losing of [a] game."[8]

These highly conservative views met with much resistance from women athletes and also other physical educators. In rural areas, the local citizenry and school administrators valued their female high school basketball players, and in working-class communities, girls and women enthusiastically participated in industrial and community programs. In the African American community, in both the colleges and the high schools, the female athlete was appreciated. These advocates of women's sport, plus supporters in community, park, and private club programs, either took no notice or utterly ignored the pronouncements of the CWA/SWA and the Women's Division. The Amateur Athletic Union was the most prominent advocate and promoter of women's basketball, track and field, and swimming during the 1920s and vigorously fought back against the women's physical education establishment campaign to ban AAU and Olympic competition for women.[9]

INTERSCHOLASTIC SPORTS
FOR GIRLS IN CHICAGO

Some sport historians have recently found considerable opposition to the noncompetition ideology that persisted in predominantly rural areas, such as Iowa and the South, where the playing of interscholastic basketball continued, whereas in city schools, it failed to develop or was terminated by administrators without evident resistance by the students.[10] This finding is supported by a large amount of evidence that athletics for girls in the 1920s was primarily a rural phenomenon. In Iowa, a prime example, girls' basketball was sustained in the small country schools, but was successfully suppressed in the major cities. Yet in some big urban centers, notably Chicago and Philadelphia, girls' participation in interscholastic competition was considerable, if brief, during the 1920s.

With regard to Chicago, the Illinois High School Athletic Association set the agenda for rules on girls' athletics through much of the state, adopting a bylaw in 1916 that barred all interscholastic sports contests. They were supported in this ban by the Illinois League of High School Girls' Athletic Associations, formed in 1919.[11] Chicago schools, however, did not then belong to the IHSAA, and for a few years the Chicago Public High School League followed its own muse. While the Chicago schools adhered to the noncompetitive model for team sports, for those sports that engaged the individual—namely, golf, tennis, swimming, and rifle—the city league was more progressive than the state association. But there was also considerable unsanctioned activity by Chicago schoolgirls in basketball, softball, and volleyball competition.

The Chicago Public High School League, although its schools were not IHSAA members, originally abided by the association's ban on girls' interscholastic contests and even imposed its own restrictions on girls' competition. But in the early 1920s, these strictures began to weaken, paradoxically as a by-product of the tremendous growth of Girls' Athletic Associations in Chicago schools. The GAAs did a tremendous job in building interest in girls' athletics, which in turn led to a drive to compete by the energized girls. A look back at how the GAA movement arose in Illinois is imperative. The beginnings of a statewide GAA began in 1917, when following the regular annual meeting of the High School Conference (an Illinois group of high school educators that met annually at the Illinois State Normal College in Bloomington), a special section for teachers of girls' physical education was formed. This group, after several meetings in 1919, formed the Illinois League of High School Girls' Athletic Associations (ILGAA).[12]

The women of the ILGAA were adamantly opposed to interscholastic competition for high school girls, and their first activities were to "eliminate wide-spread evils and tone down the excesses of numerous programs already in existence." At first the group was weak and undoubtedly ineffective. In 1922 the ILGAA had only 30 members, compared to the IHSAA's 623 member high schools. Girls' basketball, still being conducted interscholastically in many small towns, elicited the most attention from the ILGAA. Yet there were certain sports that were considered acceptable for interschool competition by women educators, notably archery, tennis, golf, and field hockey. In Illinois the IHSAA, not long after the formation of the ILGAA, eased its rule against interscholastic girls' competition by allowing it for archery, tennis, and golf, under the stipulation that they were "conducted under the rules prescribed by the Illinois League of High School Girls' Athletic Associations."[13]

The ILGAA eventually flourished through an alliance with the IHSAA. The ILGAA approached the group for assistance at the IHSAA's

1926 annual meeting. The upshot was that the IHSAA Board of Control agreed to finance the league and fund the position of director for the ILGAA. Pauline Kapp of Oak Park High was chosen, and during her term (1927–1929), the organization grew to 117 members. Carrying out a program reflecting the prevailing ideology for women's athletics, the ILGAA prohibited interscholastic contests, except for golf, tennis, and archery. Intramural sports were encouraged, but modified to what were deemed acceptable standards of physiological capabilities of women. Thus, only line basketball was played, and track and field events were modified in distance and weight for women. The organization promoted dancing and recreational activities, such as hiking, horseback riding, and ice skating."[14]

As for the Chicago Public High School League programs for girls, league officials were most accommodating to interschool competition in tennis and golf. The league introduced golf competition in 1922, when it allowed the girls to compete in the annual boys' tournament in June for the league title. The girls would play the same number of holes as the boys, on the same course, in an "open" tournament. Girls would be awarded first-, second-, and third-place medalist prizes. The first year, only two girls, both from Hyde Park, took advantage of the opportunity and participated. In 1923 the tournament attracted competitors from several schools, and officials awarded an individual title and team title (although only one full team participated). The tournament produced a similarly meager turnout the following year. Interest in the girls' competition was not what the league had hoped.[15]

In 1925 girls' golf picked up considerably, and newspapers reported on a few dual meets, as Senn, Lake View, and Schurz all fielded full golf teams. At the league meet in June, the individual title was won by Florence Beebe, from Schurz, who was fast developing a reputation as one of the state's top junior golfers. The summer after the tournament, she would gather huge galleries and garner headlines for her accurate long drives, one of which went 310 yards. Beebe repeated as individual medalist in 1926, beating out Mildred Hackl of Senn High; both of them would become future stars in women's golf. The *Chicago Tribune* showed a foursome on a green from the high school tournament, two girls and two boys. The girls who are putting are Beebe and Hackl. The photo is stunning in its modernity, high school young men and women participating in a sport together on wholly equal terms. In terms of progressive attitudes toward schoolgirl sports, the golf competition was one of the few bright spots in interscholastic activity for girls in Illinois. The girls received sizable coverage in the newspapers, they were lauded by their schools, and they played alongside boys in mixed tournaments.[16]

The most thriving sport for Chicago high school girls in the 1920s was tennis, and the newspapers gave regular coverage to league activity, which ended in a championship match in late June of each year. Beginning in 1909, the city schools had sponsored tennis competition for girls, but abandoned girls' competition after the war. Chicago school authorities decided to revive tennis for girls in 1922, and it took off more strongly than did golf. The league championship was usually held in late June, but two months of dual-meet competition preceded the city championship series. In 1926

22. Waller High girls' tennis team, 1922, the initial year when the Chicago High School League began sponsoring tennis competition for girls, which eventually engaged thirteen teams. Courtesy of the Chicago History Museum.

the girls' league was up to thirteen schools in four sections—North, South, West, and Central.[17]

Under the prevailing views of the day, most Illinois schools did not adopt swimming as a competitive activity for girls, and it was not approved by the IHSAA. The Chicago Public High School League said it "sponsored" interschool competition for girls only in golf and tennis competition, omitting the mention of swimming, which means only that the league did not support a league championship. School authorities not only allowed Chicago schoolgirls to compete in dual swim meets (and sometimes in triple meets), but also authorized the awarding of letters for competition and totaled these contests in the annual report. As early as 1921, the *Chicago Tribune* reported on Hyde Park competing against Lindblom, but most notices of swimming competition appeared in the high school student newspapers and yearbooks. There were such reports in 1925, when Parker, Englewood, and Lindblom participated in a triple swim meet, at Lindblom, consisting of a variety of races and diving contests. The school's principal gave a speech to the girls after the meet, perhaps lauding the efforts of the girls and putting value on the competition. The schools occasionally produced champion swimmers who made their names in outside competition, and the schools' newspapers and yearbooks proudly promoted them as local stars. The league reported that girls' swim teams during the 1925–1926 school year had conducted a total of fifty dual meets.[18]

Famed swim coach William Bachrach of the Illinois Athletic Club had started working with female swimmers shortly after the AAU approved female competition in 1916. He produced a number of women champions. His most notable protégé was Sybil Bauer, whom he discovered swimming for Schurz High as a freshman. She joined his IAC team and soon was setting national records in the backstroke. In the 1924 Olympics, she easily overpowered the field and won the backstroke. Another protégé was freestyler Ethel Lackie of University High, who in the 1924 Olympics won two gold medals. Another top Chicago-area Olympian was Jane Fauntz of Hyde Park, who while still a student participated in the 1928 Olympics in the breaststroke. Although there was limited competitive swimming for girls in the high schools, elsewhere they had many opportunities, notably

23. Lindblom High girls' swimming team from 1925, when the Chicago High School League was sponsoring some fifty dual and multiple-team meets a year for girls, despite such competition being banned in the rest of the state. Courtesy of the Chicago Public Library, Special Collections and Preservation Division, ECC 3/6.

at the Illinois Woman's Athletic Club, formed in 1926 and one of the biggest sponsors of girls' competitive swimming. Industrial firms, such as Western Electric, formed girls' swim teams. The newspapers regularly reported on high school–age girls' achievements at meets sponsored by clubs and two amateur organizations, the Amateur Athletic Federation and the Central AAU.[19]

Track and field was banned as an interscholastic activity throughout the state by secondary-school educators, but the high school girls found many opportunities to compete, sometimes even under the banner of their school. The Chicago Park District, private clubs, Turner organizations, and church leagues were all sponsoring competition for women and girls when, in 1923, the Central AAU opened its annual indoor meet to women's competition. Some fifty women and girls participated in the high jump and 50-yard-dash events. Among the competitors was an extraordinary high school runner, Helen Filkey, who as a freshman at Lake View High competed for a park-district team. Chicago schoolgirl competitors in the Central AAU 1924 meet were future AAU national champ Nellie Todd, running for Lucy Flower High, and Norma Zilk of Lake View High, running "unattached." Chicago high school girls occasionally listed their high school as their affiliation when competing, and sometimes they competed head-to-head under their school colors, as when Helen Filkey, representing Lake View, raced against Nellie Todd, representing Lucy Flower, in a 1924 meet. In 1925 a team of Senn High girls at an AAU meet competed in a relay and individual running events. Thus, during the years 1923–1926, the girls were coming close to interscholastic competition in track, but not quite, as there was no unambiguous league-supported competition under school colors.[20]

24. Lake View High schoolgirls compete in track and field, 1924, in an amateur contest while representing their school, an illegal activity, as school track and field competition was barred during the 1920s. Courtesy of the Chicago History Museum.

All through the 1920s, the local newspapers covered the girl track and field contestants without condescension and without qualification. Readers learned about star high school runners, and in their schools their fellow students learned about their achievements in the school newspapers and yearbooks. Helen Filkey by 1926 was attending Senn High and was national champion and record holder in the broad jump, the 100-yard dash, and 60-yard hurdles. She had become the biggest female athletic star in Chicago. Filkey did not compete as a Senn athlete, but instead worked as the assistant coach, probably more knowledgeable about track than the teacher coach. Most of the elite Chicago high school runners were coached not by their gym instructors, but by Canadian Tom Eck, the veteran long-distance coach at the University of Chicago since 1915 who had taken a special interest in developing female track and field talent. After Eck died in 1926, the city's top female track competitors gravitated for their training and club competition to the Illinois Women's Athletic Club.[21]

Whereas the Chicago Public High School League did not sponsor a single meet during the 1920s, the grammar schools conducted an annual track and field meet for boys and girls. Once the girls entered high school, the interschool competition halted. But there was a slight glimmering of interscholastic competition, which was greatly overshadowed by the girls' vigorous participation in the park-district and club programs and pointed to future possibilities.[22]

Basketball was one of the most visible sports in the schools, and one of the most popular with the girls. School authorities were particularly vigilant about interschool play. But the girls from the public high schools were driven to compete, particularly when they looked around and saw all kinds of basketball competition readily available to girls their age. The newspapers reported daily during the winter months on a welter of games by amateur clubs and teams representing private and parochial high schools, park districts, church leagues, industrial leagues, and the AAU, all who vigorously competed against each other, with no adverse effects, and playing by men's rules as well. Chicago had a number of highly visible amateur club teams, to which the newspapers gave a lot of ink, notably the Uptown Brownies, Tri Chi Girls, and the Jewish People's Institute team.

The women played for Chicago, midwestern, and national championships in large venues before thousands of fans.[23]

Reflecting the attitudes of the almost universally male sportswriter fraternity, a *Chicago Tribune* columnist in 1926 reported favorably on one of the games he saw: "In appearance the girls were attractive and decidedly not of the 'hard boiled' variety. We expected the girls to slow up from exhaustion, but they stood it better than most boys' teams and seldom took time out except for bumps. We do not know what after effect such strenuous and nervous physical exercise has for girls, but Principal Page of the Edmonton [Grads], accompanying the team, asserts no ill effects have been observed in twelve years of play. . . . [W]e're no longer a skeptic." Regarding the use of men's rules for girls, sports reporter Harland Rohm wrote, "[The] girls game, in which each girl plays in a certain section of the floor like an animated checker, still survives, but it won't do for the girl of the present day." Did the male sportswriters have a better sense of what girls of the day should experience in sports than the physical educators? It appears so.[24]

The African American community supported many amateur girl teams, most notably the Roamer Girls. The star of the Roamers was Isadore Channels, who was a student at Phillips High and also a four-time national American Tennis Association champion. Phillips did not sponsor girls' basketball, so Channels played on the intramural captain-ball team. She must have felt ridiculous playing this basketless game, when outside the school she was playing basketball by men's rules. When the Phillips High boys played big intersectional games, as against Armstrong from Washington, DC, the game was usually preceded by the Roamers playing another amateur team, such as the Harvey Bloomers.[25]

The public-school girls, it would seem, looked enviously at their private- and parochial-school counterparts, who throughout the decade played occasional interschool contests against one another. Newspaper reports, often in agate type at the bottom of the page, revealed games by such Catholic secondary schools as DePaul, St. Thomas Aquinas, and Providence Academy, as well as by Luther Institute. The game became so popular that a number of Catholic girls' schools formed a basketball league in 1927.[26]

Chicago public high school girls, apparently oblivious to the rule against interschool basketball competition, occasionally competed, but such games were so underwater that they never made the newspapers, though reports of the games did appear in student publications. In 1922 Senn High played a game against Schurz and every year thereafter played one other outside game against another school, as did Marshall High, which each year routinely played Schurz High. A girls' basketball season in these particular schools typically involved intramural matches, and near the end of the school year, an all-star team was selected. And what can an all-star team do other than play another school's all-star team?[27]

More extensive activity was found on the city's South Side, where four schools—Calumet, Bowen, Fenger, and Morgan Park—formed a league in 1923 and for four years played home and away games with each other, at least six games a season, for the "District Championship." Bowen High, for example, in 1925 played nine games, seven against public high schools

25. Marshall High girls' basketball team from 1925, when many Chicago school-girl teams engaged in interschool games, although such competition was ostensibly barred by the Chicago school authorities. Courtesy of the Chicago Public Library, Special Collections and Preservation Division, EGP 8/5.

and two against Catholic high schools, Longwood Academy and St. Xavier's Academy. The yearbook extolled interscholastic games, saying, "We invite our neighboring teams for practice and real games, having social good times, making new friendships and learning our shortcomings in the art of the game." These pieces of evidence indicate that there was a level of interschool girls' basketball competition not fully apparent to Chicago school authorities at the time.[28]

Rifle marksmanship was one other sport considered by Chicago school authorities to be acceptable for girls to compete against other schools. The meets were conducted two ways, either by actually meeting the school at a shooting gallery and tallying the scores or by shooting at one's home gallery and telegraphing the score to one's opponent. Although there was no league competition, Chicago-area schools competed against each other both ways and also competed in national tournaments sponsored by the National Rifle Association in Washington, DC. In 1925, for example, Waller High vied for a "national title" against Crosby High of Connecticut in a telegraphic meet. The girls and boys would sometimes compete in the same meet, as when the Chicago schools competed for both girls' and boys' titles at an outdoor exposition held at the Coliseum. Lake View High's Mary Ward garnered national fame in the mid-1920s as "Sure Shot Mary" for her perfect scores in high school contests while competing on the boys' team. Evanston High, north of the city, had a girls' team that competed in local, state, and national matches. The school's yearbook noted that the rifle meets "are the only chances the girls have for competition with other schools, and competition of this sort is always worthwhile and enjoyable."[29]

Some other sports featured interscholastic activity as well. The Parker High student newspaper of 1925 not only was filled with girls' interschool contests in tennis, golf, and swimming, but also had reports on its girls' baseball (meaning softball) and volleyball teams playing games against nearby Normal College. Harrison High formed a girls' speed-skating team with plans to compete against other high schools. By and large, however, the girls largely competed in interclass contests, which many girls considered a poor substitute for interschool contests. A Parker girl complained of the lack of participation of seniors in the annual interclass volleyball contests. Trying to put her finger on the reason, she noted, "Do our girls grow more individualistic as they grow to womanhood or is it the fault of the training? Girls trained in our public playgrounds are much more dependable—better sports." Thus, the competition that the educational establishment decried as being inimical to the essential nature of girls was not looked at the same way by at least one high school girl.[30]

By 1926 girls in the Chicago Public High School League were engaged in far more extensive interscholastic athletic activity than publicly recognized. The GAA, ironically, which had been established to provide the intramural alternative to the interscholastic model of competition, with its tremendous success in bringing girls sports competition, undoubtedly encouraged forays into interschool competition. In 1925 more than thirty thousand girls were involved in intramural sports in the Chicago schools. By 1926 Englewood saw a growth to more than one thousand girls and Lindblom to more than two thousand girls, one-third of the school population. Identification with one's graduating class as opposed to one's school has much less emotional pull, so that those girls who had a natural desire to compete, notwithstanding the educators' contrary views, were looking at nearby schools and saying, "We must determine who is best."[31]

INTERSCHOLASTIC SPORTS IN THE NORTHEAST

Both Detroit and Philadelphia sponsored interschool sports for girls in the 1920s. Whereas Detroit officially sponsored track and field, tennis, and golf, Philadelphia had a combination of officially sanctioned and unsanctioned interscholastic competition similar to the situation in Chicago. Beginning in 1921 with the launching of a track and field meet by three schools, a number of public high schools in the city and the suburbs within two years established a program of unsanctioned competition among themselves in field hockey (1922), baseball (1923), basketball (1923), and volleyball (1923). Leading schools in girls' interscholastic sports were Southern (South Philadelphia High for Girls), Frankfort, Germantown, and Swarthmore. As the Philadelphia Public League did not sponsor championships in any of these sports, the schools went ahead and formed their own leagues (as in baseball) and unofficially recognized champions with the best records (as in field hockey). Tennis, captain ball, and swimming were subsequently adopted by some of the schools. In 1924 the Germantown Fathers' Association introduced a cup to be awarded to the school that won the most girls' championships.[32] The Philadelphia Public League sponsored a championship only in one sport for girls, track and field, and beginning in 1922 annually conducted the Interscholastic Field Meet. As the meet was open to all Philadelphia public-school members, such schools as West Philadelphia and Girls' High School, which never participated in any other interscholastic sports for girls, entered teams. Thus, by the mid-1920s, girls competed in interscholastic sports (albeit moderately) in both Chicago and Philadelphia.[33]

NATIONAL AND STATE TOURNAMENTS

Controlling interscholastic basketball during the 1920s consumed much of the energies of the women's physical educational establishment, which had greater success in the universities and colleges than in the high schools in getting interschool competition banned. Nonetheless, in the 1920s, the high school game for girls was much more circumscribed than it had been a decade earlier. Only in certain areas of the country were girls playing the game by boys' rules, and in many places interscholastic competition was entirely banned. By 1925 ten states conducted state basketball tournaments for their high school girls. Two were in the East (Delaware and Connecticut), one in the Midwest (Iowa), and seven in the South (Virginia, South Carolina, Florida, Tennessee, Kentucky, Texas, and Oklahoma). In three other states—Pennsylvania, Nebraska, and Arkansas—the state associations regulated the sport. In ten other states, notably New York, New Jersey, Massachusetts, and Illinois, some communities sponsored interschool teams, often illegally. Girls' interscholastic basketball was being played in more than half the states, but it was now a three-court line game, involving six players, two each confined to each section of the court. In the 1924–1925 and 1925–1926 *Spalding* basketball guides, a survey of 1,600 schools was conducted on their participation and attitude regarding interscholastic competition for girls, and the results showed more than half of the schools voicing approval for such participation.[34]

Iowa at this time was the premier center for girls' basketball. In the first two decades of the twentieth century, the game mushroomed in the smallest towns of Iowa rather than the large cities, and by 1920 the Iowa High School Athletic Association (IHSAA) found there was enough interest to establish a state tournament for girls. A boys' tournament had been played since 1912, and in 1923 the IHSAA also took over sponsorship of the boys' tournament.[35]

Iowa was not immune from the debate over the role of women in athletics, and during 1924 and 1925 many Iowa educators, particularly from the schools in the larger cities, questioned whether girls should be engaged in interschool contests, let alone a state tournament series. After contentious debate over the issue at the 1925 meeting of the IHSAA, the majority of the 259 schools voted to eliminate girls' competition. This vote did not go down well with many rural administrators who highly prized their girl athletes and the enjoyment that they brought to their small towns. They also valued the game for all the traditional virtues that organized sports are thought to confer—healthful exercise, character building, and the development of social skills that come from performing with a team. One irate administrator at the IHSAA meeting before the fateful vote warned, "Gentlemen, if you attempt to do away with girls basketball in Iowa, you'll be standing in the center of the track where the train runs over!" That powerful train started up when four superintendents rebelled and set up the Iowa Girls High School Athletic Union for the express purpose of continuing the girls' tournament. In the first year of the tournament, 1926, 159 schools participated. The schools in the larger cities had dropped out of girls' interscholastic basketball, but the game continued to grow in the state, but largely among the small-town schools.[36]

Just north of Iowa, in Minnesota, girls were competing vigorously in basketball, but also in swimming. As in Iowa, girls' interscholastic sports predominated in the rural high schools, but not in Minneapolis or St. Paul, both of which had supported interscholastic girls' basketball before the war. The state did not sponsor a girls' state championship in basketball, but it supported a girls' state championship in swimming, beginning in 1924. Minnesota was the only state to have conducted such a tournament during the 1920s, and one of fewer than a handful that actually supported interscholastic swimming for high school girls. The hotbed of swimming in Minnesota was the iron-mining region in the northern part of the state, where taxes from the mines went to the construction of schools with elaborate athletic facilities, including swimming pools. As a result of this bounty, the region became a hotbed for swimming excellence in Minnesota as well as nationwide. Such schools as Hibbing and Chisholm produced national record holders and champions with their boys' teams and future Olympians with their girls' teams, notably Ann Govednik (who competed in the 1932 and 1936 Olympic Games).[37]

State basketball championships for girls were pioneered in three states in 1919—West Virginia, South Carolina, and Oklahoma. The West Virginia tournament was initiated by Spencer High, a small school in the west-central part of the state. West Virginia girls did not play the six-player three-court game, but played a more athletic two-court version with five players, with a roving center. The state tournament in its first year attracted ten teams, from both big cities and rural hamlets, and Spencer High lavished special treatment on the attending teams, holding a reception in the ballroom of the Spencer State Hospital for the Insane and a dance at the Spencer Country Club. The following year, twenty-five teams competed. By 1921 and 1922, Spencer was hosting thirty-four teams each year. The 1923 tournament was broken up into sectionals, and only twenty-four teams went to Spencer. When the host Spencer girls won the 1923 tournament, the local citizens, oblivious to amateur rules, lavished gifts and cash awards on the girls (each player received forty dollars). By 1924 the West Virginia High School Athletic Association was casting a leery eye on the tournament, which again featured twenty-four teams drawn from sectionals.[38]

As early as 1906, Texas high schools were fielding girls' basketball teams, whereby typically each year, competing claims for the titular state championship would be heard and occasional challenge matches played to settle them. Teams originally played line basketball, but by 1910 some teams loosened the game up by incorporated some men's rules. The

University Interscholastic League (UIL) was formed in 1912 to manage and sponsor high school athletics and by 1914 sponsored girls' basketball competition, as well as track and field, up to the county level. Later, tennis competition was added. Under pressure from female physical educators, however, the UIL in 1920 discontinued its support of girls' basketball and track, but elevated tennis competition to a state-level championship. Girls' high school basketball competition, however, continued vigorously, especially in rural areas. New sponsoring organizations arose to sponsor girls' basketball, and they soon had the girls competing regularly for the state championship. Texas prospered with many female AAU teams, and the high schools competed not only among themselves but also against AAU amateur squads and college teams, with teams at all levels receiving extensive press coverage.[39]

Kentucky was one of the exceptions to the use of line basketball. Residents of the largely rural state saw no problem with their farm girls playing by boys' rules. Because the state made no provision for public schools until 1908, Kentucky had been slow in adopting basketball. Around 1910 such schools as Paris, Somerset, and Maysville were playing basketball. As one historian put it, the girls in the state "took to basketball like a thoroughbred at the starting gate," and the game spread throughout the state. In 1917 the Kentucky High School Athletic Association (KHSAA) was formed, and the following year the organization started a boys' state tournament. In 1921 the KHSAA started the girls' tournament and had the girls playing by boys' rules. By the following year, fifty-one girls' teams participated. The small rural Kentucky communities felt pride over the basketball achievements of their girls and never gave a thought that they were playing under supposedly unsuitable boys' rules.[40]

Girls' interscholastic basketball also thrived in Tennessee. The game had developed such interest by the 1920s that an invitational state tournament was established in 1922 and conducted in Nashville. Unlike their Kentucky counterparts, the girls played the line game. In 1925 the Tennessee Secondary School Athletic Association was formed, and the following year the girls' tournament came under the aegis of that organization.[41]

Florida had a prospering state championship series during the 1920s. In the large cities such as Miami, girls competed only on an intramural basis, but interschool competition prospered in the rural schools. The annual championship was a huge event in the state's small communities, who boosted their hometowns by cheering on their girls' teams.[42]

In the separate segregated world of the South and border states, basketball for high school girls thrived in the black high schools. Throughout the 1920s, African American girls organized high school teams and played interschool games with other black high schools in their states and nearby black college teams. In Kentucky the girls' game was particularly popular, and like their counterparts in the white schools, the girls played under boys' rules. Attucks (Hopkinsville), Clinton (Frankfort), Dunbar (Lexington), and Central (Louisville) competed against each other as well as against the Kentucky Normal School. In Missouri and Kansas, such schools as Lincoln (Kansas City), Northeast (Kansas City), and Douglass (Columbia) played interscholastically and by boys' rules. In Texas, South Carolina, and Florida, which had interscholastic basketball programs for girls in the white high schools, the black schools similarly competed. The fewer black schools had less league organization and tended to have more colleges on their schedules. In the northern states, African American high school girls played for amateur teams, although they often got their training in their local high schools.[43]

In the New York–New Jersey area, the public schools in New York City since 1905 had denied interschool competition for girls. Many suburban schools took their cue from the big city and likewise abolished interschool competition, but a small number of suburban schools continued to engage in basketball competition, which by the mid-1920s was flourishing. They adapted to the changing trends, however, by switching to line basketball to make it more acceptable. Westchester County, Long Island, and New Jersey featured regular competition, including challenge matches for the state championship.[44]

In 1923, halfway across the continent in Oklahoma, Guthrie High, after winning the girls' state title, proceeded to play a series of challenge matches for the national championship. The school first traveled to Iowa to beat Audubon High in a three-game series, in a two-court game as opposed to the prevailing three-court game, and then swept the New York challenger, Croton High, in a series held in Guthrie. In response, in 1924, Westfield High of New Jersey, after claiming the eastern championship, offered a prize, the "Westfield Challenge Cup," for the winner of a series of games for the girls' national championship. Local businessmen put up two thousand dollars to pay travel expenses for the Guthrie girls to ensure their participation. The girls on their way east stopped in Washington, DC, to be introduced to President Calvin Coolidge, who called them a "robust group of girls." Arriving in New Jersey, Guthrie beat Westfield in a best-of-three series, followed by an exhibition staged for the Fox and Pathé News cameras.[45]

In 1925 the national championship became a tournament competition—the Girls National Interscholastic Basketball Tournament—and was held at Hempstead High, on Long Island. The following year, the tournament was moved to Youngstown, Ohio, home of Struthers High, the second-place team in 1925. The Ohio location, which required a long trip for the defending champion, Hempstead High, however, was too problematic for the school's educators. The principal denied the girls permission to participate in the tourney. He asserted, "I can't see any reason for barnstorming a group of little girls out to Ohio to play basketball under conditions I know nothing about. I wouldn't send my own daughter on such a trip as that I don't feel justified in sending anyone else's daughter." A petition was drawn up and submitted by a group of local businessmen requesting a reconsideration, but the principal remained adamant. From the area, a New Jersey school, Mount Holly, was chosen to participate in a nine-team field that included schools from Pennsylvania, Virginia, South Carolina, Tennessee, West Virginia, Kansas, and Ohio.[46]

In 1927 and 1928, the final two years of the tournament, the national championship was held in Wichita, Kansas, and most of the entries were drawn from western states—Kansas, Nebraska, Oklahoma, Wyoming, and Idaho. Despite being a hotbed of girls' basketball, Iowa did not send a team. Eastern entries came from West Virginia and Pennsylvania. The 1928 tournament was apparently the last for the Girls National Interscholastic. State and league championships continued to be contested in sports around the country, and in the New York–New Jersey area, girls' basketball continued to thrive, where league champions were regularly crowned.[47]

THE SUPPRESSION OF
INTERSCHOLASTIC COMPETITION

The termination of the girls' national basketball tournament after 1927 was a part of the overall trend toward ending women's interschool competition at all levels. The unrelenting campaign throughout the decade by women's physical educators to curb interscholastic and intercollegiate athletics ultimately bore fruit at the end of the decade. They attained their best success on the collegiate level, eliminating interschool competition in most areas of the country, except in the African American schools. The reformers had a more mixed success on the secondary-school level, whereby fourteen states discontinued their state basketball tournaments for girls during 1931–1939, but nine states in the South and Midwest continued to hold state tournaments. Two factors explain why reformers were able to abolish girls' interschool competition in basketball: the exploding popularity of boys' basketball and the rise of state high school associations. The growth in boys' basketball found many schools adding a lightweight class to their heavyweight program, or frosh-soph and junior-varsity levels to their varsity programs, and school authorities welcomed the freeing up of courts by the elimination of girls' programs. At the same time, the 1920s saw both a growth in state high school associations and a rise in the number of takeovers by state associations of girls' athletics, takeovers for the purpose of curtailing interschool activity.[48]

In West Virginia, for example, the West Virginia High School Athletic Association had grown in power so that it was able both to terminate the tournament sponsored by Spencer High and to force the girls to abandon their more athletic five-player game for the six-player three-court game. The West Virginia authorities believed that the tournament and the style of play were detrimental to the girls' health. The movement to abolish girls' basketball in the state continued to gain strength so that by the end of the decade, it had died out in West Virginia.[49]

The movement to suppress interschool competition met with tremendous success, and reformers in journals regularly ran reports in most triumphant tones on their latest victories, about such-and-such state discontinuing its girls' tournament. What the physical educators did not count on was the country girl and the supporting rural culture that appreciated the physical abilities of their high school girls. A 1928 survey published in the *School Review* on the northwestern states found a huge correlation between small schools and a high degree of girls' participation in interscholastic sports. In a range of six school sizes, the lowest, mostly rural schools of fifty to ninety-nine students, had an 83 percent participation rate; the highest, mostly city schools of five hundred to two thousand students, had a 33 percent participation rate, a result that could be extrapolated to apply to the entire country. The author of the survey report explained that "smaller communities, lacking in opportunities for diversion that are enjoyed by larger communities look to the schools as the source of community enterprise."[50]

Across the country, the rural communities provided the resolve and sustenance to preserve female competitive basketball in the high schools, including state championship competition. A 1927 survey in the *American Physical Education Review* found that more than half of the small-town schools favored interschool basketball contests extending beyond league and county, while the vast majority of the large town and city schools rejected such contests. Even in the South and Southwest, there were successes by the reformers, as in 1932, when Kentucky abolished its state tournament in favor of intramural basketball. But some states that had jumped on the reform bandwagon in abolishing their girls' state tournaments reversed themselves because of opposition from the schools, particularly the ones in rural areas, and in a few short years reintroduced their state competitions. For example, Oklahoma abolished its state tournament in 1933 but resumed it in 1934, and South Carolina abolished its tourney in 1931 only to revive it in 1933.[51]

In Chicago, a typical area of large urban high schools, the suppression of girls' basketball was complete by the late 1920s, the city schools having joined with their suburban counterparts in acquiescing to the reformers' intramural model. It came about as a result of the increased power of the state high school association, the IHSAA, which had been steadily growing with its sponsorship of the state basketball meet. In 1926 the association assumed cosponsorship with the University of Illinois of its annual track and field, tennis, and golf tournaments. Chicago schools, which were not members of the IHSAA, were now forced to join the organization if they wanted to continue to participate in those spring contests. In March 1926, the IHSAA took in new members Lake View, Schurz, Hyde Park, Tilden, Lindblom, and Englewood, among which were some of the biggest supporters of girls' competition in the city. Although it is unclear the extent to which the IHSAA forbade interscholastic competition—in theory it allowed archery, tennis, and golf—it is significant that after the Chicago schools joined the IHSAA, all official girls' interschool competition was terminated before the 1927 season. Chicago school authorities suppressed the illegal activities by cracking down on the underground volleyball and basketball games and barring the wearing of school colors in track competition.[52]

The suppression of interscholastic sports in Philadelphia, which began in 1924, was not abrupt as in Chicago but more gradual, and year by year schools dropped one sport after another under pressure from school authorities. For example, they first forced the girls to drop boys' rules in basketball for girls' rules and then followed with a ban on interschool competition altogether. In 1933, when Philadelphia ended the Interscholastic Track Meet, interschool sports for girls were essentially over in the city. In a curious departure from the rest of the nation, Philadelphia's suburban high schools, however, saw not only no decline in their interscholastic sports programs but a positive growth during the 1930s. The influence of the anticompetitive ideology of educators was felt, however, in the suburban schools' policy that games and meets must emphasize learning and instruction and that no league titles would be at stake. This demand did not prevent the girls, in their urge to compete, from making claims to unofficial championships.[53]

The physical education establishment across the land organized in the place of interschool competition their model of "democratic sport," namely, "play days." These competitions were bigger in the colleges than in the high schools, where it took hold primarily among the larger schools in the metropolitan areas. Athletes from different high schools would gather together either at a local college or at one of the attending high schools to compete in a particular sport, be it basketball, volleyball, field hockey, or track, or in a variety of sports. The players on the day of the meet would divide into mixed teams of players from several schools. Typically, each team would be designated with a color. By such means, the educators sought to diminish the competitive fire in sports contests that playing for one's school might engender. After the competition, the girls gathered to socialize and enjoy refreshments. For example, in 1929 150 girls representing twenty-six New Jersey secondary schools met at the New Jersey College for Women and competed in basketball, baseball, relay running, volleyball, and track competition. The girls were divided into six teams of yellow, blue, green, orange, purple, and red. In between the competition, college girls gave exhibitions of riding, soccer, and archery.[54]

The ILGAA, like its counterparts in the East, initiated a vigorous promotion of "play days" in the late 1920s. And in tune with the anticompetitive philosophy behind play days, the Illinois High School Athletic Association head, Charles W. Whitten, enthused over their merits, "The spirit of play and cooperation is practiced throughout. . . . [N]o special consideration, honors, or awards are given to 'star' players, and all attempts to promote commercialism or exhibitionism are discouraged or prohibited."[55]

In the Chicago area, play days for girls took firmer root in the suburbs than in the city, becoming common among the suburban North Shore public and private schools by 1926. That year Roycemore, an Evanston private school, hosted a field-hockey play day to invitees Evanston High and two private schools, Chicago Latin and North Shore Country Day, and Evanston played host for a "basketball carnival" that included sixty girls from New Trier, Roycemore, and North Shore Country Day. After both events, refreshments were served and a dance held. In 1927 New Trier for the same schools hosted a "splash party," involving some

26. Illinois play-day baseball (softball) game, 1932, when almost all girls' inter-school contests had been banned in favor of play days, which lessened competitiveness by ending contests that represented schools. Courtesy of the Illinois High School Association.

twenty girls. The Evanston reporter commented on the event, a bit wistfully, "Although girls are not allowed to hold interscholastic contests in Illinois, they may have parties." In 1928 the Women's Athletic Association of Northwestern University hosted an athletic field day in track and swim for Senn, Deerfield, New Trier, Evanston, and Roycemore. The ILGAA began sponsoring play days in 1928, with five play days, involving fifty schools and four hundred girls the first year, and fourteen play days, involving sixty-six schools and twelve hundred girls, the following year. The ILGAA itself directly conducted two annually, in the fall and in the spring.[56]

Another alternative to interscholastic competition offered up by the physical education reformers was the telegraphic or postal meet. The concept had been used for decades in both boys' and girls' rifle meets, where schools on a given day would report their results via telegraph or by mail. In rifle the results were shooting scores, but as extended to other sports, it was free-throw shooting percentage in basketball, racing times in swimming and track, distance and height measurements in track, and

27. Illinois Girls' Athletic Association member competing in archery, 1932, after the Illinois High School Athletic Association ended interschool competitions and turned them into postal contests. Courtesy of the Illinois High School Association.

final scores in bowling. By having the girls represent their schools in such competition, the reformers believed they could satisfy the girls' desire to compete by comparing athletic records, but without the face-to-face competition that could lead to excessive physical intensity and aggressiveness. In 1928, in Illinois, the ILGAA introduced a postal basketball shooting tournament, involving seventy-six schools the first year, and in later years added bowling and archery.[57]

The reformers won the cultural war of the 1920s and the battle for control. Most triumphant was their conception of what constituted good character and good sportsmanship in the high school athletic female of the 1920s. That conception was a girl who enjoyed modest interclass competition for the mere enjoyment of the game and did not strive for championships and victories. She did not play in front of screaming crowds, making a "spectacle" of herself. Nor did she play like a boy, using boys' rules and competing at boys' levels, and instead played under moderate standards designed for girls. In a minority of high school programs, notably in rural areas, girls participated in interschool competition in front of townspeople who believed their participation was just as character building as boys' interscholastics.

By the end of the 1920s, interscholastic sports for girls were thus in retrenchment, as most of the girls' competitive programs that dotted the country only a few years earlier had been eliminated, and many state tournaments in basketball had been discontinued. With the onset of the Depression, high school programs facing greater budgetary constrictions curtailed sports sponsorship overall, further reducing girls' programs. Not until the early 1970s, with a resurgence of interscholastic sports for girls across the land, would the American girl finally enjoy a full opportunity for participation in high school sports competition, something that she had tasted a bit of in the 1920s, only to have it cruelly taken away.

13

THE SEPARATE AND UNEQUAL
WORLD OF AFRICAN AMERICAN
INTERSCHOLASTIC SPORTS

African American high school sports came to fruition during the 1920s. The experience of African Americans in the creation of interscholastic sports was varied, depending on the section of the country. In the Deep South, black high schools suffered from rigid segregation and a white establishment that kept the black schools impoverished. Those schools lacked athletic facilities, and the development of high school athletics in the black schools in such states as Mississippi, Alabama, and Georgia lagged far behind white schools in the South and their black counterparts in other parts of the country. In the border regions—such as the District of Columbia, Missouri, and Kansas—segregation was still a fact, but economic support for the black schools was far superior than in the Deep South, and interscholastic sports thrived in those areas in the 1920s. In the northern and western states, although the black population had a continual struggle against social segregation and discrimination, their young men and women who attended integrated schools, notably in Chicago and New York, had the opportunity to experience interscholastic sports on predominantly white teams. Also, northern predominantly black schools (through de facto segregation) had the opportunity to compete against predominantly white schools.

As in the mainstream educational establishment, African American educators sought to provide interscholastic sports for much the same reasons, as a means of building physical health and vitality, building strength of character, and understanding American democratic values, at least in their ideal conception. And with adult supervision, they would play in an environment free of professionalism, rowdyism, and corruption. But in a dimension not faced by their white counterparts, black educators also wanted to build the mental and physical strength of Africa American youth to be able to hold themselves up in the world (that is, "moral stamina"), where they could handle everyday impediments, slights, and hostilities from a prejudicial and discriminatory white society.[1]

THE AFRICAN AMERICAN EXPERIENCE IN THE NORTH

A look at the experience of black schools in Illinois captures both the northern and the border-state experience. Illinois is commonly considered a northern state. It is also an extremely long one that extends four hundred miles south from the Wisconsin border to the Ohio River, as deep into the South as southern Kentucky and southern Virginia. Illinois, like the rest of America in the 1920s, was hardly a nirvana for blacks, but compared to the South, its treatment of blacks was relatively enlightened and democratic. In most of the state, integration prevailed in the public schools, and the African American youth enjoyed opportunities to participate in the extracurriculum, although it should be recognized that a large proportion of blacks of high school age were not in school. For many black students, the law was not always there to ensure equal opportunity, and they faced social barriers that prevented them from enjoying the full benefits of high school sports. However, in the far-southern part of the state, known as Egypt—with such town names as Cairo, Dongola, and Karnak—legal segregation prevailed, and African American high schools students were forced to compete only on all-black athletic teams and against other black teams. As with other border states, the African American schools in Egypt developed viable athletic programs.

Chicago's first public secondary school—Chicago High School—was formally integrated in 1861, when, after a bitter division, the Chicago School Board voted to accept a black student into the school. At the time, there was pervasive discrimination throughout the state that kept African American children out of the public schools. In 1872 Illinois enacted a free-school law that made the school board responsible for providing a sufficient number of free schools for "all" children and the "right and opportunity to an equal education in all such free schools." On the other hand, the new legislation empowered the school board to "assign" pupils to several schools in their districts, thereby giving them the freedom to set up segregated schools. In Egypt this isolation is exactly what transpired, as all the schools there became as rigidly segregated as any in the Deep South. Elsewhere in the state, there was a vast reduction in instances of blacks being excluded from the public schools following 1874 legislation putting a bit more teeth in the law against educational discrimination.[2]

CHICAGO'S PHILLIPS HIGH COMPETES IN THE NORTH AND SOUTH

Black prominence in Chicago high school athletics dates back to around the turn of the century. In 1901 the first Cook County League championship basketball team, Hyde Park, featured an outstanding black athlete, Sam Ransom, who subsequently led his school to a national football championship and league baseball titles. The school sometimes had to face teams that demanded Ransom be taken out of the lineup. Hyde Park, as did other Chicago schools, to their credit, denied such requests and would instead cancel games.[3]

With the advent of World War I, Chicago, like many northern cities, experienced the first wave of the "Great Migration," where tens of thousands of blacks migrated north from the rural, segregated South to enjoy the thriving job opportunities opened up by the war boom. Between 1916 and 1919, some fifty thousand blacks moved to Chicago, creating two large settlements on the South and West Sides. Phillips High, on the South Side, was impacted by this migration, being transformed from a virtually all-white school to one that was two-thirds black by 1917. Racial conflict boiled up in the high school and in the city, and during 1917–1921 there were fifty-eight racially motivated bombings in the city. In 1919 Chicago experienced one of the worst race riots in the history of the North.[4]

By 1922 Phillips was virtually 100 percent black, and the city's newspapers routinely began referring to its athletic teams as "all-colored," as

28. Hyde Park High baseball team, 1903, in which the presence of an African American player, Sam Ransom, as the captain of the team proved that in Chicago and most northern cities, African Americans were not barred from competition by a color line. Courtesy of the Chicago History Museum.

they regularly referred to the individual black athletes by their color. In basketball Phillips achieved particular prominence and produced many highly talented basketball players who later achieved fame with college and professional teams. The school's football teams were not as successful as its basketball teams, but the *Chicago Defender* regularly championed Phillips's teams and individuals in all sports as being representative of racial achievement.[5]

In the 1920s and 1930s, most high school programs were not divided into varsity and frosh-soph divisions but rather into heavyweight and lightweight divisions. By 1922, when the Phillips heavyweight team won the Central Division title in the Chicago Public High School League, the *Chicago Defender* had "adopted" Phillips as the black community's high school. Thereafter, as Phillips High went from success to success during the decade, the newspaper's headlines got higher, the stories grew longer, and the photos ballooned larger. Phillips's emergence as a black school, however, brought a degree of social conflict at the games with the white schools. Racially motivated slights and injustices directed at the Phillips teams and fans did not go unnoticed by the *Defender*. In March 1923, for example, the paper decried the officiating that allowed Marshall to win a close game against Phillips by repeatedly fouling Phillips players most blatantly, "souring the fair-minded public." The paper's readers knew what "public" was being referred to; the subtext of racial bias did not need to be articulated. In 1923 a new tradition was added, an annual banquet given to the Phillips basketball teams by the *Defender*. Businessmen, professional people, and representatives of various black clubs, the YMCA, and fraternal organizations all attended to show their solidarity to their basketball representatives in the Chicago school league.[6]

The Phillips heavyweight team of 1924 received extensive coverage by the *Defender*, which believed that the team was destined to win the city championship. Much to the community's dismay, this richly talented Phillips team was smashed by Lane Tech, 18–4. Phillips that year started a new tradition of playing a postseason game with a notable African American school from a distant city. The team in late March went down to Kansas City, Missouri, to play Lincoln High. Then in late April, the team traveled to Washington, DC, and played Armstrong High.[7]

The often present racial tension boiled over during the 1925 season, with clashes erupting at heavyweight games against Lindblom and Hyde Park. League authorities punished Phillips for these outbreaks, and just prior to the playoffs in February 1925, the school was forced to withdraw its team from further competition. Phillips resorted to completing the season in the segregated black basketball world. The *Chicago Defender* sponsored a trip by Armstrong High from DC to play Phillips. The game drew forty-five hundred fans, and the fifty-five box seats at the Eighth Regiment Armory were filled with the "elite of Chicago's social and business world." Phillips brought in its fifty-four-member band as well as its booster orchestra. The *Defender* devoted two pages of its broadsheet to cover the game, including a separate article on what members of society came to watch the game. The contest was a huge event in the black

29. Phillips High heavyweight basketball team, 1925, when it represented Chicago's black community in competition against white high school teams in the city and against black schools nationwide. Courtesy of the Archives, Chicago Board of Education.

community, but mainstream newspapers only minimally mentioned the contest.[8]

The commercial world of professional athletics was an enticement that occasionally brought trouble to the school's program. The 1925 heavyweight team saw two members, Tommy Brookins and Randolph Ramsey, enticed to go professional by the Eighth Regiment semipro team, located only blocks from the high school. The 1927 team was forced to forfeit its games because of an overage player, but would have had to forfeit its games anyway for playing a semipro team in Cleveland, Ohio, during the season.[9]

A Chicago public high school championship finally came to Phillips in 1928, when its lightweight team destroyed a fine Harrison team to win the title. The team, typically, experienced at least one disturbance at one of its games, involving Hyde Park, when students poured out of the stands in a melee after Phillips's star player, Al "Runt" Pullins, squared off against a Hyde Park player. The first all-black championship team opened a lot of eyes in the city. Said a *Chicago Tribune* reporter, "Speed that was dazzling, accurate shooting that was almost amazing, and a stout defense that thwarted Harrison . . . Phillips, with its quintet of rangy fast players, is easily the best lightweight team the city league has had for several years." Pullins eventually became a founding member of the legendary Harlem Globetrotters. In January 1929, Abe Saperstein formed the Harlem Globetrotters, using mostly ex-Phillips players.[10]

The first black team to win the heavyweight title was the Phillips squad of 1930, defeating Morgan Park High. According to the *Tribune*, the Phillips team had been the "favorite for the title since the opening of the schedule" two months earlier. The *Chicago Defender*, in its extensive coverage of this breakthrough for the black community, publicly asked Amos Alonzo Stagg to invite Phillips to its national interscholastic tourney. In 1930 the biggest postseason tourney in Chicago was not the state tournament, which was largely a tournament of downstate schools, but Stagg's national tournament at the University of Chicago. Every year in the Stagg tourney, the public-league champion was an automatic entry—that is, until 1930, when the color line reared its ugly head. Morgan Park received the invitation that should have gone to Phillips. The Stagg tourney in 1930 was facing increasing resistance from educators, and many states, especially from the North, refused to send their champions. The southern states were still eager participants, and barring Phillips was an obvious but reprehensible way to keep the tourney alive. The *Defender* pointed this out, saying that "the university athletic department had bowed to the will of the ex-Confederates and their offspring."[11]

In 1931 the Phillips heavyweights were rated to repeat their public-league championship. In the title game, however, Phillips met an insurmountable barrier—six-foot-eight center and future Hall of Famer Robert Gruenig of Crane Tech. At this time, the center jump was still employed after each basket, and Gruenig won every one of them, and Crane prevailed. Phillips gained a bit of consolation for their loss of the public-league title by entering again the separate world of black interscholastic sports, when on March 21 at Hampton, Virginia, they won the championship of the national black invitational, called the National Interscholastic Basketball Tournament.[12]

Phillips's football program, like its basketball program, during the regular season would participate in the white world, but in postseason play, it had to enter the segregated black world. In the 1920s, it was customary for winning schools at the end of the regular football season to engage an opponent in another state or another section of the country. Phillips was forced to find all of its postseason opponents among the segregated schools in the border or southern states. In 1925 the school began an annual Thanksgiving-game contest against Louisville Central (a black school). The following year, Phillips played two Kentucky opponents, Louisville Central again, on Thanksgiving Day, and Owensboro Western Colored, two days later.[13]

In 1927 Phillips was reminded why it needed to seek out opponents among its fellow black schools in the South. During a scrimmage practice against the Hyde Park team, a fight broke out between members of the two squads, and then it spread to the spectators. The fight, which was broken up with police fire hoses, made it over the Associated Press wires, which reported that six persons were injured and noted that "even knives were used." Postseason games continued through the 1930s and 1940s, and Phillips traveled to Louisville, Memphis, Kansas City, and Tulsa. In 1933 Phillips's postseason game with Booker T. Washington of Tulsa was considered an event even among its white population. The *Tulsa World* pointedly noted that the game drew a crowd that consisted of "3,000 white customers and the well-filled colored section." In league competition, Phillips also competed in tennis and baseball, and the *Defender* dutifully covered all their achievements. In 1927 the school's baseball team received considerable attention when it reached the league's championship game, only to lose the title to Lane Tech.[14]

The *Chicago Defender* and other black papers not only extolled the athletic achievements of the predominantly African American schools, but also called attention to the achievements of black athletes from predominantly white schools. For example, the *Defender* excitingly reported on the exploits of Eugene Beatty of Detroit's Northeastern High at the Northwestern University national indoor track meet, where he won the most points to win individual honors. The reporter noted that the Froebel team of Gary, Indiana, won the meet "with nine of our boys." Because the paper had a national readership, it often featured profiles of athletes and teams from other states, such as the piece on Gus Moore, who won the New York PSAL cross-country title in 1925, and a basketball story headlined "Race Boys Shine in Cage Tourney Held in Denver," in 1935.[15]

The *Defender* reports on the achievements of wrestlers reveal a surprising aspect on race relations. Whereas northern schools were racially tolerant of team sports and noncontact individual sports, they tended to be more sensitive to individual sports where there was a lot of physical contact, namely, wrestling and swimming (contact being the sharing of water). Yet the Chicago public schools competed in an integrated environment. The *Defender,* for example, in 1927, reported on the achievements of wrestler Modest Ferrell, who as a member of the Tilden Tech team placed third in the public schools' league championship that year.

30. Phillips High baseball team, 1924, which could compete against white and integrated teams in Chicago, in contrast to Major League Baseball, where African Americans were excluded. Courtesy of the Archives, Chicago Board of Education.

In contrast to public schools' tolerance, the University of Chicago several years later barred a Tilden High black wrestler from its high school meet.[16]

SOUTHERN ILLINOIS SCHOOLS
AND THE BORDER-STATE EXPERIENCE

The border states are where we find the origin of interscholastic sports for black high schools, namely, West Virginia, Virginia, Kentucky, Missouri, and Kansas, as well as in Washington, DC, and southern Illinois. In this section of the country, where de jure segregation existed, black high school teams were barred from competing against white schools and denied membership in state interscholastic associations and participation in those associations' state meets. The border states were particularly well suited to pioneering black interscholastic competition, and understanding that history helps to explain the experience of the southern Illinois black schools.

The border states presented certain advantages to African American high schools over the Deep South. According to black sports historian Charles Herbert Thompson, these border areas were able to better finance their schools, supporting black high schools with designated taxes from the black population. He noted that as "residential compositions" changed, many border black high schools inherited superior structures with more athletic facilities. Thompson placed the locus for the first interscholastic organization of black high schools in the Washington, DC, area. High school sports developed there because of the high concentration of African Americans in the area (more than a quarter million in a fifty-mile radius counted in the 1910 census), plus a favorable tax situation, in which a law passed by Congress in 1862 required that 10 percent of all taxes paid by blacks in the District of Columbia go to black schools. Thompson saw the number of schools, their proximity to each other, and their better facilities as collectively conducive for development of an interscholastic organization.[17]

The formation of a league in the DC area was preceded by several years of informal competition. M Street High (later called Dunbar) played baseball and football before 1900 and around 1901 inaugurated the first track competition. In 1901 football competition included Colored High (later called Douglass) and Morgan College Preparatory, both in Baltimore, in addition to M Street. In baseball Wiley Bates (Annapolis), Morgan Preparatory, and M Street High competed.[18]

In 1906 six black educators in the District of Columbia formed the Inter-Scholastic Athletic Association of the Middle States to bring together African American students into athletic competition. The organization was the brainchild of Edwin Bancroft Henderson, who had joined the DC school district in 1904 as its first African American physical education instructor. Notwithstanding the organization's name, Henderson and his colleagues created a broader organization to include African American colleges along with local high schools, plus affiliated athletic clubs. Henderson envisioned the association as a means to provide training and opportunity for black Americans, especially high school students, with the idea that African Americans could break down segregation barriers by their athletic achievements. But the development of character through sports was also on the founders' minds, seeing athletics as a means toward "improvement of the youth, physically, mentally and morally."[19]

The inaugural competition was a track and field meet, held on Memorial Day in 1906. In the 1907–1908 season, the league added basketball competition. The initial league grouping consisted of eight teams—Howard Medical, Howard College, Crescent Athletic Club, Oberlin Athletic Club, LaDroit Park, and the three secondary schools of Armstrong, M Street, and Howard Academy. Colored High of Baltimore and Commercial High of DC later joined the league. Other sports added to the league schedule were baseball and football. In 1910 the Interscholastic League canceled its league format and became a sanctioning body.[20]

In December 1910, Henderson founded the first all–high school league in DC with the formation of the Public Schools Athletic League. The PSAL was modeled after the New York PSAL in that it encompassed both the District's high schools and its elementary schools and was designed not only to provide a competitive framework, but also to improve physical fitness for all the District's children, boys and girls. By 1911 the league was organized into eight grammar schools and four high schools (two outside the District). The league conducted competition in basketball, football, baseball, and indoor and outdoor track and field. By the 1920s, the high school league was called the Interstate High School Association and included schools from DC, Baltimore, and Virginia. This league was supplanted by the South Atlantic High School Association in 1930.[21]

The next major athletic association of black high schools arose in West Virginia, where in 1925 the West Virginia Colored High School Athletic Union was formed among African American schools of the state. The league was launched with a basketball tournament, which drew eleven of the state's twenty-four black high schools. This number increased to seventeen by 1927 and twenty-two by 1930. Notable high schools in the conference included Kelly Miller (Clarksburg), Genoa (Bluefield), and Douglass (Huntington). The schools also competed among themselves in baseball but not in a regular league schedule. In 1933 the union added an annual track and field meet.[22]

Missouri and Kansas are typical border states, with a history of segregated school systems but a bit more enlightenment in terms of race relations. That history meant the schools received sufficient support to provide robust athletic opportunities for their students, and they could compete occasionally against white high school teams. The Missouri Valley Interscholastic Athletic Association (MVIAA) was formed in 1918 among African American schools of Kansas and Missouri. The initial membership included six schools, three from Missouri and three from Kansas. In basketball the MVIAA pioneered league competition for both boys and girls. On the eastern side of the state was the Mississippi Valley Interscholastic Athletic Association, founded in the 1920s to provide athletic competition among the segregated schools in the St. Louis area of Missouri and Illinois.[23]

Illinois and Indiana shared the dubious distinction of being the only two northern states that had legal segregation in the schools, and the black schools in southern Illinois and throughout Indiana were forced to establish their own state organizations, Illinois in 1919 and Indiana in 1920. Indiana had a statewide organization, but in Illinois, around fifteen black schools in Egypt organized, forming the Southern Illinois Conference of Colored High Schools. The schools had played basketball and other sports since before World War I and, being excluded from competition with the white schools and their leagues, saw the need to get together to regulate the sports and award championships. Basketball was the first sport contested, but the first postseason tournament was not staged until 1925. In 1922 the league initiated an annual track and field meet.[24]

The Southern Illinois Conference schools were not initially members of the Illinois High School Athletic Association, but in 1928 they adopted the eligibility rules and conditions of competition as established by the association, and in return the association furnished the conference with team trophies and individual awards for the league's basketball and track and field competitions. In November 1928, the IHSAA Board of Control voted to admit schools of the Southern Illinois Conference to membership in the state association.[25]

Although members, the Southern Illinois Conference schools were not allowed to enter the IHSAA-sponsored state basketball tournament, and during the 1930s they were forced to find end-of-season championship competitions in various tournaments sponsored by black colleges. In 1940 Egypt's black schools petitioned the Illinois High School Association (IHSA, as it was then known) for seventy-five dollars to pay for a trip of their league champion to a national basketball tournament conducted by Tuskegee. The following year, however, the IHSA turned down the Southern Illinois Conference petition for funds, as the organization had always disapproved of intersectional contests. The state association no doubt realized that it put Egypt's segregated schools in an unfair situation, both denying them entrance into the Illinois state tournament and keeping them from playing in black end-of-season tournaments. In 1946 the IHSA brought the Southern Illinois Conference schools into the state tournament, where they competed in the border regions of Egypt (but not deep in Egypt), and in 1954 the IHSA finally ended all segregated competition, forcing full integration in the state tournament within Egypt.[26]

AFRICAN AMERICAN SCHOOLS SPONSOR INTERSCHOLASTIC TOURNAMENTS

African American colleges in the border states were naturally aware of the plethora of interscholastic tournaments sponsored by the major universities. Although many of the northern predominantly black schools participated in university-sponsored track tournaments, most of the all-black schools were barred from such participation, notably the schools in the border states. Several Negro colleges in the 1920s, notably Howard University and Hampton Institute, began sponsoring interscholastic meets, first in track and field and later in basketball. Howard University inaugurated an annual interscholastic track and field meet in 1920 at the same time it began its intercollegiate meet for Negro colleges. The meet attracted only eastern schools, from New Jersey, DC, Maryland, and Virginia. Within a few years, the meet was overshadowed by the larger and more prestigious Hampton interscholastic meets.[27]

In 1922 the Hampton Institute inaugurated its new athletic field with a combination intercollegiate and interscholastic track meet. The meet was the brainchild of the physical education director, Charles H. Williams. The high school meet, along with the intercollegiate meet, grew slowly at first, attracting only a handful of schools, but by the mid-1920s, the meet took off, becoming the preeminent track and field invitational for black high schools. In 1925 schools from North Carolina and South Carolina joined the usual entries from DC, Virginia, Maryland, and New Jersey. By 1926 the feature event for the high schools was the "National High School Mile Relay," which naturally was a black event only.[28]

While the eastern African American schools in the border states had a large venue in the annual Hampton Institute interscholastic, the midwestern border states had no comparable track meet until Lincoln University of Jefferson City, Missouri, established the Middle Western Interscholastic in 1930. This May meet attracted segregated black schools in the border states—mainly Missouri, Kansas, and southern Illinois—and the socially and legally segregated black schools in the northern cities, notably Detroit and Gary. The number of entries grew so large by 1931 that Lincoln University divided the meet into large- and small-school classes. Also in 1931, Lincoln sponsored its first interscholastic tennis tournament for black schools and in 1933 initiated a midwestern tournament in basketball, inviting schools from Illinois, Missouri, Kansas, and Oklahoma.[29]

The Tuskegee Relays was established by the Tuskegee Institute, in Alabama, in 1927. The meet featured individual and relay-team championships in events for colleges, high schools, and girls. In the 1929 meet, for example, twelve high schools participated, and relay events for the high school teams were held in the quarter-mile, half-mile, 2-mile, and medley relay. The girls' events—100-yard dash and quarter-mile relay—were opened to both high school and college girls.[30]

In basketball the premier showcase for African American schools was initially the National Interscholastic Basketball Tournament (NIBT), founded in 1929 by Charles E. Williams at Hampton. The racial-exclusion policies at the University of Chicago and other university-sponsored basketball tournaments forced the African American community to develop its own national tournament to give recognition to schools with predominantly black student bodies. The first year's tournament drew only ten teams, all from the Eastern Seaboard, coming from DC, North Carolina, Virginia, and West Virginia, but strangely not Maryland.[31]

The following year, the tournament drew a larger and more far-flung field, drawing teams from Florida, South Carolina, and Kentucky. The tournament became more national in scope in 1931, when Phillips from Chicago and Roosevelt from Gary participated, drawing in all fifteen teams from six states and the District of Columbia. The NIBT was the catalyst that produced other basketball invitationals for black schools. Beginning in 1928, for example, the Morehouse College Athletic Association sponsored an annual state meet of all Georgia black high schools.[32]

STATE ASSOCIATION FORMATION AND TOURNAMENTS IN THE 1930S

By the early 1930s, university-sponsored high school tournaments were no longer the norm. The National Federation of State High School Athletic Associations had almost totally abolished such tournaments—particularly in basketball—but in black sports the story was slightly different, where some college-sponsored meets continued to thrive. Black schools in all the border states and upper South had formed state associations by the early 1930s. The African American schools in Virginia organized a statewide association in 1928, and in North Carolina, the black schools under the leadership of W. T. "Army" Armstrong, of Fayetteville State College, organized a state league the following year. Tennessee formed its first statewide organization in 1934 to conduct state tournaments in basketball for both boys and girls. African American schools in Texas formed a state association in 1928, but not a lasting one until 1938. In Oklahoma the black schools—most all named after Booker T. Washington—formed a statewide interscholastic association in 1931. In the Deep South, the development of associations was slower, generally from the mid-1930s to the late 1940s.[33]

The development of interscholastic sports in Kentucky is instructive of the challenges that African American schools in the South faced in forming interscholastic associations. The experience in Kentucky was less like the one of the border states and more like a typical southern state in that it provided a low level of support in its segregated system. Most of the state's growth in black high schools occurred only after World War I, and many were only two-year institutions. Such schools were able to provide interscholastic sports programs only after their conversion to four-year institutions during the late 1920s and early 1930s. Support from the state and local governments was anemic for black schools, and most were direly impoverished and small, without gymnasiums and other sport facilities. At many of the schools, basketball was played on an outdoor gravel-surface area. Only a handful of the schools could support a football team. Kentucky black schools received considerable support from northern philanthropy, notably from Julius Rosenwald, the head of Sears, Roebuck, who during the 1920s contributed to the construction of fifty-three hundred schools, shops, and teachers' homes in black areas of the southern states. Local blacks contributed 17 percent to the cause, and local white officials were shamed into providing 64 percent from public funds. At least five Kentucky high schools serving an African American population were named after the famed philanthropist.[34]

As of the mid-1920s, fewer than twenty black high schools in Kentucky were competing against one another, but during the late 1920s and early 1930s, an additional thirty schools were soon engaged in sports competition. This rapid increase in numbers was owing to growth in support of education for blacks that resulted in the founding of many new high

schools, increased enrollments, the change from two-year to four-year programs, and the increased facilities afforded the schools, much of it because
of Rosenwald support. As a result, in 1932 leading African American educators in the state formed the Kentucky High School Athletic League.
Membership was limited to only four-year schools, and approximately fifty
joined in the first years, eventually reaching a high of sixty-nine.[35]

The league regulated competition in three sports—basketball, football, and track and field. The only state championship sponsored by the
Kentucky league, however, was the annual basketball tournaments for
boys, held at the Kentucky State College in Frankfort. Girls' basketball
was not supported by the Kentucky league, but the schools sponsoring
girls' teams would sometimes compete for a state championship. The
league also sponsored football competition, but few schools participated.
This pattern of development of interscholastics in Kentucky was replicated
throughout the South during the 1920s and 1930s.[36]

In the border states of the Midwest, the midwestern meets in track,
tennis, and basketball, sponsored by Lincoln University, in Jefferson City,
Missouri, gave way to state meets in the area. In 1933 all the Missouri
schools came together to form the Missouri State Negro Interscholastic
Athletic Association, which held track and basketball tournaments at Lincoln University. In the troubled National Interscholastic Basketball Tournament, the 1932 meet was canceled, but revived in 1933. The Depression
years impinged on the finances of Hampton, and the institution had to
give up the tournament, so that in 1934 and 1935, tournament sponsorship
was assumed by Roosevelt High of Gary, Indiana, and after several shifts
in sponsorship, the last tournament was held in 1942 in Durham, North
Carolina.[37]

Meanwhile, the Tuskegee Institute in 1935 augmented its national track
and field meet for girls and boys with a basketball tournament in which
there were separate competitions for boys and girls. The initial meet drew
ten boys' teams and six girls' teams. The tournament was at first called the
Southern Interscholastic Basketball Tournament (SIBT), but beginning
in 1937 it grew more national in scope. With the decline of the NIBT,
the SIBT changed its name to the National Invitational Interscholastic

Basketball Tournament in 1941. The tournament remained at Tuskegee one more year before travel restrictions during World War II ended it. The National Invitational was revived in 1945 in Nashville. The prosperity of the Tuskegee Institute meets in both track and field and basketball was partly owing to the fact that the Deep South schools were slow in developing their own state groups and depended on Tuskegee to provide venues for competition. Tuskegee did much to bring these schools into interscholastic competition and to help them catch up with the schools in other areas.[38]

In 1934, when the NIBT came under sponsorship of Roosevelt High of Gary, Indiana, the organizers formed the National Interscholastic Athletic Association (NIAA). Their intention was to create an equivalent to the National Federation of State High School Athletic Associations, as its aim was to serve as a national governing body representing all sports and composed of all black state associations. The NIAA, however, never became an all-embracing national organization as envisioned by its founders, and it ended after the last NIBT was staged in 1942.[39]

African American schools from the country's discriminatory and segregated practices were forced to create their own separate interscholastic sports competitions, which from a combination of lesser resources and an underdeveloped educational system trailed the creation of interscholastic sports in mainstream society. In both the North and the South, the African American community nonetheless succeeded in creating a separate world of interscholastic competition for both its boys and its girls that sought to give their children, as best their resources would allow, some of the same experiences furnished to white high school students in mainstream schools, providing the requisite school programs, league championships, state championships, and national championships. The initiatives to provide sports programs also paralleled the mainstream world by establishing controls by educators, who saw their responsibilities as cleaning up unsupervised sports and preparing the moral and ethical foundation for uplifting their youth that would give them the strength of character to compete in the wider white world. African American interscholastic sports were mostly separate and mostly not equal, but they were something they could look on with pride. In the 1930s, few African Americans could even hope of a world in which interscholastic sports were conducted without regard to the color of one's skin, but that world would be partly achieved several decades later.

14

NEW NATIONAL GOVERNANCE AND THE TRIUMPH OF THE STATE HIGH SCHOOL ASSOCIATIONS

The great expansion of interscholastic sports into a national scope during the 1920s was exhilarating to many fans of sports and helped immensely in making high school sports a major audience draw during the decade. But like the overheated economy of the 1920s, it was set to crash just like the stock market of October 1929. The crash for national tournaments came the following year, fueled by several years of opposition that had been building to a boil from high school educators who saw the increasing aggrandizement and commercialization of high school sports as eroding the educational and character-building mission of high school sports. In 1927 Charles W. Whitten of Illinois became secretary-treasurer of the fast-rising National Federation of State High School Athletic Associations, headquartered in Chicago. He launched a relentless campaign that would dramatically change the governance of interscholastic sports in the next several years. The high school athletic world would soon come to reflect the assertion of authority by secondary-school administrators as they moved in their final search for control to place high school interscholastic competition into a realm deemed appropriate to the overall mission of the secondary-school educational system.

The system that had existed since the early 1900s—where colleges and universities took the responsibility of sponsoring many high school contests, particularly in swimming, track and field, and tennis—would soon come apart. The foundation for this change was the emergence of state athletic associations and their coming together in a national organization. Most of these state associations were built in sponsorship of basketball tournaments, but their aim was to take control of all high school sports and expel the universities and colleges out of the high school athletics business.

The growth of state associations had been steady the previous two decades. By 1920 all the states in the Midwest had organizations that sponsored and governed interscholastic athletics. The colleges and universities at this time, as was abundantly evident, were vigorously sponsoring interscholastic contests in such sports as basketball, track and field, swimming, golf, and tennis, and their involvement was growing year by year toward a more commercial approach, one that was becoming larger and more national in scope. The members of the state associations (educators in the schools) were looking at these developments with increasing displeasure. At this time, L. W. Smith of the Illinois High School Athletic Association believed that a broader organization that crossed state boundaries was needed to deal with what were perceived as problems in college and university sponsorship of interscholastic athletic events.

In the spring of 1920, Smith called together representatives of other state organizations in Iowa, Indiana, Michigan, and Wisconsin to a meeting in Chicago. The report of the first meeting provided the reason for their coming together: "The particular reason that brought the officials together was the fact that high school athletics were being handled in an unsatisfactory manner in contests under the auspices of colleges and universities." The organization took the name "Midwest Federation of State High School Athletic Associations," and the first rules it adopted were intended to assert the new organization's power. The federation insisted on a prohibition on member schools from sending teams to interstate meets not sanctioned by a board of control in the meet's home state and a corollary prohibition on any player competing in such meets who was ineligible to compete in his home state.[1]

The second year's meeting of the Midwest Federation in Chicago represented a rocky start for the organization, as only four states sent representatives—Illinois, Iowa, Michigan, and Wisconsin. Indiana chose to drop out. After Smith beat the bushes for greater participation, the Midwest Federation saw a leap to eleven member states in its third meeting, in

Chicago, in March 1922, adding Kansas, Minnesota, Montana, Nebraska, North Dakota, South Dakota, and Ohio. When the states of Maine, Oklahoma, Kentucky, and Mississippi sent representatives to the fourth annual meeting in Cleveland in 1923, the federation decided that even though it had a membership of only fifteen state organizations, a name change was needed to reflect its new national presence, so it became the "National Federation of State High School Athletic Associations."[2]

BRINGING DOWN STAGG'S BASKETBALL TOURNAMENT

The National Federation was now poised to play a significant role in the governance of interscholastic sports on a national level. From its inception, the federation was concerned about how colleges and universities sponsored contests for high schools, and it worked assiduously to eliminate perceived evils. Opposition to national tournaments by federation members gradually built up through the early and mid-1920s, and a special target was the two national tournaments, track and field and basketball, sponsored by the University of Chicago. As early as 1920, the basketball tournament had alienated the state associations, when its tournament manager, Pat Page, invited two Indiana schools suspended by their state association over eligibility issues, Wingate and Crawfordville, and the two ended up playing for the Stagg title. Targeting the Stagg tourney, the Indiana state association barred its schools from all post–state championship tournaments in 1922.[3]

Another bothersome issue vexing educators arose in 1923, which was the granting of valuable individual awards to winning team members in the basketball tournament—primarily the gold watches given to the first-place team members. Many state associations by this time had rules against giving awards worth more than one dollar. With the obvious intention of eliminating the "gold watch" issue as a source of opposition to his tournament, Stagg introduced a motion at a combined meeting in December 1923 of the Big Ten athletic directors and nine midwestern state high school associations to limit prizes at all tournaments and meets to "token . . . medals, cups, and watch fobs." This motion was accepted, and in the 1924 meet the first-place winners received "gold watch charm medals." Stagg's efforts could not keep the Wisconsin state association from rejecting an invitation that year, mistakenly citing the "gold watch" issue, but also contending that the national tourney had lax eligibility rules and was making excessive amounts of money.[4]

By 1927 the federation had grown considerably more powerful, and with the election that year of Charles W. Whitten, an aggressive advocate of high school control of interscholastic sports, as secretary-treasurer of the organization, members took a dramatically more forceful approach to the entire issue of collegiate sponsorship of high school athletics. With Whitten's ascension, the National Federation pursued a more unrelenting campaign that eventually ousted the universities and colleges from the business of interscholastic sports three years later. Whitten presented his views in late 1927 in an article in the *School Review,* spelling out several problems in secondary-school athletics. Many of the abuses cited

31. Amos Alonzo Stagg, as athletic director of the University of Chicago, built two national high school tournaments, in basketball and track and field. Courtesy of the Chicago History Museum.

stemmed from the overcommercialization of high school sports, where there was tremendous pressure from coaches, student bodies, local townspeople, civic groups, and newspapers to have a winning team. Such pressures produced broken eligibility rules (usually age and academic), neglected schoolwork, exploitation of star players by the press and public, lack of sportsmanship, and the overloading of schedules. The essential character-building element of high school sports was seen as being seriously eroded under abuses being fostered by this overcommercialized system. Whitten cited an example of a high school football coach, "whose whole life has been devoted to the development of character in young men," who was fired for having a "bad" season.[5]

Whitten believed that "high school principals acting individually would be impotent and helpless" in ending the abuses in high school athletics. But he saw the formation of state associations by the principals as "powerful combinations" that reformed high school athletics and ended abuses. At the time of his writing, forty-seven of the forty-eight states had statewide associations regulating high school sports, and they had effectively established eligibility rules, eliminated the tramp athlete, and maintained the amateur rule. Whitten asserted, "It is to these well-organized and powerful associations that we must look for the continued control of athletics in high schools."[6]

What particularly exercised Whitten and most of his cohorts in the state associations was collegiate sponsorship of interstate meets. He noted that the National Association of Secondary School Principals in 1925 went on record as opposing interstate contests. Said Whitten:

> The transportation of high-school teams to distant sections of the country for athletic contests seems to be a growing evil. . . . Boys are away from their school work for days at a time to what educational end? There is little enough of educational warrant in the case of high schools for the determination of the numerous local and state championships now stressed. What, then, should be said of so-called "national" meets and tournaments, which probably are never conceived either by their sponsors or by the participating schools as educational exercises but are designed primarily as advertising and sporting events throughout?[7]

The National Federation's primary concern, thus, was to address the attendant explosive growth in national tournaments, and its first action took place in December 1927 at a council meeting in Chicago that went on record as opposing any "national basketball tournament for high schools." The target was Stagg's tremendously successful and visible national tournament. In February 1928, at the federation's national meeting in Boston, the midwestern representatives asked the delegates for a resolution opposing the meet. Stagg had addressed a preconvention letter to the delegates that was apparently persuasive to a degree and answered some of their concerns over eligibility and physical strain. He argued that the University of Chicago had made repeated modifications in its eligibility rules and contended that they were now higher than the regulations of the National Federation and that the tournament did not put undue strain on young athletes, pointing out that each team played one game a day, except on the last, when they played two, which was less onerous than some state tournaments. The delegates chose not to vote on a resolution opposing the meet. Instead, they produced a resolution requesting the executive committee of the National Federation (meaning essentially Whitten) to conduct an investigation of the Stagg tournament.[8]

Whitten decided not to investigate the tournament, but rather to take a poll. He pointed out that the only complaint with the tournament's management was that "there was considerable carelessness, not to say indifference, in the matter of eligibility of both schools and participants." He figured that these matters could be handled by conferences and mutual agreements between school representatives and Stagg, so he decided to go in another direction and conduct a nationwide poll of high school principals to determine whether a national basketball tournament was actually favored by educators, and, if so, what were its benefits. A typical question Whitten wanted answered was whether "its contributions to the objectives of secondary education sufficient to justify the large expenses, the extended absence from school, and the consequent disruption of the regular school program."[9]

Whitten sent out the questionnaires to each state association, except the eight that had already voted in opposition to the national tournament. Fifteen states ignored the poll, out of either hostility or indifference. But

32. Charles W. Whitten, as secretary-treasurer of the National Federation of State High School Athletic Associations, was the chief architect in the campaign to push colleges and universities out of sponsorship of high school tournaments. Courtesy of the Illinois High School Association.

Whitten obtained participation from twenty-three state associations, who sent out the poll material to the principals. A total return from the principals was 2,334 votes, of which 1,350 (58 percent) of them opposed the tournament and 984 (42 percent) favored the tournament. A more overwhelming statistic showed that only five of the twenty-three states had returned majorities in favor of the tournament (Arkansas, Kentucky, Oklahoma, Texas, and South Dakota). The South in the later years of the tournament was the strongest bastion of support for the event, and the poll reflected that sentiment. At the National Council of the federation in

1929, in Cleveland, the members examined the poll and passed a resolution that the National Federation would refuse to sanction any "interstate basketball tournaments," by a vote of twenty to two. All colleges, high schools, athletic clubs, and other organizations conducting such tournaments were urged to discontinue the practice. The gist of the resolution focused on the size, exploitation, and commercialism of the national tournament, "for purposes devoid of any educational aims and ideals," and the additional expanded season that loaded up the schoolboy calendar with too many games and tournaments.[10]

The February resolution came too late to impact the Stagg tournament in 1929, which brought in forty teams, including twenty-eight state champions. The newspaper coverage was extravagant. There was the familiar narrative of the underdog small schools battling the big-city schools that enthralled the public, as in the *Chicago Tribune* headline "Hamlets Battle Cities in U. of C. Semi-Finals." Despite the popular and critical success of the 1929 extravaganza, there was an unsettling undercurrent that the tournament was not long for the world.[11]

After the 1929 tournament, the National Federation brought in a powerful ally, the North Central Association of Colleges and Secondary Schools, which began work on a comprehensive report on the Stagg tourney. At the March 1930 meeting of the NCAC, its delegates were presented with a complete report and heard a talk by Whitten strongly condemning interstate tournaments. The report asserted that interschool athletics were now under strong local state athletic associations that offered "completely adequate programs of interscholastic competition" and that college sponsorship not only was unnecessary, but also opened the door to evils. A frequently cited evil was that the tournaments served as "bright colored cloaks for organized moves to recruit prep athletes." The NCAC issued a resolution designed to "discourage" all member institutions from sponsoring high school meets, unless invited to by a state association. The resolution was not formally adopted because of a technicality, but it met with near-unanimous approval of the delegates and was viewed as a threat by the midwestern colleges and universities that they would be expelled if they sponsored a meet without a state association's sanction.[12]

33. The University of Chicago's National Interscholastic Basketball Tournament, 1929, was the largest basketball tournament of any kind in the 1920s and served as the focal point of the state high school associations' campaign to end collegiate sponsorship of high school sports. Courtesy of the Special Collections Research Center, University of Chicago Library.

The resolution severely crippled the Stagg tournament, as state associations withdrew their support. The 1930 tournament was a much-diminished affair, attracting only twenty-five teams. In the South, however, most state associations continued to support the tourney, because they either were not federation members or had simply chosen to defy the national organization. More than half (thirteen) were from the South (including three teams from Texas), five were from the West, three came from the East, and only four were from the Midwest. The lone Illinois entry was Morgan Park, the second-place team in the Chicago Public High School League. In deference to their southern invitees, Stagg officials chose not to invite the Chicago public-league champion, the all-black Phillips team, to ensure the participation of the teams from the South. Stagg also filled out the field with private, parochial, and military academies, institutions that had previously been excluded.[13]

The *Chicago Tribune*, a strong supporter of the Stagg tournament, vigorously campaigned for its continuance and conducted its own poll of principals in midwestern states. The *Tribune* poll, published in May, was designed to produce a favorable result, finding that eight of the twelve states supported the tournament and only four opposed. Most support came from the border states—Kentucky, Kansas, and Oklahoma—and the smaller, more rural schools.[14] Its powerful sports columnist, Arch Ward, wrote scathingly of the movement to end collegiate sponsorship of high school athletics:

> Not long ago high schools were clamoring for the assistance of colleges and universities in promoting athletics. Probably no high school in the country was giving proper athletic training to any considerable number of boys in the days when the colleges first lent a helping hand. The colleges perhaps had two thoughts in mind. First, they could help to develop athletics in their own section, and second, they would do a bit of legitimate advertising. Now it seems the officers of certain state high school associations suggest that high schools no longer need the assistance of colleges.[15]

The University of Chicago as early as February 1930 was nearing a decision on terminating Stagg's tourney based on resolutions adopted by the National Federation at the Cleveland meeting a year earlier, the third one appealing to universities and other organizations to discontinue their sponsorship of high school meets. Dean Frederic Woodward sent a letter to Stagg, saying, "In view of these resolutions and particularly the third one it seems to President [Robert Maynard] Hutchins and to me that we ought not to continue to hold the national interscholastic basketball tournament after this year." To build their case against the tournament, however, Woodward decided the university should carry out its own investigation and conduct a poll of principals whose high schools had participated in the tournament the previous ten years. The university found—possibly much to its surprise—that of these former-participant schools, eighty-nine opposed and only thirty supported the meet. In December 1930, the university, bowing to the inevitable and the consensus of opinion, elected to terminate the tournament.[16]

What Educators Wanted in Reform

The decision in 1930 to end the Stagg tournament was a direct result of the actions of the National Federation and indirectly a result of a reform atmosphere that arose from an ever-growing opposition from the educational establishment against the excesses it saw in high school athletics, thereby undergirding the National Federation's successful campaign. Various educational organizations aligned themselves with the National Federation and the professional literature, as represented by the *American Physical Education Review,* and formal reports all came to the agreement that high school sports were overcommercialized and should not be sponsored by the colleges and universities. Two important reports were by the Carnegie Foundation and by Frederick Rand Rogers, published by Columbia University. Both reports came out in 1929 and represented the consensus of opinion on what high school interscholastic sports should be.

In 1929 the Carnegie Foundation for the Advancement of Teaching published its famous report *American College Athletics,* popularly called the *Carnegie Report.* Under chief author Howard J. Savage, the report provided an all-encompassing look at the state of college athletics—its strengths, its problems, its abuses, and its evils. What was less appreciated by educators at the time and decades later is that the *Carnegie Report* had also examined the state of high school athletic programs in its chapter "Athletics in American Schools." The report was fairly favorable on the status of high school athletics, commenting that "school athletics are much more nearly an integral part of the educational process" and noting that all states except Nevada had state associations. The *Carnegie Report,* while making mention of girls as well as boys in athletics, largely overlooked the contentious issue of schoolgirls in high school interscholastics. It also treated the African American high school athlete as the "invisible man" and made no mention of the status of high school athletics in segregated and predominantly black schools.[17]

The *Carnegie Report* saw in particular the baneful influence of communities where townspeople forced high school sports into commercialization and other perceived evils. Said the report of the "townsman": "The worst influence of such a person upon high school students is probably exerted through suggestions and offers of money for coaches, equipment, extra or post-seasonal games and trips, personal trophies and awards, and extra prizes. His machinations lead readily to the use of unsuitable events in meets, heavy schedules, series of post-season games, especially the over-valuing of championships, and to ignoring the effects of especially trying contests upon the physical well-being of athletes."[18]

In regard to the commercialization of high school athletics, the report contended that financial profits from high school games were "used in materially enriching organizations or in providing buildings and playing fields" for the schools. This claim seems doubtful if it is understood that ticket fees to games were the sole source of funds for such support. The report would have been on safer ground to say that such fees augmented taxpayer funds in such construction. The report pointed out that commercialization had reached such a degree that athletic facilities in some areas of the country were built far out of proportion to the school population. Savage and his writers made mention of the phenomenon in Indiana, where small towns built huge arenas for their high school basketball teams. They gave the example of Flora, population 441, school enrollment 90, and a gym with a seating capacity of 1,200. The report also decried cups and plaques given out made of sterling silver and of local merchants sponsoring lavish banquets for high school teams and rewarding them with expensive gifts. It also found that occasional corruption of the educational process took place, with athletes being given grades they did not earn. The report did not discuss this issue to any great length, indicating that the authors did not deem it a major problem.[19]

On the question of championships, the report recognized that such events can "provide an incentive to competition, unify effort, and stimulate one kind of school loyalty." But the report decried championship competition that extended beyond the normal season and that inordinately took up students' time and engaged to an excessive degree the interests of the community so that physical education aims were utterly subordinated.[20]

The *Carnegie Report* praised the efforts of many people and a number of organizations in the high school educational establishment that engaged in combating these abuses, singling out New York City's PSAL, the New England College Conference, and the Women's Division of the National Amateur Athletic Federation. To put in contrast their laudatory behavior, the report directed its withering eye to the sponsorship of high school meets by colleges and universities. The report noted, "It is a pity that such college influences as are embodied in the championship tournaments and meets conducted in the name of the Intercollegiate Conference, the University of Chicago, the University of Pennsylvania, and many other universities, should not be directed wholly to similar ends. The doubtful value of spying out promising schoolboy athletes is scarcely a legitimate excuse for the excessive devotion to the spectacular to which such meets and tournaments contribute." The *Carnegie Report* saw as fundamental the idea that athletics should not be separated from physical education. "If it were necessary to sum up in a single phrase the worst results of that separation," said the report, "probably that phrase would be the impairment of ethical and moral standards of schoolboys through the commercialization of athletics."[21]

Frederick Rand Rogers's report, *The Future of Interscholastic Athletics*, laid out a similar reform agenda. Rogers was the New York state director of physical education and president of the state's high school athletic association. He dealt at considerable length with the issue of "championships." Much of Rogers's objection took an extreme position, questioning the existence of all championships, even on the league level. This objection was not realistic and had no chance of gaining traction with educators. But Rogers found some agreement for his arguments against state championships and found almost universal agreement for his arguments against interstate and national championships.[22]

Rogers reported on a 1929 meeting of state directors of physical education and found that of the group of seventeen, fourteen adopted a policy of "reducing emphasis on championship athletic tournaments," and twelve of them would oppose state championships, in either some or all sports. California reported that state championships in all but tennis and track had been abolished. Florida reported that a football state championship had been abolished, and it was looking into baseball. West Virginia eliminated all state championships except basketball. In 1928 the New York State Public High School Athletic Association had voted to abolish all state tournaments beginning in the 1929–1930 season, owing primarily to the strenuous advocacy of Rogers. He argued to the committee, "A city championship may be innocuous—the gains may even outweigh the losses, a league championship may do more good than harm, but a state championship among schoolboys always tends to be destructive. Of course a national championship is a major crime in education."[23]

Rogers tried to build a case that there was a trend by the states to eliminate state championships, but it was based on actual cutbacks by only four states—Florida, West Virginia, California, and New York. The latter two were special cases. Both states had large populations and great geographic spread, and high schools that participated in a state championship in one of those states often faced considerable travel and a large-event situation. What both states did was to cut back from a state championship to sectional championships to reduce the scope and size of the events.[24]

Most state associations were not interested in eliminating state championships, because in most of the states the school administrators by and large approved of these state tournaments, at least for basketball and track and field. This broad approval for state championships can be assumed by extrapolating from a 1928 poll that John M. Booth did among 310 secondary schools in the states of Washington, Oregon, Idaho, and Montana. In responses to questions on whether state tournaments should be continued in various sports, Booth found that roughly 70 percent of the schools desired to continue state basketball tournaments and roughly 75 percent wanted to continue state track and field meets. On the other hand, only about 35 percent wished to continue state football championships. The respondents maybe had in mind football, as well as hearing the rising swell of voices against the commercialization of high school athletics, compelling 60 percent to agree that championship programs had gone "too far." Booth found an overall positive attitude toward state tournaments, and the implication from his survey meant that Rogers had a minimal constituency for his campaign to abolish state tournaments.[25]

Most compellingly, most of the state associations were founded on the basis of administering and governing a state tournament, usually basketball. The issue in the state associations was not the existence of the state tournaments per se, but who would run them, whether they be local, state, or interstate—the high schools or the colleges? The state high school associations by the end of the decade were opposed to collegiate sponsorship of high school meets, and their opposition first centered on interstate tournaments sponsored by universities.

OTHER TOURNAMENTS FALL

The end of the Stagg tournament in 1930 signaled the close of collegiate sponsorship of interstate meets, and one by one like dominoes the other tournaments fell. Seemingly, almost weekly in 1930, the sports pages reported on one or more university- or club-sponsored tournament being terminated. Following the North Central Association resolution of March 1930 against university-sponsored high school tournaments, and Stagg's vow to save his tournament, the *Chicago Tribune* asked Stagg's Big Ten counterparts about the issue to measure the level of support from his colleagues. What the paper found was largely opposition. Michigan's athletic director, Fielding Yost, was adamant against such tournaments, commenting, "To have a national tournament after a strenuous regular season, including regional and state meets, seem to me to be prolonging the competition more than need be." George Little, the athletic director at Wisconsin—which was sponsoring national academy meets in basketball, swimming, and indoor track, plus a midwestern outdoor relay meet—was noncommittal but surprisingly servile to the North Central decision, saying, "We are anxious to cooperate with the North Central conference."[26]

Within a year, virtually all Big Ten–sponsored interstate meets were terminated, and elsewhere in the country the trend was the same. In early 1931, the University of Michigan ended its sponsorship of its three interstate meets—an outdoor meet (1898), an indoor track meet (1922), and a swimming meet (1924). Athletic director Yost gave as reasons the concern over "overemphasis" on high school meets and that state meets were now being sponsored by the Michigan High School Athletic Association.[27]

About the same time, Northwestern announced its abandonment of its "national" indoor track, swimming, and wrestling meets, citing the NCAC resolutions. Northwestern had earlier felt the pressure after the 1929 meets, when Michigan barred its high school athletes (which provided large contingents to the Northwestern meets) from participating in out-of-state meets. Despite the loss of the Michigan schools, Northwestern's 1930 track meet attracted fifty-one schools and 324 athletes, and the entire meet, with the addition of swimming and wrestling, featured seventy-two schools and 643 athletes. The wrestling meet drew both the Oklahoma and the Iowa state champions, plus four other Iowa schools, and almost half the swimming teams were from out of state, three from Minnesota. But the swimming meet was basically a midwestern event, as was the track meet, which drew mostly Illinois schools, with a handful of schools from neighboring states. The event was still a sizable extravaganza in 1930, which was precisely the problem and led to its termination. The University of Wisconsin that year also ended its trio of national meets for academies, as well as its midwestern outdoor-relay interscholastic.[28]

The smaller institutions of higher education in Illinois, as represented by the Little 19 Conference, likewise acquiesced to the North Central edict, and Illinois Wesleyan, Bradley, and Milliken all terminated their interscholastic track and field meets by the winter of 1931. Many high school principals and coaches, mostly representing rural schools, were not happy with the North Central decision, as the *Chicago Tribune* explained that for them, the tournaments served to promote and stimulate track in the high schools. Some announced that their schools would cease to have track teams.[29]

In the East, the close proximity of the states meant no long-distance trips by most entrants, vitiating one of the chief complaints about university-sponsored interstate meets. Nonetheless, there was a trend in the East to end such sponsorship, starting as early as 1924, when New York University ended its track interscholastic. Yale University ended interstate invitation to its track interscholastic after 1928, turning it into an all-Connecticut meet. Pennsylvania terminated its basketball meet in 1930 and its track interscholastic in 1932. A few university-sponsored meets continued. Pennsylvania's "national" meet in swimming attracted only middle-state schools, so it did not meet the disapproval of educators and continued into the 1930s, as did the tennis meets of Princeton and Pennsylvania.[30]

The last major collegiate-sponsored high school tournament to be terminated was the University of Chicago's National Interscholastic Track and Field Tournament, held since 1902. Beginning with the 1930 meet, under the new requirements for National Federation sanction, Stagg could no longer invite athletes from private academies, and the separate academy division was discontinued. That change reduced the number of entries from the more than eight hundred to about six hundred. Further attacks from the state associations further diminished the meet, as more and more state associations banned their athletes from attending the Stagg meet and other intersectional contests. Froebel High of Gary, for example, the Stagg champion in 1929 and 1930, was not allowed by the Indiana High School Association under a new regulation barring interstate contests to defend its title in the 1931 meet, a field that was further reduced to five hundred entries. Stagg sustained the meet's success in 1932, however, with a strong field that broke several national records and attracted the largest crowd since 1928, at more than eight thousand.[31]

The last year of the tournament, 1933, did not end in a whimper, either. Meet officials claimed that eleven meet records and five national interscholastic records were broken. Most notable was the presence of the soon-to-be-legendary track and field star Jesse Owens, who led his school, Cleveland East Technical, to the national title, while breaking two national interscholastic records (100- and 220-yard dashes) and breaking a meet record (long jump). Most extraordinary was that 100-yard record, which tied the men's world record at 9.4 seconds. The achievement provided the headlines for the meet. The event was returned to Soldier Field, and the tournament program probably did not endear educators with advertisements for beer, cigarettes, and cigars. University officials canceled the tournament in April 1934, in the wake of a resolution by the National Federation in their February meeting saying that the organization would no longer sanction any national high school meet sponsored by a college or university.[32]

34. The University of Chicago's National Interscholastic Track and Field Tournament, 1925, was the largest high school track and field meet in the country, and its last meet in 1933 signaled the end of national interscholastic tournaments. Courtesy of the Special Collections Research Center, University of Chicago Library.

The end of the Stagg track meet signaled the final triumph of the secondary-school establishment in reshaping athletic governance for the nation's public secondary schools. A note of triumphalism was sounded in the 1932 *Illinois High School Athlete*:

> When the colleges and independent organizations discontinued their practice of sponsoring meets for high school teams, there were many alarmists who predicted that track and field sports would die a sudden death. For a patient who was alleged to be near death's door, this one seems to be unusually lively if we can judge from the dozens of meets that have been sanctioned for this spring. This includes County Meets, Triangular ones, Relay Carnivals, Conference meets, and just meets. . . . High school coaches have shown themselves capable of standing on their own feet after having been dependent on other organizations for a number of years.[33]

The article goes on to note that high schools are able to find plenty of competition and that there are available a sufficient number of high school fields and "no scarcity of high school departments that are willing to sponsor meets."[34] With regard to indoor competition, such a rosy scenario was a bit more problematic, as there was a critical lack of high school field houses with indoor tracks. But in Illinois and other states, many high schools soon began building large field houses that could hold an indoor tournament, such as Oak Park High. The school erected a spectacular $750,000 field house in late 1927, and the *Chicago Herald and Examiner* earlier in the year gushed over the impending structure: "The field house will contain four inside gymnasiums and one outdoor on the roof, two swimming pools and eventually an auditorium to seat 1,000 people. It will be built in units, which when completed, will serve a maximum of 5,000 students. . . . The field house will measure 219 feet by 128 feet. Among other features it will contain a running track ten feet wide. It will allow 300 boys and 300 girls to take their physical training at one time."[35]

Decades later the huge Oak Park indoor track facility still inspires awe from people who first lay their eyes on it. The field house was a significant symbol of the changing of the guard in high school indoor track, that is, the shift from university to high school support of the sport. The field house in subsequent years not only helped Oak Park maintain its preeminence in track and field, but also helped immeasurably to sustain and promote indoor track in particular as a sport for all schools in the area. Oak Park began sponsoring its famed Oak Park Relays in 1931 and eventually sponsored a separate meet for facility-hampered Chicago schools.[36]

With the onset of the Depression, school district budgets were severely constricted in the ability to provide for expansion of facilities to include field houses, gymnasiums, and stadiums. Paradoxically, however, through the Works Progress Administration (WPA), a federal-government employment program established in 1935, thousands of high schools were provided with not only field houses, but stadiums and other facilities as well. By 1943 the WPA nationwide had constructed 3,026 athletic fields; 2,302 stadiums, grandstands, and bleachers; and 1,255 gymnasiums; plus making thousands of reconstructions, improvements, and expansions to existing facilities. Secondary schools were the beneficiaries in the bulk of those numbers. In the small state of Arkansas alone, the construction of more than 150 athletic plant facilities—81 gymnasiums, 38 athletic fields, and 34 stadiums, grandstands, and bleachers—were of considerable benefit to the secondary schools in the state.[37]

INTERSCHOLASTIC SPORTS IN THE
EARLY DEPRESSION YEARS

In the late 1920s and early 1930s, the United States Office of Education published a series of monographs on a number of surveys it called collectively the *National Survey of Secondary Education*. In 1932 the office published *Monograph No. 27*, authored by P. Roy Brammell, called *Intramural and Interscholastic Athletics*, a report based on a survey of 327 secondary schools conducted during the 1929–1930 school year, with visits and interviews conducted at 36 of the schools the following year. The 327 schools were not randomly selected, but were the "satisfactory" respondents of a survey sent to 760 schools that were "reported as doing promising work in the field of athletics." In any case, while the survey shows a more flourishing sports program than average in the country, it does provide a snapshot of the state of secondary sports at the end of the 1920s.[38]

The survey found that the five most popular interscholastic sports for boys, based on the total of schools that responded affirmatively as sponsoring the sport, were basketball (284 schools), football (220), track and field (199), baseball (171), and tennis (106). Golf (54) and swimming (47) trailed the big five. In girls' sports, the survey found a definite trend by school administrators in discontinuing interschool contests, but with the remaining schools, which survey reporters found to be increasingly rural, the big-five sports were basketball (124 schools), followed far behind by tennis (33), track and field (31), volleyball (14), and baseball (14), the latter meaning softball.[39]

In the financing of interscholastic sports, the schools relied on several sources of income. Most of the sports were assumed to be self-supporting, and ticket sales were considered the main income source for sustaining athletic teams in 85 percent of the surveyed schools. Another source listed "pools of funds derived from all extracurriculum activities," which was designated by 20 percent of the schools, suggesting an even higher percentage of ticket sales. Brammell makes a telling point: "It is not surprising, therefore, that in a large number of schools considerable attention is given to the development of formidable teams, so that large numbers of persons will become sufficiently interested in the competitions to pay the price of admission." Other sources he listed included board of education subsidies, student-body fees, plays and entertainments, and athletic-association membership fees. Increasingly, however, Brammell found that shortfalls in the athletic budget were being made up by subsidies from boards of education, based on the notion that athletic contests had "educational legitimacy." The survey noted in financing the athletic plant that "it is the general policy of boards of education in the United States to provide athletic fields, gymnasiums, and facilities, and the more permanent form of equipment out of funds derived from local tax levies."[40]

Brammell discovered a considerable change in the professionalism of the coaches since Lewis Hoch Wagenhorst wrote his report on interscholastic athletics in 1924. Wagenhorst had found a low level of professional background in the coaches, where he reported only 70 percent of the football coaches were college graduates, 67 percent of the basketball coaches, and 62 percent of the baseball coaches. Many such coaches, according to Wagenhorst, were not "connected in any other official capacity with the school" (he found 14 percent in football, 12 percent in basketball). During the decade, however, there was movement to raise the educational standards of coaches and make them members of the faculty and considerable pressure, according to historian Timothy Patrick O'Hanlon, to make them certified physical education teachers. Coaches were seen as valuable components in the educational mission of the schools.[41]

Brammell reported that coaches were employed by more than two-thirds of the schools in his survey, and 90 percent of those coaches were members of the school faculty. In most states, coaches were required to be faculty and have a requisite college degree. In about half the schools surveyed, the coaches received a higher salary than other teachers, reflecting their extra stipends for coaching duties. In some 70 percent of the schools, interscholastic athletics were considered a part of the physical education program. In summary, Brammell concluded that in most school systems, interscholastic sports were considered a part of the educational functions of the school and therefore required financial and institutional support.[42]

The success of the National Federation in taking control of interscholastic sports in the early 1930s, with the attendant expulsion of private clubs and universities from the business of sponsoring high school events, signaled the end of a long half-century struggle over governance, a search for control that began with their birth. Interscholastic sports in this time span came to be seen more and more as part of the educational mission of secondary schools, so that by the end of the 1920s, they were financially and institutionally supported by the nation's school systems. The educational mission since the inception of secondary schools in the late eighteenth century had always encompassed more than academic learning, but also entailed the development of the whole individual to include the building of good character, values, and citizenship, plus good health and physical vigor. Educators thus looked at high school athletic competitions as playing an intrinsic role in their mission and worked to bring them under their control at ever-higher levels. The nub of the search for control always rested ultimately over the moral worth of high school sports, the vision of which drove the state associations to ultimately assume governance on the national stage, thus completing the structure of administration and control that has remained in place virtually unchallenged since the 1930s.

EPILOGUE

When the National Federation of State High School Athletic Associations (now the National Federation of State High School Associations) in the early 1930s took over governance of all high school programs, bringing them under the purview of the secondary-school educational establishment, high school educators undoubtedly assumed it was a permanent solution to long-standing intractable problems in high school sports. In ending most collegiate sponsorship of interscholastic sports, the state associations had great success in reining in the growing expansion and commercialism of high school sports, terminating national championships, curbing long travel trips, and reducing the exploitation of high school athletes by forces outside the educational realm. And under the prevailing educational ideology of the day, interscholastic sports for girls were effectively terminated in most states, except for a few entrenched programs in the South, Iowa, and the Philadelphia area. Seemingly, the system of control of high school sports was firmly in place, but they could not escape the essential tensions from their very beginnings between the educational mission of the schools and the sponsorship of competitive sports teams. Those tensions persisted into the postwar years, eroding the educators' aims to use sports to build character. Such issues of commercialism, eligibility, long travel, expansionism, and girls' interscholastic competition would arise again and again and change the interscholastic landscape in the next several decades.

Canada in the postwar years began structuring its interscholastic governance like the system in the United States (with its state high school athletic associations), when in 1948 both Ontario and Saskatchewan formed organizations to regulate and sponsor high school sports competition.

Other provinces within the next several years likewise set up high school athletic associations, notably Alberta in 1956, Prince Edward Island and Manitoba in 1962, and British Columbia in 1968. Eventually, the Ontario high school organization grew to be the second largest in North America after California. An umbrella organization for all the provinces, the Canadian School Sport Federation, was formed in 1967.[1]

At the close of the 1920s, high school sports were essentially put on hold for some fifteen years. The Depression, which brought a halt to growth in the extracurriculum owing to limited finances, followed by World War II, with gas rationing and other wartime restrictions, effectively curtailed many interschool athletic programs in the high schools. With the end of the war, pent-up demands exploded into a prosperity boom that benefited interscholastic sports. Across the country, high schools added more levels to their programs, from freshmen through varsity, bringing more students into high school sports and raising their level of competitiveness. In football, for example, heavyweight and lightweight programs in the larger schools were generally replaced with varsity, junior-varsity, sophomore, and freshman (or sometimes freshman A, freshman B, and freshman C) programs. For the smaller or less prosperous schools, mainly two levels, varsity and freshman-sophomore, were developed.

The trend toward creating more and more competition classes based on school enrollment accelerated in many states, fueled by a long-established concern for ensuring equal competition. Thus, one could find a small state such as Rhode Island, with some fifty high schools, sponsoring state championships in four classes. Some states, such as Indiana and Illinois, resisted the multiclass trend for several decades. Beginning with the 1997–1998 school year, however, Indiana broke up its legendary single-class basketball tournament into a four-class tournament. Attendance fell for the four-game series from around seventy-five thousand in 1990 to around thirty thousand in 2000. Illinois broke up its single-class system and went to two classes for the 1972–1973 season and then went to four classes for the 2007–2008 season. By the time Illinois went to four classes, only Delaware and Kentucky conducted state tournaments with fewer than four classes.[2]

The postwar prosperity helped schools increase the number of sport offerings, so that wrestling, gymnastics, cross-country, golf, tennis, soccer, and swimming were added to the usual four of football, basketball, track and field, and baseball. What happened in Illinois was typical for the nation: even though the state already had nine sponsored sports on its calendar, the Illinois High School Association sponsored an increasing number of state tournament sports, starting with cross-country in 1947, followed by gymnastics in 1958, and soccer in 1973. In the South, Florida followed a similar trajectory, adding cross-country in 1947, wrestling in 1965, weightlifting in 1975, and soccer in 1977. Northern states and Canada added such winter sports as skiing, curling, and ice hockey to their winter calendars. Wisconsin added skiing in 1958 and curling in 1959.[3]

At the same time, the big cities saw a decline in their high school sports programs, as deteriorating inner-city schools dropped sport offerings and the middle classes abandoned the cities for the suburbs. Whereas prior to the war many city schools were competitive in such "country club" sports as swimming, golf, and tennis, the postwar years saw a gradual decline of city schools offering such sports, and also a growing lack of institutional support in coaching, equipment, uniforms, and transportation. In Illinois, for example, tennis and swimming were dominated by Chicago schools during the 1930s and early 1940s, but in the postwar years the city ceased to be a factor in the state tournament in those sports. New York City's interscholastic athletic program suffered perennial inadequate funding in the postwar years and was severely damaged by a teacher strike that temporarily shut down extracurricular activities in 1951. Many New York high schools subsequently curtailed their sports offerings. By the 1960s, inner-city schools in most major cities were competitive only in basketball and track and field.[4]

COMMUNITY BONDS BUILD HIGH SCHOOL SPORTS

In many communities outside the major metropolitan areas, the bonds between the citizens of the local town and their high school athletic teams that had represented a powerful cultural force in America for decades only accentuated during the postwar years, as small colleges dropped football and amateur town teams disappeared. To sports fans of local towns, the high school team represented their community, a devotion that often led to excess. Indiana was the preeminent hotbed of high school basketball in the 1950s and had been for many decades. The Indiana High School Athletic Association was responsible for a program reaching some eight hundred schools in a basketball-mad state where small towns built gymnasiums with outsize seating capacities, notably a town of 400 that built a 4,000-seat gym for all the farmers for miles around. New Castle—population 18,000—boasted of having the nation's largest high school gymnasium, with 9,300 seats. Basketball in Indiana helped local farm communities find redemption and uplift during a time when their way of life and economy were in decline.[5]

The state's basketball culture was superbly illustrated by the accomplishment of Milan High, when in 1954 the tiny school, with an enrollment of 167, beat Muncie Central, enrollment 2,600, for the state championship. Both a book, *The Greatest Basketball Story Ever Told* (1993), and a movie, *Hoosiers* (1986), captured the essence of 1950s Indiana basketball, reminding the nationwide audience of the same kind of feelings they may have had for their high school basketball teams during that decade.[6]

Similarly, high school football in Ohio and Texas produced the same kind of community bonds with their athletic teams, and the same kind of excess. Ohio has a rich tradition of high school football excellence, extending back to the turn of the century, and even though there was no state championship series until 1972, many of the programs built fanatical followings. Massillon represented the state's highest level of community devotion, supporting the football team of Washington High with an enrollment of 1,200 students in a city of 33,000 and having a stadium seating 22,000. By 1963 the school was playing before 120,000 to 160,000 fans a season. Besides a large stadium, the school district supplied the head coach with six assistant coaches and coaches for each of the three junior high schools.[7]

Texas high school football was the mother of all excess by the 1950s, whereby many of its schoolboys were trained in the plushest facilities, traveled on expensive private jets, played in the biggest high school stadiums in the country, learned football from the most highly paid coaches, and performed before the largest and most fanatical groups of fans. The University Interscholastic League, as the Texas state association was known, had sponsored a state football championship since 1920. In some Texas high school programs, the schoolboys would play before 20,000 or more fans many times during the regular season. Abilene High in its Class 4A championship game against Fort Worth in 1955 drew more than 30,000 fans. Writing in 1963, Bill McMurray of the *Houston Chronicle* reported that during one season, 926 schools fielded teams (the largest number in the nation), involving some 50,000 boys, and played around 4,800 games before more than 8 million fans. He commented, "Schoolboy football is big business in Texas," taking in four million dollars on a low ticket cost of fifty cents per person.[8]

In 1954 the Supreme Court in *Brown v. Board of Education* ended legal segregation in the country. Although southern school districts fought the ruling for more than a decade, school segregation greatly diminished during the 1950s and 1960s, and African Americans gradually were brought into the mainstream of interscholastic competition. First in Washington, DC, then in the border states, and then in the Deep South, all legally segregated schools were eventually closed and their leagues and state conferences disbanded, In DC the separate leagues for black and white schools were merged into one league. School sports often became the success template by which integration in the schools was navigated and by which integration in society at large was measured. Integration reduced the ranks of segregated black schools so much that by the last national black basketball tournament in 1967, only 6 schools participated. In the northern states, predominantly black schools gradually stopped competing interstate against black schools. These schools were becoming more numerous in the major urban centers, so there was no need to travel interstate to find another black school against which to compete. Also, they became more integrated into the white world of competition, participating in their state high school tournaments and finding less abuse and discrimination.[9]

The South resisted integration by organizing private high schools, called "segregation academies" by detractors. During the 1960s, these schools formed athletic leagues and state associations to conduct championship competition, and the process accelerated after the Supreme Court decision in *Alexander v. Holmes County* (1969) that ordered desegregation of the South's school systems. In Mississippi, the most segregated southern state, the number of private schools soared from 49 in 1967 to 207 in 1971, enrolling nearly 25 percent of the white student population. The schools formed the Mississippi Private School Association in 1968 to provide a statewide sponsoring organization for school athletics and activities.[10]

In sections of the country that still supported girls' interscholastics— notably the South and Midwest—there was some retrenchment in sports for girls in the immediate postwar years. In such states as North Caro- lina, which had long supported girls' basketball, the state tournament was ended in 1954 by educators, influenced by the direction that colleges in the state were going in curtailing female athletics. With a decline in girls' basketball, cheerleading grew in its place. One notable exception at this time was Iowa, which not only sponsored the most popular girls' basket- ball tournament in the nation but also expanded opportunities—softball in 1955, tennis and golf in 1956, track and field in 1962, and cross-country in 1966, soon followed by swimming, gymnastics, field hockey, and vol- leyball, all by 1970. Wayne E. Cooley, head of the Iowa Girls High School Athletic Union, said at one point during the expansion, "We now have a sport for every girl, and a girl for every sport," mocking the Women's Divi- sion motto from the 1920s in support of intramurals for girls, "A game for every girl and every girl in a game." Philadelphia in both city and subur- ban schools also added at this time interscholastic sports for girls, notably basketball, field hockey, and volleyball.[11]

Catholics at the end of World War II still constituted a predomi- nantly working-class immigrant group, of which 66 percent were ranked as "lower class," compared to 56 percent of the national population. As postwar prosperity increased and the population moved from the city to the suburbs, Catholics grew faster in socioeconomic status than any other religious group except the Jews. By 1970 Catholics were indistinguishable from the population in measures of education and occupational status and were ahead in income. Catholics had become as American as the mainstream population and had emerged out of their "Catholic ghetto." They also saw the weakening of their parallel institutions, notably their high school athletic programs.[12]

Across the nation, Catholic high schools increasingly joined state athletic associations, some of which changed their public school–only policies to encompass private schools. In Illinois, for example, Catholic population growth in the Chicago suburbs led to the creation of the Catholic Suburban High School League in 1956, and the schools voted to join the IHSA. In the city, the Chicago Catholic High School Athletic League's seventeen schools were becoming increasingly restive over their outsider status. In 1960 the four Christian Brothers schools withdrew from the league and the following year joined the IHSA. Finally, in 1974, the schools of the Catholic league, the last independent parochial league in the state, joined the IHSA.[13]

New York State, with a bit more complicated governance arrangement, saw a similar movement of Catholic schools into state competition with public schools. By the 1970s, the principal statewide high school athletic association was the New York State Public High School Athletic Association, which despite its name had been adding private and parochial school members for years. Three organizations were not part of the association—the Public Schools Athletic League of New York City, the New York State Catholic High Schools Athletic Association (which included the Catholic High School Athletic Association of New York City), and the Athletic Association of Private Schools. In 1973 an umbrella organization was formed called the Federation of New York State High School Athletic Associations, which began a state basketball tournament in 1979 and gradually added cross-country, golf, indoor and outdoor track, swimming, gymnastics, tennis (for both boys and girls), and wrestling for boys. While the melding of the Catholic high school leagues into the state association was never as full and complete as in other states—the New York Catholic schools kept their own state championships—their new participation in federation and state-association competition brought an end to the old Catholic-ghetto system.[14]

Wherever students competed during the 1950s and 1960s, the pervasive culture saw sports as uplifting and character building, serving as an antidote to what was perceived as a wave of juvenile delinquency in the 1950s and social rebellion in the 1960s. Students who participated in sports, it was universally understood, received moral guidance from their coaches, acquired lessons for life, developed good character, learned to accept rules and discipline, and discovered teamwork, sportsmanship, and the value of hard work and effort. They could read about these salutary values of sport in their daily newspaper, via a comic strip that debuted in 1958, *Gil Thorp*, about a high school coach at Milford High who not only turned around straying teens through sports but won state championships to boot.[15]

TITLE IX EXPLODES FEMALE EXPANSION IN HIGH SCHOOL SPORTS

By far the most significant change in high school sports took place in the 1970s, when across the nation state high school athletic associations introduced sports competition and greatly expanded opportunities for girls to participate. The women's movement of the 1960s, which was partly inspired and motivated by Betty Friedan's book *The Feminine Mystique* (1963), advocated equal opportunity, equal pay, and equal treatment in American society for women. The movement's fruition by the early 1970s produced many changes in the country's laws and customs, including how women were to be treated in the sports arena. In 1972 Title IX of the Education Amendments Act banned sexual discrimination by all school districts and institutions of higher learning that received federal money. Although unanticipated by the law's sponsors, Title IX had profound consequences for women in sport.[16]

Under the nondiscrimination standard spelled out by the new act, state athletic associations were impelled to make available interscholastic sports competition to girls as much as they had done for boys. The growth was dramatic. During the 1970–1971 school year, according to National Federation membership surveys, 294,015 girls compared to 3,666,917 boys participated in interscholastic sports. Only 7.4 percent of all participants were girls, and only eight states sponsored basketball tournaments. By 1980–1981 girl participants had risen to 1,853,789, constituting 35 percent, and by 2009–2010 participants numbered 3,172,637, reaching 41.5 percent. Women's sport historian Pamela Grundy reported a tenfold increase in girls' participation in basketball, from 400,000 in 1972 to 4.5 million in 1982, based on overall participation figures that encompassed non–National Federation schools.[17]

While Title IX spurred growth in most girls' sports, some boys' sports, competing for resources and gym space, went into decline, notably gymnastics (Illinois was left with the only notable program). Rifle marksmanship had been in decline for decades, but the Columbine High School shooting-death massacre of 1999 spurred educators nationwide to ban the sport. Only Georgia survived with a substantial rifle-marksmanship program. Some boys' sports significantly increased in participation, notably lacrosse, soccer, and ice hockey, reflecting increasing popularity of those sports in the college and amateur ranks. In some sports, because of their costs and inability of schools to provide facilities, notably ice hockey, schools did not officially field teams, but allowed students to form club-sponsored teams, as long as faculty members were involved.[18]

THE NEW WORLD OF HIGH SCHOOL SPORTS

Interscholastic sports during the 1980s began to repeat the excesses of the 1920s, creating highly competitive, pressurized sports environments, with increasingly commercialized programs that became national in scope. High school athletic programs, especially the basketball programs, moved into alliances with corporate sponsors, the companies typically supplying shoes, uniforms, and equipment for the athletic teams. Such support proved invaluable in helping impoverished school districts to make athletics available to students. The sometimes-intense competition between shoe companies in supplying footwear to high-profile basketball programs, however, was distasteful to many educators, who saw shoe companies withdraw support once the team started losing. Corporate support also involved purchasing rights for naming stadiums or gymnasiums and donations for sponsorship of regional, sectional, or state tournaments. The National Federation of State High School Associations, which encouraged such giving, was sponsored by at least nine official sponsorships (called "corporate partners") in 2010.[19]

National rankings, beginning with the *USA Today* football poll in 1982, grew to include ever more sports and more ranking organizations, so that there are three or four national ranking services each in football, boys' and girls' basketball, baseball, and softball. These rankings fueled a boon in intersectional matches—particularly in football and basketball—along with attendant national television exposure. Some state associations dropped their decades-old travel bans on interstate travel. Notable football powers, such as De La Salle of Concord, California, and Evangel Christian of Shreveport, Louisiana, traveled across the country to match themselves against other "national powers." Such travel, because of the lower costs, was even more common in basketball, where tournaments in Chicago, St. Louis, New York, and California drew teams nationwide.[20]

Although national tournaments continued to be opposed by the National Federation of State High School Associations, such tournaments arose in such sports as wrestling, golf, and soccer, drawing private schools and some public schools with teams disguised as private clubs. The National High School Coaches Association (NHSCA), founded in 1989, introduced a national individual wrestling championship in 1999, where competitors represented their states but not their high schools. By 2001, however, the NHSCA also introduced a "final four" national championship that pitted four of the top-ranked wrestling schools in a dual-meet competition at Easton, Pennsylvania. The NHSCA introduced a national golf tournament in 2005. Nike began sponsoring a national cross-country meet in 2004, drawing such national powers as the York High boys team of Elmhurst, Illinois (competing as the backward-named Kroy team), and the Saratoga Springs High girls team of New York (competing as the Kenetic Racing Club). In the desire for college scholarships and an eventual professional career, students increasingly specialized in one sport, attending expensive sports camps during the summers and private clubs during the school year. Some students traveled hundreds of miles to attend special private secondary schools with fifth-year programs designed to hone sports skills.[21]

Television exposure on the national level for high school sports increased after the start of the twenty-first century, augmenting the various all-star games that had showcased individual talent for a couple of decades. Many state associations also increased television coverage to more of their state tournaments. In 2002–2003 ESPN2 broadcast two high school games showcasing a nationally famous player, LeBron James, of St. Vincent–St. Mary of Akron, Ohio. Games in Ohio were broadcast on pay-per-view television, and his team played road games in Philadelphia, Pittsburgh, Greensboro, and Los Angeles. At the end of his high school career, he was drafted into the National Basketball Association and hailed as the "next Michael Jordan."[22]

The expansion of competition to a national scope, the coast-to-coast travel, and increased television coverage of high school sports were sources of growing concern to many educators. They saw potential damage to their students in the excess media coverage and star treatment of young immature players and teams, heightening the pressure for them to perform and win and to get scholarships. Commented Gordon Gillespie, a Chicago-area coach in 2006, who had won five state titles, "There is a demand to play football, and parents are buying into it. They are caught up with the baloney, the exposure camps that cost $600 a pop. Someone is exploiting the hell out of these kids, and it's all based on the idea that you won't get a Division I scholarship if you don't show up. It has become more important than becoming a doctor or lawyer."[23]

The educational mission of secondary schools was too often forgotten in communities seeking to build athletic programs to win championships. For both boys and girls, the aim of interscholastic sports increasingly went beyond the building of strength and health and good character to providing opportunity to full-ride college admissions.[24] For example, in a best-selling book, *Friday Night Lights: A Town, a Team, and a Dream* (1990), the author, H. G. Bissinger, examined for one year the football program of Permian High of economically depressed Odessa, Texas, and saw skewed priorities. The townspeople had built a $5.6 million twenty-thousand-seat stadium for the school, which won several state championships. However, the school failed to build an educational institution with the same consideration, allowing standards to fall and underbudgeting needed school supplies.[25]

The pressure to perform at the high school level saw emulation by athletes and coaches of some abuses that existed at the collegiate and professional levels. By the first decade of the new century, the issue of performance-enhancing drug abuse, which for a couple of decades had been building in the collegiate and pro ranks, had reached down into the interscholastic world. Inspired by their sports heroes, high school students were increasingly turning to drugs to improve their performances. By 2008 four states had drug-testing policies for their high school athletes—Illinois, New Jersey, Florida, and Texas—as well as hundreds of secondary schools nationwide. Testing is done on anabolic steroids (which build strength and endurance); ephedra, caffeine, creatine, and other stimulants (which produce quick energy and promote aggressiveness); diuretics (which speed weight reduction); and peptide hormones (which provide bursts of energy). Many of these drugs were available in increasingly popular and thoroughly legal energy drinks and dietary supplements.[26]

Despite the overall growth and prosperity of secondary-school sports in the postwar years, many towns and cities experienced significant decline in their interscholastic programs. Many rural towns suffered economic decline as the family farm decayed and young people migrated to the cities for employment, and many large cities saw their schools decline as neighborhoods deteriorated and were engulfed in poverty. As a result, inner-city and rural schools continued to trail behind suburban schools in the level and variety of sports offered to their students. Helping to stem these declines is that in many of these schools, educators encourage participation in interscholastic sports as a means by which to keep students in school.

The dire straits of big-city programs were most tellingly related in a series of articles that appeared in the *Chicago Tribune* on the Chicago Public High School League sports program in 1991. For example, each Chicago high school received from the board of education a $6,700 annual equipment allowance plus a small stipend of $1,500 or $2,500 for each teacher who coached a sport. The athletic budgets of the city schools, augmented by fund-raising and student fees, generally ran from $20,000 to $25,000. In contrast, suburban schools such as Evanston High supported its teams with a budget of $160,000 and stipends of $4,000 to $5,500 for coaching teams. Because of declining resources, the Chicago high school sports program saw a decrease in participation from 33 percent of the students in 1979 to 25 percent in 1991. Chicago suburban schools generally had much greater facilities, with multiple gymnasiums, swimming pools, tennis courts, and a variety of athletic fields for soccer, baseball, and football.[27]

In New York City, the *New York Times* ran a similar series in 1999, pointing out the decline of the PSAL, following budget slashing in the 1970s. By the late 1990s, many New York schools had greatly reduced the number and levels of their sports offerings. In New York, each school was expected to finance its athletic budget to a much greater degree than in Chicago, and thus each school received only about $2,500 plus small stipends for the coaches from the central office. The great disparity in programs in the PSAL was revealing: whereas a near-suburban school such as Tottenville High on Staten Island had a $75,000 budget supporting forty-one sports programs, inner-city Jefferson High had to make do with a $12,500 budget supporting eighteen programs.[28]

By the 2009–2010 school year, total participation in interscholastic sports in the United States was 7,628,377, which included 4,455,740 boys and 3,172,637 girls (these figures reflect multiple numbers for multiple sports athletes). Boys' participation was greatest in eleven-player football (1,109,278 participants), outdoor track and field (572,123), basketball (540,207), baseball (472,644), and soccer (391,839). Girls' participation was greatest in outdoor track and field (469,177), basketball (439,550), volleyball (403,985), fast-pitch softball (378,211), and soccer (356,116). The overall growth in student participation in interscholastic sports was also tempered by a growing trend of students (especially students in suburban areas) leaving high school athletic programs to participate in private-club programs.[29]

The United States built its current structure of interscholastic sports governance in steps during the half century from approximately 1880 to 1930, producing a social institution that by the early twenty-first century impacts virtually every aspect of our society and its culture. High school sports have become so important that they are a touchstone of conflict over race, religion, gender, class, and virtually every other social division that rents our society. Yet at the same time, high school sports bring our communities together, from the camaraderie on the football field to the shared experiences of the townspeople in backing their teams. The values and ethics in our society as a whole are reflected in our schools and most publicly on the athletic fields and courts.

The very term *interscholastic sports* inherently poses the contradiction in an educational institution sponsoring sports for high school students, having them play before spectators, charging admission, and financing expensive programs with seemingly no educational purpose—with educational moneys going for coaches, uniforms, bands, cheerleaders, gymnasiums, playing fields, and stadiums. But interscholastic sports have become so thoroughly infused throughout our secondary-school system that it would be unthinkable that they would ever dramatically be reformed, let alone removed. And providing the undergirding of support for high school sports is the broadly and long-held belief that they help build character, and particularly American character, and that the values taught through the inculcation of competitive sports have helped build this country's democracy and overall moral fiber. So we are destined to live with high school sports, both with their failings and with their successes, even though their contradictions were manifest from their very inception and never did and never could go away.

Notes

Selected Bibliography

Index

Notes

Preface

1. Thomas D. Snyder and Sally A. Dillow, *Digest of Education Statistics, 2010*, 15, 19; National Federation of State High School Associations, "2007–2008 High School Athletics Participation Survey." A clean number of total participants is not possible. The National Federation listed a total of 7,429,381 participants for the school year 2008–9, but this figure reflected multiple-sport athletes.

2. Timothy J. L. Chandler, review of *Muscle and Manliness: The Rise of Sport in American Boarding Schools*, by Axel Bundgaard, *Journal of Sport History* 33, no. 3 (2006): 359–61.

1. Baseball and Football Pioneer High School Sports

1. Bundgaard, *Muscle and Manliness*, 6–9, 12; Curtis C. Stone, "High School Athletics: A History and Current Problems"; James Alfred Montgomery, "The Development of the Interscholastic Athletics Movement in the United States, 1890–1940."

2. Bundgaard, *Muscle and Manliness*, 12; Stone, "High School Athletics," 56–58, 70–71.

3. Bundgaard, *Muscle and Manliness*, 13–16.

4. Ibid., 34–36, 39–40, 44–45.

5. Ibid., 18–19; Axel Bundgaard, "Tom Brown Abroad: Athletics in Selected New England Public Schools, 1850–1910," 28–29.

6. Bundgaard, *Muscle and Manliness*, 52, 83; Elmer Ellsworth Brown, *The Making of the Middle Schools*, 433.

7. Brown, *Making of the Middle Schools*, 397.

8. Bundgaard, *Muscle and Manliness*, 87–93.

9. Brown, *Making of the Middle Schools*, 295–96.

10. Ibid., 353–66.

11. Stone, "High School Athletics," 75; Brown, *Making of the Middle Schools*, 34, 301, 311–13, 407–8; David Ment, "Public Schools," in *The Encyclopedia of New York City*, edited by Kenneth T. Jackson (New Haven, CT: Yale Univ. Press, 1995), 957–60.

12. Brown, *Making of the Middle Schools*, 468–69; Montgomery, "Development of the Interscholastic Athletics Movement," 20.

13. Stone, "High School Athletics," 104.

14. George B. Kirsch, *The Creation of American Team Sports: Baseball and Cricket, 1838–72* (Urbana: Univ. of Illinois Press, 1989), 158, 162–63; *Chicago Times*, Oct. 10, 1869, June 11, 1971; Warren Goldstein, *Playing for Keeps: A History of Early Baseball* (Ithaca, NY: Cornell Univ. Press, 1989), 17–18.

15. Harold Seymour, *Baseball: The People's Game*, 6; Melvin L. Adelman, *A Sporting Time: New York City and the Rise of Modern Athletics, 1820–70* (Urbana: Univ. of Illinois Press, 1986), 128; Kirsch, *Creation of American Team Sports*, 144, 158–59.

16. Stephen Freedman, "The Baseball Fad in Chicago, 1865–1870: An Exploration of the Role of Sport in the Nineteenth-Century City," *Journal of Sport History* 5, no. 2 (1978): 42; "Base Ball in the West," *New York Clipper*, Jan. 5, 1867, 308; *Chicago Tribune*, Oct. 18, 20, 1869, June 1, Aug. 5, 13, 1870.

17. Seymour, *Baseball: The People's Game*, 27.

18. Bundgaard, "Tom Brown Abroad"; Seymour, *Baseball: The People's Game*, 41–42; Stone, "High School Athletics," 80–81.

19. Franklin Spencer Edmonds, *History of the Central High School of Philadelphia*, 251, 257; *New York Clipper*, Nov. 5, 1870, 242.

20. A more extensive examination of youth and high school sports in Chicago appeared in an earlier essay by the author: Robert Pruter, "Youth Baseball in Chicago, 1868–1890: Not Always Sandlot Ball." See also *Chicago Times*, Oct. 16, 1868; and *Chicago Tribune*, Oct. 28, 1928.

21. *Chicago Times*, May 18, 1870, June 16, 1871; *Chicago Times*, June 19, 1873, May 10, 24, June 14, 1874.

22. "Village Sports," *Evanston Index*, June 15, 1878; *Evanston Index*, May 4, 1878; William Grant Webster, *The Evanston Village High School* (Chicago: privately printed, 1907), 123.

23. *Evanston Index*, June 15, 1878, May 5, 26, 1879, May 29, 1880; Webster, *Evanston Village High School*, 45–52.

24. Harriet I. Spalding, *Reminiscences*, 82–83; Peter Levine, *A. G. Spalding and the Rise of Baseball: The Promise of American Sport* (New York: Oxford Univ. Press, 1985), 6–7.

25. Thomas W. Gutowski, "Student Initiative and the Origins of the High School Extracurriculum: Chicago, 1880–1915," 55–65.

26. *Sixteenth Biennial Report of the Superintendent of Public Instruction of the State of Illinois, July 1, 1884—June 30, 1886*, 179–80.

27. "West Division High School," *High School Journal* 1, no. 1 (1884): 5; "Sports and Pastimes," *Hyde Park Herald*, May 17, 1884; "Base Ball at Home," *Hyde Park Herald*, June 6, 1885; "Hurrah for Hyde Park," *Hyde Park Herald*, May 30, 1885; "Evanston High School," *High School Journal* 6, no. 3 (1886): 7.

28. [Letter from "Earnest"], *High School Journal* 6, no. 4 (1886): 4; "Early High School Days," *Tabula*, Apr. 2, 1895, 1.

29. *Evanston Index*, May 5, 12, 26, June 2, 1888; *Chicago Tribune*, May 22, 26, 30, June 5, 10, 16, 1889.

30. "High School Items," *Evanston Index*, Apr. 28, 1888; "High School Items," *Evanston Index*, May 19, 1888.

31. "Evanston," *High School Journal* 8, no. 8 (1889): 67; "Principal Henry L. Boltwood, Evanston (Ill.) High School"; Charles L. Brown, "Athletics," *High School Journal* 9, no. 6 (1890): 87.

32. Melvin I. Smith, *Evolvements of Early American Foot Ball: Through the 1890/91 Season*, 39–46, 57, 70; Bundgaard, *Muscle and Manliness*, 57–74; Bundgaard, "Tom Brown Abroad."

33. Edmonds, *Central High School of Philadelphia*, 254; M. Smith, *Evolvements of Early American Foot Ball*, 225, 233, 239.

34. "The Game of Football," *Washington Post*, Nov. 24, 1889; "Coaches Corner," *Scholastic Coach* 28, no. 1 (1958): 62; Jeffrey Mirel, "From Student Control to Institutional Control of High School Athletics: Three Michigan Cities, 1883–1905," 86–89; Lewis L. Forsythe, *Athletics in Michigan High Schools: The First Hundred Years*, 49.

35. "High School Items," *Evanston Index*, Nov. 1, 15, 1879; "University Items," *Evanston Index*, Dec. 13, 1879, 37; "High School Items," *Evanston Index*, Dec. 3, 1881; "High School Items," *Lake View Telephone*, Dec. 17, 1881.

36. "Football in the S.D.H.S.," *High School Journal* 4, no. 3 (1885): 4.

37. "South Division High School," *High School Journal* 2, no. 2 (1884): 5.

38. "H.S.F.B.L.," *High School Journal* 4, no. 2 (1885): 8; "North Division High School," *High School Journal* 4, no. 3 (1885): 5; "H.S.F.B.L.," *High School Journal* 4, no. 4 (1886): 8; M. Smith, *Evolvements of Early American Foot Ball*, 131–32, 136.

39. "N.D.H.S.—Foot-ball," *High School Journal* 6, no. 2 (1886): 5; "Lake View Athletics," "W.D.H.S.," and "N.D.H.S.," *High School Journal* 6, no. 3 (1886): 5; "N.D.H.S." (letter), *High School Journal* 6, no. 4 (1886): n.p.

40. Victor Frankenstein, "South Division," *High School Journal* 8, no. 4 (1888): 27; "A Game of Football," *Chicago Tribune*, Oct. 26, 1888; "Sporting Notes," *Inter Ocean*, Oct. 28, 1888; "The High School," *Evanston Index*, Dec. 1, 1888; "A Football League," *Chicago Tribune*, Sept. 28, 1889.

41. M. Smith, *Evolvements of Early American Foot Ball*, 178–79, 184, 540; Stephen Hardy, *How Boston Played* (Boston: Northeastern Univ. Press, 1982), 112–15; "Schoolboys to Have Football League," *New York Times*, Oct. 19, 1893.

42. "The Cutlers Defeated," *New York Times*, Nov. 18, 1888; "Thanksgiving Day Games," *New York Times*, Nov. 28, 1888; "Stevens Win the Pennant," *New York Times*, Dec. 15, 1889; "Interscholastic Football League," in *Brooklyn Daily Eagle Almanac, 1891* (Brooklyn: Brooklyn Daily Eagle, 1891), 59; "Both Teams on Their Mettle," *New York Times*, Nov. 15, 1892; "Schoolboys Have Crack Teams," *New York Times*, Oct. 31, 1893.

2. The Rise of Schoolboy Track and Tennis

1. "Hyde Park," *High School Journal* 7, no. 7 (1888): 109.

2. "W.D.H.S.," *High School Journal* 6, no. 4 (1886): n.p.; "Scholars in the Field," *Chicago Tribune*, June 7, 1888.

3. "Field Day," *High School Journal* 8, no. 8 (1889): 62–63.

4. "Hyde Park," *High School Journal* 8, no. 8 (1889): 66.

5. "Field Day," *High School Journal* 8, no. 8 (1889): 63; "High School Athletes," *Chicago Tribune*, July 3, 1889.

6. Ibid.

7. "High-School Pupils in the Field," *Chicago Tribune*, June 25, 1890.

8. Felix Durant, letter, *High School Journal* 10, no. 7 (1891): 106.

9. Frank C. Tracy, "Athletic Notes," *Voice*, Apr. 1891, 29; "High School Field Day," *Chicago Tribune*, June 13, 1891.

10. "High School Athletes"; "High-School Pupils in the Field"; "School Boys in Competition," *Chicago Times*, June 14, 1893; "Lake View High School Wins," *Chicago Tribune*, June 14, 1893.

11. "Athletics," *Englewood High School Journal* 1 (Feb. 1893): 9; "At Champaign," *High School Weekly* 1 (June 12, 1893): 19.

12. "At Champaign," 19.

13. "Hints on Athletic Training," *High School Journal* 8, no. 8 (1889): 63; Fred A. Hayner, "A Review of Athletics, '90–'91," *Voice*, June 1891, 50–51; "Athletics," *Libethrian* (1895): 97–103; "Big Field Days," *Chicago Tribune*, May 15, 1898.

14. "High School League Closed," *Chicago Tribune*, June 13, 1891.

15. "Tournament at Morgan Park" and "Field Day at Highland Park," *Chicago Tribune*, June 9, 1891; "De La Salle Athletic Club Games," *Chicago Tribune*, June 17, 1893; "De La Salle Athletes in the Field," *Chicago Tribune*, June 17, 1894; "Preparatory School Athletics," *Chicago Tribune*, June 8, 1895; "Hold an Academic Field Day," *Chicago Tribune*, May 24, 1896.

16. "Plan High School Meets," *Chicago Tribune*, Mar. 15, 1903; "Important Meet Proposed," *Chicago Tribune*, Mar. 2, 1902.

17. "Hold an Academic Field Day," *Chicago Tribune*, May 24, 1896; "Morgan Park Academy," *University of Chicago Weekly*, Apr. 1, 1893, 7–8.

18. "Gossip of the Academy Boys," *Chicago Tribune*, Dec. 20, 1903; "Rule Out 'Prep' Players," *Chicago Tribune*, Oct. 18, 1897; "Interacademic League Formed," *Chicago Tribune*, Feb. 4, 1900.

19. "Athletics," *Cherry Circle*, May 1, 1895, 4; "Preparatory School Athletes," *Chicago Tribune*, June 8, 1895; "Adopt a Football Schedule," *Chicago Tribune*, Oct. 8, 1895; "Princeton-Yale Again Champion," *Chicago Tribune*, May 24, 1896; "Wins 'Championship' in Final," *Chicago Tribune*, Feb. 10, 1903.

20. "Interpreparatory Tennis Games," *Chicago Tribune*, June 13, 1897; "School Golfers at Play," *Chicago Tribune*, May 26, 1901; "Chicago Latin Again Winner," *Chicago Tribune*, June 10, 1906.

21. "Tournament at Phillips," *Boston Globe*, Oct. 21, 1878; "Berkeley Athletics Contesting," *New York Times*, May 12, 1885; "Athletics," *Outing* 8, no. 4 (1886): 485–88; "Adelphi Association Games," *New York Times*, June 9, 1888; "Sports at St. Paul," *New York Times*, June 1, 1893; Walter M. Ostrem, "The Beginnings of Track and Field Sports in Minnesota," 18–19.

22. "School Boys as Athletics," *New York Times*, May 18, 1879.

23. Ibid.; "Competing in Athletic Games, Spring Meeting of the Scottish-American Club—School-Boys in Rivalry," *New York Times*, May 16, 1880; "City and Suburban News," *New York Times*, Mar. 9, 1885; "Cutler Wins the Cup," *New York Times*, May 23, 1886.

24. "Harvard School Wins the Cup," *New York Times*, June 9, 1892; "Schoolboys Have Crack Teams," *New York Times*, Oct. 31, 1893; "Among School Athletes," *New York Times*, Jan. 13, 1897.

25. "Meeting of Schoolboy Athletes," *New York Times*, Mar. 3, 1894; "Have a New Constitution," *New York Times*, Jan. 15, 1896; "Among School Athletes," *New York Times*, Jan. 13, 1897; "The Interscholastics Meet," *New York Times*, Dec. 15, 1897.

26. "Schoolboys Have Crack Teams," *New York Times*, Oct. 31, 1893; "School Boy Athletes," *Brooklyn Eagle*, May 26, 1894; "St. Paul's by 24 Points," *Brooklyn Eagle*, May 15, 1898.

27. "Latin School Wins Tennis," *Brooklyn Eagle*, June 5, 1894; "Handball and Basketball Tourney," *New York Times*, Nov. 20, 1897; "Last League Meeting," *Brooklyn Eagle*, June 4, 1898; "Schoolboy Athletes Meet," *Brooklyn Eagle*, Mar. 4, 1899.

28. "Inter-Scholastic Sports," *Brooklyn Eagle*, Sept. 26, 1899; "Public High School Games," *New York Times*, May 21, 1899; "Athletic Schoolboys," *New York Times*, Mar. 18, 1900.

29. "Inter-Scholastic Sports."

30. "Eight Nines in the Interscholastic League," *Boston Globe*, Mar. 17, 1889; "How the Cup Has Been Won," *Boston Globe*, Oct. 31, 1897; "Schoolboy Records of 1898," *Boston Globe*, Mar. 5, 1899; Stephen Hardy, "Exercise and Sports for the Schools."

31. "Ice Polo League," *Boston Globe*, Jan. 10, 1892; "Schoolboy Records of 1898."

32. "Championship Awarded," *Philadelphia Inquirer*, Mar. 9, 1900; "Friends' Central Football Team of 1900," *Philadelphia Inquirer*, Jan. 3, 1901.

33. "New-Jersey Interscholastic League," *New York Times*, Feb. 9, 1896; "Sporting News in Brief," *New York Times*, Mar. 25, 1896; "New-Jersey School Contests," *New York Times*, June 6, 1896; "The Championship Game," *New York Times*, Oct. 25, 1896.

34. "Lake View High School," *High School Journal* 2, no. 1 (1884): 6; "Evanston High School," *High School Journal* 6, no. 3 (1886): 7; "Lake View Athletics," *High School Journal* 6, no. 3 (1886): 5; "Scholars in the Field," *Chicago Tribune*, June 7, 1888; H. A. Tracy, "Tennis in W.D.," *Voice*, May 1891, 35.

35. W. M. Dean, "Athletic Notes," *Voice*, May 1894, 10; "The Tennis Tournament," *Voice*, June 1894, 19; "Cook County High School Tennis," *Chicago Tribune*, June 19, 1894.

36. *Spalding's Lawn Tennis Guide for 1896* (New York: American Sports Publishing, 1896), 50–51; "Inter-Scholastic Tennis Meeting," *Chicago Tribune*, Mar. 15, 1896.

37. William Dana Orcutt, "The Interscholastic Movement"; "Tennis Champion R. D. Wrenn," *Chicago Tribune*, Sept. 3, 1893; "Three Tennis Tourneys," *Chicago Tribune*, Aug. 16, 1896.

38. "Ojai Valley Tennis," *Los Angeles Times*, Mar. 13, 1899; "High Schools Tackle Tennis," *Los Angeles Times*, May 19, 1904; "Donnell's New Honor," *Los Angeles Times*, May 16, 1906.

39. "Active Young Athletes," *New York Times*, Feb. 20, 1892; "Interscholastic Athletics," *New York Times*, Feb. 28, 1892; "Long Island Schoolboys' Games," *New York Times*, Mar. 1, 1896.

40. "St. Paul's School Won," *New York Times*, Mar. 29, 1896; "Worcester Athletes Won," *New York Times*, Mar. 28, 1897; "Public School Athletic Triumph," *New York Times*, Dec. 27, 1903.

41. "Schoolboy Records of 1898," *Boston Globe*, Mar. 5, 1899; "Brookline High Wins the First Preparatory School League Meet," *Boston Globe*, Mar. 1, 1906; "A.A.U. Told to Mind Its Own Affairs," *Boston Globe*, Mar. 11, 1906.

42. "C.A.A.'s Indoor Meet," *Inter Ocean*, Mar. 3, 1895; "Pupils at the Games," *Chicago Tribune*, Apr. 7, 1895.

43. "Purple and White Win," *Chicago Tribune*, Apr. 5, 1896.

44. "Indoor Meet a Success," *Chicago Tribune*, Mar. 15, 1896; "Athletes in Fine Trim," *Chicago Tribune*, Feb. 27, 1897; "U. of C. Is Victor," *Inter Ocean*, Mar. 6, 1898.

45. "First Regiment Company to Hold First Annual Indoor Meet," *Chicago Tribune*, Feb. 16, 1896; "Soldiers' Indoor Meet," *Chicago Tribune*, Jan. 23, 1898; "Athletes in Fine Form," *Chicago Tribune*, Feb. 21, 1897.

46. "Soldiers Wins the Meet," *Chicago Tribune*, Jan. 29, 1899; "Madison Team Wins Meet," *Chicago Tribune*, Mar. 6, 1904; "Seven Thousand Cheer Athletes," *Inter Ocean*, Mar. 29, 1905.

3. THE PHYSICAL EDUCATION MOVEMENT
AND THE CAMPAIGN FOR CONTROL

1. Guy Lewis, "Adoption of the Sports Program, 1906–39: The Role of Accommodation in the Transformation of Physical Education," 36–37.

2. This is the standard "melting pot" explanation given for Progressive Era reform, as exemplified in the work of Lawrence A. Cremin in his chapter "Culture and Community," in *The Transformation of the School: Progressivism in American Education, 1876–1957*, 58–89. See also Ellwood Cubberley, *Public Education in the United States: A Study and Interpretation of American Educational History*, 502–4; and Ira Katznelson and Margaret Weir, *Schooling for All: Class, Race, and the Decline of the Democratic Ideal*, 96–99.

3. Joel H. Spring, *The American School, 1642–1990*, 2nd ed. (New York: Longman, 1990), 155–57. Spring cites Ellwood P. Cubberley's work as being representative of this "altruistic" view of the role of the high school, although the reports and articles by earlier educators in the first decade of the twentieth century are suffuse with such views. See, for example, Gilbert B. Morrison, "Secret Fraternities in High Schools," 488; and F. D. Boynton, "Athletics and Collateral Activities in Secondary schools," 206–7, the latter which argues that the extracurriculum could serve as a melting pot to instill democratic and American values.

4. Robert Knight Barney, "Physical Education and Sport in North America," 196.

5. Quoted in Roberta J. Park, "Science, Service, and the Professionalism of Physical Education, 1885–1905."

6. Barney, "Physical Education and Sport," 196.

7. Emmett A. Rice, John L. Hutchinson, and Mabel Lee, *A Brief History of Physical Education*, 249–51; Deobold B. Van Dalen and Bruce L. Bennett, *A World History of Physical Education*, 401.

8. Dudley A. Sargent, "Ideals of Physical Training"; Park, "Science, Service, and Professionalism," 7–10, 15; Van Dalen and Bennett, *World History of Physical Education*, 403–8, 439–40; Natalie Marie Shepard, *Foundations and Principles of Physical Education*, 141, 149.

9. Dudley A. Sargent, "Athletics in Secondary Schools," 60.

10. Frederick Whitton, "Higher Ideals in Secondary Education," 266.

11. Joel H. Spring, "Mass Culture and School Sports," 487–91; Shepard, *Foundations and Principles*, 156–58; Barney, "Physical Education and Sport," 211.

12. J. M. Sarver, "Inter-School Athletics," 420–23.

13. G. S. Lowman, "The Regulation and Control of Competitive Sport in Secondary Schools of the United States: I. Public High Schools," 241.

14. Ibid., 345; G. S. Lowman, "The Regulation and Control of Competitive Sport in Secondary Schools of the United States: II. Private Schools and Academies," 308.

15. Lowman, "Public Schools," 246; Lowman, "Private Schools," 309.

16. Lowman, "Public Schools," 246; Lowman, "Private Schools," 310.

17. Lowman, "Public Schools," 246–49; Lowman, "Private Schools," 311–13.

18. Lowman, "Public Schools," 250–51; Lowman, "Private Schools," 313–15.

19. James Huff McCurdy, "A Study of the Characteristics of Physical Training in the Public Schools of the United States," 212.

20. Lowman, "Public Schools," 254; Lowman, "Private Schools," 317–18.

21. William Orr, "The Place of Athletics in the Curriculum of Secondary Schools for Girls and Boys," 53–54; "Uses and Abuses of Athletics."

22. George L. Meylan, "Athletics," *American Physical Education Review* 10, no. 2 (1905): 160.

23. Sargent, "Athletics in Secondary Schools," 62–68.

24. Lowman, "Public Schools," 254; Lowman, "Private Schools," 318.

25. Meylan, "Athletics," 158; W. J. S. Bryan, "Principals' Conference," 486.

26. Sargent, "Athletics in Secondary Schools," 62–68.

27. Meylan, "Athletics," 159; Bryan, "Principals' Conference," 486–87.

28. Earl Cline, "Advisability of Inter-High-School Contests in Athletics," 23–24.

29. Meylan, "Athletics," 159; Henry S. Curtis, "A Football Education," 263; Charles W. Larned, "Athletics from a Historical and Educational Standpoint," 4.

30. An extended discussion of adolescent sexuality and school sports can be found in Joel H. Spring's "Mass Culture and School Sports." See also Frank Herbert Beede, "School Athletics"; and E. H. Nichols, "Competitive Athletics," 594.

31. Bryan, "Principals' Conference," 486.

32. Sargent, "Athletics in Secondary Schools," 63; Nichols, "Competitive Athletics," 593–94. The most comprehensive explanation of how interscholastic athletics served the modern industrial state in producing compliant productive workers can be found in Timothy Patrick O'Hanlon, "Interscholastic Athletics, 1900–1940: Shaping Citizens for Unequal Roles in the Modern Industrial State" (article). O'Hanlon argues that the very structure of interscholastic athletics, placing students in various levels of competition, mirrored the world of work and thus socialized students into their future roles in industrial capitalism. Spring, in "Mass Culture and School Sports," also presents a social control theory that emphasized the need to "control a growing urban proletariat."

33. Curtis, "A Football Education," 263, 266.

34. Larned, "Historical and Educational Standpoint," 4–8. Timothy O'Hanlon, in "School Sports as Social Training: The Case of Athletics and the Crisis of World War I," extends his social control theory to encompass the needs of not only the modern industrial state but also the modern military, saying, "The attributes necessary for an industrial society and for military preparedness often turned out to be remarkably similar" (20).

4. Educators Impose Institutional Control

1. Bryan, "Principals' Conference," 488.

2. Sargent, "Athletics in Secondary Schools," 61–62.

3. Sarver, "Inter-School Athletics," 423–25; Edmonds, *Central High School of Philadelphia*, 221.

4. Edward L. Harris, C. A. Waldo, and J. E. Armstrong, "Report of the Committee on Athletics."

5. E. V. Robinson, "Discussion."

6. J. Thomas Jable, "The Public Schools Athletic League of New York City: Organized Athletics for City Schoolchildren, 1903–1914," 217–38; "Public School [*sic*] Athletic League"; [Elizabeth Burchenal], "The City Child Is Handicapped by Restricted Play," *New York Times*, Feb. 23, 1913, 57.

7. Jable, "Public Schools Athletic League," 221–22; Luther Halsey Gulick, "Athletics for School-Children," 201.

8. Jable, "Public Schools Athletic League," 223–25; "High School Championships," n.p.

9. Jable, "Public Schools Athletic League," 227.

10. Ibid., 235.

11. "School Basketball," *Philadelphia Inquirer*, Jan. 20, 1900; "Schoolboys Meet," *Philadelphia Inquirer*, Mar. 8, 1900; "Football Games To-day," *Philadelphia Inquirer*, Nov. 24, 1898; "Clearing House for School Ills," *Philadelphia Inquirer*, May 7, 1911.

12. "Government of Athletics in Philadelphia"; "Alumni Oppose Board Direction of School Sport," *Philadelphia Inquirer*, May 15, 1912; "Greatest All-Scholastic Basketball Team," *Philadelphia Inquirer*, Mar. 10, 1912.

13. "Fifth Annual Field Day of Philadelphia Public Schools, May 25, 1912, Belmont Plateau, Fairmont Park"; "Belmont Wins Schoolboys' Meet," *Philadelphia Inquirer*, May 5, 1910; "Schoolboy Soccer," *Philadelphia Inquirer*, Dec. 12, 1911.

14. "To Include All Boston Schools: It Is Proposed to Organize a New Interscholastic Athletic League," *Boston Globe*, Jan. 9, 1905; "New School League," *Boston Globe*, Feb. 14, 1905; "Starts Out on New Basis," *Boston Globe*, Mar. 8, 1907.

15. Stephen Hardy, "Exercise and Sports for the Schools," 118–19; "Boston Rules Governing Athletics."

16. "Athletics for All," *Boston Globe*, Mar. 29, 1910.

17. Edwin Bancroft Henderson, "Report of Secretary of the Public Schools Athletic League of Washington, D.C."; David K. Wiggins, "Edwin Bancroft Henderson: Physical Educator, Civil Rights Activist, and Chronicler of African American Athletes," 90.

18. Gulick, "Athletics for School-Children," 205; Jable, "Public Schools Athletic League," 235.

19. This account of the Chicago school regulatory reform originally appeared in an earlier and longer treatment by the author: Robert Pruter, "Chicago High School Football Struggles, the Fight for Faculty Control, and the War against Secret Societies, 1898–1908." See also Harold M. Mayer and Richard C. Wade, *Chicago: Growth of a Metropolis* (Chicago: Univ. of Chicago Press, 1969), 176–78.

20. "Athletics," *Echo* 2, no. 6 (1898): 14; "High School League Formed," *Chicago Tribune*, Feb. 5, 1898.

21. Ibid.

22. "Hyde Park 105, Brooklyn Poly, 0," *Chicago Tribune*, Dec. 7, 1902; "Chicago Schoolboys Win," *New York Times*, Nov. 29, 1903; "North Division Swamps Brooklyn," *Inter Ocean*, Nov. 29, 1903.

23. "Expels South Division," *Chicago Tribune*, Oct. 18, 1901; "Hyde Park Will Not Compete," *Chicago Tribune*, May 16, 1902; "High Schools in Defeat," *Chicago Tribune*, Nov. 25, 1904; "Defeats Are a Surprise: High School Teams End Season in Unexpected Fashion," *Chicago Tribune*, Nov. 27, 1904.

24. "Rules to Govern School Games," *Chicago Tribune*, Jan. 23, 1901; "Blow to School Teams: New Order Issued Regarding Football Players," *Chicago Tribune*, Oct. 25, 1901; "New High School Rules," *Chicago Tribune*, Feb. 11, 1902; "Schoolboys Are Stubborn," *Chicago Tribune*, Oct. 5, 1902.

25. "School Eleven a Wreck: North Division Weakened by Scholarship Rule," *Chicago Tribune*, Sept. 27, 1902.

26. "New High School League," *Chicago Tribune*, Oct. 3, 1902; "Schoolboys Are Stubborn," *Chicago Tribune*, Oct. 5, 1902; "Boy Strikers Are Firm," *Chicago Tribune*, Oct. 9, 1902.

27. "To Settle High School Fight," *Chicago Tribune*, Oct. 8, 1902; "High School Boys Disband," *Chicago Tribune*, Oct. 16, 1902.

28. "High School Teams Active," *Chicago Daily News*, Sept. 15, 1902; "Close Call for the Maroons," *Chicago Daily News*, Sept. 25, 1902; "Ginger in Hyde Park's Work," *Chicago Daily News*, Oct. 2, 1902; "Schoolboys Are Stubborn"; "Eckersall a Future Maroon," *Chicago Tribune*, Oct. 26, 1902; "Pick Hyde Park to Win," *Chicago Tribune*, Nov. 22, 1902; "Has Hyde Park at Sea," *Chicago Daily News*, Dec. 3, 1902.

29. Harry Keeler, "The Financial Responsibility of High School Managers of Athletics," 316–17.

30. Ibid., 317.

31. Ibid., 318–20.

32. "New Rules Are Disliked: Rigid Regulations Confront High School Athletics," *Chicago Tribune*, Mar. 13, 1904.

33. "New Rules Are Disliked"; Board of Control, *Cook County High School Athletic League Constitution and By-Laws* (New York: American Sports Publishing, 1906), 10; "Oak Park Is Now in Fold," *Chicago Tribune*, June 10, 1908.

34. Albert L. Clark to Amos Alonzo Stagg, Jan. 18, 1904, Amos Alonzo Stagg Papers, Box 71, Folder 31, Special Collections Research Center, University of Chicago Library.

35. Clark to Stagg, Dec. 14, 1904, ibid.; Stagg to C. J. Zeller, Care Dieges & Clust, New York Jewelers and Silversmith, ibid.; "Indoor Meets at an End," *Chicago Tribune*, Mar. 27, 1904.

36. Jable, "Public Schools Athletic League," 225.

37. "Indoor Meets Are Marked Success," *Inter Ocean*, Mar. 20, 1905.

38. [Amos Alonzo Stagg], "Notes on Cook County High School Meets, Winter Quarter 1911," Stagg Papers; "Indoor Meets," *Inter Ocean*. Amos Alonzo Stagg Papers, Box 74, Folder 31, Special Collections Research Center, University of Chicago Library.

39. Forsythe, *Athletics in Michigan High Schools*, 104, 265–68; Eric L. Cowe, *Early Women's Athletics: Statistics and History*, 8.

40. Lewis Hoch Wagenhorst, *The Administration and Cost of High School Interscholastic Athletics*, 21–23; Forsythe, *Athletics in Michigan High Schools*, 152.

41. Wagenhorst, *Administration and Cost*, 3–5; Nelson Campbell, "Pioneers and Bloomer Girls."

42. Charles W. Whitten, *Interscholastics: A Discussion of Interscholastic Contests*, 4–6.

43. Wagenhorst, *Administration and Cost*, 5.

44. Richard V. McGehee, "Educational Competition? School Sport in Texas"; Roy Bedichek, *Educational Competition: The Story of the University Interscholastic League of Texas*, 28–29.

45. Wagenhorst, *Administration and Cost*, 21–23; Bedichek, *Educational Competition*, 24–25, 465–68.

46. Wagenhorst, *Administration and Cost*, 9–10; Bedichek, *Educational Competition*, 27.

5. Student Resistance to Control and Reform

1. Elbert K. Fretwell, *Extra-Curricular Activities in Secondary Schools*, 409; Mirel, "From Student Control to Institutional Control," 94; Hardy, *How Boston Played*, 119–20 (see chap. 1, n. 41); Jable, "Public Schools Athletic League," 226; Gutowski, "Student Initiative," 70–71.

2. Forsythe, *Athletics in Michigan High Schools*, 75. Mirel pointedly differs with Forsythe's "mixed reaction" assessment, but this author thinks Forsythe got it right.

3. Helen Lefkowitz Horowitz, *Campus Life: Undergraduate Cultures from the End of the Eighteenth Century to the Present* (New York: Alfred A. Knopf, 1987); Burton Clark and Martin Trow, "The Organizational Context," in *College Peer Groups: Problems and Prospects for Research*, edited by Theodore M. Newcomb and Everett K. Wilson (Chicago: Univ. of Chicago Press, 1966), 17–70.

4. A more comprehensive version of the Chicago schools' war on the secret societies appeared in an earlier essay by the author: Pruter, "Chicago High School Football Struggles." See also "School 'Frat' May Go," *Chicago Tribune*, May 26, 1904; and "Societies Are Not Wanted," *Chicago Tribune*, Oct. 22, 1904.

5. Gutowski, "Student Initiative," 57; "West Division High School," *High School Journal* 1, no. 5 (1884): 4; "Types of the High School Student," *High School Journal* 7, no. 6 (1888): 93; Gilbert B. Morrison, "Report of the Committee on 'Secret Fraternities,'" 447.

6. Gutowski, "Student Initiative," 57; *High School Student* 1 (May 12, 1893): 4; "Events in Chicago Society," *Chicago Tribune*, June 29, 1898; *High School Life* (Chicago: High School Life Publishing, 1900), 14, 18, 22, 24–25; "Inter-Fraternity Baseball," *Libethrian* (1904), n.p.; "Fraternity Elevens Draw," *Inter Ocean*, Dec. 1, 1907.

7. *Forty-First Annual Report of the Board of Education for the Year Ending June 28, 1895* (Chicago: Board of Education, 1895): 34–35; *Fifty-First Annual Report of the Board of Education for the Year Ending June 30, 1905* (Chicago: Board of Education, 1906): 179; Mary J. Herrick, *The Chicago Schools: A Social and Political History*, 117; "High School Honors to Hyde Park Again," *Chicago Record-Herald*, June 26, 1906; Spencer C. Smith, "Report of the Committee on the Influence of Fraternities in Secondary Schools," 4, 8; Seward S. Travis, "High School Fraternities," 519.

8. S. Smith, "Influence of Fraternities," 6; Morrison, "Report of the Committee," 447; "Politics in Brooklyn School," *New York Times*, Mar. 2, 1905; "Plan to Abolish School Fraternities," *New York Times*, Feb. 8, 1911; "Abolition Highly Judicious" (editorial), *New York Times*, Jan. 10, 1913.

9. "The Public Schools," in *Encyclopedia of New York City*, edited by Jackson, 917 (see chap. 1, n. 11).

10. A. F. Nightingale, "The Place of the High School in Our System of Education," 151.

11. "Ban Put on 'Frats' in the High Schools," *Chicago Record-Herald*, Mar. 12, 1908; Henry D. Sheldon, *Student Life and Customs*, 298–99.

12. Morrison, "Secret Fraternities in High Schools"; Morrison, "Report of the Committee."

13. S. Smith, "Influence of Fraternities"; Gilbert B. Morrison, "Social Ethics in High-School Life"; William Bishop Owen, "The Problem of the High School Fraternity"; "The Washington Decision on the High-School Fraternity Question"; Travis, "High School Fraternities"; "A Discussion of High-School Fraternities and Sororities."

14. *Proceedings Board of Education, City of Chicago, July 8, 1903, to June 22, 1904* (Chicago: Board of Education, 1904), 734.

15. Ibid., 734; "Secret Societies in the High Schools," *Fifty-Third Annual Report of the Board of Education* (Chicago: Board of Education, 1907), 133.

16. *Proceedings, 1904*, 734; "Secret Societies in the High Schools," in *Fifty-Third Annual Report*, 133.

17. *Proceedings, 1904,* 734; "Secret Societies," 133–34.

18. Owen, "Problem of the High School Fraternity," 502; "Secret Societies," 133; Morrison, "Social Ethics," 449.

19. William Hard, "High-School Fraternities: Farce, Tragedy, and Statesmanship"; L. Clark Steelye, "The Influence of Sororities"; Grace Latimer Jones, "The Evils of Girls' Secret Societies."

20. *Proceedings, 1904,* 733–34.

21. "Boys May Evade Anti 'Frat' Rule," *Chicago Tribune,* Sept. 15, 1904; "School Boys Win Legal Battle," *Chicago Tribune,* Oct. 25, 1904; "'Frat' Order Is Entered," *Chicago Tribune,* Oct. 26, 1904; "School Battle Now On: Real Fight for the Cook County Football Pennant Begins," *Chicago Tribune,* Oct. 30, 1904.

22. "'Frat' Boys Help Teams: Granting Injunction Will Improve School Elevens," *Chicago Tribune,* Oct. 16, 1904; "School Boys Win a Legal Battle," *Chicago Tribune,* Oct. 25, 1904; "School Battle Now On"; *Fifty-First Annual Report of the Board of Education* (Chicago: Board of Education, 1906), 130; "'Frat' Boys Seek to Enjoin Board: Ask Judge to Stop Repressive Measures Which Aim to Abolish Societies," *Chicago Tribune,* Nov. 29, 1906.

23. "Give Football a Body Blow," *Chicago Daily News,* June 22, 1906; "School 'Frats' Must Go, Says Board's President," *Chicago Tribune,* Nov. 18, 1906; *Proceedings Board of Education, City of Chicago, July 5, 1906, to June 26, 1907* (Chicago: Board of Education, 1907), 477–78.

24. "Football Shows Life in Schools," *Inter Ocean,* Sept. 30, 1906; "Many High School Games, Scheduled for Today," *Chicago Tribune,* Oct. 27, 1906; "Call Off Preparatory Games," *Inter Ocean,* Oct. 28, 1906; "New Rules Are Disliked: Rigid Regulations Confront High School Athletics," *Chicago Tribune,* Mar. 13, 1904.

25. "Fight after Boys' Game," *Chicago Tribune,* Nov. 4, 1906; "North Siders Win County Honors," *Inter Ocean,* Dec. 2, 1906; "Exeter 12, Haverhill R., 0," *Boston Globe,* Oct. 4, 1906; "South Boston 5, Dorchester 4," *Boston Globe,* Oct. 14, 1906; "Everett H.S. 16, Cambridge Latin 0," *Boston Globe,* Nov. 4, 1906.

26. "High School Elevens Form League," *Chicago Record-Herald,* Sept. 26, 1907; "School Boys Open Football Season," *Inter Ocean,* Oct. 20, 1907.

27. "Revive High School League," *Inter Ocean,* Sept. 22, 1907.

28. "Football Outlook," *Oak Leaves,* Sept. 21, 1907; "High School Elevens Form League," *Chicago Record-Herald,* Sept. 26, 1907.

29. "Gives 'Frats' a Blow," *Chicago Record-Herald,* Nov. 12, 1907; "'Frat' Boy Loses in Legal Fight," *Chicago Tribune,* Nov. 12, 1907; "High School Fraternities" (editorial), *Chicago Tribune,* Nov. 13, 1907; *Proceedings Board of Education, City of Chicago, July 3, 1907, to June 17, 1908* (Chicago: Board of Education, 1908), 205–8.

30. "Death Knell for School Societies," *Chicago Tribune,* Jan. 4, 1908; "Blow at School Fraternities," *Chicago Daily News,* Mar. 6, 1908; "Appellate Court Decision on Control of Fraternities," Apr. 30, 1908, in *Proceedings, 1908,* 750–53.

31. "To Fight Ban on Fraternities," *Chicago Record-Herald*, July 4, 1908; "War on School Board," *Chicago Record-Herald*, Sept. 13, 1908; "'Frats' in Rupture with School Board, Employ Attorneys," *Inter Ocean*, Sept. 13, 1908; "'Frat' Pupils Return Pending Court Fight," *Chicago Record-Herald*, Sept. 15, 1908; "'Frat' Crisis Today, 500 Face Expulsion from High Schools," *Inter Ocean*, Sept. 14, 1908; "Frats Seek Court Aid, $15,000,000 Backs Pupils' War," *Inter Ocean*, Sept. 15, 1908; *Proceedings Board of Education, City of Chicago, July 1, 1908, to July 7, 1909* (Chicago: Board of Education, 1909), 183–84.

32. "Judge Rules against 'Frats,'" *Chicago Tribune*, Oct. 4, 1908; "Fraternities Lose Case; School Board Has Right to Expel," *Inter Ocean*, Oct. 4, 1908.

33. "Ban Put on 'Frats' in the High schools," *Chicago Record-Herald*, Mar. 12, 1908; Travis, "High School Fraternities," 525; Mirel, "From Student Control to Institutional Control," 98.

34. "Boys Equal Girls in High Schools," *Chicago Tribune*, Sept. 8, 1909; "A New School Year" (editorial), *Chicago Tribune*, Sept. 8, 1909; "'Prep' Football Today's Big Card," *Chicago Tribune*, Oct. 2, 1909; "High School Teams Play Football Matches Today," *Chicago Tribune*, Oct. 9, 1909; *Proceedings Board of Education, City of Chicago, July 14, 1909, to June 29, 1910* (Chicago: Board of Education, 1910), 72; *Proceedings Board of Education, City of Chicago, July 13, 1910, to June 28, 1911* (Chicago: Board of Education, 1911), 875; *Proceedings Board of Education, City of Chicago, July 12, 1911, to June 26, 1912* (Chicago: Board of Education, 1912), 1004; *Proceedings Board of Education, City of Chicago, July 2, 1912, to June 27, 1913* (Chicago: Board of Education, 1913), 1037–38; *Proceedings Board of Education, City of Chicago, July 8, 1914, to June 30, 1915* (Chicago: Board of Education, 1915), 456–58; *Proceedings, 1915*, 679–70; "Frats Admit Defeat, Students Seek Peace," *Chicago Record-Herald*, Jan. 21, 1913.

35. Gutowski, "Student Initiative," 59.

36. "High School Fraternities Widely Banned"; William Graebner, "Outlawing Teenage Populism: The Campaign against Secret Societies in the American High School, 1900–1960."

37. "Trip Stirs School Board," *Chicago Tribune*, Dec. 19, 1908; "Englewood Team Wins Butte Game," *Chicago Tribune*, Dec. 20, 1908; "Englewood Loses to Longmont, 13–0," *Chicago Tribune*, Dec. 26, 1908, "Praise for Englewood Team," *Chicago Tribune*, Dec. 29, 1908; "Chicago Boys in Trouble," *Chicago Tribune*, Jan. 5, 1907.

38. "Row on School Gridiron," *Chicago Tribune*, Nov. 21, 1909; "Urion Says 'No Junkets,'" *Chicago Tribune*, Dec. 15, 1909.

39. "Football Junket," *Oak Leaves*, Dec. 24, 1910; "Oak Park Eleven Crushes Everett in Clash for Title," *Chicago Tribune*, Dec. 1, 1912; "Wendell Phillips Eleven Leaves for Games in West," *Chicago Tribune*, Dec. 21, 1912; "DePaul Beats Beverly Teams by 30–7 Score," *Chicago Tribune*, Dec. 5, 1915.

40. "High School Boys in Athletic War," *Chicago Tribune*, Jan. 16, 1908; "Fights a Menace to School Sport," *Chicago Tribune*, Jan. 17, 1908.

41. "Hyde Park Star Called 'Pro,'" *Chicago Tribune*, Nov. 18, 1910; "Will Clean Up 'Prep' Ranks," *Chicago Tribune*, Nov. 23, 1910.

42. "J. C. Reed to Head Board of Control," *Chicago Tribune*, June 9, 1908; "Halas Is Declared a 'Pro,'" *Chicago Tribune*, Mar. 17, 1910.

43. "Will Clean Up"; "Will Not Award H.S. Flag," *Chicago Tribune*, June 22, 1911; "Oak Park Loses Crane Case," *Chicago Tribune*, May 18, 1911.

6. Winter Indoor Sports Fill the Void

1. Albert G. Applin II, "From Muscular Christianity to the Market Place: The History of Men's and Boys' Basketball in the United States, 1891–1957," 36; "Y.M.C.A. News," *Inter Ocean*, July 16, 1892; "Morgan Park Academy," *University News*, Mar. 7, 1893.

2. "The University Team Wins—Other Athletic Events," *University News*, Mar. 23, 1893; standings of City Basketball League, *University of Chicago Weekly*, Feb. 15, 1894, 7; "Chicago Too Much for Iowa," *Chicago Tribune*, Jan. 19, 1896.

3. "Morgan Park Academy," *University News*, Mar. 7, 1893; "University Boys Win," *Inter Ocean*, Mar. 19, 1893; "With the Athletic Editor," *University of Chicago Weekly*, Feb. 15, 1894, 7.

4. *Cook County High School Indoor Baseball League, Secretary's Record: Minutes, Dec. 12, 1895–Feb. 19, 1899, Plus Constitution and By-Laws,* Chicago History Museum Archives; "YMCA Basketball Games," *Chicago Tribune*, Jan. 12, 1896.

5. "High School Basketball League," *Chicago Tribune*, Dec. 9, 1900; "Spalding Team Wins Banner," *Chicago Tribune*, Mar. 5, 1901; G. W. Ehler, "Basketball in Chicago."

6. "Winter Sport of Schools," *Chicago Tribune*, Jan. 12, 1902; "Medill Team Is the Champion," *Chicago Tribune*, Mar. 30, 1902; "Adopt High School Schedule," *Chicago Tribune*, Jan. 11, 1903; "North Division's Pennant," *Chicago Tribune*, Apr. 27, 1903; "Evanston Team Out of Race," *Chicago Tribune*, Jan. 30, 1907; "Basketball Schedule Out," *Chicago Tribune*, Dec. 18, 1906; "To Control Academic Sport," *Chicago Tribune*, Feb. 10, 1907.

7. "Twenty-Six Fives in Pennant Race," *Chicago Tribune*, Nov. 23, 1910; "Basket Schedule Draws 33 Teams," *Chicago Tribune*, Nov. 23, 1912.

8. "School Fives Start Play," *Chicago Tribune*, Mar. 28, 1908; "State Basketball Tourney," *Oak Leaves*, Mar. 7, 1908; Scott Johnson, "Learning to Fly, 1908–1929," 6–11; Scott Johnson, "From the Y to the U."

9. "Growth of Basketball," *Brooklyn Eagle*, Mar. 7, 1897; "Scholastic Sport," *New York Times*, Jan. 15, 1899; "Morris School Games," *New York Times*, Mar. 30, 1900; "School League Formed," *New York Times*, Nov. 25, 1903; "Boys Receive Athletic Cup," *New York Times*, Feb. 5, 1905; Nelson Campbell, "The Weird and the Wondrous," 138.

10. "Sports at Show," *Boston Globe*, Mar. 2, 1900; "Holyoke the Champion," *Boston Globe*, July 11, 1901; "Highland Interscholastic League," *Boston Globe*, Jan. 22, 1903;

"Unruly Crowd," *Boston Globe*, Feb. 25, 1904; "Nine Teams: Boys Form Basket-Ball League," *Boston Globe*, Oct. 28, 1904.

11. "Basketball Notes," *Philadelphia Inquirer*, Feb. 6, 1897; "Temple and Central High," *Philadelphia Inquirer*, Jan. 30, 1898; "Interscholastic Standing," *Philadelphia Inquirer*, Mar. 11, 1899; "Interscholastic League Standing," *Philadelphia Inquirer*, Jan. 11, 1901.

12. Applin, "From Muscular Christianity to the Market Place," 77–78.

13. Nelson Campbell, "Pioneers and Bloomer Girls"; Herb Schwomeyer, *Hoosier Hysteria*, 50–51.

14. John M. Booth, "An Investigation in Interscholastic Athletics in Northwestern High Schools," 697–98; Bozeman Bulger, "The Army of Basket Ball," 43.

15. "Swim in Record Times," *Chicago Tribune*, July 4, 1897; "Swimming," *Cherry Circle*, Feb. 15, 1898, 10; "Swimming," *Cherry Circle*, Apr. 15, 1898, 13.

16. "Lowers the Record," *Inter Ocean*, July 24, 1898; "Ladies' Day Program," *Cherry Circle*, Feb. 18, 1899, 5; "Swimming," *Cherry Circle*, Apr. 1, 1899, 7; "Hyde Park Team Defeated," Feb. 9, 1899; "CAA Team Defeats Armour," *Chicago Tribune*, Mar. 1, 1900; "For Water Polo Championship," *Chicago Tribune*, Mar. 15, 1900; "Schedule of Water Polo Games," *Chicago Tribune*, Feb. 17, 1901.

17. "Games at the Coliseum," *Chicago Tribune*, Mar. 10, 1901; "Water Races at Coliseum," *Chicago Tribune*, Feb. 10, 1902; "Triangular Athletic Meet," *Chicago Tribune*, Jan. 2, 1903; "To Hold Aquatic Contests," *Chicago Tribune*, June 7, 1903; "Local Athletes in Annual Meet," *Chicago Tribune*, Jan. 2, 1904.

18. "Maroons Win Tank Meet," *Chicago Tribune*, Mar. 4, 1905; "Yale Swimmers Defeat Maroons," *Chicago Tribune*, Apr. 25, 1905; "Sanctions Swimming League," *Chicago Tribune*, Mar. 2, 1906; "Chicago Wins Aquatic Meet," *Inter Ocean*, Mar. 17, 1906; "Oak Park Swimmers Winners," *Chicago Tribune*, Apr. 15, 1906.

19. "Evanston Academy Wins," *Inter Ocean*, Feb. 13, 1908; "Aquatic Meet to Evanston High," *Chicago Tribune*, Jan. 21, 1909.

20. Frank J. Sullivan, "Swimming Records Stand," *Chicago Tribune*, Dec. 27, 1908.

21. "Swimming Notes," *Illinois Athletic Club Magazine* 3, no. 7 (1913): 49.

22. Chauncey A. Hyatt, "Interscholastic Swimming in the Middle West, 1915–16," 111, 115.

23. Ibid.

24. "Sportsmen's Show Opens," *New York Times*, Mar. 2, 1900; "Swimming Championships," *New York Times*, Sept. 21, 1902; "West Phila. Win Swimming Honors," *Philadelphia Inquirer*, Jan. 16, 1916; "Schoolboys Race in Tank," *New York Times*, Feb. 16, 1913; "Local Lads Best Swimmers," *New York Times*, Apr. 6, 1913.

25. "Commerce Swimmers Lead," *New York Times*, Feb. 27, 1907; "Harris Hall Boys Win," *New York Times*, Nov. 28, 1908.

26. "Swimmers Are after Records," *Los Angeles Times*, June 2, 1910; A. G. Waddell, "Swimming Championships Decided in Beach Tank," *Los Angeles Times*, May 9, 1913; "High School Swimmers Settle Titles Tonight," *Los Angeles Times*, Apr. 17, 1914; "State Meet to Be in Month," *Los Angeles Times*, May 17, 1916.

27. "Water Polo Stars," *Los Angeles Times*, Apr. 30, 1913; "The Late Sports," *Los Angeles Times*, Feb. 3, 1918.

28. Terrence Cole, "'A Purely American Game': Indoor Baseball and the Origins of Softball"; Morris Bealle, *The Softball Story*; Paul Dickson, *The Worth Book of Softball: A Celebration of America's Pastime*.

29. Bealle, *The Softball Story*, 7.

30. "Indoor Baseball Notes," *Chicago Tribune*, Nov. 22, 1891; *Indoor Baseball League Minutes*.

31. *Indoor Baseball League Minutes*; "Evanston High School Winner," *Chicago Tribune*, Mar. 18, 1896; "West Division Wins Pennant," *Inter Ocean*, Mar. 5, 1900.

32. "Crane Boys Arrested during Indoor Game," *Chicago Record-Herald*, Feb. 22, 1907.

33. "'Prep' Title to Crane Nine"; "New Age Limit for 'Preps,'" *Chicago Tribune*, Feb. 7, 1914.

34. "Indoor Baseball," in *The Annual Voice*, 1914 (Chicago: McKinley High, 1914), 112–14; "Catholic 'Prep' Leaguers Frame Charts at Meeting," *Chicago Tribune*, Nov. 21, 1912.

35. Seymour, *Baseball: The People's Game*, 364–66; *Spalding's Indoor Baseball Guide for 1906* (New York: American Sports Publishing, 1906), 74, 94; *Spalding's Indoor Baseball Guide, 1913* (New York: American Sports Publishing, 1913), 68; *Spalding's Indoor Baseball Guide, 1913–14* (New York: American Sports Publishing, 1913), 128.

36. Charles Phelps Cushing, "The Baseball of the City Urchin."

37. "Boom for Playground Ball," *Chicago Tribune*, Dec. 8, 1907.

38. "Ice Skating," in *Encyclopedia of New York City*, edited by Jackson, 579–80 (see chap. 1, n. 11); "Outlook for Skaters," *New York Times*, Dec. 13, 1895; "Hockey in Brooklyn," *New York Times*, Dec. 30, 1897.

39. "Among School Athletes," *New York Times*, Jan. 13, 1897; "Schoolboys' Skating Races," *New York Times*, Mar. 16, 1900; "High School Boys Champions," *Brooklyn Eagle*, Mar. 21, 1897; "Lively Skating Races," *Brooklyn Eagle*, Feb. 12, 1898; "Skating Races Go to Poly.," *Brooklyn Eagle*, Mar. 7, 1903.

40. "Hockey and Speed Skating," *New York Times*, Feb. 5, 1905; "St. Nicholas Rink Races," *New York Times*, Feb. 9, 1906; "Young Skaters in Championships," *New York Times*, Mar. 16, 1907; "Public School and College Athletes," *New York Times*, Feb. 7, 1909; "Schoolboys on Skates," *New York Times*, Nov. 27, 1910; "Ice Carnival on Saturday," *New York Times*, Feb. 15, 1917; "Comment on Current Events in Sports," *New York Times*, Feb. 26, 1917.

41. Melville W. Webb Jr., "Schoolboy Records of 1898," *Boston Globe*, Mar. 5, 1899; Stephen Hardy, "'Polo at the Rinks': Shaping Markets for Ice Hockey, 1880–1900"; Stephen Hardy, "Long before Orr: Placing Hockey in Boston, 1897–1929," 247–49.

42. "Champions of the Merrimac Valley," *Boston Globe*, Mar. 15, 1902; "Missed Chance for Championship," *Boston Globe*, Mar. 3, 1904; "Sustained Only One Defeat," *Boston Globe*, Mar. 2, 1904; "Fast Team Likely," *Boston Globe*, Dec. 15, 1906.

43. "Scholastic Sport," *New York Times*, Oct. 30, 1898; "Poly Prep Wins L.I.I.L. Hockey Championship," *Brooklyn Eagle*, Feb. 22, 1899; "Boys' High Champions," *New York Times*, Feb. 25, 1906; "Schoolboys Beat Seventh Regiment," *New York Times*, Feb. 23, 1915.

44. "Gain for Hockey in 1917," *New York Times*, Dec. 30, 1917; "Manual Seven in Lead," *New York Times*, Mar. 3, 1917; "MacPhee to Head League," *New York Times*, Nov. 2, 1917; "Hockey under P.S.A.L.," *New York Times*, Dec. 6, 1917; "Hockey Title to Erasmus," *New York Times*, Mar. 22, 1919; "P.S.A.L. Hockey Dates Officially Announced," *New York Times*, Nov. 23, 1923.

45. "Interscholastic Hockey Championship a Tie," *Brooklyn Eagle*, Mar. 11, 1899; "New York Schoolboys Win at Hockey," *New York Times*, Mar. 22, 1901; "Big Season Promised in Hockey," *New York Times*, Nov. 29, 1903; Hardy, "'Polo at the Rinks.'"

46. "Preps Form Hockey Team," *Chicago Tribune*, Jan. 12, 1916; "Hockey," in *The Aitchpe* (1916), 108; "Ice Hockey, 1916–17," in *The Aitchpe* (1917), 102.

47. "At Sportsmen's Show," *New York Times*, Mar. 18, 1902, "Sportsmen's Show Ends," *New York Times*, Mar. 8, 1903.

48. "Girl Swimmers in Garden Pool," *New York Times*, Feb. 25, 1908; "Schoolboys Close Successful Shoot," *New York Times*, Jan. 5, 1908.

49. "School Athletics on a Big Scale," *New York Times*, Nov. 29, 1903; "Gen. R. Wingate, Youths' Friend, Dies" and "Notes of the Schoolboys," *New York Times*, Dec. 1, 1907; "Stuyvesant Gunners Win," *New York Times*, Nov. 9, 1919; Jable, "Public Schools Athletic League," 229–30.

50. "Scholastic Rifle Shoot," *New York Times*, Mar. 28, 1909; "Iowa City H.S. Champion Shooters," *New York Times*, May 16, 1913.

51. "Shooting for Schoolboys," *New York Times*, Dec. 6, 1910; "Western Schools Lead in Shooting," *New York Times*, Mar. 11, 1913; "Iowa City Boys Rifle Champions," *New York Times*, Mar. 17, 1914; "Rifle Champions New Mexico Boys," *New York Times*, Mar. 7, 1915.

52. "Organize Rifle League," *Washington Post*, Mar. 1, 1910; "Rifle Team for Girls," *Washington Post*, Nov. 15, 1912; "Central High Riflists Win U.S. Title," *Washington Post*, May 21, 1929.

53. "Big Entry for Rifle shoot," *Chicago Tribune*, Mar. 24, 1910; "A. P. Lane Best Revolver Shot in Sportsman's Club Tourney," *Chicago Tribune*, June 9, 1915; "Heubner Wins Illinois Title in Rifle Meet," *Chicago Tribune*, May 18, 1916.

54. "Handball," in *The Encyclopedia of Sports*, edited by Frank G. Menke, revisions by Suzanne Treat (New York: A. S. Barnes, 1975), 537–39; "Hand Ball and Racket: The

Games in This City—How They Are Played," *New York Times*, Jan. 23, 1876; "Polys' Easy Victory: Won Every Game of Handball from Bryant & Stratton Players," *New York Times*, Mar. 3, 1895; "Pratt and St. Paul's Will Battle To-morrow," *Brooklyn Eagle*, Oct. 21, 1902; "Erasmas Girls Win Lively Handball Match," *New York World*, Dec. 11, 1902.

55. "No Handball in the Schools," *New York Times*, Jan. 22, 1908; "Public Schools Athletics," *New York Times*, Apr. 4, 1909; "James Madison Wins in P.S.A.L. Handball," *New York Times*, Nov. 28, 1926; "Handball Crown to James Madison," *New York Times*, June 19, 1927.

7. New Outdoor Sports Advance the Educational Mission

1. George B. Kirsch, *Golf in America* (Urbana: Univ. of Illinois Press, 2009), 3–4; Herbert Warren Wind, *The Story of American Golf*, vol. 1, *1888–1941* (1948; reprint, New York: Callaway Editions, 2000), 18–19, 30–36, 43; W. Chick Evans, "Evans Traces Start of U.S. Golf to 1794," *Chicago Herald and Examiner*, May 8, 1934.

2. Kirsch, *Golf in America*, 75–76; Tom Govedarica, *Chicago Golf: The First Hundred Years* (Chicago: Eagle Communications, 1991), 27–38, 58–64; Herbert Warren Wind, "Golfing in and around Chicago," *Chicago History* 4 (Winter 1975–76): 244–51; "New Golf Club Organized," *Chicago Tribune*, Aug. 27, 1893; "First Game of Golf," *Chicago Tribune*, Aug. 5, 1894; "Chicago Golf Club Organized," *Chicago Tribune*, Mar. 15, 1895; "Chicago Golf Club," *Chicago Tribune*, June 30, 1895; J. G. Davis, "Great Advance by Public Golf in Twenty Years," *Chicago Tribune*, Dec. 6, 1914; "Public Golf Links Open," *Chicago Tribune*, May 12, 1899; Alexis J. Colman, "The Golf Clubs of Chicago," *Outing*, July 1899, 354–65.

3. Govedarica, *Chicago Golf*, 63–66, 166; "Western Golf Association," *Chicago Tribune*, Apr. 28, 1899.

4. "Students Play Good Golf," *New York Times*, July 10, 1897; "Interscholastic Tournament," in *Spalding's Official Golf Guide* (New York: American Sports Publishing, [1898]), 45.

5. "Interscholastic Golf," *Outing*, May 1899, 212; "Golfers Busy with Games," *New York Times*, Apr. 9, 1899; "Growth of Golf in Colleges," *Chicago Tribune*, Oct. 29, 1899.

6. "Vardon's Play Is Good," *Chicago Tribune*, Mar. 4, 1900.

7. "School Golfers at Play," *Chicago Tribune*, May 26, 1901; "University Defeats Rugby," *Chicago Tribune*, May 30, 1901.

8. "Golf on Many Links," *Inter Ocean*, June 4, 1899; "Evanston High School Golf Team," *Chicago Tribune*, Apr. 12, 1900; "Is a Great Golfer," *Inter Ocean*, July 16, 1899; "Golfer Holabird the Star in a New Role," *Chicago Tribune*, Jan. 27, 1901; "School Golfers at Play," *Chicago Tribune*, May 26, 1901; "University Defeats Rugby," *Chicago Tribune*, May 30, 1901.

9. "Louis N. James Takes National Golf Championship at Glenview," *Inter Ocean*, July 20, 1902.

10. Joseph Edmund, "Golf in the Middle West," 68; "Olympic Golf Championships," in *Spalding's Official Athletic Almanac for 1905*, compiled by James E. Sullivan (New York: American Sports Publishing, 1905), 231–33.

11. "Clow Is First in Golf Tourney," *Chicago Tribune*, June 30, 1903; "Golf on the Local Courses," *Chicago Tribune*, June 4, 1904; "Program for School Golfers," *Chicago Tribune*, May 31, 1908.

12. "Western Interscholastic Golf Association," in *Spalding's Official Golf Guide for 1909* (New York: American Sports Publishing, 1909), 147–49.

13. J. G. Davis, "Golf Honors to Lane Team," *Chicago Tribune*, June 13, 1911; "'Prep' Golfers to Compete for Title on Saturday," *Chicago Tribune*, June 10, 1912; "Hyde Park Wins Golf Title," *Chicago Tribune*, June 8, 1913.

14. "One Easterner Is Left at Wheaton," *Inter Ocean*, Sept. 9, 1909; Tom Bendelow, "Golf around Chicago," 140.

15. "Travers Wins Interscholastic Golf," *New York Times*, May 19, 1904; "Youngsters Meet for Golf Honors," *New York Herald*, May 18, 1906; "Legg Wins Interscholastic," *New York Times*, May 23, 1907.

16. "School Golf," *Boston Globe*, Mar. 1, 1902; "Competitions," *American Golfer*, Aug. 1910, 235.

17. Bunker Hill, "New England Notes," *American Golfer*, Aug. 1910, 197.

18. John G. Anderson, "Massachusetts Amateur Championships," *Golf Illustrated & Outdoor America*, Aug. 1914, 41; "Western Junior Championship," in *Spalding's Official Golf Guide of 1915* (New York: American Sports Publishing, 1915), 119; "Brandt of Hyde Park Leads Prep Golfers in Illinois Tourney," *Chicago Tribune*, May 14, 1916.

19. Bunker Hill, "New England Notes," *American Golfer*, Mar. 1911, 5; Bunker Hill, "New England Department," *American Golfer*, Mar. 1915, 422; "Big Entry for Boys' Tourney," *New York Times*, June 24, 1912.

20. Gabe Logan, "The Rise of Early Chicago Soccer"; "Sunday's Association Football Games," *Chicago Tribune*, Nov. 4, 1894.

21. "Association Football Season Opens Today," *Inter Ocean*, Mar. 19, 1905.

22. Ibid.

23. Henry S. Curtis, "A Plea for Association Football," 2–7; Sir Ernest Cecil Cochrane, "Association Foot Ball," in *Spalding's Official Association "Soccer" Foot Ball Guide* (New York: American Sports Publishing, 1907), 5–11.

24. "Englewood Wins Soccer Match," *Chicago Tribune*, Nov. 25, 1906; "Soccer in the High Schools," *Chicago Tribune*, Apr. 17, 1909; Archibald Birse, "Soccer Foot Ball in Chicago," in *Spalding's Official Association "Soccer" Foot Ball Guide, 1912–13* (New York: American Sports Publishing, 1912), 187; "High School Soccer League," *Chicago Tribune*, Feb. 25, 1912.

25. "Oak Park Eleven Takes Cook County Title," *Chicago Tribune*, May 18, 1913; "Four to Play for Peel Cup," *Chicago Tribune*, Apr. 26, 1914; "Lake View Gets into Cup Event," *Chicago Tribune*, Nov. 29, 1914; Keene Gardiner, "Stars of Crane Sweep Card at Sport Carnival," *Chicago Tribune*, June 6, 1915; "Soccer Minors Play Today," *Chicago Tribune*, Dec. 11, 1915.

26. "'Soccer' Tourney for High School Boys," *New York Times*, Nov. 6, 1906; "Public Schools Athletic League Championships of Greater New York," in *Spalding's Official Association "Soccer" Foot Ball Guide* (New York: American Sports Publishing, 1908), 17–19; "Soccer Football at Los Angeles, Cal., High Schools," in *Spalding's Official Soccer Foot Ball Guide, 1913–14* (New York: American Sports Publishing, 1913), 287; "Baltimore Public League School," in *Spalding's Official Soccer Foot Ball Guide, 1917–18* (New York: American Sports Publishing, 1917), 74–75.

27. "Westchester Hare and Hounds Club," *New York Times*, Nov. 26, 1878; "Harvard Hares and Hounds," *New York Times*, Dec. 7, 1879; "In and about the City," *New York Times*, Nov. 27, 1885; "An Old English Sport," *Chicago Tribune*, Dec. 19, 1886; "Paper Chases Popular," *New York Times*, Apr. 4, 1887.

28. "The Hares and Hounds," *Chicago Tribune*, June 19, 1887; "Northwestern Cross Country Club," *Chicago Tribune*, Nov. 9, 1895; "New Chicago-Purple Contest," *Chicago Tribune*, Jan. 14, 1902; "Cross Country Running," *New York Times*, Nov. 19, 1900.

29. "Cross Country Run," *Oak Leaves*, Dec. 7, 1906.

30. "Heneage First in Oak Park Run," *Chicago Tribune*, Dec. 9, 1905; "Barnes Wins the Long Race," *Chicago Tribune*, Dec. 8, 1906; "Distance Run Won by Barnes," *Chicago Tribune*, Nov. 9, 1907.

31. "Crane High Runners Win," *Chicago Tribune*, Nov. 28, 1908; "Cross Country Run to Crane," *Chicago Tribune*, Nov. 27, 1910.

32. "Interscholastic Sports," *New York Times*, Feb. 5, 1899; "Interscholastic Sport," *New York Times*, Mar. 26, 1899; "Trede Won across Country," *New York Times*, Apr. 2, 1899; "Jones Finished First in Cross-Country Run," *New York Times*, Dec. 23, 1906; "Vessie Leads Field in Cross Country," *New York Times*, Dec. 4, 1910; "Barringer Boys Win," *New York Times*, Oct. 29, 1911; "Columbia Race to Morris High," *New York Times*, Nov. 19, 1911.

33. "Cornell Team Is in Poor Shape," *Chicago Tribune*, Nov. 26, 1896; "Cross Country Run Is Ayres," *Philadelphia Inquirer*, Nov. 29, 1901; "High School Won," *Philadelphia Inquirer*, Dec. 1, 1905; "Mercersburg Wins Interscholastic Run" and "Gallagher Wins Run," *Philadelphia Inquirer*, Nov. 30, 1906; "Philadelphia Boys Win," *New York Times*, Nov. 27, 1908.

34. Thomas C. Mendenhall, *A Short History of American Rowing*, 25–26; Robert F. Kelley, *American Rowing: Its Background and Traditions*, 20–23, 48–73; Ronald A. Smith, *Sports and Freedom: The Rise of Big-Time College Athletics*, 26–51.

35. "Harvard Freshman Crew," *New York Times*, Feb. 4, 1878; "Yale and Her Athletes," *New York Times*, Dec. 7, 1890; "Faults of Yale's Crew," *New York Times*, June 4, 1896.

36. Mendenhall, *Short History of American Rowing*, 28; "Harvard Freshman Crew."

37. Edmonds, *Central High School of Philadelphia*, 259; "Schoolboy Records of 1898," *Boston Globe*, Mar. 5, 1899.

38. "Big Events in Rowing," *New York Times*, Feb. 1, 1903; "American 'Henley' Races," *New York Times*, July 3, 1903; "Great Rowing at Henley Regatta," *Philadelphia Inquirer*, May 31, 1904.

39. "Boat Race for Schoolboys," *New York Times*, Mar. 19, 1907; "Schoolboys Train for Rowing Races," *New York Times*, Apr. 7, 1907; "Columbia Crews Lead on Harlem," *New York Times*, May 31, 1907; "Crews on the Harlem," *New York Times*, May 30, 1901; Kelley, *American Rowing*, 32.

40. "Schoolboy Athletics," *New York Times*, Mar. 15, 1908; "No High School Crews This Year," *New York Times*, Mar. 7, 1915; "Schoolboy Crews Boated," *New York Times*, May 2, 1916; "Schoolboy Crews to Race," *New York Times*, Mar. 5, 1918; "Zola Scores Twice in Harlem Regatta," *New York Times*, May 31, 1925; "High School Crews Banned by League," *New York Times*, Apr. 21, 1926.

41. Donald M. Fisher, *Lacrosse: A History of the Game*, 22–54.

42. Ibid., 65–66, 70–71.

43. Ibid., 82–83.

44. "Lacrosse for Football," *New York Times*, Nov. 25, 1909; Fisher, *Lacrosse*, 75, 80; "Boys' High Lacrosse Team Wins," *New York Times*, Apr. 21, 1906; *Brooklyn Daily Eagle Almanac, 1908* (Brooklyn: Brooklyn Daily Eagle, 1908), n.p.

45. "New Lacrosse League," *New York Times*, May 4, 1917; "Lacrosse Title for St. John's," *New York Times*, June 24, 1917.

46. Fisher, *Lacrosse*, 84.

8. The New Athletic Girl and Interscholastic Sports

1. The framework for my discussion of high school athletics for girls is derived from Susan K. Cahn in her *Coming on Strong: Gender and Sexuality in Twentieth-Century Women's Sports, 1900–1960*, particularly her chapter "The New Type of Athletic Girl," 7–30.

2. Ibid., 13–15.

3. "All Work and No Play Makes Jane a Dull Stenographer," *Chicago Tribune*, Apr. 17, 1910; [Elizabeth Burchenal], "The City Child Is Handicapped by Restricted Play," *New York Times*, Feb. 23, 1913, 57; Cahn, *Coming on Strong*, 17–18.

4. Among the many articles and books on the playground movement, three relating to Philadelphia, Boston, and Chicago are particularly worthwhile investigating: Mark A. Kadzielski, "'As a Flower Needs Sunshine': The Origins of Organized Children's Recreation in Philadelphia, 1886–1911," *Journal of Sport History* 4, no. 2 (1977): 169–88; Stephen Hardy, "Playgrounds for Children," in *How Boston Played*, 85–106 (see chap. 1,

n. 41); Benjamin McArthur, "The Chicago Playground Movement: A Neglected Feature of Social Justice," *Social Service Review* 49, no. 3 (1975): 376–95; Cindy L. Himes, "The Female Athlete in American Society, 1860–1940," 149–50.

5. Cahn, *Coming on Strong*, 19.

6. J. Parmly Paret, "Exercise for Women"; Dudley A. Sargent, "How Can I Have a Graceful Figure?"; Jessie H. Bancroft, "The Need of Exercise among American Girls," *New York Times*, Sept. 29, 1906; Minna Thomas Antrium, "The Masculinization of Girls"; Dudley A. Sargent, "Are Athletics Making Girls Masculine?"; "Perils That Women Find in Athletics," *New York Times*, Mar. 31, 1906; Cahn, *Coming on Strong*, 20–21; Himes, "Female Athlete in American," 132–33.

7. Cahn, *Coming on Strong*, 23–25.

8. Betty Spears, "Send Berenson Abbott: New Woman, New Sport," in *A Century of Women's Basketball: From Frailty to Final Four*, edited by Joan S. Hult and Marianna Trekell (Reston, VA: American Alliance for Health, Physical Education, Recreation, and Dance, 1991), 19–36; Joan Paul, "Clara Gregory Baer: Catalyst for Women's Basketball," in *Century of Women's Basketball*, edited by Hult and Trekell, 37–52.

9. Kara Lynn Knight, "Basketball and Bloomers," *Illinois History* 12, no. 4 (1959): 80; *High School Aegis* (Bloomington, IL: Bloomington High School, 1897): 7; Scott Johnson, "The Girls Were First"; "Hull House Girls Win at Austin," *Chicago Tribune*, Mar. 13, 1896; "Basket Ball," *Tabula*, Dec. 1896, 56; "Englewood Girls Victorious," *Chicago Tribune*, Apr. 18, 1897; "Basketball," *Tabula*, Nov. 1896, 39; Florence Speakman, "Girls' Athletics," *Voice*, Oct. 1899, 10.

10. "Athletics," *Echo* 2, no. 6 (1898): 14–15; Frances A. Kellor, "Growth of Basket Ball," *Chicago Tribune*, Feb. 25, 1900.

11. Kellor, "Growth of Basket Ball"; "Girls to Give a Circus," *Chicago Tribune*, Feb. 29, 1901.

12. "Girls' Athletics," *Voice*, Feb. 1900. 14; Veva Padden, "Girls Athletic Association," *Voice*, Sept. 1901, 15; "Girl Teams Arrange Schedule," *Chicago Tribune*, Jan. 18, 1906.

13. "Girls a Factor in Sport," *Chicago Tribune*, Jan. 25, 1903; "Change in the Division," *Chicago Tribune*, Jan. 17, 1904.

14. "High School Girls' Basketball Teams," *Chicago Tribune*, Dec. 11, 1904; "Hyde Park Champion," *Chicago Tribune*, Apr. 20, 1905; "Breakers Ahead for Girl Fives," *Chicago Tribune*, Jan. 17, 1906; "Schedule for Girls' Teams," *Chicago Tribune*, Feb. 14, 1906; "Oak Park Girls Champions," *Chicago Tribune*, Mar. 17, 1906.

15. "Hyde Park H.S., 29; Dwight, 18," *Chicago Tribune*, Apr. 22, 1905; "Trip for Oak Park Girls' Team," *Chicago Tribune*, Mar. 25, 1906.

16. "School Heroine," *Oak Leaves*, May 20, 1904; photo of 1906 Oak Park girls team, *Oak Leaves*, Apr. 28, 1906; "Hyde Park High School Girls' Basketball Team," *Chicago Tribune*, Apr. 2, 1905.

17. *University High Weekly,* Nov. 27, 1906, 20; Jan. 8, 1907, 11; Mar. 5, 1907, 9.

18. "Pratt Girls Defeat Jamaica," *Brooklyn Eagle,* Feb. 27, 1898; "Girls Play Basket Ball," *New York Times,* Mar. 4, 1897.

19. "Girl Scholastic Athletes," *New York Times,* Nov. 20, 1899; "Girls Tennis Tournament," *New York Times,* Apr. 29, 1900.

20. "East Orange Girls in Basket Ball," *New York Times,* Dec. 14, 1903; "Local Girls Lost at Basket Ball," *New York Times,* Jan. 18, 1904; "Basket Ball for Women," *New York Times,* June 5, 1904; "Girl Athletes Rough It," *New York Times,* Feb. 12, 1905; "Girl Athletes Rough It," *New York Times,* Feb. 12, 1905.

21. "Basket Ball for Women," *New York Times,* June 5, 1904.

22. "Lynn 17, Cushing Academy 11," *Boston Globe,* Mar. 3, 1899; "Basket Ball Notes," *Boston Globe,* Mar. 3, 1902; "Basket Ball Notes," *Boston Globe,* Mar. 10, 1902; "Piled Up 83 Points," *Boston Globe,* Feb. 28, 1904; "Norwood Girls 71, Sharon Girls 2," *Boston Globe,* Mar. 7, 1908.

23. "Girls Win, Boys Lose," *Boston Globe,* Feb. 27, 1904; "Two Games at Hyde Park," *Boston Globe,* Feb. 28, 1904; "Has Won Seven Games Out of the 10 Played This Season," *Boston Globe,* Feb. 23, 1904; "Girls' Basket-Ball Team," *Boston Globe,* Dec. 8, 1906.

24. Lynne Fauley Emery and Margaret Toohey-Costa, "Hoops and Skirts: Women's Basketball on the West Coast, 1892–1930s."

25. Ibid., 146–48; "Basket Ball League Is to Be Formed," *Los Angeles Times,* Feb. 9, 1903; "Rough Basketball," *Los Angeles Times,* May 15, 1904; "Amendments to Athletic Laws," *Los Angeles Times,* Dec. 18, 1904; "Ventura Girls Lose Game," *Los Angeles Times,* Mar. 5, 1905; "Final Girls Honors," *Los Angeles Times,* Mar. 14, 1908; "Santa Ana Wins Championship," *Los Angeles Times,* Mar. 15, 1908; "Compton's Good Record," *Los Angeles Times,* Mar. 15, 1908.

26. "Fair Maids in Brain-Storms," *Los Angeles Times,* June 1, 1907. Note that the game in Southern California was played with five players, which was a far more customary number for the game under boys' rules. The game in Northern California was played with six players and was more decorous.

27. Milo S. Walker, "Indoor Base Ball for Women," 87.

28. Ibid., 85–87; "Girls to Play Indoor Baseball: League Is Formed among the West Side Schools," *Chicago Tribune,* Feb. 22, 1901.

29. Veva J. Padden, "Girls' Athletics," *Voice,* Dec. 1901, 8; Veva J. Padden, "Girls' Athletics," *Voice,* Jan. 1902, 12; Keene Gardiner, "Athletic Misses Play Baseball," *Chicago Tribune,* Feb. 15, 1912; "Phillips Girls Again Victorious," *Chicago Tribune,* Mar. 9, 1912.

30. Gertrude Dudley and Frances A. Kellor, *Athletic Games in the Education of Women,* 212–13; "Girls' High School No. 2 Team, New Orleans P.S.A.L.," caption in *Spalding's Official Indoor Base Ball Guide,* 1912, edited by R. L. Welch (New York: American Sports Publishing, 1912, 128.

31. "Girls in Olympic Games," *Chicago Tribune*, May 26, 1900.

32. "Lake View High School Pupils Brave the Rain and Hold Their Field Day Exercises," *Chicago Tribune*, June 7, 1902; "Mr. Groener and Fair Play," *Red and White*, Jan. 1922, 56.

33. "Coeds in a Track Meet," *Chicago Tribune*, June 18, 1905; "Wendell Phillips Scholars Engage in Big Track Meet," *Chicago Tribune*, June 15, 1907; "Girl Athletes Amaze Crowd," *Chicago Tribune*, June 3, 1909.

34. Cowe, *Early Women's Athletics*, 8–10; "Fifth Annual Field Day."

35. "[Athletic Notes]," *Voice*, May 1891, 37; "[Athletic Notes]," *Voice*, June 1896, 37; "[Athletics]," in *N.D. Annual, 1910* (Chicago: North Division High School), n.p.; "Adopt H.S. Schedule," *Chicago Tribune*, May 19, 1911; "The 1912 Tennis Season," in *The Oracle* (1913), 120.

36. "Los Angeles Takes All Tennis Honors," *Los Angeles Times*, June 2, 1907; Lynne Fauley Emery, "From Social Pastime to Serious Sport: Women's Tennis in Southern California in the Late 19th and Early 20th Centuries."

37. Quoted in Steveda Chepko, "The Domestication of Basketball."

38. Dudley and Kellor, *Athletic Games*, 69–77.

39. Chepko, "The Domestication of Basketball," 116; Nancy Cole Dosch, "'The Sacrifice of Maidens' or Healthy Sportswomen? The Medical Debate over Women's Basketball"; Himes, "Female Athlete in American," 135–41.

40. "Basketball Girls in a Fight," *Chicago Tribune*, Feb. 10, 1903.

41. Dudley and Kellor, *Athletic Games*, 149–52.

42. Ibid., 179–87.

43. Quoted in Chepko, "The Domestication of Basketball," 114; Dudley and Kellor, *Athletic Games*, 51–53.

44. "Bars Girls from Basketball," *Chicago Tribune*, Nov. 3, 1907; "Girls Basketball in Doubt," *Chicago Tribune*, Nov. 19, 1911; "Girls' Basketball," in *Red and White* (1910), 26–27; "Girls' Basketball," in *The Aitchpe* (1914), 167.

45. "Newark Girls Win at Basketball," *New York Times*, Nov. 30, 1906; Augusta Lane Patrick, "Relative Merit of the Y.M.C.A. Rules and Women's Rules"; "Flushing Girls Play Fine Basket Ball," *New York Times*, Feb. 23, 1907.

46. "Girls' Athletic League," *School Journal* 71, no. 23 (1905): 659; "Athletics for Girls Out of School Hours," *New York Times*, Dec. 16, 1905; "Girls Need Athletics," *New York Times*, Mar. 30, 1906; "Schoolgirls in Athletics," *New York Times*, Feb. 5, 1911.

47. "Perils That Women Find in Athletics," *New York Times*, Mar. 31, 1906; "New Kind of Athletics for City Schoolgirls," *New York Times*, May 9, 1906.

48. *Brooklyn Daily Eagle Almanac, 1906* (Brooklyn: Brooklyn Daily Eagle, 1906), 184; "School Girls Plan Games," *New York Times*, Apr. 13, 1907; "40,000 Girls in Athletics," *New York Times*, July 4, 1915; "Girls Branch and Its Work," *New York Times*, Mar. 12, 1916.

49. "Girls Skilled at Basketball," *Boston Globe*, Mar. 13, 1911; "Keen Race for Girls' Title," *Boston Globe*, Dec. 16, 1912; "Suburban Girls' Basket League Not to Enlarge," *Boston Globe*, Dec. 14, 1922.

50. "Rough Playing Is Eliminated," *Los Angeles Times*, June 6, 1907.

51. "Alhambra Wins in Basketball," *Los Angeles Times*, Mar. 4, 1908; Emery and Toohey-Costa, "Hoops and Skirts," 149–50.

52. "Athletic Misses Play Baseball," *Chicago Tribune*, Feb. 15, 1912; "Girls' Indoor," *Voice*, 1916 15, no. 7 (1916): 123–25; Edna Bowles, "Girls' Indoor Baseball," in *The Aitchpe* (1916), 166; Barbara N. Noonkester, "The American Sportswoman from 1900 to 1920," 185–86.

53. "Dancers at High School Field Day and Victorious Sprinter," *Chicago Tribune*, June 7, 1911.

54. "Hyde Park Girls Triumph," *Chicago Tribune*, June 28, 1914; "Girls' Tennis," in *The Aitchpe* (1915), 169; "Hyde Park Girl Athletic Star Eats before Bed," *Chicago Tribune*, Oct. 11, 1916; "Girls' Tennis Title for Miss Leighton in H.S. Tournament," *Chicago Tribune*, Oct. 21, 1917.

9. INTERSCHOLASTICS AND THE GOLDEN AGE OF SPORTS

1. *Cardinal Principles of Secondary Education, Bulletin 1918, No. 35*, 8, 24; Ellwood Cubberley, revised by Walter Crosby Eels from 1925 edition, *An Introduction to the Study of Education*, 331–32.

2. *Cardinal Principles*, 15, 21–23; Cubberley, *Introduction to the Study of Education*, 338.

3. Raymond Schmidt, "Rise of the Intersectionals," in *Shaping College Football: The Transformation of an American Sport, 1919–1930*, 26–38.

4. Survey conducted by author on Illinois high schools' football intersectional matches was made from consulting newspapers, mostly from Chicago, and high school yearbooks and newspapers.

5. "Account of Games," in *The Scottonian* (1923), 174–82; "Cedar Rapids at Toledo for Title Prep Go Today," *Chicago Tribune*, Dec. 8, 1923; "Scott Topples Cedar Rapids Eleven, 24 to 21," *Chicago Tribune*, Dec. 9, 1923; "Waite Trounces Boston Preps in Grid Battle," *Chicago Tribune*, Dec. 7, 1924; Waite High School record book, untitled and undated.

6. Rockwell R. Stephens, "Eastern Trips Boost School Football," *Chicago Tribune*, Nov. 28, 1921.

7. "Englewood Is Sunk, 13–0, in Eastern Mud," *Chicago Tribune*, Dec. 6, 1925; "Pine Bluff Beats Englewood, 7–6, in Last Period," *Chicago Tribune*, Nov. 29, 1929; "Lindblom Wins by 14 Touchdowns," *Chicago Tribune*, Nov. 28, 1925.

8. James Crusinberry, "Proviso Beats Bay State Boys in Hot Tilt, 14–7," *Chicago Tribune*, Nov. 14, 1920; "Proviso Shifts Earn 13–6 Win at Fitchburg," *Chicago Tribune*,

Nov. 27, 1921; Larry Dailey, "Proviso Trims Eastern Preps, 24–9," *Chicago Tribune*, Nov. 5, 1922; "Eastern Preps Crush Proviso Eleven by 20–6," *Chicago Tribune*, Nov. 2, 1924; Rockwell B. Stephens, "Eastern Trips Boost School Football," *Chicago Tribune*, Nov. 28, 1921.

9. "St. James Eleven Defeats DePaul by 21–10 Count," *Chicago Tribune*, Dec. 5, 1920; "DePaul Drops Hard Battle at Haverhill, 14–7," *Chicago Tribune*, Nov. 27, 1921; "St. James High Trims DePaul in Belated Rally," *Chicago Tribune*, Oct. 19, 1924; "DePaul Eleven Swamped, 36–0, by Texas Boys," *Chicago Tribune*, Dec. 22, 1928.

10. W. H. Perry Jr., "Central Crushes Phillips 7 to 0," *Chicago Defender*, Nov. 28, 1925; Edward Meacham, "Kentuckians Fall before Phillips Hi," *Chicago Defender*, Dec. 4, 1926; "Phillips Slips Defeat to Owensboro," *Chicago Defender*, Dec. 3, 1927; "Central High Turns Back Wendell Phillips," *Chicago Defender*, Dec. 8, 1928.

11. Joe Davis, "Lake View Golfers Sweep Prep Tourney," *Chicago Tribune*, Feb. 23, 1924; Morrow Krum, "Lake View High Golf Club to Have Regular Classes," *Chicago Tribune*, Mar. 5, 1925; "Golf Now an Extra Course in a Chicago High School," *New York Times*, Mar. 6, 1925; "Chicago Public High School Championships," Chicago Public High School League files (undated mimeograph manuscript from league files).

12. Mike Chapman, *Encyclopedia of American Wrestling*, 2–3; "Hammond High Wrestlers Win Indiana Title," *Chicago Tribune*, Mar. 3, 1935.

13. "Playground Boys in Mat Bouts," *Chicago Tribune*, Feb. 12, 1911; "Park Mat Titles at Stake," *Chicago Tribune*, Mar. 20, 1911; "Hyde Park Boxers Thump St. Cyrils in First Prep Meet," *Chicago Tribune*, Mar. 28, 1916; "Tilden Sweeps Bowen Five from Title Path, 18–6," *Chicago Tribune*, Feb. 23, 1923; "166 Wrestlers Enter City H.S. Mat Tourney," *Chicago Tribune*, Mar. 28, 1926; Rob Sherrill, *Mat Madness: 60 Glorious Years of Illinois High School Wrestling*, 1–2.

14. "Froebel Takes Track Title in Northwestern Prep Meets," *Chicago Tribune*, Mar. 24, 1929; "Froebel Takes N.U. Track Title; Chisholm Swim Winner," *Chicago Tribune*, Mar. 23, 1930.

15. B. E. Wiggins, "Should High School Wrestling Be Encouraged?"

16. "Gymnasium," *Cherry Circle*, June 1903, 8; "Many Enter Gymnastic Meet," *Chicago Daily News*, Nov. 29, 1911; Gerald R. Gems, *The Windy City Wars*, 66–68; Wilma Jane Pesavanto, "A Historical Study of the Development of Physical Education in the Chicago Public High Schools, 1860 to 1965," 46, 63, 85.

17. "Interscholastic Sport," *New York Times*, Jan. 1, 1899; "Gymnastics at Columbia," *New York Times*, Apr. 14, 1901; "Columbia Gymnasts Compete," *New York Times*, Apr. 10, 1902; "Gymnastic Championship," *New York Times*, Apr. 10, 1903.

18. "Newark Second in Penn Gym Meet," *New York Times*, Apr. 6, 1924; "School Gym Crown Won by Dickinson," *New York Times*, May 22, 1926.

19. "School Gym Crown Won by Dickinson," *New York Times*, May 22, 1926; "Met. Gym Title Won by Dickinson High," *New York Times*, Apr. 7, 1929; "Dickinson Gymnasts

Win New Jersey Title," *New York Times*, Mar. 10, 1929; "Gymnastic Meets Listed," *New York Times*, Nov. 9, 1930; "Vetreno Scores in Gym Contests," *New York Times*, Apr. 5, 1931.

20. "Englewood, Senn Win in Prep Gym, Fencing Meet," *Chicago Tribune*, May 25, 1924; "Englewood and Lindblom Win Prep Gym Meets," *Chicago Tribune*, May 24, 1925; "Coaches' Corner," *Chicago Tribune*, Apr. 26, 1951; "Lindblom Wins 13th Straight City Gym Title," *Chicago Herald and Examiner*, Apr. 17, 1938; Leonard Green, "Senn Reaches More Heights in High School Competition," *Chicago Herald American*, Feb. 8, 1942.

21. James Crusinberry, "New York Prep Nine, sans Suits, Bats, Sure Stars," *Chicago Tribune*, May 23, 1920; James Crusinberry, "Prep Champs of New York Want Ball Game Here," *Chicago Tribune*, May 25, 1920; "Local 'Preps' Want to Play New Yorkers for Baseball Title," *Chicago Tribune*, May 27, 1920; "Sounds Tocsin for Prep Nine to Play Gotham," *Chicago Tribune*, May 31, 1920.

22. James Crusinberry, "New York Preps Down Lane Tech in Hitfest, 12–6," *Chicago Tribune*, June 27, 1920.

23. "Chicago Schoolboys Trounce N.Y. Nine," *New York Times*, June 19, 1921; "George Washington Beats Chicago Nine," *New York Times*, June 25, 1922; "Local School Wins Title before 40,000," *New York Times*, June 30, 1923; James Crusinberry, "Schurz Takes Prep Title by Beating Gotham," *Chicago Tribune*, June 24, 1924; James Crusinberry, "50,000 Yelling Boys and Girls See Lane Beat Flushing High in N.Y. 3–1 on One Hit," *Chicago Tribune*, June 25, 1925.

24. "Lane Tech Again Wins City Prep Baseball Title," *Chicago Tribune*, June 19, 1926; Frank Schreiber, "New York Nine Beats Lane in Title Game, 10–2," *Chicago Tribune*, June 26, 1926; Frank Schreiber, "Renew Efforts to Stage Prep Game with N.Y.," *Chicago Tribune*, June 14, 1927; "Rain Stops Lane, Phillips Game; Play Saturday," *Chicago Tribune*, June 22, 1927.

25. "Delaporte Goes West for Physical Education Meet," *Chicago Evening American*, June 19, 1925.

26. US Weather Bureau, *Climatic Summary of the U.S. Supplement for 1931 through 1952* (Washington, DC: Government Printing Office, 1961), 28–60; Bureau of the Census, *Fourteenth Census of the United States, Taken in the Year 1920*, vol. 3, *Population* (Washington, DC: Government Printing Office, 1922), 248, 508, 681, 772, 857, 1122; *Bureau of the Census, Fourteenth Census of the United States Taken in the Year 1920*, vol. 2, *Population*, 1920 (Washington, DC: Government Printing Office, 1922), 934–46; Eddie Schroeder, telephone interview with the author, Apr. 1, 1999.

27. "Anderson Sets New Record in Skating Meet," *Inter Ocean*, Jan. 23, 1905; "Silver Skates Derby," in *General Skating Information*, 16–18; Julian T. Fitzgerald, "America Is Turning More and More to Out-of-Door Winter Sports," in *General Skating Information*, 1.

28. "School Boy Competition," in *General Skating Information*, 11–13; "Chicago Schoolboy Skating Teams Leave for New York Feb. 3," *Chicago Tribune*, Jan. 15, 1921;

"Eighteen Boys Named to Skate N.Y. School Team," *Chicago Tribune*, Feb. 13, 1921; "Local Kid Skaters Romp Away with Cleveland Races," *Chicago Tribune*, Mar. 1, 1921; "Jimmy Thomson Star as Chicago Skaters Win at Philadelphia," *Chicago Tribune*, Mar. 4, 1921; "Kid Skaters of Chicago Sweep Rivals Off Ice," *Chicago Tribune*, Mar. 6, 1921.

29. Frank Schreiber, "Chicago's Lads for Inter-City Ice Meet Chosen," *Chicago Tribune*, Jan. 29, 1922; "School Boy Ice Skaters of 4 Cities Arrive This Week," *Chicago Tribune*, Feb. 19, 1922; Frank Schreiber, "Chicago Schoolboys Win Ice Title," *Chicago Tribune*, Feb. 26, 1922.

30. "Club, Boy Skaters in Three Derbies Today," *Chicago Tribune*, Jan. 13, 1923; "Englewood and Austin Share Skate Honors," *Chicago Tribune*, Jan. 14, 1923; "Austin Cleans Up H.S. Titles," *Chicago Tribune*, Jan. 27, 1924; "Fifteen Girls Are Organized as 1926 Tech Skate Team," *Harrison Herald*, Jan. 15, 1926, n.p.

31. "Select Skaters for Adirondack Gold Cup Meet," *Chicago Tribune*, Feb. 5, 1928; "Schoolboy Ice Team Ready for Eastern Races," *Chicago Tribune*, Feb. 12, 1928; *Proceedings Board of Education, City of Chicago, July 13, 1927, to June 27, 1928* (Chicago: Chicago Board of Education, 1928), 896–97; "Chicago Skaters Win Team Title," *Chicago Tribune*, Feb. 19, 1928.

32. "Saranac Lake Wins Honors in Skating," *New York Times*, Feb. 4, 1932; Wagenhorst, *Administration and Cost*, 27.

33. Frank Schreiber, "Steps Taken for Intercity Sport in All Branches," *Chicago Tribune*, Feb. 27, 1922.

34. "Mendenhall Wins Cross Country Run," *Philadelphia Inquirer*, Nov. 25, 1903; "Mercersburg Now Real Live Champs," *Philadelphia Inquirer*, Dec. 1, 1916.

35. "Columbia Race to Morris High," *New York Times*, Nov. 19, 1911; "165 Schoolboys Run on the Drive," *New York Times*, Nov. 14, 1915; "Mercersburg Wins Prep School Run," *New York Times*, Nov. 12, 1922; "Schenectady High Wins Columbia Run," *New York Times*, Nov. 10, 1929.

36. "Newark Prep Run Blanks Out," *New York Times*, Nov. 21, 1926; "St. Benedict's Prep Wins Newark Race," *New York Times*, Nov. 26, 1926; "Jordan Home First in Newark Prep Run," *New York Times*, Nov. 25, 1926; "Schenectady Boys Favorites in Run," *New York Times*, Nov. 28, 1929.

37. "I.A.C. Wins at Polo, Beating C.A.A. for A.A.U. Swim Honors," *Chicago Tribune*, Mar. 5, 1920; "Lindblom Wins National Swim Title," *Chicago Tribune*, Mar. 5, 1926; "Tilden High Swimmers Win National Meet," *Chicago Tribune*, Mar. 4, 1927; "Schurz Churns to Title in I.A.C. Prep Swim Meet," *Chicago Tribune*, Mar. 2, 1928.

38. "Lane Tech Wins Prep Water Meet; New Trier Second," *Chicago Herald and Examiner*, Mar. 28, 1920; "Atlantic City Wins National Prep Swim Meet," *Chicago Tribune*, Mar. 22, 1925; "Delaware Prep Swimmers 1st in N.U. Meet, *Chicago Tribune*, Mar. 27, 1927.

39. "To Seek National Title," *New York Times*, Jan. 28, 1922; "Mercersburg Wins in Schoolboy Swim," *New York Times*, Feb. 26, 1922; "Schoolboy Swim to Lawrenceville," *New York Times*, Jan. 20, 1923; "School Swimmers Break Two Marks," *New York Times*, Jan. 28, 1923; "Mercersburg Wins School Swim Meet," *New York Times*, Mar. 2, 1924; "Mercersburg Takes School Swim Title," *New York Times*, Jan. 31, 1926.

40. "U.S.L.T.A. Awards 229 Tournaments," *New York Times*, Apr. 9, 1923; "Whitbeck Annexes Lawn Tennis Title," *New York Times*, June 28, 1923; "Scott and Jones in College Final," *New York Times*, June 27, 1924; "U.S.L.T.A. Holds Session Saturday," *New York Times*, Feb. 1, 1925; "McKnight Wins Net Final," *New York Times*, May 15, 1928; "Oshinsky Defeated in Penn Net Final," *New York Times*, May 5, 1929; "Hebard Is a Victor in Scholastic Tennis," *New York Times*, May 11, 1929; "Shields Is Winner in Harvard Tennis," *New York Times*, June 1, 1929.

41. Clyde Bruckman, "McCormack and Barber Stars," *Los Angeles Times*, May 24, 1914.

42. "Illini to Stage Sports Carnival for Prep Stars," *Chicago Tribune*, Apr. 30, 1916; "Chicago Preps Win Illinois Tennis Titles," *Chicago Tribune*, May 22, 1927; "Hyde Park Net Men Victors in Maroon Meet," *Chicago Tribune*, May 30, 1928.

43. "Evanston Preps Only Home Five Left on Midway," *Chicago Tribune*, Mar. 17, 1917; "Evanston Preps Annex Title in Midway Tourney," *Chicago Tribune*, Mar. 18, 1917.

44. "Wingate Wins Prep Title from Crawfordsville Five," *Chicago Tribune*, Mar. 23, 1920; Albon Holden, "Lane Wins Way to Semi-Final Meet at Midway," *Chicago Tribune*, Mar. 12, 1921; Charles "Chic" Hess, *Prof Blood and the Wonder Teams: The True Story of Basketball's First Great Coach*, 80–84; "Kentucky School Boys Take Basket Title," *Chicago Tribune*, Apr. 9, 1922.

45. "Drawings Made for Maroon National Basket Tourney," *Chicago Tribune*, Apr. 1, 1923; George Buckley, "Prep Champs of U.S. Fight for Title Tomorrow," *Chicago Tribune*, Apr. 2, 1923; "Kansas Preps Grab Tourney," *Los Angeles Times*, Apr. 8, 1923; "National Scholastic Court Teams Named," *New York Times*, Apr. 9, 1923; *National Interscholastic Basket-Ball Tournament, under the Auspices of the University of Chicago, Bartlett Gymnasium, Apr. 4, 5, 6, and 7, 1923* (Chicago: Univ. of Chicago, 1923), n.p., Stagg Papers.

46. Harland Rohm, "Morton Preps Win U.S. Basket Title," *Chicago Tribune*, Apr. 3, 1927; "Field of Forty Prep Teams in U.S. Title Race," *Chicago Tribune*, Mar. 29, 1929; Timothy O'Hanlon, "Interscholastic Athletics, 1900–1940: Shaping Citizens for Unequal Roles in the Modern Industrial State" (PhD diss.), 8; David Kindred, "The Legend of Carr Creek"; "World's Greatest Basketball Interscholastic" postcards, Stagg Papers.

47. "Passaic Five Wins Northeastern Title," *New York Times*, Apr. 5, 1925; "Central High of Washington Wins Penn Basketball Title," *New York Times*, Mar. 6, 1927; Emmett Sizemore, "Stars Enter Auburn Meet," *Atlanta Constitution*, Feb. 19, 1922.

48. "Title Meet in Newark," *New York Times*, Mar. 2, 1918; "Thomson Captures High Hurdle Race," *New York Times*, Feb. 15, 1920; "National Mark Set in Schoolboy Jump," *New York Times*, Mar. 16, 1924; "New Utrecht-Hill Tie in Title Meet," *New York Times*, Mar. 15, 1925.

49. "Prep Stars in Big Meet Here," *Chicago Tribune*, Mar. 26, 1920; "300 Athletes Enter N.U. Meet This Week," *Chicago Tribune*, Mar. 16, 1924; "Marks Tumble in Purple Prep Meets," *Chicago Tribune*, Mar. 23, 1924; "N.U. Prep Games Lure Champions of Nine States," *Chicago Tribune*, Mar. 17, 1929; "Froebel Takes Track Title in Northwestern Prep Meets," *Chicago Tribune*, Mar. 24, 1929.

50. "300 Schools Invited to Meet at Harvard," *New York Times*, May 2, 1926; "Mercersburg Won Sports—Records Were Sent Flying," *Philadelphia Inquirer*, May 24, 1903; "Mercersburg Academy Wins Mid-States Meet," *Chicago Tribune*, May 23, 1920.

51. "Star Athletes of Prep World Compete Today," *Chicago Tribune*, June 2, 1917; "Academy Teams Made Eligible for Stagg's Annual Prep Games," *Chicago Tribune*, Mar. 26, 1921; "1,000 Entries in Stagg Prep Meet," *Chicago Tribune*, May 23, 1921; "Kansas City High Wins Chicago U. Prep Track Meet," *Chicago Tribune*, May 29, 1921; Ted Iserman, "Records Smashed in Track Meets," *Chicago Tribune*, May 28, 1922.

52. "Athletic Cream of Prep Schools at Midway Today," *Chicago Tribune*, May 25, 1923; "California Prep Tracksters Fail to Grab Championship," *Los Angeles Times*, May 27, 1923; "Froebel Wins High School Track Meet at Stagg Field," *Chicago Tribune*, June 2, 1929.

53. Wagenhorst, *Administration and Cost*, 72; Kenneth A. Simon and W. Vance Grant, *Digest of Educational Statistics, 1968 Edition* (Washington, DC: Office of Education, 1968), 46.

10. Creation of Military Sports in the Secondary Schools

1. Dexter Perkins, *The American Approach to Foreign Policy*, rev. ed. (New York: Atheneum, 1968), 24–25, 130–32; Joan Hoff Wilson, *American Business & Foreign Policy, 1920–1933* (Lexington: Univ. Press of Kentucky, 1971), 47–48, 60–61; John D. Hicks, *Republican Ascendancy, 1921–1933* (New York: Harper & Row, 1960), 149–52; William W. Hartzog, *American Military Heritage* (Washington, DC: US Training and Doctrine Command and Center of Military History, 2001), 119–21.

2. O'Hanlon, "School Sports as Social Training"; Schmidt, *Shaping College Football*, 211, 244, 280.

3. Donald J. Mrozek, "Sport and the American Military: Diversion and Duty," 44.

4. "Report of Committee of the Boston Physical Education Society, to Suggest a Substitute for the Manual of Arms as a Means of Physical Exercise in the Military Training

of School-Boys"; Dudley A. Sargent, "Military Drill in the Public Schools"; "ROTC," in *The Forum* (1925), 140.

5. Luther Halsey Gulick, "Report of the Committee on the Status of Physical Education in Public Normal Schools and Public High Schools in the United States," 453; Jable, "Public Schools Athletic League," 228–30.

6. Michael Pearlman, *To Make Democracy Safe for America: Patricians and Preparedness in the Progressive Era* (Urbana: Univ. of Illinois Press, 1984), 33–35, 98–120; John Patrick Finnegan, *Against the Specter of a Dragon: The Campaign for American Military Preparedness, 1914–1917* (Westport, CT: Greenwood Press, 1974), 61–62, 113–14; O'Hanlon, "School Sports as Social Training," 15; Charles W. Elliott, "The 'ROTC': How the War Department's Plan of Military Training Has Developed," 12.

7. Dudley A. Sargent, "Military Training in High Schools"; Edward B. DeGroot, "Physical Education versus Military Training in Secondary Schools," 302–4.

8. O'Hanlon, "School Sports as Social Training," 16–18.

9. Ibid.; Edgar Z. Steever, "The Wyoming Plan of Military Training in the Schools"; "Military Training of School-Boys," *Outlook*, Feb. 16, 1916.

10. "High School Administration," *American School Board Journal* 53, no. 2 (1916): 65; "Report of the Department of Military Training," 58; Steever, "Wyoming Plan of Military Training," 147–49.

11. "Report of the Department of Military Training," 58.

12. Ibid., 59–60; [F. L. Beals], "Military Training," in *Public Schools of the City of Chicago: Sixty-Sixth Annual Report of the Board of Education for the Year Ending June 30, 1922* (Chicago: Board of Education, 1922), 39; Frank L. Beals, "Military Training."

13. "ROTC Rifle Match Is Half Completed," *Chicago Tribune*, Feb. 19, 1922; "126 Shooters Face Traps at Outdoor Show," *Chicago Tribune*, Feb. 28, 1922; "ROTC," in *Red and White* (1925), 108.

14. Wade Mudgett, "Rifle Team," in *Red and White* (Mar. 1928), 21; "Englewood Tops Rifle Tourney," *Chicago Tribune*, May 15, 1924; "Evanston High Wins National Rifle Trophy," *Chicago Tribune*, Mar. 4, 1924; "Evanston High Rifle Team Beats Lawrenceville Preps," *Chicago Tribune*, Feb. 16, 1923; "The Rifle Team," in *The Purple and White* (1924), 190.

15. Herman Schulze, "Reserve Officers Training Corps," in *Red and White Semiannual* (Chicago: Lake View High, Feb. 1925), 91; "ROTC," in *Red and White* (1926), 202–6; Jerome Leve, "Our Rifle Champs," in *Red and White* (May 1927), 21; "High School Marksmen Win Indoor Rifle Championship," caption in *Chicago Tribune*, Mar. 17, 1927; "Rifle Group Names Indoor Champions," *New York Times*, Mar. 23, 1931.

16. "Mrs. Wolff Wins Rifle Shoot at Outdoors Show," *Chicago Tribune*, Mar. 1, 1922; "Evanston High Wins National Rifle Trophy," *Chicago Tribune*, Mar. 4, 1924; "Rifle Trophy to Waukegan," *Chicago Herald and Examiner*, May 22, 1927; "Evanston Prep Rifle Team Wins First in N.R.A. Shoot," *Chicago Tribune*, Nov. 30, 1930.

17. "Jamaica High Wins School Gun Title," *New York Times*, Dec. 19, 1920; "Evander Childs Winner," *New York Times*, Apr. 23, 1922; "P.S.A.L. Shoot Won by Evander Childs," *New York Times*, Dec. 9, 1923; "Walsh Shoots Way to P.S.A.L. Title," *New York Times*, May 1, 1927; "P.S.A.L. Title Is Retained by Richmond," *New York Times*, Dec. 22, 1929.

18. "Announces Indoor Rifle Champions," *New York Times*, Apr. 22, 1923; "Washington High School Wins Rifle Title Again," *New York Times*, Apr. 29, 1923; "Remington Wins Title," *New York Times*, Apr. 9, 1924.

19. "Shooting Team," in *The Courier* (1926), 45; "Rifle Trophy to Waukegan," *Chicago Herald and Examiner*, May 22, 1927: "Evanston High Wins National Rifle Trophy," *Chicago Tribune*, Mar. 4, 1924; "Coast Rifle Team Victor," *New York Times*, Apr. 9, 1927.

20. "Fencing Meet at Midway Tonight," *Chicago Tribune*, Apr. 13, 1923; "Fencing Meet Today," *Chicago Tribune*, Feb. 24, 1924; "Englewood, Senn Win in Prep Gym, Fencing Meet," *Chicago Tribune*, May 25, 1924; "Fencing," in *The Forum* (1925), 170; "Fencing," in *The Forum* (1928), 166.

21. "Lindblom High Gymnasts Win," *Chicago Tribune*, May 23, 1926; "Fencing," in *The Forum* (1926), 172; "Fencing," in *The Aitchpe* (1930), 138; "Lindblom Wins Fencing Title in Foil Club Series," *Chicago Tribune*, Mar. 6, 1932. Although using names of the winners may not be fully accurate, it is telling that the Senn High team in the 1920s included the apparently Jewish names of Maurie Lazar, Elmer Friedman, Frank Friedberg, and Harold Lipsky. See "Fencing," in *The Forum* (1927), 193. See Stephen A. Riess, "Sports and the American Jew: An Introduction," in *Sports and the American Jew*, edited by Stephen A. Riess (Syracuse, NY: Syracuse Univ. Press, 1998), 31.

22. Waldo Mudgett, "Fencing," in *Red and White* (May 1927), 22; "Fencing," in *The Aitchpe* (1931), 131.

23. "Fencers Club Buys Site for New Home," *New York Times*, Mar. 3, 1929; "One Entry for Fencing Tourney," *New York Times*, Apr. 2, 1916; "Ducussi Wins with Foils," *New York Times*, Apr. 1, 1917; "Fencing Title for Swain," *New York Times*, Mar. 31, 1918; "Betancourt Wins Medal with Foils," *New York Times*, Apr. 4, 1920; "Sellaro, New York Boy Wonder, Takes National Interscholastic Foils Title," *New York Times*, Apr. 3, 1921.

24. "Fencers Club Buys Site for New Home," *New York Times*, Mar. 3, 1929; "One Entry for Fencing Tourney," *New York Times*, Apr. 2, 1916; "Ducussi Wins with Foils," *New York Times*, Apr. 1, 1917; "Fencing Title for Swain," *New York Times*, Mar. 31, 1918; "Betancourt Wins Medal with Foils," *New York Times*, Apr. 4, 1920; "Sellaro, New York Boy Wonder, Takes National Interscholastic Foils Title," *New York Times*, Apr. 3, 1921.

25. "Castello Captures School Foils Title," *New York Times*, Mar. 22, 1931; "Fencing Bid Rejected," *New York Times*, Apr. 19, 1939; "Gold, New Utrecht, Gains Foils Honors," *New York Times*, Mar. 31, 1940; "Mulligan Fencing Victor," *New York Times*, May 18, 1941.

26. "Indoor Polo Body Revises Title Dates," *New York Times*, Mar. 1, 1929; "Optimists and Harvard Gain Class a Polo Final—Berkshire Wins School Title," *New York Times*, Apr. 7, 1929.

27. "Scholastic Trios to Clash in Final," *New York Times*, Mar. 27, 1936; "Army Poloists Top Yale for Title, 8–7," *New York Times*, Apr. 2, 1939; "Princeton Opposes Yale Tomorrow at Polo for Right to Play Army in Tourney Final," *New York Times*, Mar. 18, 1941; James Roach, "Indoor Polo Group Cards 3 Tourneys," *New York Times*, Mar. 14, 1946; William J. Briordy, "Indoor Polo Title Taken by N.Y.A.C.," *New York Times*, Apr. 13, 1947.

28. "They're Not Too Proud to Fight," *Chicago Tribune*, Mar. 18, 1922; "Military Organization," in *Maroon and White* (1926), 123; "5,000 Chicago R.O.T.C. Cadets Mass in Drill," *Chicago Tribune*, June 6, 1926; "G.M.T.C.," in *The Temulac* (1926), 89.

29. "Target Shooting for Girls Stirs Board," *Chicago Daily News*, Jan. 27, 1926.

30. "School Girls' Martial Drill Stirs Storm," *Chicago Tribune*, Jan. 27, 1926.

31. "Target Shooting for Girls Stirs Board"; "School Girls' Martial Drill Stirs Storm," *Chicago Tribune*, Jan. 27, 1926; "Resolution in re Military Training Given to Girls in High Schools," in *Proceedings, Board of Education, City of Chicago, July 8, 1925, to June 23, 1926* (Chicago: Board of Education, 1926), 1337–38.

32. "School Girls' Martial Drill."

33. "Let the Girls Shoot" (editorial), *Chicago Tribune*, Jan. 30, 1926; "School Trustee Speaks a Word for Flappers," *Chicago Tribune*, Jan. 28, 1926; "The Inquiring Reporter," *Chicago Tribune*, Feb. 17, 1926.

34. "Girls' Rifle Team," in *The Red and Black* (Mar. 1926), 20.

35. Whitten, *Interscholastics*, 53, 125–27; "6 Chicago High Schools Join Illinois Ass'n," *Chicago Tribune*, Mar. 30, 1926; "City Preps Eligible for State Games," *Chicago Tribune*, Apr. 1, 1926; "5,000 Chicago ROTC Cadets Mass in Drill," *Chicago Tribune*, June 6, 1926; "6,000 High School Cadets Drill and Parade in Tourney," *Chicago Tribune*, May 29, 1927; "Pacifist Control of the Schools" (editorial), *Chicago Tribune*, Apr. 20, 1927; "The Pacifist Attack on the ROTC" (editorial), *Chicago Tribune*, Jan. 10, 1926.

36. Evidence for the clampdown comes from the examination of high school publications; the board proceedings are silent, and the superintendent's report after 1926 was no longer published owing to budgetary constraints. Letter from Rev. Donald R. Ward, *Sports Illustrated*, Mar. 24, 1975; "'Sure-Shot Mary,' Only 16, Hits Perfect 500 with Army Rifle," *New York Times*, Feb. 24, 1927; "100 Per Cent Perfect," caption in *Chicago Tribune*, Mar. 6, 1927; "Fencing Club," in *The Eagle* (1931), 203; "High School Fencers," *Chicago Tribune*, June 17, 1928.

37. "Pacifist Control of the Schools" (editorial), *Chicago Tribune*, Apr. 20, 1927; "Ten Years of the R.O.T.C.," *Chicago Tribune*, June 2, 1926.

38. "The Pacifist Attack on the ROTC" (editorial), *Chicago Tribune*, Jan. 10, 1926; "National Shoot Titles for G.U. and Central," *Washington Post*, Mar. 11, 1923; "Central's Girls Shots Have Enviable Record," *Washington Post*, Jan. 17, 1924; "U.S. Scholastic Gun Title Is Won by Western Team," *Washington Post*, Apr. 15, 1932.

11. The Private and Catholic Schools'
Parallel World of Interscholastic Sports

1. "Penn Crews Rowing Twice Daily Now," *New York Times*, Apr. 17, 1927; "Columbia's Eight Scores in Henley," *New York Times*, May 27, 1928; "W. Catholic Is Rowing Victor," *New York Times*, June 7, 1931; "Roman Catholic High Wins," *New York Times*, June 7, 1932.

2. "Plan Title Race for School Crews," *New York Times*, Apr. 8, 1934; "Kent School Crew Rows a Dead Heat," *New York Times*, June 2, 1935; "Stotesbury Cup Won by Hun School Crew," *New York Times*, May 19, 1935; "New York Schoolboy Takes Sculling Race," *New York Times*, June 28, 1939.

3. Kelley, *American Rowing*, 186–87, 202; "Kent School Eight to Row in England," *New York Times*, Feb. 17, 1927; "Kent School Beats Radley with Ease," *New York Times*, July 6, 1927; "Kent Crew Beaten in Henley Regatta," *New York Times*, July 6, 1930; "Harvard Oarsmen Beaten at Henley," *New York Times*, July 5, 1931; "Record U.S. Entry in Henley Regatta," *New York Times*, July 4, 1934.

4. "Around the Hole," *American Golfer*, May 1910, 474; Hazard, "Eastern Pennsylvania Notes," *American Golfer*, June 1910, 28; Far and Sure, "Eastern Pennsylvania Notes," *American Golfer*, July 1911, 219.

5. "Interscholastic Golf in the East," in *Spalding's Official Golf Guide*, 1914 (New York: American Sports Publishing, 1914), 103; Far and Sure, "Eastern Pennsylvania Notes," *American Golfer*, July 1911, 216; William B. Richardson, "School Golf Play Set for May 14–16," *New York Times*, Apr. 30, 1928.

6. "The Ouimet Case," *American Golfer*, June 1916, 121; "Around the 19th Hole," *American Golfer*, July 1917, 807; "Watson Low Scorer in Schoolboy Golf," *New York Times*, May 23, 1922; "Scholastic Golf Body to Meet Here," *New York Times*, Jan. 5, 1924; "Title School Golf Will Start Today," *New York Times*, May 13, 1929; "Kiski School Wins in Greenwich Golf," *New York Times*, May 20, 1930.

7. "St. Benedict's Keeps Title," *New York Times*, Nov. 2, 1924; "Kerny and Peddie Triumph on Track," *New York Times*, Mar. 4, 1928; *Virginia High School League Book of Records*, 67, 94.

8. "Private Schools Athletic League," *New York Times*, Jan. 8, 1916; "Poly Prep Annexes Swimming Title," *New York Times*, Mar. 13, 1927; "Penn Charter Wins I.A.A. Championship," *Philadelphia Inquirer*, Nov. 25, 1905.

9. "Lake Forest Preps Beat Shattuck; Claim Title," *Chicago Tribune*, Mar. 6, 1921; "St. Johns Military Academy Wins Midwest Prep Title," *Chicago Tribune*, Nov. 17, 1921; "Lake Forest Academy Eleven Wins Grid Title," *Chicago Tribune*, Nov. 23, 1924.

10. "Local Boys Take 3 Firsts at Madison," *Milwaukee Sentinel*, May 4, 1924.

11. "Country Day School Five Loses Hard Tilt in Meet," *Milwaukee Journal*, Mar. 19, 1926; "Four Records Shattered at Academy Track Meet," *Milwaukee Journal*, Mar. 21, 1926; "Shattuck Wins Swimming Meet," *Milwaukee Sentinel*, Mar. 24, 1928.

12. Harry M. Golden, "Pillsbury Five Wins National Academy Title," *Milwaukee Sentinel*, Mar. 21, 1926; "Culver Takes Caging Title," *Milwaukee Journal*, Mar. 20, 1927; "Last Wisconsin Team Out of Prep Tourney," *Milwaukee Journal*, Mar. 23, 1928; "St. John's to Play in Tourney Finals," *Milwaukee Journal*, Mar. 22, 1930.

13. "Mooseheart Wins Honors," *Milwaukee Journal*, Mar. 20, 1927; "Shattuck Wins Track Honors," *Milwaukee Journal*, Mar. 25, 1928; "Mooseheart Wins Track," *Chicago Tribune*, Mar. 23, 1930; "Culver Cops Swim Meet," *Milwaukee Journal*, Mar. 23, 1930.

14. "Wayland Wins First Midwest Track Carnival," *Chicago Tribune*, May 15, 1927; "St. Albans to Hold Midwest Basket Meet," *Chicago Tribune*, Dec. 16, 1930; Bob Starrett, "Four Private Prep Schools Form New Chicago Organization," *Chicago Daily News*, Dec. 6, 1930 (notwithstanding the headline, there were five schools in the league the first year).

15. Mark S. Massa, *Catholics and American Culture* (New York: Crossroad, 1999), 2–3; Charles R. Morris, *American Catholics: The Saints and Sinners Who Built America's Most Powerful Church* (New York: Times Books, 1997), ix.

16. Harold A. Beutow, *Of Singular Benefit: The Story of Catholic Education in the United States* (New York: Macmillan, 1970), 114; Charles Shanabruch, *Chicago's Catholics: An Evolution of an American Identity* (Notre Dame, IN: Univ. of Notre Dame Press, 1981), 58.

17. Beutow, *Of Singular Benefit*, 112, 149–52; J. A. Burns et al., *A History of Catholic Education in the United States* (New York: Benziger Brothers, 1937), 237–40.

18. Burns, *History of Catholic Education*, 243–47; William McNally, "The Secondary School," in *Essays on Catholic Education in the United States* (Washington, DC: Catholic Univ. of America Press, 1942), 123–24, 132.

19. McNally, "The Secondary School," 123; Burns et al., *History of Catholic Education*, 255.

20. Shanabruch, *Chicago's Catholics*, 103–5, 234–35.

21. Sister Mary Innocenta Montay, "The History of Catholic Secondary Education in the Archdiocese of Chicago," 136, 141–42, 189–93, 240; "Church School to Hold Jubilee," *Chicago Tribune*, Nov. 19, 1911; "De La Salle Institute Games," *Chicago Tribune*, June 16, 1894; "St. Ignatius College Ball Team," *Chicago Tribune*, Apr. 1, 1895.

22. Rev. Msgr. Harry C. Koenig, STD, ed., *Caritas Christi Urget Nos: A History of the Offices, Agencies, and Institutions of the Archdiocese of Chicago* (Chicago: Archdiocese of Chicago, 1981), 1:586–89; Montay, "History of Catholic Secondary Education," 145–46; "St. Stanislaus' Nine at Work," *Chicago Tribune*, Mar. 17, 1911.

23. Koenig, *Caritas Christi Urget Nos*, 439, 472, 477, 500, 533, 564, 610; Montay, "History of Catholic Secondary Education," 148; "St. Cyril College Basket-Ball Five, Which Has Closed the Season with a Good Record," *Inter Ocean*, Feb. 24, 1907.

24. "Prep League Lets Down Bar," *Chicago Tribune*, Sept. 19, 1911; "Catholics to Form League," *Chicago Tribune*, Oct. 3, 1912.

25. "Catholic 'Prep' Leaguers Frame Charts at Meeting," *Chicago Tribune*, Nov. 21, 1912; "St. Cyril Nine Wins Title," *Chicago Tribune*, May 25, 1913; "'Prep' Athletes to Start Grind," *Chicago Tribune*, Sept. 8, 1913; "St. John's Win from DePaul by Safety, 8–6," *Chicago Tribune*, Dec. 6, 1914; "DePaul Beats Beverly Teams by 30–7 Score," *Chicago Tribune*, Dec. 5, 1915; "DePaul Batter St. John's Eleven, 21–0," *Chicago Tribune*, Nov. 19, 1916.

26. *Chicago Catholic High School Athletic League Champions*, 3.

27. Montay, "History of Catholic Secondary Education," 119, 123–25; "DePaul Girls' Five Win," *Chicago Tribune*, Apr. 28, 1922; "Girls Basketball," Mar. 22, 1924; "Mercy Girls Win Title," *Chicago Herald and Examiner*, Mar. 27, 1928.

28. Gerald R. Gems, "The Prep Bowl: Football and Religious Acculturation in Chicago, 1927–1963." I relied on this essay in framing the arguments on how high school sports facilitated Catholic acculturation into American society.

29. Clarence Carey, "Chicago Prep Title Battle on Saturday," *Chicago Herald and Examiner*, Nov. 28, 1927; Clarence Carey, "Battle of Coaching Wits Will Feature Prep Game Saturday," *Chicago Herald and Examiner*, Nov. 30, 1927.

30. George A. Strickler, "50,000 See Mt. Carmel Beat Schurz, 6–0, for Prep Title," *Chicago Herald and Examiner*, Dec. 4, 1927; "Prep Heads to Quiz Eligibility of Tilden Star," *Chicago Tribune*, Nov. 15, 1928; "DePaul, at Peak of Shape, Waits Prep Tilt," *Chicago Tribune*, Dec. 5, 1928; "Tilden Whips DePaul, 12–0, for City Title," *Chicago Tribune*, Dec. 9, 1928; Gems, "Prep Bowl," 289.

31. "Can Irish Whip World? Say Yes at Mt. Carmel," *Chicago Tribune*, Dec. 4, 1931; Clarence Carey, "Harrison Wins Title, 44 to 6, from Carmel," *Chicago Herald and Examiner*, Dec. 6, 1931; "Harrison Beats Miami Prep Champions, 18–7," *Chicago Tribune*, Dec. 26, 1931; Gems, "Prep Bowl," 289.

32. "Fathers Halt Plans for Prep Charity Game," *Chicago Tribune*, Nov. 22, 1932; "Charity Game Chances Fade; Parents Firm," *Chicago Tribune*, Nov. 26, 1932; William R. Bowlin, letter to the editor, *Chicago Tribune*, Dec. 8, 1932.

33. Charles Bartlett, "Lindblom Defeats Leo, 6 to 0," *Chicago Tribune*, Dec. 2, 1934; Gems, "Prep Bowl," 290–92; Edward Burns, "Austin High Conquers Leo, 26 to 0, before Record Crowd," *Chicago Tribune*, Nov. 28, 1937.

34. Janis B. Fine and Joan K. Smith, "Interscholastic High School Sports: The Growth and Decline of the National Catholic Basketball Tournament (1924–1941)"; Wade Davies and Rich Clow, "The St. Francis Mission Indians and the National Interscholastic Catholic Basketball Tournament, 1924–1941."

35. Quotation from Davies and Clow, "St. Francis Mission Indians," 215; Fine and Smith, "Interscholastic High School Sports," 150; "National Catholic Cage Meet at Loyola," *Chicago Tribune*, Jan. 21, 1924.

36. Program quotation from Davies and Clow, "St. Francis Mission Indians," 216–18; Wallace Abbey, "Spalding Five Wins National Catholic Meet," *Chicago Tribune*, Mar. 31, 1924.

37. *Loyola News* quoted in Davies and Clow, "St. Francis Mission Indians," 216, 224.

38. Fine and Smith, "Interscholastic High School Sports," 151; "Joliet Quintet Wins Loyola Tourney," *Chicago Tribune*, Mar. 26, 1928.

39. Fine and Smith, "Interscholastic High School Sports," 151.

40. David M. Craine, "Image Enhancement: Three Chicago Institutions and the National Catholic Basketball Tournament, 1924–1941," 216.

41. Quotation from Davies and Clow, "St. Francis Mission Indians," 216; Fine and Smith, "Interscholastic High School Sports," 151; "Catholics Plan for National Cage Meet," *Chicago Tribune*, Dec. 14, 1924; "Central States Prep Teams Open Cage Tourney Play," *Chicago Tribune*, Mar. 5, 1926; "Catholic Meet Title Is Won by St. Mary's," *Champaign News-Gazette*, Mar. 5, 1928.

42. "Marquette Wins Badger Prep Cage Championship," *Chicago Tribune*, Mar. 10, 1928; "St. Teresa Gets State Catholic Basket Tourney," *Chicago Tribune*, Nov. 12, 1934; Schwomeyer, *Hoosier Hysteria*, 411.

43. "Minneapolis Quintet Takes National Title," *Chicago Tribune*, Mar. 23, 1931; "St. Patrick Takes National Basketball Title"; "Fenwick Beats Joliet, 30–27, for U.S. Title," *Chicago Tribune*, Mar. 22, 1937; "Leo Beats Indians, 49–41, for National Title," *Chicago Tribune*, Mar. 31, 1941.

44. Davies and Clow, "St. Francis Mission Indians," 218–21; Fine and Smith, "Interscholastic High School Sports," 154–55; "32 Prep Teams to Battle for Catholic Title," *Chicago Tribune*, Mar. 17, 1935.

45. Loyola Univ. public relations announcement, Jan. 18, 1942; "Leo Beats Indians, 49–41"; Arch Ward, "Colleges Hit Stagg and Loyola Cage Meets," *Chicago Tribune*, Mar. 21, 1930; Fine and Smith, "Interscholastic High School Sports," 152.

46. "Rain Breaks Up Catholics' Games," *New York Times*, June 8, 1913; "28 Games on Schedule," *New York Times*, Mar. 18, 1917; "Fives to Have Busy Time," *New York Times*, Oct. 26, 1919; "St. Augustine Wins Two Team Titles," *New York Times*, June 4, 1922; "Sixteen Events on List," *New York Times*, Dec. 13, 1923.

47. "Plan Athletic League for Catholic Schools," *New York Times*, Mar. 25, 1923; "Catholic Schools Organize League," *New York Times*, Mar. 2, 1926; "Catholic Schools Form Sports Body," *New York Times*, Mar. 30, 1927; "School Meet Won by Brooklyn Prep," *New York Times*, May 27, 1927.

48. "De La Salle Wins as 5 Records Fall," *New York Times*, Jan. 29, 1928; "Brooklyn Prep Wins Title," *New York Times*, Mar. 5, 1928; "Schoolboy Athletic Notes," *New York Times*, June 2, 1928; "La Salle Six Gains Hockey Title," *New York Times*, Mar. 2, 1929.

49. Burns, *History of Catholic Education*, 255.

12. Girls' Interscholastic Sports and the Exuberance to Compete

1. Himes, "Female Athlete in American Society," 221–61.

2. Cahn, *Coming on Strong*, 56.

3. "Resolutions Adopted by the Conference on Athletics and Physical Recreation Held under the Auspices of the National Amateur Athletic Federation at Washington, D.C., Apr. 6–7, 1923"; Lillian Schroedler, "Report of Progress, Women's Division, National Amateur Athletic Federation of America"; Cahn, *Coming on Strong*, 58–62, 87–88; Himes, "Female Athlete in American Society," 2176–83; Ellen Gerber, "The Controlled Development of Collegiate Sport for Women, 1923–1936," 9–11.

4. Sarah Addington, "The Athletic Limitations of Women," 147.

5. Ibid., 144. Much of this discussion is drawn from Cahn's chapter "Games of Strife: The Battle over Women's Competitive Sport," in *Coming on Strong*, 55–82.

6. Addington, "Athletic Limitations of Women," 38; Agnes R. Wayman, "Competition: A Statement by the Women's Division, National Amateur Athletic Federation." Gerber in her influential "Controlled Development" article cites the Dewey influence (12–13).

7. Cahn, *Coming on Strong*, 63–64; Winifred Van Hagen, "Everybody Play," 652.

8. Cahn, *Coming on Strong*, 67; Helen N. Smith, "Athletic Education," 608–10.

9. Cahn, *Coming on Strong*, 68, 72.

10. The rural nature of support for interscholastic competition in high schools, primarily basketball, can be found in the following: Paula Welch, "Interscholastic Basketball: Bane of Collegiate Physical Educators," 428–29; Janice A. Beran, "Iowa, the Longtime 'Hot Bed' of Girls Basketball," 185; Peggy Stanaland, "The Early Years of Basketball in Kentucky," 174; and Pamela Grundy, "From Amazons to Glamazons: The Rise and Fall of North Carolina Women's Basketball, 1920–1960," 142–43.

11. Whitten, *Interscholastics*, 119–24.

12. Ibid., 122–23.

13. Ibid., 119, 123–24; Ellen Mosbek, "The Illinois League of High School Girls Athletic Associations," *Illinois High School Athlete* 2, no. 1 (1929): 6.

14. Whitten, *Interscholastics*, 125–26.

15. "Prep Golf and Tennis Plans Mapped Out," *Chicago Tribune*, Apr. 28, 1922; "Englewood Cops Golf Tourney of High Schools," *Chicago Tribune*, June 11, 1922; "White Wins Prep Golf Title; Team Honors to Hyde Park," *Chicago Tribune*, June 17, 1923; "Lake View Golfers Win Prep Tourney," *Chicago Tribune*, June 20, 1924.

16. "Robert Stewart Wins Prep Golf Crown with 153," *Chicago Tribune*, June 14, 1925; "Golf Fans See Girl of 16 Drive 310 Yards," *Chicago Tribune*, July 29, 1925; "Hill of Bowen High Wins City Prep Golf Title," *Chicago Tribune*, June 13, 1926; "Florence

Beebe May Represent Purple on Links," *Chicago Tribune*, Mar. 28, 1928; "Big Brother Was Unwilling Golf Tutor for Mildred Hackl," *Chicago Tribune*, June 21, 1931.

17. "H.S. Girls to Play Golf and Tennis," *Chicago Tribune*, Apr. 26, 1922; "Girls Tennis Stars to Play in Annual Tennis Tournament," *Harrison Herald*, May 14, 1926; "Lindblom Girls Win City Prep Tennis Tourney," *Chicago Tribune*, June 17, 1926.

18. "Hyde Park Tankers Win," *Chicago Tribune*, Jan. 12, 1921; "Triple Swim Meet Won by Englewood; Parkerites Third," *Green and White*, Apr. 6, 1925, 3; "'Fran' Blanchard Wins Four Medals in Swimming Meet," *Green and White*, May 25, 1925, 3; E. C. Delaporte, "Physical Education High Schools."

19. William Bachrach and Clarence A. Bush, *Outline of Swimming: An Encyclopedia of the Sport*, 47–61; "Yank Swimmers Win in Olympic by Huge Margin," *Chicago Tribune*, July 21, 1924; "Jane Fauntz," in *The Aitchpe* (1928), 204; "Popular H.P. Girl Swims to Victory in Olympic Trials," *Hyde Park Weekly*, Sept. 19, 1928, 4; "A 'Medal-Some' Mermaid," *Chicago Tribune*, Dec. 19, 1920; "Hawthorne Girls Swim in Morton High Pool," *Chicago Tribune*, Mar. 28, 1923; "Twins Star in I.W.A.C. Swim Meet for Girls," *Chicago Tribune*, Dec. 12, 1926; "Four I.W.A.C. Swimmers Qualify for Olympic Trials," *Chicago Tribune*, June 16, 1928.

20. "First Lutheran Sprints to Win in Church Meet," *Chicago Tribune*, July 1, 1923; "I.A.C. Captures Record Crashing C. AAU Games," *Chicago Tribune*, Mar. 31, 1923; "World Records Crack as I.A.C. Wins AAU Meet," *Chicago Tribune*, Mar. 29, 1924; Clark Kelsey, "Ray Runs Fourth in Mile Event at Canuck Meet," *Chicago Tribune*, Aug. 31, 1924; "Osborn Breaks World Mark as I.A.C. Wins Title," *Chicago Tribune*, Mar. 21, 1925.

21. "Chicago's Greatest Girl Athlete Equals a World Record," *Chicago Tribune*, Sept. 28, 1924; "Helen Filkey Shatters Two World Marks," *Chicago Tribune*, July 12, 1925; "Training for Speed," *Chicago Tribune*, Mar. 7, 1926; Terry Wilson, "Track Star Helen Filkey DeVry, 92," *Chicago Tribune*, Dec. 4, 2000; "Tom Eck, Coach at Chicago for Eleven Years, Dies," *Chicago Tribune*, June 6, 1926; "I.A.C. Wins Track Games; Marks Fall," *Chicago Tribune*, Apr. 1, 1927; "The Woman Athlete," in *The Forum* (1928), 184.

22. "Young School Girl Sets World Record in Meet," *Chicago Tribune*, June 15, 1924.

23. "Girls' Basket Teams Organize," *Chicago Tribune*, Nov. 20, 1923; "Brownies Roll Up 156 Points in First Two Basket Games," *Chicago Tribune*, Dec. 29, 1926; "Tri Chi Girls Win 159 Games; Lose Only Four," *Chicago Tribune*, Jan. 1, 1927.

24. The famed Edmonton Grads, under Coach J. Percy Page, had been beating every amateur and semipro team since their graduation from high school in 1915. "In the Wake of the News," *Chicago Tribune*, Apr. 7, 1926; "Boys' Rules Speed Girls' Basket Games," *Chicago Tribune*, Dec. 27, 1926.

25. "Peoria Hi Beats Phillips Five," *Chicago Defender*, Mar. 6, 1926; "The Captainball Team," in *The Red and Black* (1925), 163.

26. "DePaul Girls' Five Wins," *Chicago Tribune*, Apr. 28, 1922; "Girls' Basketball," *Chicago Tribune*, Mar. 22, 1924; "St. Catherine Girl Cagers Defeat Loretta Academy," *Chicago Tribune*, Feb. 26, 1930.

27. "Basketball," in *The Centurion* (1922), 149; "Basketball," in *Schurzone* (1926), 125.

28. "Girls' Sports," in *The Temulac* (1925), 86; "Girls' Basketball Team," in *The Temulac* (1926), 95; "Bowen Girls Basketball Teams," in *The Bowenite* (1925), 123–24.

29. "Crosby High School Girls Set New National Rifle Record," *New York Times*, Jan. 17, 1925; "Englewood Tops Rifle Tourney," *Chicago Tribune*, May 15, 1924; "'Sure-Shot Mary,' Only 16, Hits Perfect 500 with Army Rifle," *New York Times*, Feb. 24, 1927; Carol Anger, "A Review of the Girls' Rifle Corps, 1923–24," *Evanstonian* 7, no. 4 (1924): 66–68.

30. "Parker Wins Volley Ball Game with Normal," *Green and White*, Apr. 13, 1925, 3; "Girls' Baseball Team Will Play Normal College," *Green and White*, May 18, 1925, 5; "Fifteen Girls Are Organized as 1926 Tech Skate Team," *Harrison Herald*, Jan. 15, 1926, n.p.; "Calumet Girls Win," *Chicago Tribune*, June 19, 1923; "Frosh and Sophs Win First Games in Volley Ball," *Green and White*, Apr. 20, 1925, 3.

31. "31,778 High School Girls Play Inter-Class Games," *Chicago Evening American*, June 18, 1925; "The G.A.A.," in *The Purple and White* (1926), 188; "Girls' Athletic News," in *The Eagle* (1926), 159.

32. Keith McClellan, "Wilma Rudolph Spotlights Women's Sports," 1–26; Catherine D'Ignazio, "The History of High School Girls' Sport in the City and Suburbs of Philadelphia, 1890–1990," 11–14.

33. D'Ignazio, "High School Girls' Sport in Philadelphia," 14–15.

34. Joan S. Hult, "The Governance of Athletics for Girls and Women: Leadership by Women Physical Educators, 1899–1949," 70–71; Wagenhorst, *Administration and Cost*, 27–28.

35. Beran, "Iowa, the Longtime 'Hot Bed.'"

36. Janice A. Beran, *From Six-on-Six to Full Court Press: A Century of Iowa Girls' Basketball*, 30–32.

37. Marian Bemus Johnson and Dorothy E. McIntyre, *Daughters of the Game: The First Era of Minnesota Girls High School Basketball 1891–1942*, 78, 215–17, 263–64.

38. South Carolina High School League, "Palmetto's Finest Record Book"; Beran, *From Six-on-Six*, 100; Steven Cooper and Bob Barnett, "The West Virginia Girls High School Tournament, 1919–1924."

39. Roxanne M. Albertson, "Basketball Texas Style, 1910–1933: School to Industrial League Competition," in *Century of Women's Basketball*, 155–59 (see chap. 8, n. 8); Bedichek, *Educational Competition*, 386–92; McGehee, "Educational Competition?"

40. Stanaland, "Early Years of Basketball in Kentucky," 167–74.

41. Tennessee Secondary School Athletic Association, "Year by Year Results for Girls Basketball: Team Champions."

42. Welch, "Interscholastic Basketball."

43. "Undefeated Western Girl Champions," *Chicago Defender*, Mar. 22, 1924; "Kentucky Normal Boys and Clinton Hi Girl Fives Win," *Chicago Defender*, Mar. 8, 1924; "West Kentucky Girls Win Form Hopkinsville," *Chicago Defender*, Feb. 12, 1927; "Sumner and Northeast Win Kan. State Championships," *Chicago Defender*, Apr. 3, 1926; "Fairview High Girls Cop," *Chicago Defender*, Mar. 27, 1926; "South Carolina State Girls Beat Booker High," *Chicago Defender*, Feb. 27, 1926; "Girls' Five Undefeated for 7 Years," *Chicago Defender*, Mar. 16, 1929.

44. "Croton Girls' Team Wins," *New York Times*, Apr. 15, 1924; "Defenders of the Girls' National Basketball Championship: The Team," caption in *New York Times*, Apr. 6, 1924.

45. Otis Wile, "Our (Almost) International Champions"; "Girls to Play for Title," *New York Times*, Mar. 27, 1924; "Westfield Girls Triumph," *New York Times*, Apr. 8, 1924; "Guthrie Girls Win Basketball Title," *New York Times*, Apr. 6, 1924.

46. "Hempstead Girls Win National Title," *New York Times*, Apr. 7, 1925; "Girls' Title Play to Ohio," *New York Times*, Dec. 5, 1925; "Town in Quick Rally for Girls Champions," *New York Times*, Mar. 14, 1926; "Girl Fives Are Drawn," *New York Times*, Mar. 24, 1926; "Pennsylvania Girls Win National Prep Cage Title," *New York Times*, Mar. 28, 1926.

47. "Sharon (PA) Girls Lose," *New York Times*, Mar. 24, 1927; "Eastern Girls Defeated," *New York Times*, Mar. 25, 1927; "Dickenson Girls Win, 37–16," *New York Times*, Dec. 17, 1927; "Lawrence Girls, Seeking 3rd Title in a Row, Begins School Basketball Campaign on Friday," *New York Times* Dec. 5, 1931; James Roach, "Women in Sports," *New York Times*, Dec. 13, 1931; Steven Cooper, e-mail to author, Aug. 16, 2011.

48. Cahn, *Coming on Strong*, 89–90; Himes, "Female Athlete in American Society," 2186–88.

49. Cooper and Barnett, "West Virginia Girls High School Tournament."

50. Booth, "Investigation in Interscholastic Athletics," 697–98.

51. W. W. Mustaine, "Tabulation of Replies to Questionnaire on Girls' Basket Ball"; "Report of the Advisory Committee on Athletics for High School Girls," 254–56; Stanaland, "Early Years of Basketball in Kentucky," 174; Cahn, *Coming on Strong*, 90–91; Beran, *From Six-on-Six*, 100.

52. Whitten, *Interscholastics*, 53; "6 Chicago High Schools Join Illinois Ass'n," *Chicago Tribune*, Mar. 30, 1926; "City Preps Eligible for State Games," *Chicago Tribune*, Apr. 1, 1926; "State Body Refuses to O.K. Chicago Rules," *Chicago Tribune*, Nov. 20, 1926.

53. D'Ignazio, "High School Girls' Sport in Philadelphia," 47–49, 152–56.

54. Cahn, *Coming on Strong*, 106; Himes, "Female Athlete in American Society," 2183–84; "High School Girls Hold a Sports Day," *New York Times*, May 4, 1929; Wayman, "Competition," 470–71.

55. Whitten, *Interscholastics*, 126–27.

56. "Chick" Mack, "The Roycemore Hockey Carnival," *Evanstonian* 9, no. 2 (1926): 32; Eleanor Hulteen, "Girls' Basketball Carnival," *Evanstonian* 9, no. 3 (1926): n.p.; Dorothy Ream, "The Splash Party," *Evanstonian* 10, no. 3 (1927): 32; Gertrude Haas, "The W.A.A. Field Day," *Evanstonian* 11, no. 4 (1928): n.p.; Ellen Mosbek, "Camp and Play Days," *Illinois High School Athlete* 2, no. 1 (1929): 6–7.

57. Cahn, *Coming on Strong*, 66; Himes, "Female Athlete in American Society," 2185; "Crosby H.S. Girls Score," *New York Times*, Apr. 4, 1925; "Central H.S. Wins Title," *New York Times*, Apr. 18, 1925; Ellen Mosbek, "Telegraphic Basket Shooting Contest," *Illinois High School Athlete* 2, no. 1 (1929): 7.

13. THE SEPARATE AND UNEQUAL WORLD OF
AFRICAN AMERICAN INTERSCHOLASTIC SPORTS

1. W. H. J. Beckett, "The Place of Athletics in Secondary Schools."

2. Robert L. McCaul, *The Black Struggle for Public Schooling in Nineteenth-Century Illinois* (Carbondale: Southern Illinois Univ. Press, 1987), 58–67, 108–24.

3. "Colored Boy to Captain Hyde Park Nine," *Chicago Tribune*, June 29, 1901; "Alumni Stand by Ransom," *Chicago Tribune*, Nov. 25, 1902.

4. Allan H. Spear, *Black Chicago: The Making of a Negro Ghetto, 1890–1920* (Chicago: Univ. of Chicago Press, 1967), 130, 211–16; "Color Question Again Raised at High School," *Chicago Tribune*, Apr. 6, 1917; "'Jim Crow' Rule or No Dances, Say Schoolgirls," *Chicago Tribune*, Jan. 6, 1915.

5. "24 High Schools Confronted with Seat Shortage," *Chicago Tribune*, Aug. 26, 1923; "Phillips Five Beats Hyde Park by 9 to 4," *Chicago Tribune*, Jan. 12, 1923. The Phillips teams of the 1920s have been examined in two previous histories: Gerald Gems, "Blocked Shot: The Development of Basketball in the African-American Community in Chicago"; and Nelson George, *Elevating the Game: Black Men and Basketball*, 42–43.

6. "Phillips High Wins Central Division Title," *Chicago Defender*, Feb. 18, 1922; "Phillips High Bows to Lane in Semifinals," *Chicago Defender*, Mar. 11, 1922; Frank Young, "Marshall Cops Game in the Closing Seconds from Phillips, 11 to 9," *Chicago Defender*, Mar. 17, 1923; "Citizens Will Honor Wendell Phillips Lads," *Chicago Defender*, Mar. 10, 1923.

7. "Lane Wins City Title; Harrison Lights Triumph," *Chicago Tribune*, Mar. 8, 1924; "Phillips High Defeats Kansas City, 23 to 13," *Chicago Defender*, Apr. 5, 1924; "Phillips High Beats Armstrong, 17–10," *Chicago Defender*, Apr. 26, 1924.

8. "Colored Pupils and White War at School Game," *Chicago Tribune*, Jan. 10, 1925; "Phillips Withdraws from Basket League," *Chicago Tribune*, Feb. 6, 1925; "4,500 See Armstrong High Beaten, 25 to 15, in Basketball Classic," *Chicago Defender*, Feb. 21,

1925; Nettie George Speedy, "Society Watches Phillips Hi Win Winter Classic," *Chicago Defender*, Feb. 21, 1925.

9. "Attention! Brookins-Ramsey," *Chicago Defender*, Feb. 28, 1925; "Phillips High Forfeits All Floor Games," *Chicago Defender*, Mar. 12, 1927.

10. "Phillips Beats Harrison to Win Prep Cage Title," *Chicago Tribune*, Mar. 11, 1928; "Police Quell Student Boxers at Cage Games," *Chicago Tribune*, Feb. 8, 1928; "Phillips High to Play for City Title," *Chicago Defender*, Mar. 3, 1928; Ben Green, *Spinning the Globe* (New York: HarperCollins, 2005), 34–50.

11. "Phillips Hi Heavies Win City Title," *Chicago Defender*, Mar. 22, 1930; "They're Chicago's Beat; What about Them, Mr. Stagg?," *Chicago Defender*, Mar. 22, 1930; John Caution, "Protest Color Line at U. of C. Cage Meet," *Chicago Defender*, Mar. 29, 1930.

12. "Crane Defeats Phillips to Win Prep Title, 30–22," *Chicago Tribune*, Mar. 29, 1931; "Phillips High Wins Hampton Title," *Chicago Defender*, Mar. 28, 1931.

13. W. H. Perry Jr., "Central Crushes Phillips 7 to 0," *Chicago Defender*, Nov. 28, 1925; Edward Meacham, "Kentuckians Fall before Phillips Hi," *Chicago Defender*, Dec. 4, 1926.

14. "Fists, Knives Used as Chi Preps Battle," *San Francisco Examiner*, Oct. 6, 1927; "Booker T. Team Defeats Chicago," *Tulsa World*, Dec. 3, 1933; Frank A. Young, "Wendell Phillips Loses to Lane Tech, 11–3," *Chicago Defender*, July 2, 1927; "Lane Tech Nine Beats Phillips to Win Title," *Chicago Tribune*, June 26, 1927.

15. David W. Kellum, "Detroit School Lad Skips over Timbers for New Mark," *Chicago Defender*, Mar. 30, 1929; "Moore Takes High School Championship," *Chicago Defender*, Nov. 18, 1925; "Race Boys Shine in Cage Tourney Held in Denver," *Chicago Defender*, Mar. 23, 1935.

16. "Wrestling Champ" (caption), *Chicago Defender*, Apr. 16, 1927; "Draw Color Line at University of Chicago," *Chicago Defender*, Feb. 6, 1932.

17. Charles Herbert Thompson, "The History of the National Basketball Tournaments for Black High Schools," 10–12.

18. Edwin Bancroft Henderson, *The Negro in Sports*, 238, 273–75; Thompson, "National Basketball Tournaments for Black High Schools," 12–13.

19. Bob Kuska, *Hot Potato: How Washington and New York Gave Birth to Black Basketball and Changed America's Game Forever*, 11–21; Robert N. Mattingly, "History of the I.S.S.A.A."

20. Lewis E. Johnson, "Basket Ball in Washington"; Kuska, *Hot Potato*, 3, 26.

21. Henderson, "Public Schools Athletic League of Washington, D.C."; "Athletes Hold Meet," *Washington Post*, Mar. 12, 1911; "Interstate High School Assn. Elects Gibson Head," *Chicago Defender*, Nov. 26, 1925; "Dunbar High Wins the South Atlantic Football Crown," *Chicago Defender*, Dec. 6, 1930; D. Wiggins, "Edwin Bancroft Henderson," 90.

22. C. Robert Barnett, "'The Finals': West Virginia's Black Basketball Tournament, 1925–1927," 30–36; F. A. Parker, "High School Quintets of West Virginia Enter Play for

State Championship," *Chicago Defender*, Mar. 20, 1926; "Kimball Hi West Va. State Champs," *Chicago Defender*, Mar. 27, 1926. Barnett's feature sheds much light on the pioneering West Virginia tournament and contributes significantly to our understanding of early black interscholastics.

23. Thompson, "National Basketball Tournaments for Black High Schools," 14–18; "Lincoln High School Five in Victory over Northeast," *Chicago Defender* (national ed.), Mar. 7, 1925; L. Jacobs, "Sumner Hi Leads Missouri Valley Interscholastic Race as Season Nears End," *Chicago Defender*, Mar. 19, 1927; "Sumner Hi Clinches Miss. Valley Title," *Chicago Defender*, Feb. 25, 1928.

24. Thompson, "National Basketball Tournaments for Black High Schools," 18; Richard B. Pierce, "More than a Game: The Political Meaning of High School Basketball in Indianapolis"; "Sumner Beats Lovejoy," *Chicago Defender*, Jan. 31, 1920; Eugene King, "Cairo Cops Championship," *Chicago Defender* (national ed.), Mar. 28, 1925; "Carbondale Wins 8th S. Illinois Prep Meet," *Chicago Defender* (national ed.), May 11, 1929; Charles W. Whitten, "The Colored High Schools of Illinois," in *Interscholastics*, 134–39.

25. Whitten, *Interscholastics*, 136–37.

26. Ibid., 137–38; Pat Heston, "More than a Game: High School Basketball's Victory over Segregation"; Taylor Bell, *Sweet Charlie, Dike, Cazzie, and Bobby Joe*, 41–44.

27. Lord Jeff, "Howard Wins Track Meet; Dunbar Tops School Lads," *Chicago Defender*, May 21, 1921; "Lincoln Wins Mile Relay in Howard's Annual Meet," *Chicago Defender*, May 17, 1924.

28. "Hampton Opens New Athletic Field May 20 with Track Meet," *Chicago Defender*, Mar. 25, 1922; "Third Annual Track Games at Hampton Institute May 17," *Chicago Defender*, May 17, 1924; Thomas W. Young, "Nine Records Smashed at Hampton," *Chicago Defender*, May 22, 1926.

29. "Entries Swell for Lincoln Track Meet," *Chicago Defender*, May 3, 1930; "40 Prep Schools May Enter Teams in Mo. Lincoln Meet," *Chicago Defender*, Apr. 25, 1931; "Mo. Lincoln to Hold Prep Tennis Tourney May 23," *Chicago Defender*, May 16, 1931; J. D. Parks, "Sumner High of Kansas City Wins Western Cage Tourney," *Chicago Defender* (national ed.), Mar. 17, 1934.

30. "11 Records Set at Tuskegee Relays," *Chicago Defender*, May 11, 1929.

31. Thompson, "National Basketball Tournaments for Black High Schools," 20–28; "1929 Interscholastic Championship to Be Held at Hampton," *Chicago Defender*, Feb. 9, 1929.

32. "Fort Valley High Quintet Cops Georgia State Honors," *Chicago Defender*, Mar. 10, 1928; Thompson, "National Basketball Tournaments for Black High Schools," 19, 28–29, 163.

33. Thompson, "National Basketball Tournaments for Black High Schools," 17–18; "Va. State to Hold State Hi Cage Play," *Chicago Defender*, Feb. 25, 1928; "Booker T. Five Captures Title," *Chicago Defender*, Mar. 4, 1933; "Johnson City Girls Win Tournament,"

Afro-American, Mar. 9, 1935; "Allen White Girls and Boys Show Class in Cage Tourney," *Chicago Defender* (national ed.), Mar. 23, 1935, 39; "Tulsa High Wins Meet," *Chicago Defender*, May 21, 1932.

34. Louis Stout, *Shadows of the Past: A History of the Kentucky High School Athletic League*, 10, 36, 39, 51, 54; Milton Golden, "Rosenwald, Julius," in *American National Biography* (New York: Oxford Univ. Press, 1999), 18:893–95.

35. Stout, *Shadows of the Past*, 10–11, 74.

36. Ibid., 12–13, 67; "Maysville Girls Win State Title," *Chicago Defender*, Mar. 31, 1934.

37. "Lincoln High Is Victor in Cinder Meet," *Chicago Defender*, May 20, 1933; "Vashon Wins Missouri's Prep Cage Tournament," *Chicago Defender* (national ed.), Mar. 16, 1935; Al Monroe, "Sumner Wins Track Relay in Missouri," *Chicago Defender*, May 15, 1937; Thompson, "National Basketball Tournaments for Black High Schools," 28–52.

38. Thompson, "National Basketball Tournaments for Black High Schools," 53–69; "Madisonville High Takes Cage Tourney at Tuskegee," *Chicago Defender*, Mar. 28, 1936.

39. Thompson, "National Basketball Tournaments for Black High Schools," 31, 36–37, 52.

14. New National Governance and the Triumph of the State High School Associations

1. Whitten, *Interscholastics*, 141–42.

2. Ibid., 142–43.

3. Letter from H. O. Crisler, tournament manager, to Tom Stephenson, *Elkhart Daily Truth*, Jan. 10, 1928, Stagg Papers.

4. *Minutes of the "Conference of Athletic Directors of the Conference Universities and Officers of the Nine State High School Athletic Associations," Dec. 1923*, Stagg Papers; F. Nevermore, Secretary of the Wisconsin Interscholastic Athletic Association, to H. O. Crisler, Univ. of Chicago, Feb. 5, 1924, Stagg Papers.

5. Charles W. Whitten, "Some Disquieting Aspects of Our Athletic Program."

6. Ibid., 748.

7. Ibid., 746.

8. Whitten, *Interscholastics*, 145–46; "Schools Favor Dropping Cage Meet at U. of C.," *Chicago Tribune*, Dec. 24, 1927; [Amos Alonzo Stagg] to the National Federation of High School Athletic Associations, Feb. 24, 1928, Stagg Papers (not signed in this copy by Stagg but clearly by him).

9. Whitten, *Interscholastics*, 146–47.

10. Ibid., 148–50; Wilfrid Smith, "C. W. Whitten Tells Stand on Cage Tourneys," *Chicago Tribune*, Apr. 9, 1930; *Minutes of the 1929 Annual Meeting of the National*

Council of the National Federation of S.H.S.A. Assoc., Cleveland Athletic Club, Cleveland, Ohio, Feb. 25, 1929, Stagg Papers.

11. Harlan Rohm, "Athens Wins National Basketball Tourney," *Chicago Tribune*, Apr. 7, 1929; Harlan Rohm, "Hamlets Battle Cities in U. of C. Semi-Finals," *Chicago Tribune*, Apr. 6, 1929; "In the Wake of the News," *Chicago Tribune*, Apr. 2, 1929.

12. Because of some objections in the wording over the issue of private and parochial schools, the resolution was not adopted; a rewrite was requested for voting on at the next meeting. Charles W. Whitten, "A Big Step in Advance"; Whitten, *Interscholastics*, 151–53; "N.C.A. Aims Blow at Prep Cage Meets," *Chicago Herald and Examiner*, Mar. 21, 1930; Don Maxwell, "Fate of U. of C. Prep Tourneys Up to Faculty," *Chicago Tribune*, Apr. 8, 1930; Arch Ward, "College Chiefs Watch Maroons," *Chicago Tribune*, May 15, 1930.

13. "Stagg Tourneys Bring Memories of Great Games," *Chicago Tribune*, Mar. 23, 1930; John Caution, "Protest Color Line at U. of C. Cage Meet," *Chicago Defender*, Mar. 29, 1930.

14. Wilfrid Smith, "Chicago Schools Vote 11 to 6 for Prep Tourneys," *Chicago Tribune*, May 19, 1930; Wilfrid Smith, "Maroons Abandon National Basket Meet," *Chicago Tribune*, Dec. 9, 1930.

15. Arch Ward, "College Chiefs Watch Maroons," *Chicago Tribune*, May 15, 1930.

16. Dean Frederic Woodward to Amos Alonzo Stagg, Feb. 19, 1930, Stagg Papers; W. Smith, "Maroons Abandon National Basket Meet." Amos Alonzo Stagg Papers, Box 65, Folder 13, Special Collections Research Center, University of Chicago Library.

17. Howard J. Savage et al., *American College Athletics*, 54, 153–54.

18. Ibid., 62–63.

19. Ibid., 61–65.

20. Ibid., 62.

21. Ibid., 63, 65.

22. Frederick Rand Rogers, *The Future of Interscholastic Athletics*, 27–28.

23. Ibid., 45–47; Frederick Rand Rogers, "State Championships Abolished."

24. Rogers, *Future of Interscholastic Athletics*, 48–50.

25. Booth, "Investigation in Interscholastic Athletics," 699.

26. "Big Ten Deserts Stagg in Prep Meet Fight," *Chicago Tribune*, Apr. 9, 1930.

27. "Abandon Prep Meets," *Chicago Tribune*, Jan. 11, 1931.

28. "103 Teams in Purple Meets; 643 Athletes," *Chicago Tribune*, Mar. 20, 1930; "Froebel Takes N.U. Track Title; Chisholm Swim Winner," *Chicago Tribune*, Mar. 23, 1930; "N.U. Gives Up 18 Year Old Prep Meet," *Chicago Tribune*, Jan. 21, 1931.

29. Arch Ward, "Big Ten Presidents to Discuss North Central Case," *Chicago Tribune*, Mar. 5, 1931.

30. "New Utrecht High Wins Track Meet," *New York Times*, Apr. 20, 1924; "Roxbury School Wins Track Title at Yale," *New York Times*, May 20, 1928; "College and School Scores," *New York Times*, May 19, 1929; "Abandon Court Tourneys," *New York*

Times, Dec. 9, 1930; "Penn Interscholastic Meet Abandoned in Economy Move," *New York Times*, Feb. 25, 1932.

31. "600 Prep Trackmen Enter 26th Stagg Interscholastic," *Chicago Tribune*, May 27, 1930; "Prep Athletes Here for Meet at Stagg Field," *Chicago Tribune*, June 11, 1931; "Arkansas City Wins U.S. Prep Track Title," *Chicago Tribune*, June 15, 1932.

32. "Schoolboy Ties World's Record for 100 Yards," *Chicago Tribune*, June 18, 1933; U.S. Prep Meet at U. of C. Is Discontinued," *Chicago Tribune*, Apr. 14, 1934; *University of Chicago Twenty-Ninth Annual Interscholastic Track and Field Games, June 17, 1933, Program*, Department of Physical Education and Athletics Records, 1892–1974, Special Collections, Joseph Regenstein Library, Univ. of Chicago. The meet claimed five national interscholastic records were broken and gave Jesse Owens credit for three of them. But Owens's long jump record of 24 feet, 9 5/8 inches broke only the existing national record in the books. Owens a week earlier in Cleveland had already bettered the national record with a leap of a little more than 24 feet, 11 inches.

33. "Track Meet Sanctions," *Illinois High School Athletic* (1932).

34. Ibid.

35. "Oak Park Gets $750,000 Gym," *Chicago Herald and Examiner*, May 21, 1927.

36. "Oak Park High to Open Prep Relays Friday," *Chicago Tribune*, Mar. 30, 1931.

37. *Final Report on the WPA Program, 1935–43*, 131; Jason Scott Smith, *Building New Deal Liberalism: The Political Economy of Public Works, 1933–1956* (New York: Cambridge Univ. Press, 2006), 114; Holly Hope, *An Ambition to Be Preferred: New Deal Recovery Efforts and Architecture in Arkansas, 1933–1943* (Little Rock: Arkansas Historic Preservation Program, 2006), 38.

38. P. Roy Brammell, *Intramural and Interscholastic Athletics: Bulletin 1932, No. 17, National Survey of Secondary Education, Monograph No. 27*, vi, 3.

39. Ibid., 50, 76.

40. Ibid., 81–85.

41. Wagenhorst, *Administration and Cost*, 81–83; O'Hanlon, "Interscholastic Athletics, 1900–1940" (PhD diss.), 215–27.

42. Brammell, *Intramural and Interscholastic Athletics*, 83, 99–100, 104.

Epilogue

1. Canadian School Sport Federation, http://www.schoolsport.ca; Sue Fleming (CSSF assistant to executive management committee), e-mail to the author, Mar. 15, 2007; Ontario Federation of School Athletic Associations, "Past Champions."

2. Applin, "From Muscular Christianity to the Market Place," 266; Troy D. Paino, "Hoosiers in a Different Light: Forces of Change v. the Power of Nostalgia"; Taylor Bell, "Four-Class Issue Isn't Going Away: System Takes Effect Next Season, but Foes Still Blasting IHSA," *Chicago Sun-Times*, Mar. 11, 2007.

3. Stone, "High School Athletics," 160–61; Illinois High School Association, "IHSA Record Book"; Florida High School Athletic Association, "FHSAA Championship Record Books"; Wisconsin Interscholastic Athletic Association, "Welcome to the Official WIAA Website."

4. Reid Hanley, "Public League Rich in History," *Chicago Tribune*, Mar. 22, 1991; Charles G. Bennett, "Closing of Schools in Fund Cut Urged," *New York Times*, Apr. 17, 1951; "Moss Group Weighs Unifying the Athletics of High Schools under Single Director," *New York Times*, Apr. 30, 1951; Leonard Buder, "City Urged to Aid School Sports by Annual Subsidy of $300,000," *New York Times*, Oct. 6, 1954.

5. Paino, "Hoosiers in a Different Light," 63–65; William F. Fox Jr., "I'll Take Hoosier Hoopla," 16, 42; Jimmie Angelopolous, "Hoosier Madness," 18–21, 71–73; Schwomeyer, *Hoosier Hysteria*, 434.

6. Paino, "Hoosiers in a Different Light," 64–65; Angelopolous, "Hoosier Madness," 20–21; Greg Guffey, *The Greatest Basketball Story Ever Told*; *Hoosiers* (Santa Monica, CA: Orion Pictures, 1986).

7. Luther Emery, "Massillon: A Rich and Glorious Tradition"; Ohio High School Athletic Association, "OHSAA All-Time State Football Tournament Results."

8. "University Interscholastic League," *Texas Almanac, 1982–1983* (Dallas: A. H. Belo, 1981), 41–45; Bill McMurray, "Texas: King Sized Football."

9. Thompson, "National Basketball Tournaments for Black High Schools," 93–127; Barnett, "'The Finals'"; David K. Wiggins, "'With All Deliberate Speed': High School Sport, Race, and *Brown v. Board of Education*," 335–37.

10. Kenneth T. Andrews, "Movement-Countermovement Dynamics and the Emergence of New Institutions: The Case of 'White Flight' Schools in Mississippi"; Anthony M. Champagne, "The Segregation Academy and the Law"; Mark Lowry II, "Schools in Transition."

11. Grundy, "From Amazons to Glamazons"; Beran, *From Six-on-Six*, 192; Shelly Lucas, "Courting Controversy: Gender and Power in Iowa Girls' Basketball"; D'Ignazio, "High School Girls' Sport in Philadelphia," 231–34, 239.

12. Morris, *American Catholics*, 223, 256; Jay Dolan, *The American Catholic Experience: A History from Colonial Times to the Present* (Notre Dame, IN: Univ. of Notre Dame Press, 1992), 357–58.

13. "New Catholic Suburb League Making Plans," *Chicago Tribune*, Dec. 13, 1956; "Four Catholic Schools Quit," *Chicago Tribune*, Feb. 28, 1961; "Catholic League to Join IHSA; Cites Competition," *Chicago Tribune*, Jan. 31, 1973.

14. "New High School Sports Federation of New York," *New York Times*, Oct. 14, 1973; "Schools Try for 2 State Titles," *New York Times*, Mar. 18, 1983; "Championship Ban Lifted," *New York Times*, Feb. 17, 1994.

15. Eldon E. Snyder, "Teaching the Sociology of Sport: Using a Comic Strip in the Classroom," *Teaching Sociology* 25, no. 3 (1997): 239–43; Patricia Hagen, "Gil's World."

16. US Commissioner on Civil Rights, "The Impact of Title IX: Participation in High School and College Competitive Athletics."

17. National Federation of State High School Associations, "The Impact of Title IX"; National Federation of State High School Associations, "2009–2010 High School Athletics Participation Survey"; Pamela Grundy and Susan Shackelford, *Shattering the Glass: The Remarkable History of Women's Basketball.*

18. "2009–2010 High School Athletics Participation Survey."

19. J. Thomas Jable, "Progress or Plight: The Growing Commercialism of High School Athletics in the United States"; National Federation of State High School Associations, "NFHS Corporate Partners."

20. Jable, "Progress or Plight"; Kelley King, "The Little School That Can't Be Beat."

21. Jable, "Progress or Plight"; National High School Coaches Association, "1999 NHSCA National Open High School All-Americans"; National High School Coaches Association, "Event History: 2001 Final Four of High School Wrestling"; Rich Gonzalez, "Never before Had Such Breathtaking Storylines Played Out Quite Like This: Champion Met Champion. Talent Met Technology. And for the First Time Ever, America Met Its True Number Ones."

22. Jable, "Progress or Plight"; Jerry Sullivan, "Star High School Basketball Player Sure to Have the Last Laugh," *Buffalo News*, Dec. 29, 2002.

23. Taylor Bell, "Pressure's on Like Never Before: Retired Coaches Say Today's Game Has Become Too Big," *Chicago Sun-Times*, Sept. 3, 2006.

24. Douglas Lederman, "Use Sports to Lure Inner-City Youths to Education, Preaches a Coach Who Directs a U. of Chicago Institute."

25. H. G. Bissenger, *Friday Night Lights: A Town, a Team, and a Dream*, 128–52, 363–64.

26. Tina Akouris, "Add Illinois to the List: State Golf Tournaments Will Mark Start of IHSA Drug Testing for Athletes," *Chicago Sun-Times*, Oct. 13, 2008; Laurel S. Garzon et al., "The School Nurse's Role in Prevention of Student Use of Performance-Enhancing Supplements"; Andrea Jensen Tatich, "Performance-Enhancing Drugs and Supplements in Women and Girls."

27. John Leptich, "Cash-Strapped System Short-Changes Athletes," *Chicago Tribune*, Mar. 23, 1991; Barry Temkin, "Public League Failures Mean Shortchanged Kids," *Chicago Tribune*, Mar. 22, 1991.

28. Kirk Johnson, "For New York, 25–Year Losing Streak," *New York Times*, Jan. 13, 1999; Kirk Johnson, "Separate but Unequal: 2 Schools' Tales," *New York Times*, Jan. 14, 1999.

29. National Federation of State High School Associations, "2009–2010 High School Athletics Participation Survey"; John Gehring, "Athletic Choice: Students Shun School Teams," 1, 15.

Selected Bibliography

Archival Sources

Chicago History Museum Archives. Chicago, IL.

Chicago Public High School League files. Chicago, IL.

Stagg, Amos Alonzo. Papers. Special Collections, Joseph Regenstein Library, Univ. of Chicago, Chicago, IL.

Government Documents

Annual Reports of the Board of Education. Chicago: Board of Education, 1895–1922.

Beals, Frank L. "Military Training." In *Department of Education: Annual Report of the Superintendent of Schools for the Year Ending June 30, 1924,* 45–46. Chicago: Board of Education, 1924.

Brammell, P. Roy. *Intramural and Interscholastic Athletics: Bulletin 1932, No. 17, National Survey of Secondary Education, Monograph No. 27.* Washington, DC: US Government Printing Office, 1933.

Cardinal Principles of Secondary Education, Bulletin 1918, No. 35. 1918. Reprint. Washington, DC: US Government Printing Office, 1937.

Delaporte, E. C. "Physical Education High Schools." In *Annual Report of the Superintendent of Schools for the Year Ending June 30, 1926,* 114. Chicago: Chicago Department of Education, 1926.

Final Report on the WPA Program, 1935–43. Washington, DC: US Government Printing Office, 1947.

"High School Championships." In *New York City Public Schools, Public Schools Athletic League, Division of High Schools.* Brooklyn: Public Schools Athletic League, [1960].

Proceedings Board of Education, City of Chicago, July 8, 1903, to June 27, 1928. Chicago: Board of Education, 1904–28.

"Report of the Department of Military Training." In *Public Schools of the City of Chicago Sixty-Fifth Annual Report of the Board of Education for the Year Ending June 30, 1919.* Chicago: Board of Education, 1919.

Sixteenth Biennial Report of the Superintendent of Public Instruction of the State of Illinois, July 1, 1884–June 30, 1886. Springfield, IL: [Superintendent of Public Instruction], 1886.

Snyder, Thomas D., and Sally A. Dillow. *Digest of Education Statistics, 2010.* Washington, DC: National Center for Education Statistics, Institute of Education Sciences, US Department of Education, 2011.

CITY AND COMMUNITY NEWSPAPERS

Atlanta Constitution

Boston Globe

Brooklyn Eagle

Buffalo News

Champaign News-Gazette

Chicago Daily News

Chicago Defender

Chicago Defender (national edition)

Chicago Evening American

Chicago Herald American

Chicago Herald and Examiner

Chicago Record-Herald

Chicago Sun-Times

Chicago Times

Chicago Tribune

Evanston Index

Hyde Park Herald

Inter Ocean

Lake View Telephone

Los Angeles Times

Milwaukee Journal

Milwaukee Sentinel

New York Clipper
New York Herald
New York Times
Oak Leaves
Philadelphia Inquirer
Philadelphia Record
San Francisco Examiner
Tulsa World
Washington Post

HIGH SCHOOL AND UNIVERSITY NEWSPAPERS

Echo (Medill High School, Chicago)
Englewood High School Journal (Englewood High School, Chicago)
Evanstonian (Evanston High School, Illinois)
Green and White (Parker High School, Chicago)
Harrison Herald (Harrison High School, Chicago)
High School Journal (Cook County high schools)
High School Life (Cook County high schools)
High School Student (Cook County high schools)
High School Weekly (Cook County high schools)
Hyde Park Weekly (Hyde Park High School, Chicago)
Red and White (Lake View High School, Chicago)
Tabula (Oak Park High School, Illinois)
University High Weekly (University High School, Chicago)
University of Chicago Weekly
Voice (West Division High School, Chicago)

HIGH SCHOOL YEARBOOKS AND RECORD BOOKS

The Aitchpe (Hyde Park High School, Chicago)
The Annual Voice (McKinley High School, Chicago)
The Bowenite (Bowen High School, Chicago)
The Centurion (Senn High School, Chicago)
The Courier (Fenger High School, Chicago)
The Eagle (Lindblom High School, Chicago)

The Forum (Senn High School, Chicago)

The Harrisonian (Harrison High School, Chicago)

Libethrian (Hyde Park High School, Chicago)

The Oracle (Hyde Park High School, Chicago)

The Purple and White (Englewood High School, Chicago)

The Red and Black (Phillips High School, Chicago)

Red and White (Lake View High School, Chicago)

Schurzone (Schurz High School, Chicago)

The Scottonian (Scott High School, Toledo, OH)

The Temulac (Calumet High School, Chicago)

Waite High School record book (Waite High School, Toledo, OH, untitled and undated)

OTHER SOURCES

Addington, Sarah. "The Athletic Limitations of Women." *Ladies' Home Journal,* June 1923, 38, 144, 147.

Albertson, Roxanne M. "Basketball Texas Style, 1910–1933: School to Industrial League Competition." In *A Century of Women's Basketball: From Frailty to Final Four,* edited by Joan S. Hult and Marianna Trekell, 155–66. Reston, VA: American Alliance for Health, Physical Education, Recreation, and Dance, 1991.

Andrews, Kenneth T. "Movement-Countermovement Dynamics and the Emergence of New Institutions: The Case of 'White Flight' Schools in Mississippi." *Social Forces* 80, no. 3 (2002): 911–36.

Angelopolous, Jimmie. "Hoosier Madness." *High School Basketball* 1, no. 1 (1964): 18–21, 71–73.

Antrium, Minna Thomas. "The Masculinization of Girls." *Lippincott's Monthly Magazine* 88 (Oct. 1911): 564–66.

Applin, Albert G., II. "From Muscular Christianity to the Market Place: The History of Men's and Boys' Basketball in the United States, 1891–1957." PhD diss., Univ. of Massachusetts, 1982.

Bachrach, William, and Clarence A. Bush. *Outline of Swimming: An Encyclopedia of the Sport.* Chicago: J. B. Bradwell, 1924.

Barnett, C. Robert. "'The Finals': West Virginia's Black Basketball Tournament, 1925–1957." *Goldenseal: A Quarterly Forum for Documenting West Virginia's Traditional Life* 9 (Summer 1983): 30–39.

Barney, Robert Knight. "Physical Education and Sport in North America." In *History of Physical Education and Sport*, edited by Earle F. Zeigler, 173–219. Englewood Cliffs, NJ: Prentice-Hall, 1979.

Bealle, Morris. *The Softball Story*. Washington, DC: Columbia, 1957.

Beckett, W. H. J. "The Place of Athletics in Secondary Schools." In *Official Handbook, Inter-Scholastic Athletic Association of the Middle States*, edited by William A. Joiner and Edwin B. Henderson, 71–72. New York: American Sports Publishing, 1910.

Bedichek, Roy. *Educational Competition: The Story of the University Interscholastic League of Texas*. Austin: Univ. of Texas Press, 1956.

Beede, Frank Herbert. "School Athletics." *School Journal* 72, no. 9 (1906): 218–19.

Bell, Taylor. *Sweet Charlie, Dike, Cazzie, and Bobby Joe*. Urbana: Univ. of Illinois Press, 2004.

Bendelow, Tom. "Golf around Chicago." In *Spalding's Official Golf Guide for 1911*, edited by Thomas Bendelow. New York: American Sports Publishing, 1911.

Beran, Janice A. *From Six-on-Six to Full Court Press: A Century of Iowa Girls' Basketball*. Ames: Iowa State Univ. Press, 1993.

———. "Iowa, the Longtime 'Hot Bed' of Girls Basketball." In *A Century of Women's Basketball: From Frailty to Final Four*, edited by Joan S. Hult and Marianna Trekell, 181–204. Reston, VA: American Alliance for Health, Physical Education, Recreation, and Dance, 1991.

———. "Playing to the Right Drummer: Girls' Basketball in Iowa, 1893–1927." *Research Quarterly for Exercise and Sport* (Centennial Issue) (Apr. 1985): 78–85.

Bissenger, H. G. *Friday Night Lights: A Town, a Team, and a Dream*. Cambridge, MA: Da Capo Press, 2000.

Booth, John M. "An Investigation in Interscholastic Athletics in Northwestern High Schools." *School Review* 34, no. 9 (1928): 696–706.

"Boston Rules Governing Athletics." *American School Board Journal* 55, no. 1 (1917): 49.

Boynton, F. D. "Athletics and Collateral Activities in Secondary Schools." In *National Education Association Journal of the Proceedings and Addresses of the Forty-Fourth Annual Meeting Held at St. Louis, Missouri, June 27–July 1, 1904*, 206–14. Winona, MN: National Education Association, 1904.

Brown, Elmer Ellsworth. *The Making of the Middle Schools*. New York: Longmans, Green, 1907.

Bryan, W. J. S. "Principals' Conference." In *National Educational Association Journal of Proceedings and Addresses of the Forty-First Annual Meeting Held at Minneapolis, Minnesota, July 7–11, 1902, 485–88.* Winona, MN: National Education Association, 1902.

Bulger, Bozeman. "The Army of Basket Ball." *Saturday Evening Post,* Jan. 9, 1932, 43.

Bundgaard, Axel. *Muscle and Manliness: The Rise of Sport in American Boarding Schools.* Syracuse, NY: Syracuse Univ. Press, 2005.

———. "Tom Brown Abroad: Athletics in Selected New England Public Schools, 1850–1910." *Research Quarterly for Exercise and Sport* (Centennial Issue) (Apr. 1985): 28–37.

Cahn, Susan K. *Coming on Strong: Gender and Sexuality in Twentieth-Century Women's Sports, 1900–1960.* New York: Free Press, 1994.

Campbell, Nelson. "Pioneers and Bloomer Girls." In *Grass Roots & Schoolyards: A High School Basketball Anthology,* edited by Nelson Campbell, 161–64. Lexington, MA: Stephen Greene, 1988.

———. "The Weird and the Wondrous: Vintage Big City." In *Grass Roots & Schoolyards: A High School Basketball Anthology,* edited by Nelson Campbell, 137–44. Lexington, MA: Stephen Greene, 1988.

Canadian School Sport Federation. http://www.schoolsport.ca.

Champagne, Anthony M. "The Segregation Academy and the Law." *Journal of Negro Education* 42, no. 1 (1973): 58–66.

Chapman, Mike. *Encyclopedia of American Wrestling.* Champaign, IL: Leisure Press, 1990.

Chepko, Steveda. "The Domestication of Basketball." In *A Century of Women's Basketball: From Frailty to Final Four,* edited by Joan S. Hult & Marianna Trekell, 109–24. Reston, VA: American Alliance for Health, Physical Education, Recreation, and Dance, 1991.

Chicago Catholic High School Athletic League Champions. Chicago: Wisklander Printing, [1959].

Cline, Earl. "Advisability of Inter-High-School Contests in Athletics." *American Physical Education Review* 15, no. 1 (1910): 22–31.

Cole, Terrence. "'A Purely American Game': Indoor Baseball and the Origins of Softball." *International Journal of the History of Sport* 7, no. 2 (1990): 287–96.

Cooper, Steve, and C. Robert Barnett. "The West Virginia Girls High School Tournament, 1919–1924." Unpublished manuscript, 2011.

Cowe, Eric L. *Early Women's Athletics: Statistics and History.* Vol. 2. Bingley, England: privately printed, 2005.

Craine, David M. "Image Enhancement: Three Chicago Institutions and the National Catholic Interscholastic Tournament, 1940–1941." *Journal of Illinois History* 11, no. 3 (2008): 205–20.

Cremin, Lawrence A. *The Transformation of the School: Progressivism in American Education, 1876–1957.* New York: Alfred A. Knopf, 1961.

Cubberley, Ellwood P. *An Introduction to the Study of Education.* Revised by Walter Crosby Eels from 1925 edition. Boston: Houghton Mifflin, 1933.

————. *Public Education in the United States: A Study and Interpretation of American Educational History.* Boston: Houghton Mifflin, 1934.

Curtis, Henry S. "A Football Education." *American Physical Education Review* 9, no. 4 (1904): 262–66.

————. "A Plea for Association Football." *American Physical Education Review* 9, no. 1 (1906): 1–7.

Cushing, Charles Phelps. "The Baseball of the City Urchin." *Colliers*, June 10, 1911, 20.

Davies, Wade, and Rich Clow. "The St. Francis Mission Indians and the National Interscholastic Catholic Basketball Tournament, 1924–1941." *International Journal of the History of Sport* 23, no. 3 (2006): 213–31.

DeGroot, Edward B. "Physical Education versus Military Training in Secondary Schools." *American Physical Education Review* 22, no. 4 (1917): 302–4.

Dickson, Paul. *The Worth Book of Softball: A Celebration of America's Pastime.* New York: Facts on File, 1994.

D'Ignazio, Catherine. "The History of High School Girls' Sport in the City and Suburbs of Philadelphia, 1890–1990." PhD diss., Temple Univ., 2010.

"A Discussion of High-School Fraternities and Sororities." *Elementary School Teacher* 6, no. 1 (1905): 47–54.

Dosch, Nancy Cole. "'The Sacrifice of Maidens' or Healthy Sportswomen? The Medical Debate over Women's Basketball." In *A Century of Women's Basketball: From Frailty to Final Four*, edited by Joan S. Hult and Marianna Trekell, 125–36. Reston, VA: American Alliance for Health, Physical Education, Recreation, and Dance, 1991.

Dudley, Gertrude, and Frances A. Kellor. *Athletic Games in the Education of Women.* New York: Henry Holt, 1909.

Edmonds, Franklin Spencer. "The Central High School of Philadelphia, 1838–1902." *School Review* 11, no. 3 (1903): 211–23.

———. *History of the Central High School of Philadelphia*. Philadelphia, PA: J. B. Lippincott, 1902.

Edmund, Joseph. "Golf in the Middle West." In *Spalding's Official Golf Guide for 1905*, edited by Charles S. Cox. New York: American Sports Publishing, 1905.

Ehler, G. W. "Basketball in Chicago." In *Spalding's Official Basket Ball Guide*, edited by Geo. T. Hepbron, 13–15. New York: American Sports Publishing, 1901.

Elliott, Charles W. "The 'ROTC': How the War Department's Plan of Military Training Has Developed." *School Life* 3, no. 9 (1919): 12–15.

Emery, Luther. "Massillon: A Rich and Glorious Tradition." *High School Football* 1, no. 1 (1963): 10–16, 80–81.

Emery, Lynne Fauley. "From Social Pastime to Serious Sport: Women's Tennis in Southern California in the Late 19th and Early 20th Centuries." *Californians* 8, no. 4 (1990): 38–42.

Emery, Lynne Fauley, and Margaret Toohey-Costa. "Hoops and Skirts: Women's Basketball on the West Coast, 1892–1930s." In *A Century of Women's Basketball: From Frailty to Final Four*, edited by Joan S. Hult and Marianna Trekell, 137–48. Reston, VA: American Alliance for Health, Physical Education, Recreation, and Dance, 1991.

"Fifth Annual Field Day of Philadelphia Public Schools, May 25, 1912, Belmont Plateau, Fairmont Park." *American Physical Education Review* 17, no. 5 (1912): 384–90.

Fine, Janis B., and Joan K. Smith. "Interscholastic High School Sports: The Growth and Decline of the National Catholic Basketball Tournament (1924–1941)." *Journal of Midwest History of Education Society* 21 (1994): 149–57.

Fisher, Donald M. *Lacrosse: A History of the Game*. Baltimore: Johns Hopkins Univ. Press, 2002.

Florida High School Athletic Association. "FHSAA Championship Record Books." http://www.flhsaa.org/records/.

Forsythe, Lewis L. *Athletics in Michigan High Schools: The First Hundred Years*. New York: Prentice-Hall, 1950.

Fox, William F., Jr. "I'll Take Hoosier Hoopla." *Saturday Evening Post*, Feb. 22, 1941.

Fretwell, Elbert K. *Extra-Curricular Activities in Secondary Schools*. Boston: Houghton Mifflin, 1931.

Garzon, Laurel S., Rebecca E. Ewald, Carolyn M. Rutledge, and Teresa Mead-
ows. "The School Nurse's Role in Prevention of Student Use of Performance-
Enhancing Supplements." *Journal of School Health* 76, no. 5 (2006): 159–63.

Gehring, John. "Athletic Choice: Students Shun School Teams." *Education
Week* 23, no. 6 (2003): 1–15.

Gems, Gerald R. "Blocked Shot: The Development of Basketball in the African-
American Community in Chicago." *Journal of Sport History* 22, no. 2 (1995):
135–48.

———. "The Prep Bowl: Football and Religious Acculturation in Chicago,
1927–1963." *Journal of Sport History* 23, no. 3 (1996): 284–302.

———. *The Windy City Wars.* Lanham, MD: Scarecrow, 1997.

General Skating Information. Chicago: Alfred's Ice King, [1923].

George, Nelson. *Elevating the Game: Black Men and Basketball.* New York:
HarperCollins, 1992.

Gerber, Ellen. "The Controlled Development of Collegiate Sport for Women,
1923–1936." *Journal of Sport History* 2, no. 1 (1975): 1–28.

Gonzalez, Rich. "Never before Had Such Breathtaking Storylines Played Out
Quite Like This: Champion Met Champion. Talent Met Technology. And
for the First Time Ever, America Met Its True Number Ones." Dyestat.
http://www.dyestat.com/3us/4xc/NTN/meet/richg.htm.

"Government of Athletics in Philadelphia." *American School Board Journal* 45,
no. 5 (1912): 47.

Graebner, William. "Outlawing Teenage Populism: The Campaign against
Secret Societies in the American High School, 1900–1960." *Journal of American History* 74, no. 2 (1987): 411–35.

Grundy, Pamela. "From Amazons to Glamazons: The Rise and Fall of North
Carolina Women's Basketball, 1920–1960." *Journal of American History* 87,
no. 1 (2000): 112–46.

Grundy, Pamela, and Susan Shackelford. *Shattering the Glass: The Remarkable
History of Women's Basketball.* New York: New Press, 2005.

Guffey, Greg. *The Greatest Basketball Story Ever Told.* Bloomington: Indiana
Univ. Press, 1993.

Gulick, Luther Halsey. "Athletics for School-Children." *Lippincott's Monthly
Magazine,* Aug. 1911, 201–10.

———. "Report of the Committee on the Status of Physical Education in Public
Normal Schools and Public High Schools in the United States." *American
Physical Education Review* 15, no. 6 (1910): 453–54.

Gutowski, Thomas W. "Student Initiative and the Origins of the High School Extracurriculum: Chicago, 1880–1915." *History of Education Quarterly* 28, no. 1 (1988): 49–72.

Hagen, Patricia. "Gil's World." *Journal of Popular Culture* 31, no. 3 (1997): 47–54.

Halas, George. *Halas by Halas: The Autobiography of George Halas.* New York: McGraw-Hill, 1979.

Hard, William. "High-School Fraternities: Farce, Tragedy, and Statesmanship." *Everybody's Magazine* 21 (Aug. 1909): 173–83.

Hardy, Stephen. "Exercise and Sports for the Schools." In *How Boston Played: Sport, Recreation, and Community, 1865–1915,* 107–23. 1982. Reprint, Knoxville: Univ. of Tennessee Press, 2003.

———. "Long before Orr: Placing Hockey in Boston, 1897–1929." In *The Rock, the Curse, and the Hub,* edited by Randy Roberts, 245–72. Cambridge, MA: Harvard Univ. Press, 2005.

———. "'Polo at the Rinks': Shaping Markets for Ice Hockey, 1880–1900." Paper presented at the North American Society for Sport History annual conference, May 28, 2005, Green Bay, WI.

Harris, Edward L., C. A. Waldo, and J. E. Armstrong. "Report of the Committee on Athletics." *School Review* 11, no. 5 (1903): 348–49.

Henderson, Edwin Bancroft. *The Negro in Sports.* Rev. ed. Washington, DC: Associated Publishers, 1939.

———. "Report of Secretary of the Public Schools Athletic League of Washington, D.C." In *Official Handbook, Inter-Scholastic Athletic Association of the Middle Atlantic States,* edited by Edwin B. Henderson and William A. Joiner, 17–27. New York: American Sports Publishing, 1911.

Herrick, Mary J. *The Chicago Schools: A Social and Political History.* Beverly Hills, CA: Sage, 1971.

Hess, Charles "Chic." *Prof Blood and the Wonder Teams: The True Story of Basketball's First Great Coach.* Newark, NJ: Newark Abbey, 2003.

Heston, Pat. "More than a Game: High School Basketball's Victory over Segregation." In *100 Years of Madness: The Illinois High School Association Boys' Basketball Tournament,* 58–61. Bloomington: Illinois High School Association, 2006.

"High School Fraternities Widely Banned." *Journal of Education* 113 (Feb. 23, 1931): 236.

Himes, Cindy L. "The Female Athlete in American Society, 1860–1940." PhD diss., Univ. of Pennsylvania, 1986.

History of Englewood High School, 1874–1935. Chicago: Englewood High School, 1935.

Hult, Joan S. "The Governance of Athletics for Girls and Women: Leadership by Women Physical Educators, 1899–1949." In *A Century of Women's Basketball: From Frailty to Final Four,* edited by Joan S. Hult and Marianna Trekell, 53–82. Reston, VA: American Alliance for Health, Physical Education, Recreation, and Dance, 1991.

Hyatt, Chauncey A. "Interscholastic Swimming in the Middle West, 1915–16." In *Intercollegiate Swimming Guide, 1916–17,* 111–15. New York: American Sports Publishing, 1916.

Illinois High School Association. "IHSA Record Book." http://www.ihsa.org /records/index.htm.

Jable, J. Thomas. "Progress or Plight: The Growing Commercialism of High School Athletics in the United States." Paper presented at the 2004 NASSH Convention, Asilomar, CA, May 30, 2004.

———. "The Public Schools Athletic League of New York City: Organized Athletics for City Schoolchildren, 1903–1914." In *The American Sporting Experience,* edited by Steven A. Riess. Champaign, IL: Leisure Press, 1984.

Johnson, Lewis E. "Basket Ball in Washington." In *Official Handbook, Inter-Scholastic Athletic Association of the Middle Atlantic States,* edited by William A. Joiner and Edwin B. Henderson, 67–68. New York: American Sports Publishing, 1910.

Johnson, Marian Bemus, and Dorothy E. McIntyre. *Daughters of the Game: The First Era of Minnesota Girls High School Basketball, 1891–1942.* Edina, MN: McJohn, 2005.

Johnson, Scott. "From the Y to the U." In *100 Years of Madness: The Illinois High School Association Boys' Basketball Tournament,* 18–21. Bloomington: Illinois High School Association, 2006.

———. "The Girls Were First." In *Illinky: High School Basketball in Illinois, Indiana, and Kentucky,* edited by Nelson Campbell, 48–50. New York: Stephen Greene/Pelham, 1990.

———. "Learning to Fly, 1908–1929." In *100 Years of Madness: The Illinois High School Association Boys' Basketball Tournament,* 4–35. Bloomington: Illinois High School Association, 2006.

Jones, Grace Latimer. "The Evils of Girls' Secret Societies." *Ladies' Home Journal,* Oct. 1907, 26.

Katznelson, Ira, and Margaret Weir. *Schooling for All: Class, Race, and the Decline of the Democratic Ideal.* New York: Basic Books, 1985.

Keeler, Harry. "The Financial Responsibility of High School Managers of Athletics." *School Review* 11, no. 5 (1903): 316–20.

Kelley, Robert F. *American Rowing: Its Background and Traditions.* New York: G. P. Putnam's Sons, 1932.

Kindred, Dave. "The Legend of Carr Creek." In *Grass Roots & Schoolyards: A High School Basketball Anthology,* edited by Nelson Campbell, 11–14. Lexington, MA: Stephen Greene, 1988.

King, Kelley. "The Little School That Can't Be Beat." *Sports Illustrated,* Aug. 23, 2004, 78–85.

Kuska, Bob. *Hot Potato: How Washington and New York Gave Birth to Black Basketball and Changed America's Game Forever.* Charlottesville: Univ. Press of Virginia, 2004.

Larned, Charles W. "Athletics from a Historical and Educational Standpoint." *American Physical Education Review* 14, no. 1 (1909): 1–9.

Lederman, Douglas. "Use Sports to Lure Inner-City Youths to Education, Preaches a Coach Who Directs a U. of Chicago Institute." *Chronicle of Higher Education,* Sept. 19, 1990.

Lewis, Guy M. "Adoption of the Sports Program, 1906–39: The Role of Accommodation in the Transformation of Physical Education." *Quest* 12, no. 1 (1969): 34–46.

Logan, Gabe. "The Rise of Early Chicago Soccer." In *Sports in Chicago,* edited by Elliot J. Gorn, 17–42. Urbana: Univ. of Illinois Press, 2008.

Lowman, G. S. "The Regulation and Control of Competitive Sport in Secondary Schools of the United States: I. Public High Schools." *American Physical Education Review* 12, no. 3 (1907): 241–55.

———. "The Regulation and Control of Competitive Sport in Secondary Schools of the United States: II. Private Schools and Academies." *American Physical Education Review* 12, no. 4 (1907): 307–23.

Lowry, Mark, II. "Schools in Transition." *Annals of the Association of American Geographers* 63, no. 2 (1973): 167–80.

Lucas, Shelley. "Courting Controversy: Gender and Power in Iowa Girls' Basketball." *Journal of Sport History* 30, no. 3 (2003): 286, 302.

Mangan, J. A. *Athleticism in the Victorian and Edwardian Public School: The Emergence and Consolidation of an Educational Ideology.* London: Frank Cass, 2000.

Mattingly, Robert N. "History of the I.S.S.A.A. ." In *Spalding's Official Handbook, Inter-Scholastic Athletic Association of the Middle Atlantic States*, edited by William A. Joiner and Edwin R. Henderson, 15–23. New York: American Sports Publishing, 1910.

McClellan, Keith. "Wilma Rudolph Spotlights Women's Sports." Unpublished manuscript, 2007.

McCurdy, James Huff. "A Study of the Characteristics of Physical Training in the Public Schools of the United States." *American Physical Education Review* 10, no. 3 (1905): 202–13.

McElwain, Max. *The Only Dance in Iowa: A History of Six-Player Girls' Basketball*. Lincoln: Univ. of Nebraska Press, 2004.

McGehee, Richard V. "Educational Competition? School Sport in Texas." Paper presented at the 2009 NASSH Convention, Asheville, NC, May 23, 2009.

McMurray, Bill. "Texas: King Sized Football." *High School Football* 1, no. 1 (1963): 6–8.

Mendenhall, Thomas C. *A Short History of American Rowing*. Boston: Charles River Books, [1980].

Meylan, George L. "Athletics." *American Physical Education Review* 10, no. 2 (1905): 157–63.

Mirel, Jeffrey. "From Student Control to Institutional Control of High School Athletics: Three Michigan Cities, 1883–1905." *Journal of Social History* 16, no. 2 (1982): 83–100.

Money, Tony. *Manly and Muscular Diversions: Public Schools and the Nineteenth-Century Sporting Revival*. London: Gerald Duckworth, 1997.

Montay, Sister Mary Innocenta. "The History of Catholic Secondary Education in the Archdiocese of Chicago." PhD diss., Catholic Univ. of America Press, 1953.

Montgomery, James Alfred. "The Development of the Interscholastic Athletics Movement in the United States, 1890–1940." EdD diss., George Peabody College for Teachers, 1960.

Morrison, Gilbert B. "Report of the Committee on 'Secret Fraternities.'" In *National Education Association Journal of the Proceedings and Addresses of the Forty-Fourth Annual Meeting Held at Asbury Park and Ocean Grove, New Jersey, July 3–7, 1905*, 445–51. Winona, MN: National Education Association, 1905.

———. "Secret Fraternities in High Schools." In *National Education Association Journal of Proceedings and Addresses of the Forty-Third Annual Meeting*

Held at St. Louis, Missouri, June 27–July 1, 1904, 484–91. Winona, MN: National Education Association, 1904.

———. "Social Ethics in High-School Life." *School Review* 13, no. 5 (1905): 361–70.

Mrozek, Donald J. "Sport and the American Military: Diversion and Duty." *Research Quarterly for Exercise and Sport* (Centennial Issue) (Apr. 1985): 38–45.

Mustaine, W. W. "Tabulation of Replies to Questionnaire on Girls' Basket Ball." *American Physical Education Review* 32, no. 1 (1927): 41–45.

National Federation of State High School Associations. "The Impact of Title IX." "NFHS Participation Figures Search." http://www.nfhs.org/custom /participation_figures/default.aspx.

———. "NFHS Corporate Partners." http://www.nfhs.org/content.aspx?id=3250 &terms=corporate + partners.

———. "2007–2008 High School Athletics Participation Survey." http://www .nfhs.org.

———. "2009–2010 High School Athletics Participation Survey" http://www .nfhs.org.

National High School Coaches Association. "Event History: 2001 Final Four of High School Wrestling." http://www.nhsca.com/events_history_show.php ?id=20117.

———. "1999 NHSCA National Open High School All-Americans." http:// www.nhsca.com/events_history_show.php?id=20127.

Nichols, E. H. "Competitive Athletics." *American Physical Education Review* 14, no. 9 (1909): 589–99.

Nightingale, A. F. "The Place of the High School in Our System of Education." *School Review* 14, no. 2 (1906): 142–52.

Noonkester, Barbara N. "The American Sportswoman from 1900 to 1920." In *Her Story in Sport: A Historical Anthology of Women in Sports*, edited by Reet Howell, 178–222. West Point, NY: Leisure Press, 1982.

O'Hanlon, Timothy. "Interscholastic Athletics, 1900–1940: Shaping Citizens for Unequal Roles in the Modern Industrial State." *Educational Theory* 30, no. 2 (1980): 89–103.

———. "Interscholastic Athletics, 1900–1940: Shaping Citizens for Unequal Roles in the Modern Industrial State." PhD diss., Univ. of Illinois, 1979.

———. "School Sports as Social Training: The Case of Athletics and the Crisis of World War I." *Journal of Sport History* 9, no. 1 (1982): 7–29.

Ohio High School Athletic Association. "OHSAA All-Time State Football Tournament Results." http://www.ohsaa.org/sports/history/FT/state_results.htm.

Ontario Federation of School Athletic Associations. "Past Champions." http://www.ofsaa.on.ca/site/index.cfm?DSP=Chapter&ID=716.

Orcutt, William Dana. "The Interscholastic Movement." *American Lawn Tennis* 1, no. 5 (1898): 65–66.

Orr, William. "The Place of Athletics in the Curriculum of Secondary Schools for Girls and Boys." *American Physical Education Review* 12, no. 1 (1907): 49–59.

Ostrem, Walter M. "The Beginnings of Track and Field Sports in Minnesota." *Minnesota History* 39, no. 1 (1964): 18–23.

Owen, William Bishop. "The Problem of the High School Fraternity." *School Review* 14, no. 7 (1906): 492–504.

Paino, Troy D. "Hoosiers in a Different Light: Forces of Change v. the Power of Nostalgia." *Journal of Sport History* 28, no. 1 (2001): 63–80.

Paret, J. Parmly. "Exercise for Women." *Harper's Bazaar*, Apr. 6, 1901, 932–36.

Park, Roberta J. "Science, Service, and the Professionalism of Physical Education, 1885–1905." *Research Quarterly for Exercise and Sport* (Centennial Issue) (Apr. 1985): 7–20.

Patrick, Augusta Lane. "Relative Merit of the Y.M.C.A. Rules and Women's Rules." In *Spalding's Official Women's Basket Ball Guide*, 1905–1906, 91–95. New York: American Sports Publishing, 1906.

Pesavanto, Wilma Jane. "A Historical Study of the Development of Physical Education in the Chicago Public High Schools, 1860 to 1965." PhD diss., Northwestern Univ., 1966.

Pierce, Richard B. "More than a Game: The Political Meaning of High School Basketball in Indianapolis." In *Sport and the Color Line: Black Athletes and Race Relations in Twentieth-Century America*, edited by Patrick B. Miller and David K. Wiggins, 191–209. New York: Routledge, 2004.

"Principal Henry L. Boltwood, Evanston (Ill.) High School." *Academy* 3 (June 1888): 319.

Pruter, Robert. "Chicago High School Football Struggles, the Fight for Faculty Control, and the War against Secret Societies, 1898–1908." *Journal of Sport History* 30, no. 1 (2003): 47–72.

———. "Youth Baseball in Chicago, 1868–1890: Not Always Sandlot Ball." *Journal of Sport History* 26, no. 1 (1999): 1–28.

"Public School [*sic*] Athletic League." *School Journal* 71, no. 18 (1905): 492–93.

"Report of Committee of the Boston Physical Education Society, to Suggest a Substitute for the Manual of Arms as a Means of Physical Exercise in the Military Training of School-Boys." *American Physical Education Review,* nos. 1–2 (1896): 43–49.

"Report of the Advisory Committee on Athletics for High School Girls." *American Physical Education Review* 33, no. 4 (1928): 254–60.

"Resolutions Adopted by the Conference on Athletics and Physical Recreation Held under the Auspices of the National Amateur Athletic Federation at Washington, D.C., April 6–7, 1923." *American Physical Education Review* 28, no. 6 (1923): 284–88.

Rice, Emmett A., John L. Hutchinson, and Mabel Lee. *A Brief History of Physical Education.* 4th ed. New York: Ronald Press, 1958.

Robinson, E. V. "Discussion." *School Review* 11, no. 5 (1903): 346–47.

Rogers, Frederick Rand. *The Future of Interscholastic Athletics.* New York: Teachers College, Columbia Univ., 1929.

———. "State Championships Abolished." *American Physical Education Review* 34, no. 3 (1929): 132–33.

Sargent, Dudley A. "Are Athletics Making Girls Masculine?" *Ladies' Home Journal,* Mar. 1912, 11, 71–73.

———. "Athletics in Secondary Schools." *American Physical Education Review* 8, no. 2 (1903): 57–69.

———. "How Can I Have a Graceful Figure?" *Ladies' Home Journal,* Feb. 1912, 15–16.

———. "Ideals of Physical Training." *School Journal* 62, no. 18 (1901): 478.

———. "Military Drill in the Public Schools." *American Physical Education Review* 1, no. 2 (1896): 50–59.

———. "Military Training in High Schools." *American School Board Journal* 51, no. 6 (1915): 36–37.

Sarver, J. M. "Inter-School Athletics." *Education* 22, no. 7 (1902): 420–25.

Savage, Howard J., et al. *American College Athletics.* New York: Carnegie Foundation for the Advancement of Teaching, 1929.

Schmidt, Raymond. *Shaping College Football: The Transformation of an American Sport, 1919–1930.* Syracuse, NY: Syracuse Univ. Press, 2007.

Schroedler, Lillian. "Report of Progress, Women's Division, National Amateur Athletic Federation of America." *American Physical Education Review* 29, no. 6 (1924): 305–10.

Schwomeyer, Herb. *Hoosier Hysteria.* Indianapolis: privately printed, [1997].

Seymour, Harold. *Baseball: The People's Game*. New York: Oxford Univ. Press, 1990.

Sheldon, Henry D. *Student Life and Customs*. 1901. Reprint, New York: Arno Press and *New York Times*, 1969.

Shepard, Natalie Marie. *Foundations and Principles of Physical Education*. New York: Ronald Press, 1960.

Sherrill, Rob. *Mat Madness: 60 Glorious Years of Illinois High School Wrestling*. Scottsdale, PA: Laurel Group Press, 1996.

Smith, Helen N. "Athletic Education." *American Physical Education Review* 32, no. 8 (1927): 608–11.

Smith, Melvin I. *Evolvements of Early American Football: Through the 1890/91 Season*. Bloomington, IN: AuthorHouse, 2008.

Smith, Ronald A. *Sports and Freedom: The Rise of Big-Time College Athletics*. New York: Oxford Univ. Press, 1988.

Smith, Spencer C. "Report of the Committee on the Influence of Fraternities in Secondary Schools." *School Review* 13, no. 1 (1905): 1–10.

South Carolina High School League. "Palmetto's Finest Record Book." http://www.schsl.org/palfine.htm.

Spalding, Harriet I. *Reminiscences*. East Orange, NJ: privately printed, 1910.

Spring, Joel H. *The American School, 1642–1985*. New York: Longman, 1986.

———. "Mass Culture and School Sports." *History of Education Quarterly* 14, no. 4 (1974): 483–98.

Stanaland, Peggy. "The Early Years of Basketball in Kentucky." In *A Century of Women's Basketball: From Frailty to Final Four*, edited by Joan S. Hult and Marianna Trekell, 167–79. Reston, VA: American Alliance for Health, Physical Education, Recreation, and Dance, 1991.

Steelye, L. Clark. "The Influence of Sororities." *Ladies' Home Journal*, Sept. 1907, 12.

Steever, Edgar Z. "The Wyoming Plan of Military Training in the Schools." *School Review* 25, no. 3 (1917): 145–50.

Stone, Curtis C. "High School Athletics: A History and Current Problems." EdD thesis, Pennsylvania State Univ., 1963.

Stout, Louis. *Shadows of the Past: A History of the Kentucky High School Athletic League*. Lexington, KY: Host Communications, 2006.

Tatich, Andrea Jensen. "Performance-Enhancing Drugs and Supplements in Women and Girls." *Current Sports Medicine Reports* 6, no. 6 (2007): 387–91.

Tennessee Secondary School Athletic Association. "Year by Year Results for Boys Basketball: Team Champions." http://www.tsaaa.org/schdir/records/GetThe Record.cfm.

———. "Year by Year Results for Girls Basketball: Team Champions." http://www.tsaaa.org/schdir/records/GetTheRecord.cfm.

Thompson, Charles Herbert. "The History of the National Basketball Tournaments for Black High Schools." PhD diss., Louisiana State Univ., 1980.

Travis, Seward S. "High School Fraternities." *Education* 29, no. 8 (1909): 515–27.

Tynes, Jarred R. "Performance Enhancing Substances: Effects, Regulations, and the Pervasive Efforts to Control Doping in Major League Baseball." *Journal of Legal Medicine* 27, no. 4 (2006): 493–509.

US Commissioner on Civil Rights. "The Impact of Title IX: Participation in High School and College Competitive Athletics." In *The American Sporting Experience*, edited by Steven A. Riess, 386–97. Champaign, IL: Leisure Press, 1984.

"Uses and Abuses of Athletics." *School Journal* 62, no. 19 (1901): 529.

US Lacrosse. "About Lacrosse." http://www.lacrosse.org/the_sport/index.phtml.

Van Dalen, Deobold B., and Bruce L. Bennett. *A World History of Physical Education.* 2nd ed. Englewood Cliffs, NJ: Prentice-Hall, 1971.

Van Hagen, Winifred. "Everybody Play." *American Physical Education Review* 31, no. 2 (1926): 652–57.

Virginia High School League Book of Records. 11th ed. Charlottesville: Virginia High School League, 2006.

Wagenhorst, Lewis Hoch. *The Administration and Cost of High School Interscholastic Athletics.* New York: Columbia Univ. Press, 1926.

Walker, Milo S. "Indoor Base Ball for Women." In *Spalding's Official Indoor Base Ball Guide, 1903,* 85–88. New York: American Sports Publishing, 1903.

"The Washington Decision on the High-School Fraternity Question." *School Review* 14, no. 10 (1906): 739–45.

Wayman, Agnes R. "Competition: A Statement by the Women's Division, National Amateur Athletic Federation." *American Physical Education Review* 34, no. 8 (1929): 469–71.

Welch, Paula. "Interscholastic Basketball: Bane of Collegiate Physical Educators." In *Her Story in Sport: A Historical Anthology of Women in Sports,* edited by Reet Howell, 424–31. West Point, NY: Leisure Press, 1982.

Westlake, Edward G. "Supremacy of the Golfing Kids." *Cherry Circle,* Aug. 1910, 39–40.

Whitten, Charles W. "A Big Step in Advance." *Kansas State High School Athletic Association Bulletin* 2, no. 8 (1930): 4–5.

———. *Interscholastics: A Discussion of Interscholastic Contests.* Chicago: Illinois High School Association, 1950.

———. "Some Disquieting Aspects of Our Athletic Program." *School Review* 35, no. 10 (1927): 736–50.

Whitton, Frederick. "Higher Ideals in Secondary Education." *School Review* 8, no. 4 (1900): 261–67.

Wiggins, B. E. "Should High School Wrestling Be Encouraged?" *American Physical Education Review* 32, no. 8 (1927): 612–13.

Wiggins, David K. "Edwin Bancroft Henderson: Physical Educator, Civil Rights Activist, and Chronicler of African American Athletes." *Research Quarterly for Exercise and Sport* 70, no. 2 (1999): 90–112.

———. "'With All Deliberate Speed': High School Sport, Race, and *Brown v. Board of Education.*" *Journal of Sport History* 37, no. 3 (2010): 329–46.

Wile, Otis. "Our (Almost) International Champions." *Oklahoma Today*, Winter 1971–72, 17–19.

Wisconsin Interscholastic Athletic Association. "Welcome to the Official WIAA Website." http://wiaawi.org/.

INDEX